A HANDBOOK
on
PAUL'S SECOND LETTER
to the
CORINTHIANS

The Handbooks in the **UBS Handbook Series** are detailed commentaries providing valuable exegetical, historical, cultural, and linguistic information on the books of the Bible. They are prepared primarily to assist practicing Bible translators as they carry out the important task of putting God's Word into the many languages spoken in the world today. The text is discussed verse by verse and is accompanied by running text in at least one modern English translation.

Over the years church leaders and Bible readers have found the UBS Handbooks to be useful for their own study of the Scriptures. Many of the issues Bible translators must address when trying to communicate the Bible's message to modern readers are the ones Bible students must address when approaching the Bible text as part of their own private study and devotions.

The Handbooks will continue to be prepared primarily for translators, but we are confident that they will be useful to a wider audience, helping all who use them to gain a better understanding of the Bible message.

Helps for Translators

UBS Handbook Series:

A Handbook on . . .

Leviticus

The Book of Joshua

The Book of Ruth

The Book of Job

The Book of Psalms

Lamentations

The Book of Amos

The Books of Obadiah, Jonah, and Micah

The Books of Nahum, Habakkuk, and Zephaniah

The Gospel of Matthew

The Gospel of Mark

The Gospel of Luke

The Gospel of John

The Acts of the Apostles

Paul's Letter to the Romans

Paul's First Letter to the Corinthians

Paul's Second Letter to the Corinthians

Paul's Letter to the Galatians

Paul's Letter to the Ephesians

Paul's Letter to the Philippians

Paul's Letters to the Colossians and to Philemon

Paul's Letters to the Thessalonians

The Letter to the Hebrews

The First Letter from Peter

The Letter from Jude and the Second Letter from Peter

The Letters of John

The Revelation to John

Guides:

A Translator's Guide to . . .

Selections from the First Five Books of the Old Testament

Selected Psalms

the Gospel of Mark

the Gospel of Luke

Paul's Second Letter to the Corinthians

Paul's Letters to Timothy and to Titus

the Letters from James, Peter, and Jude

Technical Helps:

Old Testament Quotations in the New Testament

Short Bible Reference System

New Testament Index

The Theory and Practice of Translation

Bible Index

Fauna and Flora of the Bible

Marginal Notes for the Old Testament

Marginal Notes for the New Testament

The Practice of Translating

A HANDBOOK ON

Paul's Second Letter to the Corinthians

by Roger L. Omanson
and John Ellington

UBS Handbook Series

United Bible Societies
New York

Books in the series of **Helps for Translators** may be ordered from a national Bible Society or from either of the following centers:

United Bible Societies
European Production Fund
W-7000 Stuttgart 80
Postfach 81 03 40
Germany

United Bible Societies
1865 Broadway
New York, NY 10023
U.S.A.

L.C. Cataloging-in-Publication Data

Omanson, Roger L. (Roger Lee), 1946-
    A Handbook on Paul's second letter to the Corinthians / by Roger L. Omanson and John Ellington.
        p.   cm. — (UBS handbook series) (Helps for translators)
    Includes bibliographical references and index.
    ISBN 0-8267-0162-0
    1. Bible. N.T. Corinthians, 2nd—Commentaries. 2. Bible. N.T. Corinthians, 2nd—Translating.   I. Ellington, John.   II. Title.
III. Series. IV. Series: Helps for translators.
BS2675.3.048 1993
227'.3077—dc20   93-4494
                                                                CIP

ABS-10/93-500-EB-1-105034

Contents

PAUL'S 1st AND 2nd JOURNEYS

- - - - - First Journey

———— Second Journey

© United Bible Societies 1978

vi

Preface

A Handbook on Paul's Second Letter to the Corinthians, like others in the
UBS Handbook Series, concentrates on exegetical information important for
translators, and it attempts to indicate possible solutions for translation
problems related to language or culture. The authors do not consciously
attempt to provide help that other theologians and scholars may seek but
which is not directly related to the translation task. Such information is
normally sought elsewhere. However, many church leaders and interested
Bible readers have found these Handbooks useful and informative, and wo
hope that this volume will be no exception.

The Revised Standard Version (RSV) and the Today's English Version (TEV)
are shown at the beginning of each section so that the translator may compare
the two approaches to structure of the discourse and to paragraph division.
The two versions are shown again at the beginning of the comments on each
verse, so that they may be compared in detail. However, the discussion follows
RSV, and quotations of RSV words and phrases from the verse under discussion
are printed in **boldface** so that the translator can easily locate desired
information. TEV is kept before the translator as one of several possible models
for a meaningful translation. Quotations from TEV and other translations, as
well as quotations from elsewhere in RSV, are displayed within quotation
marks.

A limited Bibliography is included for the benefit of those interested in
further study. The Glossary explains technical terms according to their usage
in this volume. The translator may find it useful to read through the Glossary
in order to become aware of the specialized way in which certain terms are
used. An Index gives the location by page number of some of the important
words and subjects discussed in the Handbook, especially where the Handbook
provides the translator with help in rendering these concepts into the receptor
language.

The publication of *A Handbook on Paul's Second Letter to the Corinthians*
is part of a plan to complete those Handbooks in the series that will cover New
Testament books. Meanwhile work on Handbooks for the books of the Old
Testament continues. The editor of the United Bible Societies' Handbook Series
will be happy to receive comments from translators and others who use these
books, so that future volumes may benefit and may better serve the needs of
the readers.

Abbreviations Used in This Volume

General Abbreviations, Bible Texts, Versions, and Other Works Cited
(For details see Bibliography)

AB	Anchor Bible	NAB	New American Bible
A.D.	Anno Domini (the year of our Lord)	NASB	New American Standard Bible
AT	American Translation	NBE	*Nueva Biblia Española*
Brc	Barclay	NCV	New Century Version
BRCL	Brazilian Portuguese common language version	NEB	New English Bible
		NIV	New International Version
CEV	Contemporary English Version	NJB	New Jerusalem Bible
BJ	*Bible de Jérusalem*	NRSV	New Revised Standard Version
FRCL	French common language version	NVSR	*Nouvelle version Segond révisée*
GECL	German common language version	Phps	Phillips
		REB	Revised English Bible
GNC	God's New Covenant	RSV	Revised Standard Version
GNW	Good News for the World		
ITCL	Italian common language version	RVR	*Reina-Valera revisada*
		SE	*La Sainte Bible* (Segond)
KJV	King James Version	SPCL	Spanish common language version
LB	Living Bible		
LBI	*La Biblia Interconfesional*	TEV	Today's English Version
		TNT	Translator's New Testament
LPD	*El Libro del Pueblo de Dios*	TOB	*Traduction œcuménique de la Bible*
Lu	Luther (revised, 1984)		
Mft	Moffatt	UBS	United Bible Societies

Books of the Bible

Gen	Genesis	Hos	Hosea
Exo	Exodus	Matt	Matthew
Lev	Leviticus	Rom	Romans
Num	Numbers	1,2 Cor	1,2 Corinthians
Deut	Deuteronomy	Gal	Galatians
Josh	Joshua	Eph	Ephesians
1,2 Sam	1,2 Samuel	Phil	Philippians
1,2 Kgs	1,2 Kings	Col	Colossians
Psa	Psalms	1,2 Thes	1,2 Thessalonians
Pro	Proverbs	1,2 Tim	1,2 Timothy
Isa	Isaiah	Heb	Hebrews
Jer	Jeremiah	Rev	Revelation
Ezek	Ezekiel		

Translating 2 Corinthians

Information about this Handbook[1]

The purpose of this and other Handbooks is to provide Bible translators in various parts of the world with help in understanding and translating the Scriptures. This means that the Handbooks are both less and more than other commentaries.

They are less than other commentaries because they do not normally include much material on the historical background or literary criticism of the various books of the Bible; nor do they systematically describe the ways in which biblical passages have been interpreted in different church traditions and at different times. Still less do they claim to discuss the importance of the biblical text for systematic theology or religious philosophy. To these limitations of content may be added certain limitations of form. The Handbooks are intended to be read by translators, some of whom have only a limited knowledge of Hebrew and Greek, and most of whom do not speak English as their mother tongue. For this reason Hebrew and Greek words are seldom quoted, even in transliteration; and some explanations are given which a native speaker of English would not need, for example, explanations of idioms quoted from English translations of the Bible.

These limitations on the form and content of this Handbook are deliberate. They reflect an overriding concern for helping translators to understand the meaning of the biblical text as a necessary condition for translating it. Even in this area it is necessary to be selective. We do not claim to have mentioned every possible meaning of every text. Our guiding principle has been to provide translators with material for answering the two questions that are vital for their work: "What does the text mean?" and "How can we translate it?" Church workers, pastors, and scholars will no doubt find things of value for their purposes in Handbooks such as this, even though the information is not directed toward fulfilling their needs.

In agreement with this aim, this Handbook is based on the fourth revised edition (1993) of the United Bible Societies' (UBS) *Greek New Testament*. Its text is the same as that of the Nestle-Aland *Novum Testamentum Graece*, 26th

---

[1] The comments which follow concerning the information about this Handbook reproduce with only minor changes the excellent introduction, "Translating 1 Corinthians," in *A Handbook on Paul's First Letter to the Corinthians,* by Ellingworth and Hatton.

edition 1979, as corrected in 1981. In these editions square brackets— [ ] —are used to enclose words, or parts of words, whose presence or position in the text is disputed.

Although this Handbook is based on the Greek text, every effort has been made to explain the text in such a way that the Handbook can be used by translators who know little or no Greek.

Two English translations of 2 Corinthians are printed in this Handbook: the Revised Standard Version (RSV) and Today's English Version (TEV). RSV is a rather literal translation and therefore a good guide to the *grammatical structure* of the Greek text. Because RSV is more literal than the New Revised Standard Version (NRSV), RSV has been printed as the base text, but NRSV is frequently cited in the commentary. TEV is an accurate representation of the *meaning* of the text and is a useful example of how it may be restructured in translation.

This Handbook often refers to translations of 2 Corinthians in other languages, mainly European, such as French, German, and Spanish. These are quoted in a rather literal English translation. Our purpose in doing this is not to suggest that European languages are in any way more developed, or that translations in them are better, than those in other parts of the world. We have used these translations in two main ways: first, to illustrate how different interpretations of the Greek text affect the translation; and second, to provide examples of how the meaning of the text has been expressed in particular translations.

Occasionally there are quotations from non-Western languages which are usually left unnamed. These also may serve as models for the target language in certain cases. The back-translation of these renderings may sometimes sound strange to readers in other parts of the world, but their structure or idiom may be extremely helpful to those working in languages that are similar.

References to other translations, whether in English or in other languages, should be understood as suggestions and possible helps, not as perfect models to be followed without question. The responsibility for finding the closest natural equivalent of the original text belongs to the translators. No translation in another language, no commentary, and no Handbook can take this responsibility away.

The Background and Content of 2 Corinthians

Following his first visit to Corinth, during which time he established the church there, Paul wrote a letter that is now lost. He refers to this letter in 1 Cor 5.9-13. Later the Corinthians wrote to Paul concerning a number of matters, and 1 Corinthians was written in part in response to those questions. At the time that he wrote 1 Corinthians, Paul expected to visit Corinth later (1 Cor 16.3,5-6), and he promised to send Timothy to Corinth, probably sending 1 Corinthians with Timothy.

Paul next made a second visit to Corinth, which turned out to be a painful visit, and he left with much tension between himself and the church there. Paul refers to this painful visit in 2 Cor 2.1. Rather than make another visit as he had planned (2 Cor 1.15–2.1), Paul wrote from Ephesus a forceful letter to Corinth, somewhat critical in tone, but filled with anguish and tears (2 Cor 2.4).

Paul then travelled from Ephesus to Troas (2 Cor 2.12); but because he was concerned about not meeting there with Titus, he continued on to Macedonia. There he met Titus, who was coming from Corinth with the good news that the Corinthians had had a change of heart in their relationship with Paul (2 Cor 7.5-13). 2 Corinthians was written following the good news of reconciliation that Titus brought. Paul apparently sent Titus back to Corinth, sending 2 Corinthians with him, with instructions for Titus to help the Corinthians finish raising money for the collection being taken among Paul's Gentile churches for the Jewish Christians in Jerusalem (2 Cor 8.16-20).

Chapters 10–13 are very different in tone from chapters 1–9. In these final four chapters Paul writes a letter in which he defends himself and strongly attacks his opponents in Corinth. Using sarcasm and irony to defend his apostolic authority, he calls his opponents "superapostles" (2 Cor 11.5; 12.11), though in fact he considers them to be "false apostles" (2 Cor 11.13). It is possible that this part of the letter was written after receiving further news from Corinth that was more negative in character than that which Titus had brought.

2 Corinthians shows that Paul's reputation in the Corinthian church was being damaged. This happened both because actions on his part were misunderstood, and because rivals were increasing their influence, as they compared themselves to Paul by sharply criticizing his apostleship.

Unity of 2 Corinthians

Various theories have been proposed concerning whether or not 2 Corinthians was one single letter from the very first or whether it is made up from parts of several letters that Paul wrote. (1) Some interpreters consider 2 Corinthians to be exactly in the same form as Paul wrote it.[2] (2) Other interpreters consider chapters 10–13 to have been written as part of a letter separate from and prior to chapters 1–9.[3] They would identify chapters 10–13 as part of Paul's letter of tears that he refers to in 2 Cor 2.4. Such a view is not as common today as it was a generation ago, but it still has its advocates. (3) Several recent interpreters suggest that chapters 10–13 formed part of a separate letter written some time after chapters 1–9.[4] Other interpreters have

---

[2]For an extensive defense of this traditional view, see the Introduction in Hughes, especially pages xxi-xxxv.

[3]For discussions and defense of this view, see Talbert, pages xviii-xxi; and Strachan, pages xvi-xxii.

[4]For lengthy discussions and defense of this view, see Bruce, pages 163-170; Barrett, *The Second Epistle to the Corinthians,* pages 5-21; Furnish, *II Corinthians* pages 29-48; and Martin, pages xxxviii-lii.

found parts of as many as five or six separate letters in 2 Corinthians, but the three views just mentioned are the most widely held options.

One possible way of representing the relationship between Paul and the Corinthian Christians is found in the following outline. But as already indicated, not all scholars agree with this particular scheme.

VISITS AND REPORTS TO PAUL	LETTERS WRITTEN BY PAUL
Paul's FIRST VISIT to Corinth (Church established—Acts 18)	
	A lost letter written (referred to in 1 Cor 5.9)
Oral reports of Church problems	
	1 Corinthians written (from Ephesus; see 16.8)
Paul's SECOND VISIT to Corinth (the "painful visit")	
	The "tearful letter" written (now lost *or* part of 2 Cor)
Positive report from Titus	
	2 Cor 1–9 written (from Macedonia)
Negative report	
	2 Cor 10–13 written (from Macedonia)
Paul's THIRD VISIT to Corinth (proposed—2 Cor 12.14; 13.1)	

After Titus brought his positive report, and before chapters 1–9 were sent, it is possible that the negative report arrived, and that chapters 10–13 were simply added to the existing letter. Or these final chapters may have originally been a separate letter that was later added to the first nine chapters. In any case translators must deal with the letter as a whole, as we now have it.

This Handbook will not discuss the arguments for and against finding several originally separate letters, since the translation of 2 Corinthians is for the most part not affected by one's conclusions on the unity of the letter. It should be noted, however, that such theories do affect the translation of 2 Corinthians in a few verses; and for this reason translators should be aware of the arguments about the unity of 2 Corinthians. This Handbook will take note of the difficulties in those places where they occur.

A couple of examples may be given to show that theories about the unity of 2 Corinthians do indeed have some relationship to translation:

(1) 9.2 may be translated as "Achaia has been ready since last year" (so New American Bible [NAB] and *Traduction œcuménique de la Bible* [TOB]). But since such a statement seems to contradict the statement to the Corinthian Christians in Achaia in 8.10 ("complete what you began a year ago"), some

interpreters propose that chapter 9 was a separate letter written later than chapter 8. However, 9.2 may be translated as "Achaia has been ready to help since last year" (see TEV and New International Version [NIV]). Whereas NAB and TOB state that the Christians in Achaia had the money collected and ready "since last year," TEV and NIV do not say that the Achaians had the collection ready last year, only that they were ready to help since last year. The TEV and NIV translations thereby avoid a contradiction with the implied statement in 8.10 that the Christians in Achaia did not in fact have the collection ready yet.

(2) If chapters 8 and 9 were originally separate letters or parts of separate letters, then "the brothers" mentioned in 9.3,5 may not be the same brothers mentioned in 8.16-24. If that is the case, the translation "these brothers" in 9.3,5 (TEV, French common language version [FRCL]), rather than "the brothers," is incorrect.

Special Problems in Translating 2 Corinthians

While the problems discussed here are not exclusive to 2 Corinthians, they are particularly difficult ones that occur very frequently in this letter. Therefore they deserve special mention here.

1. EPISTOLARY PLURAL

In Greek of the New Testament period, it was customary for writers sometimes to use the first person plural pronoun (and first person plural forms of verbs), even though the first person singular was intended. Grammarians call this the "epistolary plural." That Paul used the epistolary plural elsewhere is beyond question (1 Thes 3.1). It is not always clear from the context, however, when Paul was referring to himself only and when he was referring to himself and his companions.[5] Some translators, especially Moffatt (Mft), Goodspeed (American Translation, AT), and *Parola del Signore: La Bibbia in lingua corrente* (ITCL), regularly use the first person singular pronoun when they think that the plural pronoun in Greek is the epistolary plural. Translators will need to decide in which cases he means "I" if and when Paul uses the plural pronoun "we." It should be said here at the outset that the context in 2 Corinthians almost never provides enough information for translators to know for sure whether Paul means "I" when he writes "we." The fact that Paul changes from "I" in 1.23 to "we" in 1.24, and then back to "I" in the following verses suggests that "we" is probably an epistolary plural in 1.24. But such switching between singular and plural forms also suggests that the plural forms at the beginning of chapter 1 may also be epistolary plurals.

The difficulty of deciding can be seen in a comparison of Mft, AT, and ITCL. Mft and AT begin using first person singular pronouns and verbs in 2 Cor 1.4 and continue through 1.14, even though the Greek has first person plural pronouns and verbs in these verses. ITCL, however, begins using the first person singular in verse 8 rather than in verse 4. Apparently the ITCL translators decided that the plural forms in 1.4-7 were true plurals that

---

[5]See Carrez, 1980, pages 474-486.

included the readers. Beginning at verse 8 and continuing through verse 14, the plural forms clearly do not include the readers and may well be epistolary plurals.

Similarly in chapter 7, Paul begins by using the plural "we" and "us" but almost immediately begins alternating between "I" and "we" in the rest of that chapter. Mft, AT, and ITCL all keep the plural forms in 7.1, on the understanding that the "we" forms include the readers. But in the rest of chapter 7 (verses 2-16) Mft, AT, and ITCL all use the pronouns "I" and "me," even when the Greek has plural forms.

Because it is so difficult, if not impossible, for interpreters to know when Paul is using the epistolary plural, the writers of this Handbook are reluctant to encourage translators to follow the examples of Mft, AT, and ITCL. Our own preference, however, is the models provided by these three translations in English and Italian.

If translators agree that Paul is using the epistolary plural, they must decide whether or not their readers will understand that Paul means "I." In other words, does the receptor language have something like the Greek epistolary plural? To further complicate the translation of 2 Corinthians, it is not always clear when the plural includes the readers (inclusive usage) and when it includes only Paul and his co-workers with him (exclusive usage). For many verses the context is so very ambiguous that it is not possible to be certain. In languages that use separate forms for inclusive and exclusive first person plural pronouns, the translation will involve a certain amount of guesswork.

2. INCLUSIVE/EXCLUSIVE FIRST PERSON PLURAL PRONOUNS

To further complicate the translation of first person plural pronouns in 2 Corinthians, it is not always clear when the plural includes the readers (inclusive usage) and when it includes only Paul and his coworkers with him (exclusive usage). For example, in 5.10 the pronoun "we" includes the readers; but in 5.11,12,13 the pronouns "we" and "us" exclude the readers and refer only to Paul (and his associates?). It is clear in verses 11-13 that "we" does not include the readers, because Paul writes of "we" and "you" in these verses.

In 5.14,16,18, however, it is not immediately clear whether the pronouns "we" and "us" include the readers. In 5.20 (and in 5.11-13) "we" does not include the readers, so probably "we" does not include the readers in verses 14-19 either. But in 5.21 "we" almost certainly does include the readers.

For many verses the context is so very ambiguous that it is not possible to be certain. In languages that use separate forms for inclusive and exclusive first person plural pronouns, the translation will involve a certain amount of guesswork. If translators decide in a given verse that the first person plural pronouns do not include the readers, they still must decide whether the plural pronoun includes the people with Paul or whether Paul has used an epistolary plural.

3. EPISTOLARY AORIST

C.F.D. Moule describes the "epistolary aorist" as an "idiom . . . whereby the writer courteously projects himself in imagination into the position of the reader, for whom actions contemporaneous with the time of writing will be past."[6] In chapters 8, 9, and 12 of 2 Corinthians, translators must decide whether Paul uses the epistolary aorist. That is, does he use a verb in the past tense with present tense meaning, when he says that he "sent" someone to Corinth? Had he, in fact, already sent the persons mentioned, or was he going to be sending them in the near future, but before the letter would arrive? One's view on the original unity of 2 Corinthians may affect one's conclusions on the question of whether Paul has used the epistolary aorist.[7] At the relevant points in the Handbook on 2 Corinthians, this difficulty will be noted.

4. SARCASM AND IRONY

Of all of Paul's letters 2 Corinthians is most characterized by the use of sarcasm and irony, especially chapters 10–13. In some languages a literal translation of passages containing sarcasm will be understood to have just the opposite meaning of the intended meaning. With sarcasm the speaker or writer says one thing but in fact means just the opposite. Use of irony or sarcasm may shatter complacency and may hurt or ridicule. In speech one's voice inflection helps the listener to recognize sarcasm. In written texts it may be the context alone that signals the presence of sarcasm. Some languages have special markers to indicate that the usual sense is not intended. Other languages use other devices to alert the reader to the use of sarcasm.

When there is the possibility that readers will fail to recognize the use of sarcasm, there are several ways in which translators may help the reader. One way, used by the translators of *El Libro del Pueblo de Dios* (LPD), is to state in comments under a section heading that the following verses contain sarcasm. LPD, for example, has a major section heading for 2 Cor 10–13, and under the heading is a summary of the contents of these chapters. The summary indicates that in some places Paul uses irony. But such a solution does not identify for the reader the specific verses where irony is present.

Another approach is followed by Charles B. Williams, whose translation uses footnotes to explain that certain verses are sarcastic in tone (11.4-5,19-20; 12.13). A third approach is to translate in such a way that readers will recognize that Paul is using irony or sarcasm. At the relevant places in 2 Corinthians, the Handbook will note when Paul is using irony or sarcasm, and will make suggestions for translation. Finally it may be possible simply to translate the intended meaning of the irony or sarcasm without any consideration of the actual form.

---

[6]Moule, page 12.

[7]See the brief but excellent discussion concerning the epistolary aorist in Hughes, pages 467-469.

Outline of 2 Corinthians

A. Introduction. 1.1-11
B. Paul and the Church at Corinth 1.12–7.16
    1. Paul explains his past actions. 1.12–2.4
    2. A plea for reconciliation. 2.5-17
    3. Paul's apostolic commission and ministry. 3.1–6.13
    4. Warnings against pagan influences. 6.14–7.1
    5. Paul's joy. 7.2-16
C. The collection for the Jewish Christians in Jerusalem. 8.1–9.15
    1. Christian giving. 8.1-15
    2. Titus and his companions. 8.16-24
    3. Help for fellow Christians. 9.1-15
D. Paul's defense of his apostolic authority. 10.1–13.10
    1. Paul defends his ministry. 10.1-18
    2. Paul and the false apostles. 11.1-15
    3. Paul's sufferings as an apostle. 11.16-33
    4. Paul's visions and revelations. 12.1-10
    5. Paul's concern for the Corinthians. 12.11-21
    6. Final warnings and greetings. 13.1-10
E. Conclusion. 13.11-14

Title

The title of this book, like most of the letters of the New Testament, should consist of information about the writer and the people to whom it is addressed. This information should be given in the most natural way possible in the receptor language. The title of this book, however, has the additional detail that it is considered the second letter that Paul wrote to the same group of people. Some possible models are "The second letter that Paul wrote to the people of Corinth," "Paul's second writing to the believers in Corinth" or "The second message written to the church in the city of Corinth by the Apostle Paul." It will also be helpful for translators to compare this title with the forms used in other cases where more than one letter has been written to the same recipients, such as 2 Thessalonians.

A. Introduction

(1.1-11)

1.1-2

REVISED STANDARD VERSION

TODAY'S ENGLISH VERSION

1 Paul, an apostle of Christ Jesus by the will of God, and Timothy our brother.

To the church of God which is at Corinth, with all the saints who are in the whole of Achaia:

2 Grace to you and peace from God our Father and the Lord Jesus Christ.

1 From Paul, an apostle of Christ Jesus by God's will, and from our brother Timothy—

To the church of God in Corinth, and to all God's people throughout Achaia:

2 May God our Father and the Lord Jesus Christ give you grace and peace.

At the time when Paul wrote, Greek letters began with the form "A to B, greetings." The first half of verse 1 corresponds to "A," telling who sent the letter and something about the person or persons sending the letter. The second half of the verse corresponds to "B" and gives information about who is to receive the letter. The second verse is a Christian expansion of the greeting in a normal Greek letter. In some languages it may be necessary to supply certain implied information and break down this formula into two separate sentences. The first part may read something like "This letter is from me, Paul, an apostle of Christ Jesus" or ". . . from me, Paul, the one whom Christ Jesus commissioned to be his messenger."

An apostle of Christ Jesus: the word **apostle** is related to a Greek verb meaning "send" and often means "someone sent as a messenger."

Christ Jesus: some older translations such as the King James Version (KJV), which were based on the Textus Receptus (see Glossary), read "Jesus Christ." More recently the Living Bible (LB) also follows this order, but most scholars today consider the order "Christ Jesus" to be original, though there may be no difference in meaning. While the word "Christ" is sometimes a title elsewhere in the New Testament, it appears to be used as a name in this case. This order of the names occurs ninety times in the New Testament and is actually more frequent in the epistles than "Jesus Christ." Except for Acts 24.24, all occurrences of "Christ Jesus" are in the epistles. A note in TOB on this verse indicates that, when Paul uses the order "Christ Jesus," he has Jewish readers in mind. If, however, the reader is likely to think that Christ Jesus refers to a different person from Jesus Christ, then it may be necessary to use the more common order here. But where possible it is good to maintain the distinction made by Paul.

By the will of God: it was God's will that Paul be an apostle. In some cases this type of clause has to be translated by a verbal expression such as "It was because God wanted it so that [I became an apostle]."

Timothy our brother: the Greek says literally "Timothy the brother," with only the definite article where the possessive pronoun appears in English. The same is true for Sosthenes in 1 Corinthians. *Bible de Jérusalem* (BJ) avoids the pronoun with "one of the brothers," but the New Jerusalem Bible (NJB) reverts to "our brother." In some languages kinship terms such as **brother** require that a possessive pronoun be used with them. In other languages, such as English, "the brother" may sound unnatural. Though most translations say **our brother**, perhaps Paul was thinking of Timothy more in his relationship to the Corinthians: "Timothy, your brother" (so the God's New Covenant translation [GNC]). If translators follow the example of RSV and TEV, the word **our** should be inclusive, that is, it includes the readers of the letter. In some languages there is no general word for **brother**, only specific words for "younger brother" or "older brother." Timothy was probably younger than Paul (1 Tim 4.12).

Timothy is mentioned along with Paul as a sender of this letter. Translators may wish to follow the model of Barclay: "This is a letter from Paul . . . and from Timothy" (so also Phillips [Phps]). Even though Timothy was a co-sender of this letter, parts of the letter are written in the first person singular, and Paul alone is clearly the writer (1.15–2.13, for example). Timothy apparently is mentioned not as a co-writer but rather as one who agrees with the contents of this letter and gives his support to what Paul has written.

When verbs and pronouns in the first person plural occur in this letter, it is not always clear whether these are plural in meaning (Paul and Timothy) or whether Paul is using the epistolary plural, that is, speaking of himself in the plural form. Therefore some translators may have to say "my brother" here, and "I" or "me" elsewhere, where "we" or "us" occur (see discussion of epistolary plural, pages 5 and following).

To the church of God: in the New Testament the word **church** may refer either to a local congregation, as in this verse, or to all Christians everywhere. Translators should avoid a word for church that means only the building where Christians meet for worship. The expression **the church of God** occurs first in Paul's farewell speech to the elders at Ephesus (Acts 20.28) and frequently in the first Corinthian letter (1.2; 10.32; 11.22; 15.9). The root meaning of the word is "assembly," "gathering," or "meeting." The term appears nine times in this letter. In almost every case (except 11.28) it seems to refer to the local congregation.

Corinth was the capital city of the province of Achaia. Paul's reference to Achaia in 9.2 includes the Corinthian Christians. Depending on the structure of the receptor language, it may be more natural to begin a new sentence here, and it may also be necessary to add the classifier term "city" with the geographical name **Corinth**; for example, "the city Corinth" or "the city of Corinth."

With all the saints who are in the whole of Achaia: this indicates a larger group of recipients in addition to the church in Corinth. Paul apparently expected that this letter, like 1 Corinthians, would be read by Christians not only in the city of Corinth but also in other cities and towns of the Roman province of Achaia. Achaia included the Isthmus of Corinth and all the land south of it, including the cities of Athens and Cenchreae. (Note the map of the area, page vi.) Some translations have rendered Achaia as "southern Greece," but it would be misleading to say simply "Greece" as in LB and early versions of TEV and FRCL.

The word **saints** expresses the idea that Christians belong to God and are set apart to serve his purposes alone. In some languages "saint" has come to mean a person who is exceptionally moral or ethical in conduct. Such a translation should be avoided. In many languages this term is translated simply "God's people" (as in TEV) or something similar that will indicate their belonging to God. In those languages that break down the introductory formula into separate sentences, this second part may read "We are [I am] sending this letter to the assembly of God's people who are in the city of Corinth and to all of God's people in the region of Achaia."

Verse 2 is identical with Rom 1.7b; 1 Cor 1.3; Eph 1.2; Phil 1.2; 2 Thes 1.2; and Philemon 3, and should be rendered the same in each case, unless there are good contextual reasons for making a difference. Translators should consult the Handbooks on these other letters.

Grace to you and peace: in the original word order the personal pronoun goes with the first word, but Paul is clearly wishing both qualities to the readers of his letter. The term for **grace** (*charis*) is related to the word for "greeting" (*chairein*) that was normally used at the beginning of letters written in Greek. Since **grace** is not a standard greeting-word in either Greek or Jewish letters, perhaps Paul was playing with words when he replaced the word *chairein* with the word *charis*. The wish of **grace** is a wish for God's love and favor to those who do not deserve it. In languages where a suitable single word does not exist, a translation such as "May God be kind and generous toward you" or "May God show his goodness to you" may be used. **Peace** was commonly used in Jewish letters. As in the Old Testament, the word **peace** means more than an absence of war or peaceful feeling that a person may have. It refers to a total state of well-being that God gives to a person or a community.

Our Father: the pronoun **our** includes the readers.

In languages that require a possessive pronoun with the word **Lord**, the inclusive pronoun "our" should be used.

This whole verse is an expression of Paul's desire for the Church at Corinth; it is a kind of prayer for the well-being of these Christians. So in many languages it will be most natural to use a structure like that of TEV, beginning with "May God . . . ," or the Contemporary English Version (CEV), which reads "I pray that God our Father and the Lord Jesus Christ will be kind to you and bless you with peace."

1.3-11

RSV	TEV
	Paul Gives Thanks to God

3 Blessed be the God and Father of our Lord Jesus Christ, the Father of mercies and God of all comfort, 4 who comforts us in all our affliction, so that we may be able to comfort those who are in any affliction, with the comfort with which we ourselves are comforted by God. 5 For as we share abundantly in Christ's sufferings, so through Christ we share abundantly in comfort too. 6 If we are afflicted, it is for your comfort and salvation; and if we are comforted, it is for your comfort, which you experience when you patiently endure the same sufferings that we suffer. 7 Our hope for you is unshaken; for we know that as you share in our sufferings, you will also share in our comfort.	3 Let us give thanks to the God and Father of our Lord Jesus Christ, the merciful Father, the God from whom all help comes! 4 He helps us in all our troubles, so that we are able to help others who have all kinds of troubles, using the same help that we ourselves have received from God. 5 Just as we have a share in Christ's many sufferings, so also through Christ we share in God's great help. 6 If we suffer, it is for your help and salvation; if we are helped, then you too are helped and given the strength to endure with patience the same sufferings that we also endure. 7 So our hope in you is never shaken; we know that just as you share in our sufferings, you also share in the help we receive.
8 For we do not want you to be ignorant, brethren, of the affliction we experienced in Asia; for we were so utterly, unbearably crushed that we despaired of life itself. 9 Why, we felt that we had received the sentence of death; but that was to make us rely not on ourselves but on God who raises the dead; 10 he delivered us from so deadly a peril, and he will deliver us; on him we have set our hope that he will deliver us again. 11 You also must help us by prayer, so that many will give thanks on our behalf for the blessing granted us in answer to many prayers.	8 We want to remind you, brothers, of the trouble we had in the province of Asia. The burdens laid upon us were so great and so heavy that we gave up all hope of staying alive. 9 We felt that the death sentence had been passed on us. But this happened so that we should rely, not on ourselves, but only on God, who raises the dead. 10 From such terrible dangers of death he saved us, and will save us; and we have placed our hope in him that he will save us again, 11 as you help us by means of your prayers for us. So it will be that the many prayers for us will be answered, and God will bless us; and many will raise their voices to him in thanksgiving for us.

SECTION HEADING: TEV has the section heading as "Paul Gives Thanks to God." Following the normal form of letter writing in his day, Paul includes a statement of thanksgiving following the greeting. All of Paul's letters except Galatians contain a thanksgiving section. Unlike this section in his other letters, Paul focuses here on the comfort that God has given, both to the apostles and to the Corinthians in times of trouble (verse 8). For this reason some translators may prefer a section heading like "Thanksgiving after affliction" (NAB) or, focusing on the reason for the thanksgiving, "Comfort in trouble."

1.3   RSV   TEV

Blessed be the God and Father of our Lord Jesus Christ, the Father of mercies and God of all comfort,

Let us give thanks to the God and Father of our Lord Jesus Christ, the merciful Father, the God from whom all help comes!

While God is the one to be **blessed**, the Greek does not make explicit who does the blessing. In Hebrew thought, human beings blessed God by praising him (Gen 14.20; Psa 28.6). But in many languages God cannot be the object of the verb "to bless." So the translation will have to use a verb like "praise," "honor," or "glorify," as seen in many modern English versions. This formula is repeated in Eph 1.3 and 1 Peter 1.3. TEV makes the subject explicit, "Let us give thanks . . . ," that is, Paul, Timothy, and the Corinthian readers.

There are two ways to understand the Greek words translated by RSV as **the God and Father of our Lord Jesus Christ**. (1) God is both the God and the father of Jesus Christ. This interpretation is reflected in both RSV and TEV. (2) The words **of our Lord Jesus Christ** qualify only the word **Father**. This interpretation is reflected in AB: "Blessed is God, the Father of our Lord Jesus Christ" (so also Barrett). If this second interpretation is followed, some will prefer to say something like "God who is the Father of . . ." or "the Father God . . . ."

The structure of the Greek favors the first interpretation. On the other hand, while Paul frequently refers to God as the Father of Jesus, only in Eph 1.17 is God called the God of Jesus. If translators follow the first interpretation (RSV, TEV), they must be careful not to give the impression that Paul is referring to two different beings.

Our Lord: our includes the readers.

The Father of mercies: this has been rendered "the all-merciful Father" (New English Bible [NEB], Revised English Bible [REB]) and "a gentle Father" (Jerusalem Bible), but NJB and Knox have simply "the merciful Father." In some languages it may be necessary to use a verbal expression like "the Father who feels pity" or "the Father who cares very much." The description of God as **the Father of mercies and God of all comfort** finds expression in the Old Testament also (see Psa 103.13; Isa 51.12; 66.13). In the context of 2 Corinthians, this description is especially appropriate for Paul's own situation. God is the one who acts with mercy and who provides comfort for his people.

Comfort: this word occurs as a verb or noun ten times in verses 3-7 and again several times in chapters 2, 7, and 13. The Greek word has several components of meaning, including the idea of consoling someone in trouble or sorrow and the idea of giving active help or encouragement. It comes from the same root as the name given to the Holy Spirit in John (14.16,26; 15.26; 16.7), translated "Counselor" in RSV. TEV has emphasized the aspect of active help ("from whom all help comes"). NRSV and REB emphasize the idea of consoling ("the God of all consolation").

Since some languages may require verbal expressions for the noun phrases in this verse, the following model is suggested: "Let us praise God, who is the God and the Father of our Lord Jesus Christ. He is the Father who has mercy on us; he is the God who always puts an end to the sadness of people."

1.4   RSV   TEV

who comforts us in all our affliction, so that we may be able to comfort those who are in any affliction, with the comfort with which we ourselves are comforted by God.	He helps us in all our troubles, so that we are able to help others who have all kinds of troubles, using the same help that we ourselves have received from God.

It is not certain whether the pronouns **us . . . our . . . we . . .** in this verse include the readers or only Paul and Timothy. The same ambiguity exists in verse 5. The liturgical sound of the language in verses 4-5 leads some interpreters to take the pronouns as including the readers. On the other hand, in Greek the words **in all our affliction** refer to specific afflictions and not afflictions in general. If the reference is to the afflictions mentioned in verses 6-11, then the pronouns do not include the readers. Furthermore, since verse 6 distinguishes between Paul and Timothy on the one hand, and the Corinthians on the other, it is more likely that these pronouns do not include the readers.

Comforts: in the translation of this Greek word, TEV again emphasizes the element of giving active help, while NRSV and REB emphasize the element of consolation: "who consoles us" (see comments on verse 3). Note that NJB uses the verb "support" throughout this section.

Affliction may refer to either external suffering or internal, mental anguish, or both. Since Paul provides very little specific information about the nature of this hardship, it is probably good to use the most general term available for "trouble" or "adversity" in the receptor language.

So that may express either purpose or result. If the former, the sense is that God comforts in order that, or for the purpose that, those who are comforted should then in turn comfort others. If, however, these words express result, the sense is that, as a result of being comforted by God, they will be able in turn to comfort others. The latter interpretation indicating result is probably to be preferred. One way of showing this connection may be to make two or three separate sentences saying something like this: "He comforts us in all our troubles. Because of this we are able to comfort other people, no matter what kind of trouble they may have. We comfort them as God has comforted us."

1.5   RSV   TEV

For as we share abundantly in Christ's sufferings, so through Christ we share abundantly in comfort too.[a]

Just as we have a share in Christ's many sufferings, so also through Christ we share in God's great help.

[a] Or, *For as the sufferings of Christ abound for us, so also our comfort abounds through Christ.*

For: the transition word may be important in the receptor language. Here it indicates a close causal relationship with what has just been said. A number of translations render the word **For** explicitly, while others depend on the structure to show this relationship. Still others use words like "indeed" (Phps), or "in effect" (FRCL and TOB), or "it is true" (Knox).

We share abundantly in Christ's sufferings is literally "the sufferings of Christ abound to us." There are two possible interpretations here: (1) The meaning may be that Paul and Timothy have suffered much because of their preaching about Jesus Christ, and Paul considers this suffering to be a part of the sufferings of Jesus through their union with Christ (so RSV, TEV). Or (2) the meaning may be that, as Christ's suffering was great on behalf of the senders of the letter (REB: "extends to us"), so Paul and Timothy's consolation is great on behalf of the Corinthians (so NRSV, REB, and the reading in the footnote of RSV). NRSV says "For just as the sufferings of Christ are abundant for us, so also our consolation is abundant through Christ." Either interpretation seems equally possible in terms of grammatical structure and context. Translators should feel free to choose the interpretation that seems correct to them.

So: because of the difference between sharing in suffering and sharing in comfort, it may be necessary in some languages to use a conjunction marking that contrast at this point. CEV, for example, has "but also . . . ."

We share abundantly in comfort too may mean that Paul and Timothy are abundantly comforted by God (RSV) or that they themselves give abundant comfort to others (so NRSV, REB, and the reading in the footnote of RSV). Some English versions have taken the word twice translated "abound" or **share abundantly** as meaning "overflow" (see NJB, NIV, NEB, and the translation by Barclay [Brc]). The whole verse then yields something like "Because just as the sufferings of Christ are spilling over into our lives, in the same way comfort through Christ is also spilling over to us." It is, however, equally probable that the last part of the verse may mean "spilling over *from* us."

Through Christ: according to verse 4 God is the source of comfort. Christ is the intermediary through whom God comforts.

On the pronoun **we** see the comments on verse 4.

1.6   RSV   TEV

If we are afflicted, it is for your comfort | If we suffer, it is for your help and salvation; if we are helped, then you too are helped and given the strength to endure with patience the same sufferings that we also endure.
and salvation; and if we are comforted, it is for your comfort, which you experience when you patiently endure the same sufferings that we suffer.

Beginning in this verse and continuing through verse 21a, the pronoun **we** does not include the readers.

If we are afflicted: the word **If** does not imply doubt on Paul's part, as if he is referring to something hypothetical. The sense is "Whenever we are afflicted." Anchor Bible (AB) says "When we are being afflicted."

The words translated as **afflicted** and **suffer** in RSV represent two different Greek words. Since the words appear to be nearly synonymous here, TEV translates both words with one English word, "suffer." The first is passive in form but should probably be transformed into an active form in many languages.

For means "for the sake of" or "in favor of." The sufferings of Paul and Timothy are seen as benefiting the people of God in Corinth and the rest of Achaia. In some languages there are benefactive verb forms that will help to convey this meaning.

Comfort and **comforted**: see comments on verse 3.

Salvation: in this context the focus is not on eternal salvation that Christians will receive but rather on the present spiritual well-being of the Corinthians. Phps translates this as "your spiritual protection."

The Corinthians experience **the same sufferings** in that they are also suffering because of their loyalty to Christ.

KJV translates a text found in no known Greek manuscript. Therefore it should not be followed by modern translators.

1.7   RSV   TEV

Our hope for you is unshaken; for we | So our hope in you is never shaken; we know that just as you share in our sufferings, you also share in the help we receive.
know that as you share in our sufferings, you will also share in our comfort.

Our hope: the possessive pronoun here does not include the Corinthians, since it involves something Paul and Timothy hope for them. The **hope** to which Paul refers is the hope that the Corinthian Christians will continue in their faith despite the afflictions and suffering that they experience. In English the word **hope** often suggests a degree of uncertainty. But in the New Testament the sense is more often that of "confidence" or "assurance." In some languages the noun **hope** has to be translated by a verbal expression such as "we put our hearts on you . . ." or something similar.

For you: note, however, that TEV has "in you." This probably does not reflect a difference in meaning in these two versions. Both indicate confidence that the Corinthian Christians will stand firm in times of trouble and affliction.

Unshaken: another way of saying this is "Our hope for you is certain (or secure, or firmly grounded)" (AB, NJB, REB), or in some languages it may be necessary to use the adjective "strong." If a verbal phrase is used to translate **hope** as suggested above, an adverb like "firmly" or "completely" may be used to translate this word. Note that CEV renders this whole clause as "you never disappoint us."

We know that is literally "knowing that." Though TEV does not make explicit the relationship between the two parts of this verse, the participle "knowing" introduces the cause or reason that their hope is unshaken. RSV adds the word **for** in order to express clearly this relationship.

Our suffering . . . our comfort: Paul does not actually say *our* suffering *. . . our* comfort in spite of the renderings of RSV and TEV. The introduction of the possessive pronoun is misleading, according to some commentators (AB, page 112). REB reads "if you share in the suffering, you share also in the comfort." But the use of the definite article in Greek (reflected in REB) seems to indicate that some particular suffering is in view. So "the suffering" and "the comfort" probably do refer to those of Paul (and Timothy). But the **sufferings** that Paul mentions are not made specific here. Though the distress may have been caused by a severe illness, the following verses suggest that the suffering was a result of external forces.

As you share in our sufferings: as with the last part of verse 6, the meaning is that they suffer the same kind of suffering as Paul and Timothy. Some languages will require that this be made more explicit by saying something like "when you suffer as we have, you will also receive comfort just as we have."

You will also share in our comfort: literally "thus also in the comfort." The meaning may be that the Corinthians will be able to comfort others, but the parallelism with the preceding phrase favors the sense that they will receive the same comfort that Paul and Timothy receive. Following the latter interpretation, translators may want to follow the model of Phps and make explicit that the help comes from God: "then, like us, you will find the comfort and encouragement of God."

1.8	RSV	TEV

For we do not want you to be ignorant, brethren, of the affliction we experi-

We want to remind you, brothers, of the trouble we had in the province of

enced in Asia; for we were so utterly, unbearably crushed that we despaired of life itself.

Asia. The burdens laid upon us were so great and so heavy that we gave up all hope of staying alive.

Verse 8 begins with the word **For**, which connects the mention of suffering in general in verse 7 with mention of specific suffering in verses 8-10. REB translates this word as "In saying this."

We do not want you to be ignorant: in Greek two negatives are used: "We do not want you not to know." In English this is expressed more naturally with a positive expression such as "we want you to know," or "we want you to be quite certain" (NJB), or more dynamically, "Make no mistake . . ." (Knox). CEV takes this as an epistolary plural and thus translates "I want you to know." Parallel expressions occur in Rom 1.13; 11.25; 1 Cor 10.1; 12.1; and 1 Thes 4.13, but with a first person singular subject.

Brethren: in his letters Paul frequently addressed his readers with the word "brothers." The context in many instances supports the view that Paul most likely was addressing both men and women. While there is an unmistakable male bias in most of the biblical books, some modern translations prefer to translate "brothers" with a word that does not exclude women when it seems that Paul was including women along with the men. So REB and CEV translate "brothers" in this verse as "my friends." (See also 8.1,23; 9.3,5; 11.9,26; 13.11.) The English word "siblings" includes both men and women, but this word would sound very unnatural in English translations. Many languages, however, do have a commonly used word that includes women and men; and in the above verses translators may want to use that word rather than a word such as "brothers," which does not include women. Note that NRSV translates "brothers and sisters." In some languages it will be necessary to add a possessive pronoun and say either "my brothers [and sisters]" or "our brothers [and sisters]."

Though Paul does not indicate here whether **the affliction** was sickness or external dangers against his life, the latter seems more probable. **Affliction** may be translated as "trouble" (TEV, REB) or "hardships" (NJB).

We experienced . . . we were . . . we despaired: perhaps Paul is speaking about himself only, using the epistolary plural (so AT: "the distress that I experienced . . . I was . . . I despaired"). If translators choose to retain the plural subject, it should be taken as including only Timothy and not the recipients of the letter.

Asia is the Roman province (see TEV and REB) of which Ephesus was the chief commercial center. It included most of the western part of Asia Minor. In modern geography Asia Minor corresponds to the peninsula that forms the western half of the country of Turkey. **Asia** in Paul's letters should not be confused with the modern continent that we call Asia.

We were so utterly, unbearably crushed: Paul is using figurative language here. The Greek is literally "excessively, beyond [our] power [to cope] we were burdened." Some possible models for translation into the receptor language may be "we were under great pressure, far beyond our ability to endure" (NIV) or "the burdens on us were so heavy that there was no way that we could tolerate them."

We despaired of life itself: some models other than TEV may be "we lost hope that we could possibly survive" or "we felt certain that we were going to die."

1.9	RSV	TEV

Why, we felt that we had received the sentence of death; but that was to make us rely not on ourselves but on God who raises the dead;	We felt that the death sentence had been passed on us. But this happened so that we should rely, not on ourselves, but only on God, who raises the dead.

Why . . . : this RSV rendering may be misleading, and TEV has no overt transition marker at all, but in Greek this verse begins with a word that expresses a contrast with the preceding verse. The sense is "Instead of feeling that we had hope, on the contrary we felt that we had received the death sentence." NRSV and REB begin verse 9 with the word "Indeed," while NJB and CEV have "In fact," both of which underscore the sense of despair mentioned in verse 8.

We felt that we had received: literally "but we have (or, had) the sentence of death in ourselves." If Paul was referring to a physical illness, then the verb "we have" may indicate that the results of the illness continued to bother him. If so, a better translation will be "we ourselves have received within ourselves" (so Barrett). But the tense of the verb may refer to an action already completed (as in 2.13), in which case the RSV and TEV translations are correct.

The sentence of death is, as TEV makes clear, "the death sentence." Probably this is figurative language. Paul had not actually received a legal sentence of death from a judge; rather his affliction was so great that he felt the way he would have felt if he had in fact received a legal sentence of death. Another way of saying this may be "we really thought that the time had come for us to die."

But that was: these three words in RSV translate one word in Greek that expresses purpose. The second half of this verse expresses the purpose for which they had "received the death sentence." The word **that** refers to the belief that they had received the death sentence. Both TEV and NIV attempt to supply this information by saying "But this happened so that . . . ," and REB has "This was meant to teach us . . . ."

Rely . . . on: the verb so translated may also be rendered "put [our] trust in" (Brc) or "place [our] confidence in" (GNC). The verb "trust" is also used by CEV, Knox, and NCV.

Who raises the dead: Judaism praised God's power as being able to raise the dead to life in this world (see 1 Sam 2.6; 1 Kgs 17.17-22; 2 Kgs 4.32-37). Since God is able to bring dead people back to life, surely he is able to protect those who suffer or are in serious danger. Some translations insert the word "can," that is, "who can even raise the dead" (AT, so also Phps). However, such an insertion may suggest that, though God is able to raise the dead, he does not do so. But Paul is affirming that God does raise the dead.

1.10   RSV   TEV

he delivered us from so deadly a peril, and he will deliver us; on him we have set our hope that he will deliver us again.

From such terrible dangers of death[a] he saved us, and will save us; and we have placed our hope in him that he will save us again,

[a] terrible dangers of death; *some manuscripts have* terrible death.

As the note in TEV indicates, some manuscripts have the plural (literally "such terrible deaths"), while others have the singular. It is difficult to decide which reading is more likely to have been original, though the meaning is basically the same in either case.

Other differences occur in the Greek manuscripts of this verse. Some omit the words **and he will deliver us**. Other manuscripts read "he delivers us" (KJV, RVR) instead of **he will deliver us**. This provides a neat past, present, and future use of the same verb, but most scholars prefer the reading followed by RSV and TEV. Some languages must distinguish between the near future and the distant future; here Paul seems to be referring to the near future. The verb translated **deliver** may also be rendered "preserve" or "rescue." This same term is found in 2 Tim 4.17 in the sense of being rescued from the jaws of a lion. The word used here is not the one usually translated "save" in English. Some languages may say something like "snatched us from the jaws of death," or "pulled us out of the way of death," or "turned us from the road of death."

We have set our hope: this English expression represents a single verb 'in Greek that has the same root as the noun in verse 7. In a number of languages it will be rendered something like "we have placed our hearts [on him]," or the whole phrase may read "we trust him [God] to rescue us from the dangers to come."

That he will deliver us again: these words express the content of the hope or the object of the verb to hope (RSV, TEV). Some Greek manuscripts, however, omit the word **that**. Translations that follow the manuscripts without the word **that** begin a new sentence with this clause: "and he will deliver us again, he on whom our hope is fixed. Yes, he will continue to deliver us" (REB). The Greek text, as represented by REB, does not state explicitly what the content of the hope is. Nor does the Greek state explicitly the grammatical object of the verb **deliver** in this case. It is, however, easily supplied from the first verb in this verse. This may be done by repeating "deliver us from death" or by adding a different expression synonymous with death or destruction. Other languages may say "prevent us from dying" or "keep us alive."

1.11   RSV   TEV

You also must help us by prayer, so | as you help us by means of your
that many will give thanks on our be- | prayers for us. So it will be that the
half for the blessing granted us in an- | many prayers for us will be answered,
swer to many prayers. | and God will bless us; and many will
| raise their voices to him in thanksgiving
| for us.

TEV rearranges the order of the clauses in this verse to present the ideas
in a logical or chronological order. In the RSV translation it sounds as if the
many prayers have already been answered when Paul writes. The thought is
rather that: (1) the people will pray for Paul and Timothy; (2) God will answer
the prayers and will bless Paul and Timothy; and (3) other people will thank
God.

Verse 11 begins with a participle in Greek. Several options exist for
translating this participle. (1) Sometimes participles have the force of an
imperative, as in RSV, "You also must help us." (2) Participles may also express
the means by which an action is accomplished, or may express the circumstances under which an action is accomplished. This latter use of the participle
is reflected in TEV, "as you help us." Similar to TEV is NRSV, "as you also join
in helping us" (so also REB). (3) Participles may express a condition: "if you too
cooperate on our behalf" (Barrett). The context does not favor one interpretation over the others, but the third option, "if you too cooperate," is probably the
most widely accepted by recent interpreters.

You also must help us by prayer: literally "you also cooperating in
helping us by prayer." The Greek does not state with whom the Corinthians
cooperate. With one another? With Paul and Timothy? With God? REB seems
to suggest that they cooperate with God: "Yes, he will continue to deliver us,
while you cooperate by praying for us."

On our behalf: as the note in NIV indicates, many manuscripts read "on
your behalf." The meaning would then be that many Christians gave thanks
for the intercessory prayers of the Corinthians. Such a reading makes very
little sense in the context and is not likely to be original.

For the blessing granted us: as noted above, Paul is referring to
blessings from God that have not yet been granted (see TEV). The granting of
blessings and the thanksgiving that will follow will come after the prayers that
Paul is urging in this verse. The RSV translation is not a good model here. It
is better to follow TEV with the future tense of the verb "to bless," or to say
something like "for the blessing that God will give [bestow on] us."

B. Paul and the Church at Corinth

(1.12–7.16)

B-1. Paul explains his past actions
1.12–2.4

RSV

TEV

The Change in Paul's Plans

12 For our boast is this, the testimony of our conscience that we have behaved in the world, and still more toward you, with holiness and godly sincerity, not by earthly wisdom but by the grace of God. 13 For we write you nothing but what you can read and understand; I hope you will understand fully, 14 as you have understood in part, that you can be proud of us as we can be of you, on the day of the Lord Jesus.

15 Because I was sure of this, I wanted to come to you first, so that you might have a double pleasure; 16 I wanted to visit you on my way to Macedonia, and to come back to you from Macedonia and have you send me on my way to Judea. 17 Was I vacillating when I wanted to do this? Do I make my plans like a worldly man, ready to say Yes and No at once? 18 As surely as God is faithful, our word to you has not been Yes and No. 19 For the Son of God, Jesus Christ, whom we preached among you, Silvanus and Timothy and I, was not Yes and No; but in him it is always Yes. 20 For all the promises of God find their Yes in him. That is why we utter the Amen through him, to the glory of God. 21 But it is God who establishes us with you in Christ, and has commissioned us; 22 he has put his seal upon us and given us his Spirit in our hearts as a guarantee.

23 But I call God to witness against me—it was to spare you that I refrained from coming to Corinth. 24 Not that we lord it over your faith; we work with you for your joy, for you stand firm in your faith. *(Chapter 2:)* 1 For I made up my mind not to make you another painful visit. 2 For if I cause you pain, who is there to make me glad but the one whom I have pained? 3 And I wrote as I did, so that

12 We are proud that our conscience assures us that our lives in this world, and especially our relations with you, have been ruled by God-given frankness and sincerity, by the power of God's grace and not by human wisdom. 13-14 We write to you only what you can read and understand. But even though you now understand us only in part, I hope that you will come to understand us completely, so that in the Day of our Lord Jesus you can be as proud of us as we shall be of you.

15 I was so sure of all this that I made plans at first to visit you, in order that you might be blessed twice. 16 For I planned to visit you on my way to Macedonia and again on my way back, in order to get help from you for my trip to Judea. 17 In planning this, did I appear fickle? When I make my plans, do I make them from selfish motives, ready to say "Yes, yes" and "No, no" at the same time? 18 As surely as God speaks the truth, my promise to you was not a "Yes" and a "No." 19 For Jesus Christ, the Son of God, who was preached among you by Silas, Timothy, and myself, is not one who is "Yes" and "No." On the contrary, he is God's "Yes"; 20 for it is he who is the "Yes" to all of God's promises. This is why through Jesus Christ our "Amen" is said to the glory of God. 21 It is God himself who makes us, together with you, sure of our life in union with Christ; it is God himself who has set us apart, 22 who has placed his mark of ownership upon us, and who has given us the Holy Spirit in our hearts as the guarantee of all that he has in store for us.

23 I call God as my witness—he knows my heart! It was in order to spare you that I decided not to go to Corinth. 24 We are not trying to dictate to you what you must believe;

when I came I might not suffer pain from those who should have made me rejoice, for I felt sure of all of you, that my joy would be the joy of you all. 4 For I wrote you out of much affliction and anguish of heart and with many tears, not to cause you pain but to let you know the abundant love that I have for you.

we know that you stand firm in the faith. Instead, we are working with you for your own happiness.

Chapter 2

1 So I made up my mind not to come to you again to make you sad. 2 For if I were to make you sad, who would be left to cheer me up? Only the very persons I had made sad. 3 That is why I wrote that letter to you—I did not want to come to you and be made sad by the very people who should make me glad. For I am convinced that when I am happy, then all of you are happy too. 4 I wrote you with a greatly troubled and distressed heart and with many tears; my purpose was not to make you sad, but to make you realize how much I love you all.

SECTION HEADING: TEV "The Change in Paul's Plans." Many interpreters see verse 12 as the beginning of a major section that continues through the end of chapter 7, and the outline of this Handbook follows that interpretation. NAB, for example, uses a major heading for 1.12–7.16 and calls it "The Crisis between Paul and the Corinthians." NJB calls this section "Some Recent Events Reviewed." But in those translations where more than one level of section heading is used, the NAB model seems preferable.

While nearly all interpreters consider verse 12 to be the beginning of a major section, they differ in how they divide this unit into smaller sections. REB, for example, groups 1.12–2.17 under the heading "Paul's concern for the church at Corinth." NAB groups 1.12–2.13 under the heading "Past Relationships." NIV, in agreement with TEV, ends this section at 2.4 and calls this section "Paul's Change of Plans." The section heading in TEV and NIV does focus on the major issue that Paul deals with in 1.12–2.4. However, ending the division at verse 4 obscures the fact that the offender mentioned in 2.5-11 seems to have been responsible for the earlier painful visit that led Paul to change his travel plans (see 2.3,9).

If the section division of TEV is followed, translators may wish to be more precise in the title of the heading. The TOB heading for 1.12–2.4 is "Why Paul put off his visit." NJB heads this section "Why Paul changed his plans." But in some languages it may be appropriate to state more specifically what Paul's intention was: "Paul Decides to Delay his Visit to Corinth" or, as the German common language version (GECL) puts it, "Why Paul did not return to Corinth."

1.12	RSV	TEV

For our boast is this, the testimony of our conscience that we have behaved in the world, and still more toward you, with holiness and godly sin-

We are proud that our conscience assures us that our lives in this world, and especially our relations with you, have been ruled by God-given frank-

cerity, not by earthly wisdom but by the
grace of God.

ness[b] and sincerity, by the power of
God's grace and not by human wisdom.

[b] frankness; *some manuscripts have*
holiness.

Verses 12-14 are transition verses from the introductory section (1.1-11) to the theme of Paul's travel plans and his relationship to the church at Corinth. As the following verses suggest, some people in Corinth thought that Paul was not being honest or straightforward in his relationship with them. In verses 12-13 Paul assures the readers that his conscience is clear, and that he has been guided in his decisions by God's grace and not by his own human wisdom.

Verse 12 begins in Greek with the word **For**. Though this word sometimes expresses a causal relationship between two phrases, it may also function as an introductory word without connecting what follows with what precedes. Here the Greek word appears to function only to introduce a new movement of thought. The word may be omitted in some languages (so TEV and REB) or translated with an introductory word such as "Now" (AB). In some languages the presence of a new section heading serves much the same purpose as this transition word. If the word is translated overtly, the receptor language word or phrase used should be one that serves to introduce an important point or that indicates a point of transition.

Boast: this noun and the related verb are very common in 2 Corinthians and may be considered a key word in this letter. In this context **boast** may refer to "that which one boasts about" (RSV, NIV, NRSV, REB) or "the reason that one is proud." The former seems more likely. While it is a noun, it may be better translated by a verbal expression, as in TEV. Here the idea of "boasting" may be expressed in some languages in terms of "pride," but in other cases it will be necessary to soften this by using an expression like "we must say something good about ourselves . . ." or "something that makes us feel good about ourselves is . . . ."

Both Nestle-Aland and the UBS *Greek New Testament* place the words **the testimony of our conscience** within commas. This punctuation is accepted by Phps: "Now it is a matter of pride to us—endorsed by our conscience—that our activities . . . ." That is, Paul is stating that he is proud that his life has been ruled by God's grace, and his conscience agrees with, or endorses, his boast. This interpretation and punctuation are followed also in NRSV: "Indeed, this is our boast, the testimony of our conscience: we have behaved . . ." (so also TOB, Nouvelle version Segond révisée [NVSR]).

On the other hand, both RSV and TEV make the words **the testimony of our conscience** a part of that about which Paul boasts, that is, he is proud that his conscience assures him that his life has been ruled by God's grace (so also REB, Spanish common language version [SPCL], FRCL). Both interpretations make good sense, and the grammar and context do not point more strongly to one interpretation over the other. In most languages it will not be possible to maintain the ambiguity of the Greek, and translators must simply choose one interpretation, knowing that the other is equally possible.

The word **conscience** presents serious problems for translators in many languages. It occurs in Paul's speeches in Acts (23.1 and 24.16) and is used frequently by Paul in his letters—especially to the Corinthian Christians. It is also found in the letter to the Hebrews and in 1 Peter. It involves knowledge based on contemplation of one's past actions. In some cases it is qualified by the adjectives "good" or "clean"—if those actions have been acceptable—and as "evil" if they are unacceptable. In 1 Peter 2.19 RSV translates the same term "mindful," and in Heb 10.2 it is rendered "consciousness." So the meaning is something like "awareness," either of having done wrong or of having done nothing wrong. In this verse it clearly involved Paul's feeling that he had done no wrong. It is translated "conscientious conviction" by NJB. In many languages the nominal expression **the testimony of our conscience** may be rendered by a verbal expression like "our heart tells us" or something similar.

We have behaved: the verb used here involves a person's actions and relationships with other people. Some languages may say "our conduct has been . . ." or "we have lived . . . ."

The words **in the world** here are not negative, as if the world is an evil place. Paul is simply referring to his daily life among people.

With holiness and godly sincerity is literally "with holiness and sincerity of God." The words "of God" may modify the second noun only (RSV, NRSV) or both nouns (TEV; NIV "in the holiness and sincerity that are from God"). Some manuscripts have a word meaning "frankness" in place of **holiness** here. In Greek the two words are spelled almost the same. In this case the word "frankness" would be virtually synonymous with **sincerity**. This is reflected in a variety of translations, including KJV, NRSV, and Translator's New Testament (TNT), as well as TEV. The reading "frankness" is recommended by the editors of the UBS *Greek New Testament* as the word that fits the context better. "Frankness" may be expressed as "openness," "absolutely above board" (Phps), or, in some cases, by a full verbal expression like "we have not hidden anything from you." The alternative term **holiness** presents special problems in many languages. If translators follow the texts that have **holiness** (as in RSV, NIV, and REB), it may be necessary to restructure the whole phrase and say something like "we have always lived as those who belong to God [or, in obedience to God] and with a sincerity that comes from God."

Earthly wisdom: literally "fleshly wisdom" (KJV). Paul sometimes uses the word "fleshly" to refer to that which is typical of human nature. Some other possible models may be "the wisdom of this world" (CEV) or simply "human wisdom" (TNT).

The grace of God: on the term **grace** see verse 2 above. The expression "the grace of God" occurs nineteen times in Acts and the New Testament letters. It refers to God's kindness or goodness to human beings, who can do nothing to earn it. In this context Paul is saying that his good behavior is not due to anything in himself but to God's goodness to him.

A model for this verse as a whole may be something like the following:

In our own hearts we know that in everything we have done in this world we have done it all with an honest and pure heart given by God. And this is especially true of what we have done in our relations with you. We are very proud of this. But we have done this by the grace of God and not by human wisdom.

1.13-14   RSV   TEV

13 For we write you nothing but what you can read and understand; I hope you will understand fully, 14 as you have understood in part, that you can be proud of us as we can be of you, on the day of the Lord Jesus.

13-14 We write to you only what you can read and understand. But even though you now understand us only in part, I hope that you will come to understand us completely, so that in the Day of our Lord Jesus you can be as proud of us as we shall be of you.

RSV follows the order of the Greek in verses 13-14, while TEV restructures the order (so also REB).

For is explanatory. In the previous verse Paul stated that his behavior was "with holiness and godly sincerity." Verse 13 explains that his letters have been written in the same way and are not intended to deceive or fool the reader.

We write: the pronoun **we** at the beginning of this verse is taken by some as an epistolary plural. Mft, for example, restructures the phrase but talks about "my letters." And AT has "what I am writing." While the verbal expression **we write** may refer to what he is now writing, it probably refers to what he habitually writes in his letters to the Corinthians. REB makes this second interpretation explicit: "There is nothing in our letters to you . . ." (so also Phps, LPD). Translators working in languages that have habitual verb forms may wish to use such a form here.

Nothing but what you can read and understand: Phps captures well the sense of Paul's words here: "Our letters to you have no double meaning—they mean just what you understand them to mean when you read them." Brc adds the words "—no hidden meaning." LPD says "Our letters are not ambiguous: there is nothing more in them than what you can read and understand." And Mft uses a well-known English idiom that also conveys the sense of the text: "You don't have to read between the lines of my letters." Another English idiom is "we did not beat around the bush." But some languages may say something like "we talked straight to you," "our words were not crossed [complicated]," or "our arrows were not crooked when we wrote to you."

I hope: the shift from the plural pronoun to **I** may be taken as support for those who see the above plural as epistolary. And in a number of languages the verb **hope** will have to be translated idiomatically, as in verse 10 above.

Understand fully: the words thus translated in RSV may also be taken as meaning "understand to the end." If taken with the words **in part**, the sense is that they now understand **in part**, but Paul hopes that they will **understand fully**. If taken with the words **on the day of the Lord Jesus**, the sense is that Paul hopes that they will go on understanding "to the end," that is, until Jesus returns (so Barrett). Though both translations fit the context, most interpreters prefer the first of the two possible meanings, as in RSV and TEV.

As you have understood in part: the Greek verb **you have understood** may be taken as referring to the present time or to a time in the past. TEV understands these words to refer to the present situation: "even though you now understand . . ." (so also REB "you do understand us in some measure"). Following this interpretation TEV has inserted the word "now," which is not written in the Greek. Paul may, however, be referring to a time in the recent past. In Greek the pronoun "us" follows the verb **have understood**. RSV has left this pronoun untranslated, but translators may wish to translate it, as TEV does.

That you can be proud . . . : the Greek word translated by **that** in RSV introduces the content of Paul's hope: **that you can be proud of us as we can be of you**.

You can be proud of us as we can be of you is literally "we are your boast just as you are ours." In some languages the clause containing the expression "to be proud of" may have to be translated something like "you will be honored because of us, just as we will be honored because of you" or "we will receive recognition because of you, but you will also receive recognition because of us."

On the day of the Lord Jesus occurs also in 1 Cor 5.5, and without the name "Jesus" in 1 Thes 5.2; 2 Thes 2.2. NJB indicates that **the day of the Lord Jesus** is in the future ("when the Day of our Lord Jesus comes") but does not make clear that this day is the day when Jesus himself will come (so GNC "on the day when the Lord Jesus comes"; see also GECL). To avoid suggesting that this is Jesus' first coming, CEV says "when our Lord Jesus returns."

The Lord Jesus: some Greek manuscripts read **the Lord Jesus** (followed by RSV, NRSV, NIV) in verse 14, and others have the possessive pronoun "our Lord Jesus" (followed by TEV, NJB, and REB). The evidence for both readings is about equal, and NAB reflects the uncertainty by placing the word "our" within brackets in the translation, as do the editors of the UBS *Greek New Testament*. Some languages must use a possessive pronoun with the noun "Lord" regardless of the correct Greek text. "Our" here seems to include the readers.

1.15	RSV	TEV

Because I was sure of this, I wanted to come to you first, so that you might have a double pleasure;[b]

I was so sure of all this that I made plans at first to visit you, in order that you might be blessed twice.

[b] Other ancient authorities read *favor*

Because I was sure of this: that is, sure that they would understand his motives and purpose. In some languages this will have to be restructured to begin "I knew this very well," followed by a "therefore . . ." or "for this reason . . . ." CEV makes clear what the demonstrative pronoun **this** refers to by saying "I was so sure of your pride in us that . . . ."

Paul states in verse 16 that he had planned to visit the Corinthians first on his way to Macedonia and then visit them a second time on his return trip from Macedonia. The Greek word **first** may be connected closely to the words **to you,** as in RSV, NRSV, and REB, and mean that he wanted to visit the Corinthians first before going to visit the Macedonians. Or the word **first** may mean "originally" in the sense of Paul's original intention (so TEV, GNC, FRCL, and TNT). Greek word order seems to favor the TEV translation, but the overall context (see verse 16) is more decisive and favors that of RSV.

Some Greek manuscripts have the word "joy" (translated as **pleasure** in RSV), and some have "grace" (NAB, translated as "blessed" in TEV). Except for one letter, the spelling of the two words is identical in Greek. Either reading makes sense in the context, and both have good manuscript support. But the UBS *Greek New Testament* favors the reading followed by TEV. This is also adopted by NIV, REB, and NJB, which use the English word "benefit" in translation.

Whether read as **double pleasure** or "blessed twice," the word **double** refers to the two visits mentioned in the next verse which he had planned to make to Corinth. CEV says "In this way you would have the blessing of two visits from me."

1.16 RSV	TEV
I wanted to visit you on my way to Macedonia, and to come back to you from Macedonia and have you send me on my way to Judea.	For I planned to visit you on my way to Macedonia and again on my way back, in order to get help from you for my trip to Judea.

The trip to Judea mentioned here is the same trip referred to in 1 Cor 16.1-4, during which the money for the Jewish Christians in Jerusalem was to have been delivered. Corinth was south of the province of Macedonia, whose capital city was Thessalonica. Paul had planned to go to Corinth first, then north to Macedonia, and then back to Corinth, before sailing east for Judea. (See the map, page vi.)

The Greek verb translated as **send . . . on** in RSV often has the additional meaning of helping someone on the journey with food, money, by arranging for travel companions and supplies (see also Rom 15.24, "to be sped on"). Since that meaning seems probable here, TEV says "in order to get help from you." In some languages it may be a good idea to make this a separate sentence: "In that way you could have helped me on my journey on to Judea."

Translators should be careful to distinguish the spelling of **Judea** and Judah. "Judah" is usually an Old Testament term referring to the kingdom in the southern part of the Holy Land consisting of the tribal areas of Judah and Benjamin; the kingdom of Judah was created following the death of Solomon and the dissolution of the United Kingdom (1 Kgs 12ff). Sometime reference to Judah is found in the New Testament in quotations or references to the Old Testament area. However, **Judea** is the Greek and Latin form of the term Judah, and this name came to have a more restricted sense referring to a much smaller area around Jerusalem, namely, a Roman province in the southern part of the Holy Land.

1.17 RSV	TEV
Was I vacillating when I wanted to do this? Do I make my plans like a worldly man, ready to say Yes and No at once?	In planning this, did I appear fickle? When I make my plans, do I make them from selfish motives, ready to say "Yes, yes" and "No, no" at the same time?

REB begins this verse with "that was my intention," indicating that Paul had wanted to visit Corinth, and implying that he had not done so. This may be a good model for certain other languages.

Since Paul canceled the return trip (see 1.23), he was accused by some in Corinth of **vacillating**, or being "fickle." REB says "Did I lightly change my mind?" Literally the Greek says "This therefore intending, did I act with the fickleness?" The presence of the definite article "the" before the noun "fickleness" may indicate that Paul is responding to a specific accusation that he was fickle or vacillating.

To do this refers to his plans to visit the Corinthians both on his way to Macedonia and on his return from there. In some cases it may be helpful to spell out what the word **this** means in the first part of the verse rather than waiting to read **my plans** in the second part. The second question is, in fact, more general. Here the reference is to his specific plan to visit Corinth. Translators may consider saying something like "Do you think that I decided on this trip without thinking?" or "When I made these plans, did that mean that I lacked determination?"

Do I make my plans . . . ? This second question is less restricted in nature than the first. Here Paul is not talking only about his specific plan to visit the Corinthians but about plans in general. The habitual verb form should probably be used in those languages that have it.

Like a worldly man is literally "according to the flesh." "Flesh" in this context, as elsewhere in Paul's writings, means humankind in its opposition to God. So TEV says "from selfish motives." But in some languages it may be most natural to translate "like the people of this world," if this gives the idea of self-interest.

The form of both questions presupposes that only a negative answer is appropriate. If this will not be clear in the receptor language in this context, it will be better to translate the questions as negative statements: "I was not

fickle when I planned to visit you. And I do not make my plans like the people
of this world . . . ."

Paul had planned to return to Corinth after his trip to Macedonia, but
in 1.23–2.1 he indicates that he did not return to Corinth as he had planned.
Originally Paul had planned to go to Macedonia first before he visited Corinth
(1 Cor 16.5-8). Then he changed his plans and visited Corinth before going to
Macedonia, intending to return through Corinth again on his return home from
Macedonia. Then he again changed his plans and did not return to Corinth
after his visit to Macedonia. Because of these changes in his plans, Paul was
criticized by some people in the Corinthian church.

Ready to say Yes and No at once? Though some manuscripts say **Yes
and No** (followed by RSV), the original form was probably "Yes, yes and No, no"
(followed by TEV, NRSV). The meaning is the same either way. Most translations add the words "at the same time" (TEV, NRSV, TOB, similarly NIV) to make
explicit what Paul leaves implicit. By this rhetorical question Paul declares
that he does not say one thing and then deny it all in the same breath.

Yes and No: in the context of these verses, the word **Yes** refers to his
promise to visit Corinth, and **No** refers to his decision not to visit as planned.
REB says "First saying 'Yes, yes' and then 'No, no'?" In some languages it may
be more natural and more easily understood to say "saying 'Yes' and then 'No'
or 'No' and then 'Yes' " or "saying 'Yes' when I mean 'No' and 'No' when I mean
'Yes.' " And in some cases the use of the words "Yes" and "No" in such a
context may be unnatural. In such cases one may translate more dynamically,
using verbal expressions: "agreeing and refusing all at the same time" or
"accepting and rejecting the same idea in a short time."

1.18 RSV	TEV
As surely as God is faithful, our word to you has not been Yes and No.	As surely as God speaks the truth, my promise to you was not a "Yes" and a "No."

As surely as God is faithful: the sense seems to be that it is not only
Paul himself who bears witness to his integrity; God, who can be trusted,
likewise bears witness to Paul's integrity. Barrett makes this implicit
information explicit in his translation: "God is to be trusted, and he will bear
witness that our word to you is not Yes and No." Another possible model can
be "Just as God never deceives [people] . . . ."

Our word: though the primary reference is to Paul's "promise" to visit the
Corinthians (so TEV), **our word** probably includes also the Good News that they
preach (1.19-20). Perhaps TEV limits the meaning too much.

Our word to you has not been Yes and No: as in verse 17, the sense is
that Paul is not saying contradictory things at the same time. AT says "there
has been no equivocation about our message to you." REB says "What we tell
you is not a mixture of Yes and No." Other models can include "We (or, I) did
not agree and refuse at the same time" or "our (or, my) promise to you was not

made with two hearts (or, minds)." The plural possessive pronoun is very likely epistolary and should be translated as a singular (so ITCL).

1.19	RSV	TEV

For the Son of God, Jesus Christ, whom we preached among you, Silvanus and Timothy and I, was not Yes and No; but in him it is always Yes.	For Jesus Christ, the Son of God, who was preached among you by Silas, Timothy, and myself, is not one who is "Yes" and "No." On the contrary, he is God's "Yes";

Paul has defended his integrity in the preceding verses, and now he defends the integrity of his gospel.

The Son of God, Jesus Christ: Paul rarely refers to Jesus as "Son of God." RSV maintains the focus of the Greek text by placing **Jesus Christ** in apposition to **the Son of God**. TEV unnecessarily shifts the focus to the name "Jesus Christ" rather than keeping the focus on the title "the Son of God." But in some languages it is considered more natural to give a person's name before his or her title. In such cases it will be better to say "Jesus Christ, the Son of God."

Whom we preached among you, Silvanus and Timothy and I: literally "who among you by us was preached, through me and Silvanus and Timothy." Many translations in English change the order of the names and place Paul after Silvanus and Timothy, since English etiquette requires that the speaker mention himself or herself last. Both RSV and TEV fail to reflect a subtle but important aspect of the Greek sentence: by mentioning himself first, Paul emphasizes his own role. AB captures this well: "who was preached among you by us—by myself, and also by Silvanus and Timothy." Translators are encouraged to follow the order of the names in the Greek (as in the 1984 German revision of the Luther translation [Lu], TOB, NJB).

Further, the Greek sentence suggests that the listing of the names was something of an afterthought, intended to clarify the words "by us." TEV (also FRCL, TOB) unnecessarily smooths out the sentence. By inserting the words "that is," NJB shows that the names are intended to clarify: "who was proclaimed to you by us, that is, by me and by Silvanus and Timothy." But translators should not structure this phrase in an unnatural way in the receptor language simply to try to reflect the form of the Greek. And in languages where it is not possible to reflect the passive of the original and TEV, one may translate actively along the lines of RSV, **whom we preached to you . . . .**

RSV transliterates the Greek name **Silvanus**, which TEV always changes to "Silas," the form better known from the book of Acts. Paul always uses the name "Silvanus," and Acts, the name "Silas." There is little doubt that the same person is referred to.

Was not Yes and No: or, in keeping with the translation of the Yes–No statements above, one may translate "he did not come with two hearts (or, minds)" or "he does not agree and refuse at the same time."

In him it is always Yes: the translation of this clause should also conform to the rendering to the above Yes–No statements. Here one may consider the following models: "he always has only one heart (or, mind)" or "he always agrees."

1.20	RSV	TEV
For all the promises of God find their Yes in him. That is why we utter the Amen through him, to the glory of God.	for it is he who is the "Yes" to all of God's promises. This is why through Jesus Christ our "Amen" is said to the glory of God.

All the promises of God: or, more literally, "as many as [are] the promises of God." This is not the more usual way of saying "all." The idea is that "no matter how many promises God has made, they are Yes in Christ" (NIV).

Find their Yes in him: the pronoun **him** in this verse refers to Jesus Christ (verse 19), although TNT takes it to refer to God. In some languages it may not be possible to carry through the formal connection with the Yes–No statements in the previous verses. But the meaning is not essentially changed if one translates "For he is the one who fulfills all the promises of God."

That is why we utter the Amen through him: the Greek is literally "this is why through him the Amen to God for glory through us." The pronoun **we** in this verse includes the readers. "Through us" seems to mean "when we say the word 'Amen' (in community worship)." **Through him** may mean when his name is said. Barclay probably correctly captures the liturgical meaning of this verse: "That is why when to the glory of God we say 'Amen' we say it through him—'through Jesus Christ our Lord.' "

The word **Amen** is well known in the church but may be considered ecclesiastical jargon in some languages. It was common practice in synagogue worship for the congregation to give assent to statements of praise to God. This was carried over into the early church. The meaning of the term is simply "It is true!" or "Indeed!" While the borrowed term "Amen" may be well known in many languages, the meaning understood by the average person is probably something like "the prayer is finished." But since this is not the meaning of the biblical word, it is a good idea to look for a common language equivalent for this term rather than using the transliterated form.

To the glory of God is a fixed phrase used mostly in church circles. To give it its full meaning, one may say "so that God will be honored" (see also 4.15; 8.19).

1.21   RSV   TEV

But it is God who establishes us with
you in Christ, and has commissioned us;

It is God himself who makes us, together with you, sure of our life in union
with Christ; it is God himself who has
set us apart,

But: the transition word is left untranslated in TEV and a number of
other versions. In REB and Mft it is rendered "and," while NIV has "now . . . ."
CEV translates "and so . . ." in an effort to show the logical connection with
what precedes. Translators should seek the most natural connecting word, but
in spite of the RSV rendering, there does not seem to be a sharp contrast with
what goes before.

The first **us** clearly excludes the readers, though the second **us** may
include the readers. Most interpreters understand the plural pronouns in
verses 21b and 22 to include the readers, though some understand them to be
exclusive, as in the preceding verses, that is, including only the apostles. It is
possible that, even though Paul uses the plural here, he may be referring to
himself; so Mft translates the plural pronouns in verses 21-22 as "me."

Establishes us with you in Christ: the verb **establish** means "to make
firm" or "to make sure." The meaning seems to be that God assures Paul and
his companions, along with the Corinthians, that they are firmly united to
Christ. The present tense of the verb is important here. AB uses the present
progressive in English to highlight it: "the one who is confirming us along with
you . . . ."

In Christ and "in Christ Jesus" are common expressions in Paul's letters.
Scholars debate the precise meaning of these words, but most agree that Paul
probably means that a Christian's new life depends closely and entirely on
Christ. TEV usually translates this expression as "in union with Christ," which
seems to capture the basic idea.

Commissioned is literally "anointing" (as in most versions, including
NRSV, NJB, and REB). The Greek has a word play: "God is the one establishing
us with you in the Anointed One and anointing us." When one was anointed,
one was "set apart" (TEV). Some other renderings are "chose" (CEV) and
"consecrated" (Mft and Phps).

1.22   RSV   TEV

he has put his seal upon us and given us
his Spirit in our hearts as a guarantee.

who has placed his mark of ownership
upon us, and who has given us the Holy
Spirit in our hearts as the guarantee of
all that he has in store for us.

Put his seal upon us: Paul uses a verb from the commercial world.
Placing one's seal upon something was a way of indicating ownership. TEV
makes this information explicit by adding "of ownership" (so also NIV). The

noun for **seal** is found in Rom 4.11 and 1 Cor 9.2, and the verb in Eph 1.13. It is also used in its literal sense in Matt 27.66. Some languages may require a more dynamic rendering such as "he has proven that we belong to him" or, probably better, "God has put a sign on us to show that we belong to him."

His Spirit . . . as a guarantee: the Greek is literally "the guarantee of the Spirit." The Spirit is "the Holy Spirit" (TEV) and is itself the guarantee.

Guarantee translates another word from the commercial world. The guarantee was the down payment, a partial payment of the purchase price, which guaranteed that the full price would be paid later. For Paul the gift of the Holy Spirit to Christians is God's guarantee that eventually he will fully redeem his people. See 2 Cor 5.5; Eph 1.13.

In our hearts is a literal translation of the Greek. In Semitic thought, one's heart was the innermost part of a person. It was regarded as the center of one's will, rational activity, and moral choice (see also 3.15). In some languages it may be necessary to say "in each one's heart" or "in each heart," in order not to suggest that a person has several hearts.

On the pronouns **us** and **our**, see comments on verse 21.

The placing of the seal and the giving of the Holy Spirit are seen by many as different ways of talking about the same thing. If this is true, the conjunction **and** is misleading. A good model for some languages may be CEV, which restructures this verse as follows: "and [he] put his Spirit in our hearts to show that we belong only to him."

1.23	RSV	TEV
	But I call God to witness against me—it was to spare you that I refrained from coming to Corinth.	I call God as my witness—he knows my heart! It was in order to spare you that I decided not to go to Corinth.

But: here, as in verse 21, this conjunction is not so much a marker of contrast as an indication of a change in subject. It is represented in many versions by the beginning of a new paragraph. So it may not need to be represented in any other way.

The first part of this verse contains implicit information that may be made explicit in translation: "But I call God to witness against me *if I am not telling you the truth*." The Greek is literally "to witness upon my soul (life)." The meaning is that Paul calls upon God to punish him if Paul has spoken a lie. It may therefore be better in some languages to translate "May God discipline me if I am not telling the truth" or "If I am lying, may God punish me."

It was to spare you: the meaning is not "to save your lives" but rather "to avoid causing you further pain" (see 2.1-2). So it may be preferable in some languages to say something like "I refused to return to Corinth because I did not want to cause you any more suffering" or "the reason I did not go to Corinth again was that I did not want to harm you further."

Coming to Corinth: the use of the verb "come" indicates the point of view of the readers. TEV has "go"—from the point of view of the writer. Either may be an acceptable translation, depending on the normal usage in the receptor language in such a situation. Apparently Paul did go to Corinth before he went to Macedonia; but after his trip to Macedonia, he did not return to Corinth as he had told them he would (see comments on 1.17). Though RSV and TEV are literal translations of the Greek, they give the wrong impression by implying that Paul did not go at all to Corinth. The meaning is that he did not *return* to Corinth after his first stop there while on his way to Macedonia. NRSV as well as NJB and Barrett add the word "again" ("It was to spare you that I did not come again to Corinth") to indicate that he did indeed go there once. NIV and FRCL use the verb "return," while CEV has the verbal expression "stayed away from." Mft indicates both the idea of restraint and the information that it would have been a return visit when he says "refrained from revisiting."

1.24 RSV	TEV
Not that we lord it over your faith; we work with you for your joy, for you stand firm in your faith.	We are not trying to dictate to you what you must believe; we know that you stand firm in the faith. Instead, we are working with you for your own happiness.

Paul's comments in the previous verses regarding his trips to Corinth may suggest to the readers that he considered himself to have the right to make decisions regarding their spiritual lives. However, verse 24 makes clear that Paul has no intention of being a spiritual dictator. The words **Not that** have the force of correcting any possible misunderstanding by the readers (see the same words at 3.5). Some may prefer to fill out the sense by saying "It is not true that . . . ."

Not that we lord it over your faith: the expression **lord it over** is somewhat archaic English and may be quite unnatural in the receptor language. It simply means to "dominate" or "act like a boss." And the word **faith** may be better translated by a verb phrase in many languages. TNT translates straightforwardly "we are not telling you what you must believe." The idea is "we are not bosses who tell you what to believe" (CEV) or "we are not seeking to impose on you what you must believe" (FRCL).

We work with you for your joy is literally "we are co-workers of your joy." Most interpreters do not include the readers, that is, the Corinthians, among the "co-workers." RSV and TEV make clear that the subject **we** in **we work** refers to Paul and his associates, although the added **with you** has the effect of including the Corinthians as co-workers. On the other hand it is grammatically possible that the "co-workers" include the Corinthians along with Paul and his associates. Such an interpretation may be reflected in NAB, "we work together for your joy" (see also *Nueva Biblia Española* [NBE]). However, the recommended interpretation is more like what is found in CEV,

"We [Paul and associates] are working together with you [Corinthians] to make you glad . . . ."

For you stand firm in your faith: these words may also be translated as "for it is by faith that you stand" (Barrett). According to RSV and TEV, Paul says *where* they **stand firm**. According to Barrett, Paul says *how* they **stand firm**. The latter meaning is then that they stand firm, not because Paul and his companions are their lords, but because of their faith in God. This seems to be the interpretation followed by CEV when it says ". . . because your faith is strong."

The traditional division between chapters 1 and 2 is unfortunate. There is no indication in the original that a paragraph break should be made at this point. Recent versions such as NRSV and REB reflect this fact by the format used. Translators are advised to avoid giving the impression of separation at this point.

2.1   RSV   TEV

For I made up my mind not to make you another painful visit.	So I made up my mind not to come to you again to make you sad.

For: the UBS *Greek New Testament* follows those Greek manuscripts that begin this verse with the word **For**. Some manuscripts have the word "But" (followed by KJV). The reading **For** seems to be the best reading, since 2.1 gives the reason for Paul's delay in making a trip to Corinth (1.23-24). This may be translated "So" as in TEV, REB, and others. TNT renders it more dynamically by beginning the verse "This is why . . . ."

I made up my mind: this English idiom translates a single Greek verb meaning "judge," followed by a form of the reflexive pronoun meaning "in myself." In many languages the literal "judge in myself" may be rendered by a verb meaning "I decided," or in some cases "I determined in my heart." In one language the meaning of this verb combined with the negative **not to . . .** that follows resulted in the translation "I refused [to return to you . . .]."

Not to make you another painful visit: literally "not to come to you again in sorrow." Though Acts does not mention this visit, apparently Paul had already made one visit to Corinth that turned out to be a painful visit (this visit may have occurred between the writing of 1 Corinthians and 2 Corinthians; see 2 Cor 13.2). According to TEV, the persons who experienced the pain from the painful visit were the Corinthians, not Paul: "to make you sad." Though verse 2 indicates that the Corinthians were the ones who experienced pain, verse 3 seems to include Paul also. It may therefore be better to avoid stating explicitly who would be made sad by such a visit. The painfulness would certainly be felt by both parties.

The "pain" or sadness to which Paul refers in verses 1-5 is emotional pain and not physical pain. Some languages may need to speak of "sorrow" or "pain in the heart" to make it clear that physical pain is not intended.

The TEV translation "to make you sad," if followed, should not be understood to mean that Paul's purpose in coming was to cause them sorrow. Rather the result of his visit was that they were made sad.

2.2	RSV	TEV

For if I cause you pain, who is there to make me glad but the one whom I have pained?	**For if I were to make you sad, who would be left to cheer me up? Only the very persons I had made sad.**

For if I cause you pain: most translations do not reflect the fact that the pronoun I is emphatic in Greek. The sense is " For if I, who ought to work for your joy, cause you pain . . . ."

In this verse **you** is plural in the Greek, while **the one whom I have pained** is singular, as in RSV. This combination can be misunderstood to mean that, if Paul causes pain to the Corinthian Christians, a single individual would make him glad. Though the Greek is singular in the second part of this verse, TEV changes to the plural ("the persons") in order to indicate that Paul is not here speaking about one specific person. REB uses the pronoun "you" in both parts of the verse: "who is left to cheer me up, except you whom I have offended?" This latter rendering makes very clear that the same group of people is referred to in both parts of this sentence (see verse 3).

Paul's question in this verse is a rhetorical one; the answer, **the one whom I have pained**, is provided in the question. TEV provides a separate answer by changing the last part of the sentence into a statement. In some languages it may be more appropriate to use an emphatic statement in place of the question: "For if I were to cause you pain, there would certainly be no one left to make me happy, because you are the ones I have made sad."

2.3	RSV	TEV

And I wrote as I did, so that when I came I might not suffer pain from those who should have made me rejoice, for I felt sure of all of you, that my joy would be the joy of you all.	**That is why I wrote that letter to you— I did not want to come to you and be made sad by the very people who should make me glad. For I am convinced that when I am happy, then all of you are happy too.**

The content of 1 Corinthians does not seem to fit with what Paul says in verse 4, so the letter referred to here in verse 3 is apparently another letter, now lost, written between 1 and 2 Corinthians. In any case Paul is not referring to the present letter (2 Corinthians) but to a letter that he wrote earlier and which he refers to again in 7.8–12. Though no specific time is indicated, the letter was probably written only a few months earlier, not a few years earlier. Some interpreters regard 2 Cor 10–13 to have been part of the letter referred to in 2.3, but such a view is improbable (see "Translating 2 Corinthians," page 2).

To make clear that Paul is not talking about something that he wrote in chapter 1 of 2 Corinthians, TEV adds "that letter." In some languages it may be necessary to say "another letter" or "that other letter."

I wrote as I did: TEV adds the word "to you" (also FRCL, ITCL, SPCL), since the context clearly indicates that the letter was written to the Corinthians.

The words **so that when I came** should not be misunderstood to mean that Paul is here referring to a visit that he had already made. He has not yet visited Corinth again since he wrote the letter mentioned in this verse, so the words **so that when I came** refer to a visit that he planned to make as soon as possible, and that he still plans to make. Translators may consider saying "the reason that I wrote was so that when I do visit you again . . . ," or else follow the simple form of TEV.

On **pain** see comment on verse 2.1.

From those who should have made me rejoice: an indirect reference to the Corinthian Christians. Some possible models for this part of the verse are "I did not want to be made sad by the very people who would have made me happy" or, more directly, "I did not want to visit you, because meeting with you would only make me unhappy. And you are the people who should make me happy."

That my joy would be the joy of you all: this clause tells the reason for Paul's wanting to be happy. In some languages it may be better to transpose this to the beginning of the verse, as is done in CEV: "The reason I want to be happy is to make you happy." Nearly all interpreters understand this to mean, as in TEV, that when Paul was happy, then all of the Corinthians would be happy too. It is possible, though less likely, that the sense is the following: I will be happy when you are all happy.

Knox captures the meaning of the verse as a whole, translating as follows:

> And those were the very terms in which I wrote to you: I would not come, if it meant finding fresh cause for sorrow where I might have expected to find cause for happiness. I felt confidence in you all, I knew that what made me happy would make you happy too.

2.4	RSV	TEV

For I wrote you out of much affliction and anguish of heart and with many tears, not to cause you pain but to let you know the abundant love that I have for you.	I wrote you with a greatly troubled and distressed heart and with many tears; my purpose was not to make you sad, but to make you realize how much I love you all.

For I wrote refers to the letter mentioned in the previous verse. REB says "That letter I sent you." Some translators may wish to begin this sentence with a temporal clause: "When I wrote that letter . . . ."

Much affliction and anguish of heart and with many tears: these three nominal expressions may have to be translated by verbs in a number of languages. The first of these is translated by CEV "I was suffering terribly." The **affliction** is here not external pain but rather emotional distress. Some translators may be tempted to combine the first two of these expressions in a single rendering because they are so similar in meaning, but if possible this should be avoided since the cumulative effect is important. Some possible models are "I was very sad and suffering greatly so that I was actually crying as I wrote that letter to you" or "when I wrote the letter to you I was so unhappy and troubled that I cried." One language translates the three similar expressions as follows: "Truly I wrote those things to you with [emotional] pain and sadness in my heart and tears in my eyes."

The noun phrase **anguish of heart** may be rendered "my heart was heavy," "my heart was breaking," or "I felt great sorrow in my heart." For other comments on **heart** see 1.22. The words **with many tears**, literally "through many tears," modifies the verb **wrote**. REB says "How many tears I shed as I wrote it." But in many languages it will be necessary to say something like "while I was writing I cried very much."

Not to cause you pain: a similar expression occurs in verse 2.

The abundant love that I have for you: the word **abundant** is literally "even more." In most translations **abundant** modifies the verb "to have love," as in RSV and TEV, indicating the extent of his love. In the Greek, however, **Abundant** may modify the words **for you**, indicating that his love is even more for them than for other people (so Barrett, "that you might know the love that I have specially for you"; and Mft, "to convince you of my love, my special love for you").

The pronouns **you** in this verse are all plural.

B-2. A plea for reconciliation
(2.5-17)

2.5-11

RSV | TEV
Forgiveness for the Offender

5 But if any one has caused pain, he has caused it not to me, but in some measure—not to put it too severely—to you all. 6 For such a one this punishment by the majority is enough; 7 so you should rather turn to forgive and comfort him, or he may be overwhelmed by excessive sorrow. 8 So I beg you to reaffirm your love for him. 9 For this is why I wrote, that I might test you and know whether you are obedient in everything. 10 Any one whom you forgive, I also forgive.

5 Now, if anyone has made somebody sad, he has not done it to me but to all of you—in part, at least. (I say this because I do not want to be too hard on him.) 6 It is enough that this person has been punished in this way by most of you. 7 Now, however, you should forgive him and encourage him, in order to keep him from becoming so sad as to give up completely. 8 And so I beg you to let him know that you really do love him. 9 I wrote you that letter because I wanted to find out how well

What I have forgiven, if I have forgiven anything, has been for your sake in the presence
of Christ, 11 to keep Satan from gaining the
advantage over us; for we are not ignorant of
his designs.

you had stood the test and whether you are
always ready to obey my instructions. 10 When
you forgive someone for what he has done, I
forgive him too. For when I forgive—if, indeed,
I need to forgive anything—I do it in Christ's
presence because of you, 11 in order to keep
Satan from getting the upper hand over us; for
we know what his plans are.

SECTION HEADING: TEV "Forgiveness for the Offender." Since Paul was
referring to an individual and a situation well known to the original readers,
he does not indicate here who the offender was or what specifically the person
had done. Probably the offense against Paul occurred during the "painful visit"
(2.1) and may have been the cause of the pain. SPCL specifies in the section
heading whom the offense was against: "Forgiveness for the person who had
offended Paul" (so also TOB). In some languages it may be necessary to
translate the noun "forgiveness" by a verb and indicate the subject. In those
cases the following models may be helpful: "You should pardon the one who did
wrong" or "Paul encourages the Corinthians to forgive the wrongdoer."

2.5   RSV   TEV

But if any one has caused pain, he
has caused it not to me, but in some
measure—not to put it too severely—to
you all.

Now, if anyone has made somebody sad, he has not done it to me but
to all of you—in part, at least. (I say
this because I do not want to be too
hard on him.)

But: as in 1.21 and 23, the transition word here is not intended to mark
contrast but to introduce a new topic. This is why TEV has "Now," and other
versions, such as NIV and REB, represent the conjunction only by a paragraph
break.

Though Paul uses an indefinite pronoun (**if any one**), the context
indicates that he is referring to a specific case. By adding the words "as is
actually the case," GNC makes clear that the word **if** does not refer to a
hypothetical situation: "Now if, as is actually the case, there is a man who has
been causing sorrow." The New Century Version (NCV) says "Someone there
among you has caused sadness." Some may prefer to say "Since there is a
certain person among you who [has caused trouble]." Paul does not state the
nature of the offense against him, but probably someone had challenged Paul's
apostolic authority. CEV makes explicit the fact that the offender was a
Christian from Corinth: "But if any one *of you*." The Greek in verse 7 makes
clear that the offender was a man.

Pain: see comment on verse 2.1.

Not to me: this is not meant to indicate that Paul was totally unaffected
or untroubled by what the person had done, but that it was not Paul alone who

suffered from the offender's action. For this reason Mft translates "not so much to me as to all of you."

In some measure: these words may modify the verb **has caused pain**. Paul does not want to state too strongly the degree of pain that the offender has caused to the Corinthians. The offender has caused all of them pain "to some extent" (NRSV). REB says "to some extent (I do not want to make too much of it) it has been done to you all" (so also NJB, NAB).

Another possible interpretation is to see the Greek for **in some measure** modifying the number of those to whom the offender caused pain (so TEV). Mft says "he has been causing pain not so much to me as to all of you—at any rate (for I am not going to overstate the case) to a section of you" (so also FRCL). Either interpretation is possible grammatically, and both make sense in the context. Translators may follow either of these two meanings.

Not to put it too severely: literally "in order not to overburden." This is taken by most commentators as a kind of parenthetical statement meaning that Paul did not want to exaggerate the importance of the problem. NCV follows this first interpretation: "(I do not want to make it sound worse than it really is)." Similar is AB, "(I don't want to exaggerate)."

It can, however, mean that Paul did not want to burden the Corinthians or the offender (so TEV), but this is less likely. Translators are therefore advised to follow the structure of the TEV model, putting this part at the very end of the verse and enclosing the statement in parentheses, if such punctuation is used in the receptor language. However, the interpretation of TEV is not recommended. The understanding of AB and NCV is preferable.

2.6   RSV   TEV

For such a one this punishment by the   It is enough that this person has been
majority is enough;   punished in this way by most of you.

Such a one: while Paul clearly has a definite person in mind (TEV "this person"), the Greek word means "For the kind of person [who would do this sort of thing]."

This punishment: the word **this** indicates that Paul is referring to a specific punishment known to him and to the Corinthians. Possibly the **punishment** was that of excommunication from the fellowship. Though nearly all translations say **punishment**, this word is perhaps too strong. Probably it does not indicate physical punishment, but discipline in a more general sense. The Greek word may mean "reproach" or "rebuke" (so Barrett: "this reproof"). Mft has a similar rendering, with "this censure." If possible, translators should choose a word that is sufficiently general to cover various kinds of discipline. Another possible approach is to make a verb phrase of this noun, as in TNT, which translates the whole verse "It is enough in this case that the majority have condemned him."

By the majority refers to the majority of the Christian community in Corinth (Martin: "by the majority [of church members]"). "By most of you"

(TEV) perhaps gives the impression that individuals at different times and in different ways punished the offender. Probably the punishment or reproof was carried out through a democratic procedure in a church meeting. Hence REB translates "The penalty on which the general meeting has agreed has met the offence well enough."

Enough: though most translations understand this word in terms of the severity of the punishment, **enough** may refer to the duration of the punishment. Indeed, verse 7 suggests that the punishment should no longer continue. If the latter interpretation is followed, the meaning is "this punishment by the majority has continued long enough" (so NBE).

Some languages will require the restructuring of this verse along the following lines: "Most of you have already agreed on the way this person should be disciplined, and that should be sufficient" or "The punishment which most of you decided for that person will be enough for him."

2.7	RSV	TEV
	so you should rather turn to forgive and comfort him, or he may be overwhelmed by excessive sorrow.	Now, however, you should forgive him and encourage him, in order to keep him from becoming so sad as to give up completely.

So . . . : RSV, following the original, continues the sentence begun in verse 6, but it will be much better in most languages to begin a new sentence here, as in TEV.

The pronoun **you** is plural, referring to those who will read this letter and who have been involved in the case of the offending Christian.

The word **rather** suggests a contrast with the idea of punishment in verse 6. NJB says "and now by way of contrast you should forgive and encourage him." GNC says "now you ought rather to take the opposite course, forgiving him and encouraging him"; and REB says "Something very different is called for now." NRSV uses the word "instead." A few manuscripts omit the word **rather**, but even if the word were not actually written in the Greek text, the context would still make the idea of contrast implicit.

The pronouns **him** and **he** refer to the person mentioned in verse 5. REB says "forgive the offender." Since Paul is referring to a specific situation, CEV incorrectly generalizes: "When people sin, you should forgive and comfort them."

Comfort: see 1.3. Either meaning of the Greek word fits well in this context: "to comfort" (RSV, NRSV, NIV, TOB) or "to encourage" (TEV, NJB, NAB, FRCL). AB argues that in certain contexts the Greek word has the meaning of "seek reconciliation" (see 1 Cor 4.13, where RSV translates this verb as "to conciliate," and TEV says "to answer back with kind words"), so AB says "deal kindly with him." All three translations, "to comfort," "to encourage," and "to deal kindly with" are possible meanings and each fits the context, so it is difficult to know which sense Paul intended here. Translators must simply choose one of these meanings, knowing that nothing really favors one interpretation over the others.

Or: meaning "otherwise," but in some languages this will have to be made more explicit by beginning a new sentence saying something like "If you do not do this . . . ."

Be overwhelmed: literally "be swallowed up." The implicit thought is that the offender may "give up [the faith] completely." The passive form may have to be avoided by saying something like "if you don't forgive him, he might be so sad that he quits in despair."

The **excessive sorrow** is that of the offender and not the community.

Knox restructures the last sentence of this verse, using the negative: "You must not let him be overwhelmed by excess of grief."

2.8	RSV	TEV
	So I beg you to reaffirm your love for him.	And so I beg you to let him know that you really do love him.

The word **So** links this verse with verse 7 by providing the reason why the Corinthians should let the offender know of their love for him. As in verse 7, CEV incorrectly generalizes: "You should make them sure of your love for them."

The pronouns **you** and **your** in verses 8-10 are plural again, referring to the Corinthian Christians.

I beg you: or perhaps better "I urge you" (NJB, NRSV, and REB). Some languages may have special verb forms to indicate an exhortation such as this.

Reaffirm: the Greek word is a technical term used for the legal action of formally approving something. Perhaps Paul has in mind that the Christian church in Corinth should take official action as a body to reaffirm their love for this person. The context does not tell how the Christians are to express what they decide. But "ratify" focuses on the official decision in a church meeting to "let him know that you really do love him" without saying how they let him know. Some may say "I beg you to give him some definite proof of your love for him" or "you must make him know that you care for him." AB says "I urge you to ratify your love for him." Mft says "I beg you to reinstate him in your love," suggesting also a formal decision by the church.

2.9	RSV	TEV
	For this is why I wrote, that I might test you and know whether you are obedient in everything.	I wrote you that letter because I wanted to find out how well you had stood the test and whether you are always ready to obey my instructions.

This is why: or, more literally, "For this [purpose]." Many modern versions such as TEV recast the sentence and use "because" later in the sentence.

I wrote refers to the letter mentioned in 2.3. As in 2.3, TEV adds the object "to you." Since Paul is referring to a specific letter, TEV also adds "that letter."

That I might test you and know: literally "in order that I might know the value (or, worth) of you." The term used here has to do with the proven value of something as a result of a testing process. Another rendering can be "so that I may know your true character." The "test" was to determine whether they were truly committed to Paul and to his apostolic teachings.

Paul does not state the person to whom the Corinthians are to be obedient. Most probably Paul was referring to their obedience to his instructions (so TEV) or to his authority (so REB). The implied contrast to their obedience to Paul's authority is probably not that they were self-willed, but rather that they were obedient to others who were opposed to Paul.

The pronouns **you** in verses 9 and 10 are plural, again referring to the Corinthian Christians.

2.10   RSV   TEV

Any one whom you forgive, I also for-   When you forgive someone for what he
give. What I have forgiven, if I have   has done, I forgive him too. For when I
forgiven anything, has been for your   forgive—if, indeed, I need to forgive
sake in the presence of Christ,   anything—I do it in Christ's presence
                                           because of you,

Any one whom you forgive, I also forgive is literally "But to whom you forgive anything, I also." The pronoun **I** is emphatic. In some languages it will be more natural to say "I also forgive" (so RSV) or "I also forgive him." And it may also be more natural to turn the sentence around, saying something like "I myself will forgive any person whom you forgive." If the receptor language requires the explicit statement of what is forgiven, one may add "what he has done," since we do not know exactly what the offense was.

I have forgiven: the use of the perfect tense indicates that the offender is in a continuing state of being forgiven. It apparently serves to show that Paul has already forgiven the offender, although this does not come out in the TEV rendering, which seems to imply a general rule.

The words **if I have forgiven anything** should not be understood to mean that Paul has doubts about whether he forgave the offender. The sense of these words is that Paul is not even sure that the offense was so serious as to need forgiveness. Martin says "if indeed there was anything to forgive." By making such a statement Paul was softening his criticism of the offender and helping to bring about reconciliation.

For your sake: some languages will have to say "on your account" or simply "for you." Others will include this idea in a special form of the verb (a form called "benefactive").

In the presence of Christ appears to mean that Paul acted with an awareness of what Christ would desire him to do. Paul did not only what would be best for the church but also what would please Christ. REB translates these words as "as the representative of Christ," and CEV says "with Christ as my witness."

2.11	RSV	TEV

to keep Satan from gaining the advantage over us; for we are not ignorant of his designs.

in order to keep Satan from getting the upper hand over us; for we know what his plans are.

This verse is a continuation of the sentence begun in verse 10 and states the purpose of the forgiveness. In some languages it may be better to begin a new sentence here, saying something like "I do this in order to prevent Satan from being able to trick us." RSV **gaining the advantage** actually implies treachery and cunning deception.

Many translators will simply transliterate the name **Satan**. "Satan" is the transliteration of a Hebrew word which means "accuser" or "adversary." By the last two centuries before the birth of Jesus, Judaism had come to think of him as a leader of the forces of evil. "Satan" was one of the names given to this spiritual being.

The pronouns **us** and **we** probably include the readers.

For we are not ignorant of his designs is an example of litotes, that is, of understatement for the sake of emphasis. **We are not ignorant of** means "we know only too well" (NJB) or "we know well enough" (Knox). In many languages it will be advisable to translate in this more direct manner, "we know very well."

His designs: that is, the evil purposes and intentions that Satan has for seducing those who seek to follow the will of God. In many languages it will be both natural and faithful to use a word that has negative connotations, such as "schemes" (NIV), "intrigues," "conspiracy," or "plots."

2.12-13

RSV	TEV
	Paul's Anxiety in Troas

12 When I came to Troas to preach the gospel of Christ, a door was opened for me in the Lord; 13 but my mind could not rest because I did not find my brother Titus there. So I took leave of them and went on to Macedonia.

12 When I arrived in Troas to preach the Good News about Christ, I found that the Lord had opened the way for the work there. 13 But I was deeply worried, because I could not find our brother Titus there. So I said good-bye to the people there and went on to Macedonia.

SECTION HEADING: TEV "Paul's Anxiety in Troas." When Paul did not make the planned visit to Corinth (1.16; 2.1), he apparently sent Titus instead, perhaps with the letter mentioned in 2.3-4. Then Paul himself left Ephesus and went to Troas to preach. Perhaps he had made specific plans to meet Titus in Troas; but in any case, he was hoping to meet him there. Even though there was an opportunity to preach the gospel in Troas, Paul was so concerned about Titus that he left Troas and continued on to Macedonia. The translation of this section heading may present problems in certain languages. Some may wish to use a single heading for the remainder of this chapter (as in NIV, TOB, and others). In this case it will be good to indicate in the heading that the section actually talks about the relief of Paul's anxiety as well as the anxiety itself. And the noun "anxiety" may be better rendered by a verbal expression such as "Paul is distressed" or "Paul worries . . . ." NIV ignores the situation in Troas and has a much more general title for verses 12-17: "Ministers of the New Covenant." But given the abrupt change at verse 14, it is probably better to make verses 12 and 13 a separate section.

2.12	RSV	TEV
	When I came to Troas to preach the gospel of Christ, a door was opened for me in the Lord;	When I arrived in Troas to preach the Good News about Christ, I found that the Lord had opened the way for the work there.

Troas was an important seaport city on the northwest coast of the Roman province of Asia Minor (see comments on 1.8; and see the map, page vi). Paul was probably traveling from Ephesus, a city about 200 kilometers southeast of Troas. In some languages it will be wise to add a classifier term like "city" or "port."

To preach the gospel of Christ is literally "for the gospel of Christ" (NAB). NJB says "for the sake of the gospel of Christ." Though the Greek may mean nothing more than "for the sake of the gospel" (see 1 Cor 9.23), nearly all interpreters understand the Greek to mean **to preach the gospel of Christ**. **Of Christ** means "about Christ." And the **gospel**, of course, means "the Good News" (see Mark 1.1,14, for example).

A door was opened for me in the Lord is metaphorical language (see 1 Cor 16.9). The **door** refers to the opportunity to preach the gospel. REB says "an opening awaited me for serving the Lord." Some other models may be "the Lord had already prepared the way" (CEV), avoiding the passive, or "there was an obvious God-given opportunity" (Phps).

The Greek for **in the Lord** may be translated as "by the Lord" or "in the Lord." If the former, the meaning is that the Lord was the one who opened the door (so TEV, FRCL). If the latter, the meaning is that Paul's opportunity for work was "in the Lord," that is, an opportunity "for serving the Lord" (so REB, NBE, GNC). Either interpretation is grammatically possible, but the meaning "by the Lord" is probably to be preferred.

Some translations use a word such as "sir," "chief," or "master" to translate **Lord**, and they sometimes need to add "God" or "Jesus" after "the Lord," to make clear that an ordinary human master or chief is not intended. In 2 Cor 1.2,3,14, Jesus is called "Lord." In this verse it is not immediately clear whether the reference is to the Lord God or the Lord Jesus. But if translators are forced to choose, it is probably better to say "the Lord Jesus."

2.13 RSV	TEV
but my mind could not rest because I did not find my brother Titus there. So I took leave of them and went on to Macedonia.	But I was deeply worried, because I could not find our brother Titus. So I said good-bye to the people there and went on to Macedonia.

But: this marks the contrast between Paul's yearning to remain in Troas in order to take advantage of the opportunity to preach the Good News, and his desire to go on to Macedonia to look for Titus.

My mind could not rest is literally "my spirit had no rest." As TEV indicates, the meaning is that Paul was "deeply worried." Some other possible models are: "I had no peace of mind" (Knox and NIV), "I was on edge the whole time" (Phps), or some more idiomatic expression in the receptor language indicating great distress. Languages have a variety of ways of expressing the idea of inner fear or anxiety. Some say "my heart was up" or "my mind was cooking (or, stewing)." Or, without using a figure of speech, translators may say simply "I was greatly upset."

My brother Titus: Titus, like Timothy, was one of Paul's companions and co-workers. We do not know whether Titus was younger or older than Paul. Though not mentioned in Acts, Titus is mentioned in 2 Corinthians, Galatians, and 2 Timothy and is the person to whom the letter called *Titus* was addressed.

Brother here is not to be understood as a relative in a family. REB says "my colleague," but such a term does not express the emotional intimacy suggested by the word **brother**. The Greek is literally "my brother." TEV ("our brother") incorrectly changes the sense of the Greek, in which Paul emphasizes the importance of Titus to himself. CEV has "my friend," but some translators find it necessary to say something like "Titus, who is like a brother to me."

Paul had sent Titus to Corinth, perhaps with the letter of tears (2.3-4), and was hoping to meet Titus in Troas. No doubt Paul was hoping to receive news from Corinth. In addition to that concern, he may have been concerned that robbers had attacked Titus and stolen the money being collected for the church in Jerusalem (see 8.6 and chapters 8 and 9). Not finding Titus there, he continued on to Macedonia, where he did meet Titus (7.5-16).

I took leave of them: the Greek does not have an explicit antecedent to the pronoun **them**, but the meaning is obviously "the people in Troas" (verse 12). Whether these people were new converts, his own colleagues, or both, is not clear. It is possible in many languages to say simply "I withdrew from that city," "I left Troas," or simply "So I said good-bye to the people there," as in TEV.

Went on to Macedonia: the Greek verb **went on** may be translated as **came** or **went**, depending on the perspective of the writer (see 1.23). Paul was almost certainly in Macedonia when he wrote 2 Corinthians (at least chapters 1–9; see "Translating 2 Corinthians," page 3, as well as 7.5-6 and 9.4); therefore translations should indicate that Paul is writing from Macedonia. Both RSV and TEV are incorrect. AB correctly says "and came away to Macedonia." Some translators may even wish to say "came here to Macedonia."

Macedonia was a province northwest of Asia Minor, on the opposite side of the Aegean Sea from Troas (see comments on 1.16; and see the map, page vi).

2.14-17

RSV	TEV
	Victory through Christ
14 But thanks be to God, who in Christ always leads us in triumph, and through us spreads the fragrance of the knowledge of him everywhere. 15 For we are the aroma of Christ to God among those who are being saved and among those who are perishing, 16 to one a fragrance from death to death, to the other a fragrance from life to life. Who is sufficient for these things? 17 For we are not, like so many, peddlers of God's word; but as men of sincerity, as commissioned by God, in the sight of God we speak in Christ.	14 But thanks be to God! For in union with Christ we are always led by God as prisoners in Christ's victory procession. God uses us to make the knowledge about Christ spread everywhere like a sweet fragrance. 15 For we are like a sweet-smelling incense offered by Christ to God, which spreads among those who are being saved and those who are being lost. 16 For those who are being lost, it is a deadly stench that kills; but for those who are being saved, it is a fragrance that brings life. Who, then, is capable for such a task? 17 We are not like so many others, who handle God's message as if it were cheap merchandise; but because God has sent us, we speak with sincerity in his presence, as servants of Christ.

SECTION HEADING: TEV "Victory through Christ." The abrupt change of topic in verse 14 has led some interpreters to argue that 2.14–6.13 and 7.2-4 were originally a separate letter that was combined with other separate letters to make up 2 Corinthians as we know it today. Possibly these verses were inserted here by an editor of Paul's letter. In any case, in the form of the letter as we have it, verses 2.14–7.4 are a discussion about Paul's ministry that departs from the normal flow of discourse at this point; and the relationship of 2.14–7.4 to what precedes and to what follows is not clear. The translation of these verses is not affected by one's decision regarding the unity of 2 Corinthians (see "Translating 2 Corinthians," page 3).

In verses 14-17 Paul uses the metaphor of a victorious military procession, with which his readers were familiar. Leaving aside for the moment his concern to meet Titus, Paul takes up the theme of his apostleship in

2.14–5.19, then follows with the theme of reconciliation in 5.20–7.4 before returning in 7.5 to Titus' arrival.

2.14	RSV	TEV
	But thanks be to God, who in Christ always leads us in triumph, and through us spreads the fragrance of the knowledge of him everywhere.	But thanks be to God! For in union with Christ we are always led by God as prisoners in Christ's victory procession. God uses us to make the knowledge about Christ spread everywhere like a sweet fragrance.

But: this conjunction is left untranslated by Mft, AB, and REB. Even KJV avoids the strong contrastive conjunction, using the transition word "now . . . ." In the receptor language the beginning of a new section may be sufficient to communicate what it conveys in the original.

Thanks be to God: this same basic expression is used five times elsewhere by Paul (Rom 6.17; 7.25; 1 Cor 15.57; 2 Cor 8.16; 9.15), although the word order sometimes differs. It is usually in the context of victory or liberation and is a strong affirmation of praise. Therefore the CEV rendering "I am grateful to God" seems a bit weak. Many languages will require the explicit statement of who thanks God. In such cases one may say "Let us thank God" or "We thank God," using the inclusive form of the first person plural pronoun.

Who in Christ always leads us in triumph: this relative clause will be better translated as a separate sentence in many languages, following the TEV model. Paul here uses the imagery of a victorious Roman general who leads a triumphant procession, after he has won a great victory in war. In the procession were the victorious soldiers as well as the captive prisoners. The Greek does not specify whether Paul pictured himself as one of the victorious soldiers or one of the prisoners. Most translations, however, seem to accept the latter interpretation (so TEV, REB). In any case it is God in Christ who is represented by the victorious general.

In Christ: see the comments on 1.21.

In this context the pronouns **us** and **we** of verses 14-17 probably refer to the apostles as a group but do not include the readers. However, some interpreters understand the plural pronouns as Paul's polite way of referring to himself, so they translate these pronouns in verses 14-17 with the pronoun "I" or "me" (so Mft and AT, but not ITCL).

The subject of the verb **spreads** is God, but the pronoun **him** (**the fragrance of the knowledge of him**) refers to Christ (see verse 15), as TEV makes explicit. The **knowledge of him** means "knowledge about Christ," not knowledge that Christ has.

In some languages there is no single word to represent the English **fragrance**, so it may be necessary to speak of a "good odor" in this context, although the Greek term used here is actually neutral and so may be either good or bad. The same word is used of the ointment used by Mary when she anointed Jesus' feet (John 12.3), and in the context of the sweet-smelling odor of sacrifices in Eph 5.2 and Phil 4.18. Since the language here is clearly figurative, some translators will prefer to add the word "like" in the receptor language. The knowledge of Christ is "like the smell of perfume" (CEV).

2.15	RSV	TEV
	For we are the aroma of Christ to God among those who are being saved and among those who are perishing,	For we are like a sweet-smelling incense offered by Christ to God, which spreads among those who are being saved and those who are being lost.

For introduces verse 15 as the cause of 2.14b.

The pronoun **we**, as in verse 14, probably does not include the readers.

The aroma of Christ is figurative language (so TEV says "we are like"), comparing Paul's ministry to the sweet smell that burnt offerings gave off to God. This is similar to the figurative use of "fragrance" in the previous verse. The word used here is different, but in this context the two words are practically synonymous and may have to be translated the same. The difference is that here the good odor is offered by Christ to God.

Of Christ may be translated as "offered by Christ" (TEV, REB).

Those who are being saved . . . perishing: see 1 Cor 1.18, where the same expression occurs. TEV's "lost" does not refer to people who are losing their way but to people who are on their way to destruction. The participles used in Greek are present passive. The present tense should be preserved in the receptor language, but in some cases the passive forms will have to be translated actively: "those whom God is saving" and "those who have no hope [of salvation]," "those who are on the road to destruction," or possibly in a negative way, "those whom God is not saving."

2.16	RSV	TEV
	to one a fragrance from death to death, to the other a fragrance from life to life. Who is sufficient for these things?	For those who are being lost, it is a deadly stench that kills; but for those who are being saved, it is a fragrance that brings life. Who, then, is capable for such a task?

To the one . . . to the other forms a chiastic statement with the second half of verse 15. The chiasmus may be outlined as follows:

> A: among those who are being saved
> B: among those who are perishing
> B': to one a fragrance from death to death
> A': to the other a fragrance from life to life

To the one refers to unbelievers who are perishing, and **to the other** refers to believers who are being saved. While TEV repeats the words "those who are being lost" and "those who are being saved" from verse 15, REB says "to the latter . . . to the former."

Fragrance: here Paul uses the more neutral term introduced in verse 14 above, but there is an obvious contrast in meaning indicated by the context. For this reason the same word should probably be translated differently in the receptor language. Barclay has "a deadly and poisonous stench" in the first case and "a living and life-giving perfume" in the second. CEV reverses the order by combining these elements with the first parts of the chiasmus in verse 15: "For people who are being saved, this perfume has a sweet smell and leads them to a better life. But for people who are lost, it has a bad smell and leads them to a horrible death."

The words **from death to death** and **from life to life** probably reflect a Semitic idiom in which emphasis is given by repeating a word. But in most languages this kind of repetition may be awkward and will probably not give the same meaning. Therefore a better model may be "For those who are dying it is the smell of death, but for those who are living, it is the smell of life." Or another language says "Those people who are being lost smell that odor as the odor of death which can kill them. But those people who are being saved smell it as the odor of life which can save them."

Who is sufficient for these things? This is a rhetorical question. The implied answer is "No one is!" In languages where readers will not recognize this as a rhetorical question, the sentence may need to be formed as an emphatic negative statement, "No one is adequate for this job," or as in CEV, "No one really has what it takes to do this work."

The words **these things** refer to the responsibilities of apostles which Paul talks about in verses 14-16a.

2.17	RSV	TEV

RSV	TEV
For we are not, like so many, peddlers of God's word; but as men of sincerity, as commissioned by God, in the sight of God we speak in Christ.	We are not like so many others, who handle God's message as if it were cheap merchandise; but because God has sent us, we speak with sincerity in his presence, as servants of Christ.

TEV omits the word **For**, which links verses 16 and 17. This word is important, however, in that it clearly links verse 17 to the question in the previous verse. The sense is that Paul is certainly not sufficient, since (**for**) he preaches the gospel in its purity and, unlike so many other preachers, he relies on God.

As in verses 14-16, the pronoun **we** probably does not include the readers.

Instead of the words **like so many**, some manuscripts have "like the others." The editors of the UBS *Greek New Testament* consider this second reading "too offensive an expression for Paul to have used in the context." Even so, some translations follow the reading "like the others" (Mft and AT, which reads "like most men"); and NRSV lists the reading "like the others" in the footnote.

Peddlers of God's word: the meaning is apparently that many others were preaching for the sole motive of making a profit. REB says "We are not adulterating the word of God for profit." Paul does not appear to be claiming that others were falsifying the gospel, though that is possible if 4.2 refers to the same persons. **God's word** does not refer to the Old Testament. As also in 4.2, the reference is to the message from God, especially the message about Christ.

But as men of sincerity: literally "but as from sincerity." Since Paul's associates included women as well as men, some translations avoid using the word **men** and use a word such as "persons" (NRSV), or they restructure the wording (TEV, REB) in order to avoid suggesting that Paul was referring to men only.

In the sight of God we speak in Christ: these same words occur in 12.19. "To speak in the sight of God" appears to suggest that Paul is speaking openly and truthfully before God, who judges wrongdoing. "To speak in Christ" is to speak as one who lives in union with Christ (see comment in 1.21). A possible model for this expression may be "we speak as Christians in the very presence of God." One translation restructures the whole verse as follows: "We are not like many people who add other business to the affairs [business] of God. But we speak the whole truth in the eyes of God, because we are people of Christ, and it is God who has sent us."

Some languages will require that this whole verse be restructured by saying something like the following:

> Many people treat the message from God as if it were a second-rate product for sale. But we are not like that. Rather we speak with sincerity in God's presence because he sent us as servants of Christ.

Or similarly:

> A lot of people try to get rich from preaching God's message. But we are God's sincere messengers, and by the power of Christ we speak our message with God as our witness. (CEV)

B-3. Paul's apostolic commission and ministry
(3.1–6.13)

3.1-18

RSV

1 Are we beginning to commend ourselves again? Or do we need, as some do, letters of recommendation to you, or from you? 2 You yourselves are our letter of recommendation, written on your hearts, to be known and read by all men; 3 and you show that you are a letter from Christ delivered by us, written not with ink but with the Spirit of the living God, not on tablets of stone but on tablets of human hearts.

4 Such is the confidence that we have through Christ toward God. 5 Not that we are competent of ourselves to claim anything as coming from us; our competence is from God, 6 who has made us competent to be ministers of a new covenant, not in a written code but in the Spirit; for the written code kills, but the Spirit gives life.

7 Now if the dispensation of death, carved in letters on stone, came with such splendor that the Israelites could not look at Moses' face because of its brightness, fading as this was, 8 will not the dispensation of the Spirit be attended with greater splendor? 9 For if there was splendor in the dispensation of condemnation, the dispensation of righteousness must far exceed it in splendor. 10 Indeed, in this case, what once had splendor has come to have no splendor at all, because of the splendor that surpasses it. 11 For if what faded away came with splendor, what is permanent must have much more splendor.

12 Since we have such a hope, we are very bold, 13 not like Moses, who put a veil over his face so that the Israelites might not see the end of the fading splendor. 14 But their minds were hardened; for to this day, when they read the old covenant, that same veil remains unlifted, because only through Christ is it taken away. 15 Yes, to this day whenever Moses is read a veil lies over their minds; 16 but when a man turns to the Lord the veil is removed. 17 Now the Lord is the Spirit, and where the Spirit of the Lord is, there is freedom. 18 And we all, with unveiled face, beholding the glory of the Lord, are being changed into his likeness from one degree of glory to another; for this comes from the Lord who is the Spirit.

TEV
Servants of the New Covenant

1 Does this sound as if we were again boasting about ourselves? Could it be that, like some other people, we need letters of recommendation to you or from you? 2 You yourselves are the letter we have, written on our hearts for everyone to know and read. 3 It is clear that Christ himself wrote this letter and sent it by us. It is written, not with ink but with the Spirit of the living God, and not on stone tablets but on human hearts.

4 We say this because we have confidence in God through Christ. 5 There is nothing in us that allows us to claim that we are capable of doing this work. The capacity we have comes from God; 6 it is he who made us capable of serving the new covenant, which consists not of a written law but of the Spirit. The written law brings death, but the Spirit gives life.

7 The Law was carved in letters on stone tablets, and God's glory appeared when it was given. Even though the brightness on Moses' face was fading, it was so strong that the people of Israel could not keep their eyes fixed on him. If the Law, which brings death when it is in force, came with such glory, 8 how much greater is the glory that belongs to the activity of the Spirit! 9 The system which brings condemnation was glorious; how much more glorious is the activity which brings salvation! 10 We may say that because of the far brighter glory now the glory that was so bright in the past is gone. 11 For if there was glory in that which lasted for a while, how much more glory is there in that which lasts forever!

12 Because we have this hope, we are very bold. 13 We are not like Moses, who had to put a veil over his face so that the people of Israel would not see the brightness fade and disappear. 14 Their minds, indeed, were closed; and to this very day their minds are covered with the same veil as they read the books of the old covenant. The veil is removed only when a person is joined to Christ. 15 Even today, whenever they read the Law of Moses, the veil still covers their minds. 16 But it can be removed, as the scripture says about Moses: "His veil was removed when he turned to the Lord." 17 Now, "the Lord" in this pas-

sage is the Spirit; and where the Spirit of the Lord is present, there is freedom. 18 All of us, then, reflect the glory of the Lord with uncovered faces; and that same glory, coming from the Lord, who is the Spirit, transforms us into his likeness in an ever greater degree of glory.

SECTION HEADING: TEV "Servants of the New Covenant." In this section Paul continues to defend his apostleship by contrasting his ministry with the ministry of Moses, and claims that the new covenant in Christ is far superior to the old covenant mediated by Moses. Paul develops his argument through his reading of the story of Moses' descent from Mount Sinai in Exo 34.29-35. The term "covenant" may be translated in some languages as "agreement" or possibly even "promise," but whatever term is used it should carry the idea of something that is reciprocal, that is, involving commitment from both parties. (See comments on this word at verse 6 below.) In some cases it will be unnatural to speak of "servants" of an agreement, since one cannot serve abstract ideas. In such cases it may be better to limit the heading to "The new agreement" or, more fully, "The new agreement between God and human beings."

3.1   RSV   TEV

Are we beginning to commend ourselves again? Or do we need, as some do, letters of recommendation to you, or from you?

Does this sound as if we were again boasting about ourselves? Could it be that, like some other people, we need letters of recommendation to you or from you?

This verse is made up of two questions, the second of which is rather complex in form. The main point of this verse is to deny Paul's need to introduce himself or to produce written recommendations from some third party to the people in Corinth, who already knew him well. In many languages such questions will serve the same purpose, but in some cases it will be better to drop the question form and to change them into affirmative or negative statements:

You may think that we are once again commending ourselves to you, but this is not so. Some people need letters of recommendation to you or from you. But certainly we do not need such letters.

While this overall structure may need to be adopted, the details on how to render certain elements within it will be discussed in the paragraphs that follow.

To commend ourselves again: his question anticipates the assumption that some Christians in Corinth may criticize him for boasting because of his comments in the preceding verse (2.17). The question is rhetorical and is his way of saying that they are not boasting about themselves again. **Ourselves** does not include the readers. The word **again** probably suggests that some Corinthian Christians had previously accused Paul of commending himself to them. **To commend** oneself was to state one's credentials and establish one's credibility (see also 4.2; 5.12). This, of course, should be unnecessary for someone already well known. The verb **commend** has the basic meaning "stand beside" or "stand with" but may also mean "prove" (7.11), "show," or "confirm." It is used eight times in 2 Corinthians (3.1; 4.2; 5.12; 6.4; 7.11; 10.12,18; 12.11), showing that it is a special problem in Paul's relationship with the Corinthians at the time this letter was written, but it does occur four times elsewhere in Paul's writings (Rom 3.5; 5.8; 16.1; and Gal 2.18). The reference in Rom 16.1 is most closely related to the usage here.

In Greek the form of the question **Or do we need . . . ?** implies that a negative answer is expected. AB captures the intended negative response as follows: "Surely, we do not need . . . do we?" GNC similarly shows that the intended answer is negative: "Is not the truth rather that we are in no need, as certain people are, of commendatory letters . . . ?"

Letters of recommendation were common in the ancient world (see Acts 18.27 and Rom 16.1-2). Such letters were written to introduce someone and to give approval to that person. Brc calls these "letters of introduction."

Paul does not identify who the **some** people are who needed letters of recommendation, but in the context of 2 Corinthians these are persons who came to Corinth from somewhere else with letters of recommendation from recognized authorities and who are opposed to Paul. Probably the same persons are referred to in 2.17 and 10.2. In this context the indirect reference to his opponents as "some other people" (TEV) suggests that Paul is critical of them. Phps expresses the implicit criticism well: "Do we need, as some apparently do, . . . ?"

Or from you: CEV makes explicit the purpose of letters of recommendation from the Corinthians: "Do we need letters . . . from you to tell others about us?"

3.2	RSV	TEV

You yourselves are our letter of recommendation, written on your[c] hearts, to be known and read by all men;

You yourselves are the letter we have, written on our hearts for everyone to know and read.

[c] Other ancient authorities read *our*

This verse is the answer to the question in the second half of the previous verse. The implicit answer is made explicit in REB, "No, you are the letter we need." Paul does not need a written letter from human authorities to establish his apostolic authority. The existence of the Christian community at

Corinth, the result of Paul's missionary activity there, is proof enough that Paul is a genuine apostle.

The language in this verse is figurative language. Some translators may need to say "You are *like* a letter which recommends us" and "you are *like* a letter written on our hearts." The passive idea contained in **written** may have to be made active by saying something like "which you have written" or using the impersonal "which someone wrote." But probably Paul is thinking of the Holy Spirit as the author of the figurative letter of recommendation, as in verse 3.

You yourselves are: in Greek the verb form already contains the pronoun, "you-are." However, an explicit pronoun is added by the writer, providing emphasis to the statement, as seen in RSV's **You yourselves are**. Some translations say simply "you are" (REB, NAB), but many translations correctly add the pronoun **yourselves** (FRCL, NIV). So in languages having emphatic forms of the pronoun, it should probably be used here.

Some good Greek manuscripts read **written on your hearts** (so RSV, NRSV footnote), but the editors of the UBS *Greek New Testament* regard the better reading to be "written on our hearts" (so TEV, NRSV, REB, NAB). "Our hearts" seems to fit the context better (see also 7.3). Languages differ as to whether to use the singular or plural of "heart" in such a context. In some cases the use of the plural will be understood to mean that each person had more than one heart. If this is the case, then the singular should obviously be used.

As has been noted above on 1.8, it is not clear here whether the first person plural pronoun **our** is an epistolary plural and refers to Paul alone (so Mft, AT, and ITCL), or whether it really does include his associates also. ITCL translates all of the first person plural pronouns in 3.1-6 with first person singular pronouns.

Read by all men is a literal translation. Since the context seems to include both men and women, it may be better in most languages to use a word such as "everyone" (TEV and NJB) or "everybody" (NIV). The passive verbs **read** and **known** may be easily transformed into active forms, since the agent is specifically mentioned in the text: "so that everyone may read and know . . . ."

For some translators the model provided by Knox for this verse may prove helpful: "Why, you yourselves are the letters [of recommendation] we carry about with us, written in our hearts for all to recognize and to read."

3.3   RSV   TEV

RSV	TEV
and you show that you are a letter from Christ delivered by us, written not with ink but with the Spirit of the living God, not on tablets of stone but on tablets of human hearts.	It is clear that Christ himself wrote this letter and sent it by us. It is written, not with ink but with the Spirit of the living God, and not on stone tablets but on human hearts.

This is a continuation of the figurative language of verse 2. Some languages may need to say "You are like a letter from Christ," although the RSV rendering accurately reflects the metaphor in Greek. Paul's main concern here is to show that his apostolic authority comes from Christ. Since it was Paul's preaching that led to their conversion, the Corinthians are themselves the evidence of his apostolic authority.

You show: the word thus translated may be understood in two different ways. It may be rendered actively as in RSV and NRSV, indicating that the Corinthians are in focus. But it may also be taken as a passive, in which case the meaning is impersonal, as in TEV "It is clear." This interpretation is also followed by NAB, NJB, REB, and several other versions; it should probably be followed in the receptor language.

From Christ means "Christ himself wrote this letter" (TEV).

Delivered by us is literally "ministered by us." The Greek may be understood to mean "delivered" or "sent" by us (RSV, TEV, REB), or "written" by us as Christ's secretary (NBE). Other translations retain the ambiguity of the Greek: "entrusted to our care" (NJB, TOB, GNC), "the result of our ministry" (NIV); and "administered by us" (NAB). The NIV rendering probably provides the best available model to be followed.

The passive ideas **delivered** and **written** in this verse will have to be made active in many languages. One may translate "Christ wrote . . ." and "he sent it in our hands" or "we delivered . . . ."

The contrasts, **not with ink but with the Spirit of the living God** and **not on tablets of stone but on tablets of human hearts**, indicate the divine nature of the "letter" which the Corinthian Christians are. In some languages it will be much more natural to state the positive before the negative: "Christ wrote it by the Spirit of the living God, not with ink. He wrote it on human hearts, not on tablets of stone." In certain languages the ideas **ink** and **tablets of stone** may be quite foreign. In some cases **ink** has to be rendered "the water [liquid] of the letter," and stone tablets become "large flat rocks." An explanatory footnote may be required in some cases.

The words **the Spirit of the living God** (see also 6.16) will be difficult to translate with meaning in many languages. In the Old Testament God is sometimes called "the living God" in contrast to lifeless pagan idols (see Deut 5.26; Josh 3.10; Jer 10.10), or to gods that are said to die when the dry season begins. Translated literally the expression **the living God** may sound very strange and unacceptable. Since God is alive by definition, this adjective may be better left implicit in the receptor language. But in other cases it may be stated negatively as "the God who cannot die" or "the God who never sleeps." In the Old Testament this expression is sometimes used in a way that is almost synonymous with "the true God," but in other contexts it has the idea "the God who gives life."

Tablets of human hearts: that is, the tablets are human hearts. The term **tablets** used here is found elsewhere in the New Testament only in Heb 9.4. The literal meaning is "a flat stone," as in the first occurrence here, but it is obviously used figuratively in the second instance. TEV simply says "on human hearts." Where tablets are not used for writing, translators may want to follow REB, "on the pages of the human heart."

For comments on **hearts** see 1.22.

3.4   RSV   TEV

Such is the confidence that we   We say this because we have
have through Christ toward God.   confidence in God through Christ.

Such is the confidence refers to the claims that Paul makes about the Corinthians in verses 2 and 3. REB says "It is in full reliance upon God, through Christ, that we make such claims." And Barclay, changing the order of the propositions, has "we can make such a claim because of our confidence in God through Christ."

We in this verse does not include the readers. Likewise in verses 5-6, the plural pronouns probably do not include the readers. Some interpreters understand that Paul is referring to himself by means of the plural pronoun, and they translate these pronouns with the first person singular pronouns, "I," "myself," "my" (so Mft, AT, and ITCL).

Through Christ toward God: it is through his relationship with Christ that Paul has confidence **toward God**. These last two words may indicate where Paul places his confidence ("in God" TEV) or may indicate that his confidence is expressed in the presence of God ("before God" Barrett). If the latter is the correct understanding, then **toward God** here is the same as "in the sight of God" in 2.17. NJB says "through Christ in facing God." And NIV gives essentially the same meaning with "through Christ before God." Translators choosing this option may find it more natural to say ". . . in the eyes of God."

3.5   RSV   TEV

Not that we are competent of ourselves   There is nothing in us that allows us to
to claim anything as coming from us;   claim that we are capable of doing this
our competence is from God,   work. The capacity we have comes from
                                             God;

On the pronouns, see comments on verse 4.

The words **Not that** which begin this verse indicate that Paul is clarifying his preceding words, lest the readers misunderstand (see also 1.24). GNC makes this relationship explicit by inserting the word "However": "However, it is not that . . . ." Some languages may have to begin this verse by saying "I do not mean to say that . . ." (compare NCV: "I do not mean that we are able to say . . ."). And others may say "But it is not true that . . . ."

In the context the word **anything** refers to the gospel and the call to preach the gospel, what TEV calls "doing this work."

Verse 5 consists of two parts that contrast with one another: reliance on self and reliance on God. GNC heightens the contrast that is implicit in Greek by adding the word "No" at the beginning of the second half of this verse: "No, such competence as we have comes to us from God."

The words **competence** (RSV) and "capacity" (TEV) may be particularly difficult to translate into some languages. The term has to do with adequacy for a task and is translated elsewhere in this letter as "enough" (2.6) and "sufficient" (2.16). Used with the negative in 1 Cor 15.9 it yields the meaning "unfit." Some possible models to translate this idea are as follows: "God gives us what it takes to do all that we need to do" (CEV) or, using the causative form of the verb, "but it is God who causes us to be able to do this work" or "God is the one who makes us fit for the task," but this may anticipate a form that will have to be used in the following verse. Another possible model is "all our ability comes from God" (Knox).

3.6	RSV	TEV

who has made us competent to be min-isters of a new covenant, not in a writ-ten code but in the Spirit; for the writ-ten code kills, but the Spirit gives life.

it is he who made us capable of serving the new covenant, which consists not of a written law but of the Spirit. The written law brings death, but the Spirit gives life.

This is a continuation of the sentence started at the beginning of the previous verse. However, the relative clause beginning with **who** . . . should probably be made into a new sentence in many languages. One can begin with "Indeed, it is he [God] who . . ." or something similar.

On the first person plural pronouns, see comments on verse 4.

Has made us competent: the verb tense in Greek may be translated with the perfect tense in English, as in RSV (also REB, NJB), or with the simple past tense, as in TEV. If, as seems likely, Paul is looking back to the specific call of God as in Gal 1.15-16, then the past tense of TEV better expresses Paul's thought here. If, on the other hand, Paul's focus is on the results of what God did, then a translation such as NJB expresses the thought clearly: "He has given us the competence to be ministers." If the latter interpretation is followed, the habitual verb form may be required in certain languages.

The word **ministers** does not refer to ordained clergy or even to modern-day deacons, although the word used here, *diakonos,* is the origin of our English word "deacon." The Greek word means simply "one who serves."

The concept of a **new covenant** appears in the Old Testament in Jer 31.31-34, and elsewhere in the New Testament in Luke 22.20 and 1 Cor 11.25. A covenant is an agreement, usually between two parties. As indicated in *A Handbook on the Letter to the Hebrews* (page 243-244), the term **covenant** is "the most central theological concept in the Old Testament." In the New Testament it defines the new relationship between God and human beings that has been created by the life and death of Jesus Christ. There is both continuity and difference involved in the Old and New Testament concepts. The term also means "testament" or "will" in certain contexts. In the present context it is a special contract between God and humanity. In this agreement all the conditions are determined by one party (God), but that does not indicate that the one who sets the conditions is a tyrant. While it is true that the initiative is completely God's, the benefits are completely for his people. The receptor language term chosen to translate **covenant** will almost certainly require an extensive entry in the glossary.

The words **not in a written code**, literally "not of a letter," mean that the new covenant is not an agreement that has been put in writing, as was God's written covenant expressed in the Old Testament. The word for "letter" here is not the same as in the expression "letters of recommendation" in verses 1 and 2 of this chapter but is the word for letters of the alphabet. Thus the emphasis here is on the act of writing. Note that TEV, like many other modern versions, supplies the implied word "law." Some other models are "matters written down" or "written letters" (NJB).

But in the Spirit is literally "but of spirit." This spirit is not the human spirit but the Spirit of God. RSV and TEV correctly capitalize **Spirit**. The new covenant is "spiritual" (REB, Knox, TNT). In some languages it may be necessary to say explicitly "the Spirit of God" or "the Holy Spirit" (CEV).

The written code kills but the Spirit gives life: in some languages it is necessary to state the object of the verbs **kills** and **gives life**. The meaning is that the Law of Moses leads to spiritual death of people, while God's Spirit gives people spiritual life. Also, the verb "kill" may not fit naturally in the receptor language with "written law" or "written code" as its subject. In this case it may be less awkward to say "leads to death," "causes death," or "brings death."

3.7   RSV   TEV

Now if the dispensation of death, carved in letters on stone, came with such splendor that the Israelites could not look at Moses' face because of its brightness, fading as this was,

The Law was carved in letters on stone tablets, and God's glory appeared when it was given. Even though the brightness on Moses' face was fading, it was so strong that the people of Israel could not keep their eyes fixed on him. If the Law, which brings death when it is in force, came with such glory,

RSV is a rather literal version that usually translates Greek words using the same word in English in spite of the context; however, in the case of the term *diakonia,* there are four different words used in 2 Corinthians. The first occurrences (3.7,8,9) are rendered "dispensation," but in other passages RSV translates "ministry" (4.1; 5.18; 6.3), "relief" (8.4), "offering" (9.1), and "service" (9.12,13). This variety clearly shows the different ways in which Paul uses the single Greek word.

In verses 7-11 Paul uses a form of argument used by the rabbis of his day: from the lesser to the greater. If such and such could be said concerning something relatively unimportant (the lesser), then how much more could such and such be said concerning the greater, or more important matter. The comparison in these verses is between the Law of Moses (the lesser) and the new covenant (the greater).

Verses 7 and 8 are one long and rather complicated sentence in Greek. TEV restructures the sentence and breaks it up into two sentences, and places the "if" clause at the end of verse 7 rather than at the beginning. The word **if** will suggest doubt in some languages. To avoid giving the impression that Paul was expressing doubt about whether the Law came with such splendor, some translations may need to follow the example of REB and TEV, and state unequivocally that the Law did come with splendor.

Paul's argument in these verses is based on the story in Exo 34.27-35 of Moses' encounter with God on Mount Sinai. **The dispensation of death** refers to the Law which Moses received on Mount Sinai. TEV translates **the dispensation of death** as "the Law, which brings death when it is in force." REB says "the ministry that brought death." The translation "ministry" more accurately reflects the consistent terminology of the passage, since the term used here, *diakonia,* has the same root as the one rendered "ministers" in the previous verse. Some translators may prefer "the sentence of death" (Knox). AT has "the religion of death." But in many languages it will be better to use the term "law" instead of "ministry."

On stone is literally plural, "on stones." Paul is referring to the two stone tablets of the Law of Moses (see Exo 31.18). See verse 3 above.

The Law of Moses **came with such splendor**. RSV, REB, and many other translations add the word **such**, which is not in the Greek. The remainder of this verse justifies the use of **such** in translation. **Splendor** is the word "glory" in Greek, which is used six times in this chapter alone (verses 8,9,10,11,18) as well as in 1.20. Here the focus is on the brightness or shining brilliance. CEV concentrates more on the generally positive character of the giving of the Law rather than on the aspect of brilliance: ". . . given in such a wonderful way." But this obscures the relationship between this statement and the next part of the verse, where the verb "shine" is used.

The Israelites is literally "the sons of Israel" but should probably be rendered "people of Israel" in most languages.

Though RSV says that the Israelites **could not look at** Moses' face, the Greek verb means "to look intently." TEV better captures the meaning: "could not keep their eyes fixed on him." NRSV says that they could not "gaze" at his face (so also Mft). Some other verb phrases used are "look steadily" (NIV and NJB) and "look for any length of time" (Barclay).

The word **fading** refers to the splendor of Moses' face. Some may wish to translate "even though his [Moses'] glory (or, brightness) was diminishing (or, only lasted for a short time)."

3.8   RSV   TEV

will not the dispensation of the Spirit be attended with greater splendor?   **how much greater is the glory that belongs to the activity of the Spirit!**

This is a rhetorical question. For languages in which Paul's words may be misunderstood to indicate doubt in his own mind, it may be better to change the question to a statement (so TEV, REB).

Verse 8 completes the comparison begun in verse 7. If the Law of Moses came with such splendor, how much greater is the splendor of the ministry of the Spirit.

Dispensation translates the same Greek word translated as "dispensation" in verse 7. REB says "the ministry of the Spirit." Other versions seek to show the parallel with the previous verse: "the administration of the Spirit" (Mft), and AT has "the religion of the Spirit." But Knox is unable to maintain the resemblance, translating simply "the spiritual law."

RSV slavishly maintains the future tense of the Greek verb **will . . . be**. When the Law of Moses was given, the new covenant was an event in the future. But the future tense in English suggests that the new covenant is not a present reality for Paul. For that reason TEV uses the present tense: "how much greater is the glory."

Verses 7 and 8 have been restructured as follows in one African language:

> 7 The old Laws were written on stones, and the glory of God was seen at that time. The people of Israel could not look [long] at the face of Moses, because it was shining strongly, even though this glory did not last. Therefore, if the Laws whose job is to bring death had glory like that, 8 then the work of the Spirit of God will have greater glory than the Laws. Is this not true?

The final question assumes the answer "Of course" and reflects the rhetorical character of the two verses, but only after having made the affirmation clearly.

3.9   RSV   TEV

For if there was splendor in the dispensation of condemnation, the dispensation of righteousness must far exceed it in splendor.   **The system which brings condemnation was glorious; how much more glorious is the activity which brings salvation!**

Verse 9, like verses 7 and 8, continues or repeats the argument of "from the lesser to the greater." It is actually a restatement in slightly different words of what has already been said.

For: while this conjunction is omitted in TEV and NIV, some kind of transition may be needed in the receptor language. Here it seems to mark the continuation of the argument started in verse 7.

As in verse 7, the word **if** does not mean that Paul had doubt. TEV omits the word **if** to avoid suggesting any question of doubt in Paul's statement.

Of condemnation and **of righteousness** describe the kinds of dispensation. The Law of Moses "brings condemnation," and the gospel "brings salvation" (TEV).

Righteousness stands in contrast with **condemnation** and is used here in the sense in which the equivalent Hebrew word is often used in the Old Testament: "salvation" (TEV), "acquittal" (REB, GNC), "justification" (NRSV).

The meaning of this verse is clearly expressed in CEV: "If something that brings the death sentence is glorious, won't something that makes us acceptable to God be even more glorious?" Or as Knox puts it, "If there is a splendour in the proclamation of our guilt, there must be more splendour yet in the proclamation of our acquittal." Another possible model taken from an African translation: "If the work that [habitually] gives people punishment had glory, then the work that [habitually] makes people just in the eyes of God will have even more glory."

3.10	RSV	TEV

Indeed, in this case, what once had splendor has come to have no splendor at all, because of the splendor that surpasses it.

We may say that because of the far brighter glory now the glory that was so bright in the past is gone.

Indeed: the transition, again omitted by TEV, introduces a further development of Paul's argument. In some languages this kind of clarification may be introduced by something like "Truly" or "In fact" (CEV). Mft takes the whole verse as parenthetical but introduces it with "Indeed."

In this case: literally "in this part." These words apparently refer to the preceding statement of verses 7-9. Many languages will say "in this matter."

What once had splendor has come to have no splendor is literally "what has had splendor has not had splendor." Paul refers here to the Law of Moses. **The splendor that surpasses it** refers to the glory of the gospel.

CEV serves as a good model translation of this verse: "In fact, the new agreement is so wonderful that the Law is no longer glorious at all." Another model says "In truth, the glory of the old covenant does not look like glory at all any longer because of the brightness of the present glory."

3.11 RSV	TEV
For if what faded away came with splendor, what is permanent must have much more splendor.	For if there was glory in that which lasted for a while, how much more glory is there in that which lasts forever!

As in verses 7-8 and 9, Paul uses the argument "from the lesser to the greater." In verse 7 that which faded away was the splendor of Moses' face. Here it is the whole ministry of the old covenant which faded away.

As in verses 7 and 9, **if** does not indicate doubt that **what faded away came with splendor**. Some languages may need to state "For since what faded away came with splendor . . . ." Another way of handling this may be to begin this verse by saying "It is true that there was splendor with the matter that did not last long, but . . . ."

What is permanent is parallel to the "dispensation of the Spirit" (3.8) and the "dispensation of righteousness" (3.9). Here it is contrasted with **what faded away**, which is parallel to "the dispensation of death" and "the dispensation of condemnation" which was given to Moses, whose glory was temporary. In some languages both of these veiled references to the Law and the New Covenant may have to be made explicit. **What faded away** may be translated "what was being annulled" (AB). The whole verse may have to be rendered more explicitly, as in CEV: "The Law was given with a glory that faded away. But the glory of the new agreement is much greater, because it will never fade away."

3.12 RSV	TEV
Since we have such a hope, we are very bold,	Because we have this hope, we are very bold.

The pronoun **we** here probably does not include the readers. Possibly Paul refers to himself with the plural pronoun (so Mft and AT, but not ITCL).

The word **Since** translates a Greek word which connects verse 12 closely to the preceding verses. The **hope** is based on the fact that the glory of the new covenant is permanent. The expression **have . . . hope** may have to be translated by an idiom: "we place our hearts in God regarding this matter." Compare 1.7.

We are very bold is literally "we use much boldness." The noun "boldness" frequently refers to boldness in speech. NJB says "we can speak with complete fearlessness" (similarly ITCL). REB says "we speak out boldly." Perhaps the word **bold** in RSV and TEV is too general. The meaning is that they are bold to proclaim the gospel.

In many languages this brief verse may have to be turned around to say something like "We are very courageous in speaking because we have hope like this" or "We are not afraid to speak out because we have such hope."

3.13   RSV   TEV

not like Moses, who put a veil over his face so that the Israelites might not see the end of the fading splendor.	We are not like Moses, who had to put a veil over his face so that the people of Israel would not see the brightness fade and disappear.

The beginning of verse 13 is literally "and not as Moses put a veil on his face." Translators may need to supply words such as "and we do not act like Moses" in order to make this an independent sentence instead of continuing from verse 12 as in RSV. REB begins this verse "it is not for us to do as Moses did: he put a veil . . . ." But the relationship to the idea of speaking boldly in verse 12 may still be obscure in some languages. Knox shows the relationship more clearly with "It is not for us to use veiled language, as Moses veiled his face."

Veil: the term thus translated is found only in this section (although a related verb is used in 1 Cor 11.6). The related verb means simply "to hide." It was therefore a kind of cloth used to conceal something, in this case Moses' face. In many languages the only alternative will be to use the word "cloth." Note that CEV uses the verb "cover" without indicating what kind of material fulfilled that purpose.

The Israelites is literally "the sons of Israel," but this is more naturally translated "the people of Israel" in most languages (see 3.7).

On the meaning of the word translated **see** in RSV, see comments on **could not look at** in 3.7. Here again the idea is to stare or to look for longer periods of time.

The end of the fading splendor does not mean that the splendor stopped fading and yet remained to some degree. The **end** of the fading splendor means that the splendor ceased to exist altogether. The participle translated as **the fading splendor** in RSV is neuter as in 3.11 (referring to the old covenant), and not feminine as in 3.7 (referring to the splendor).

3.14   RSV   TEV

But their minds were hardened; for to this day, when they read the old covenant, that same veil remains unlifted, because only through Christ is it taken away.	Their minds, indeed, were closed; and to this very day their minds are covered with the same veil as they read the books of the old covenant. The veil is removed only when a person is joined to Christ.

The significance of the word **But** with which verse 14 begins should not be ignored. Paul hastens to add after verse 13 that Moses is not to be blamed; rather the peoples' hearts were hardened. Knox makes the contrast even sharper, saying "but in spite of that . . . ."

The pronoun **their** refers to the Israelites of the preceding verse.

The Greek verb **were hardened** is in the passive voice. No subject is stated, though Paul most likely thought of God as the agent (see Rom 11.7). In those languages that have no passive voice, it will be necessary to seek an active form to express this idea. Elsewhere in the New Testament we find the expression "their hearts were hardened" (Mark 6.52 and 8.17), but here it is the **minds** that are hardened. REB, like TEV, speaks of their minds being "closed," while NIV has "their minds were made dull." In some languages it may be appropriate to say more bluntly "they became stupid" or "they became like people without intelligence." Or, making the implied agent explicit, one may say "God made their minds dull."

To this day, that is, "even today" or "until now." This refers to the time at which Paul was writing this letter, not to a time in the twentieth century. If this is unclear to the reader of the receptor language, one may have to say "even at the time I am writing you . . . ."

The old covenant: Paul is referring to the Hebrew Scriptures. As the parallel words "whenever Moses is read" in 3.15 show, Paul is probably not thinking of the Old Testament as a whole but only of the "books of Moses." GNC capitalizes the words "Old Covenant." TEV adds the words "books of" before "the old covenant." NJB says "the reading of the Old Testament." While the NJB translation will help readers today understand more clearly what writings Paul was referring to, it is anachronistic and probably too general, and it should be avoided. A collection of writings called "The New Testament" did not yet exist when Paul was writing, yet the translation "the Old Testament" suggests a collection of writings that presupposes the existence of the New Testament. Knox has "the old law," making the connection with the "law of Moses" in the next verse more apparent.

When they read: literally "on the reading." Probably Paul is thinking of the reading of the Old Testament writings during the synagogue services. REB reflects this understanding: "for that same veil is there to this very day when the lesson is read from the old covenant." AB says "at the public reading of the old covenant." Since the idea is very likely not one of private devotional reading, the receptor language rendering may be "when they hear someone read . . . ," where the passive "is read" would be impossible. Barclay adds ". . . in the synagogue," making the setting of the reading even more explicit.

Recent archaeological evidence suggests that the synagogue as a building did not come into existence until some time in the second century A.D. References in the New Testament to synagogues probably refer not to buildings called synagogues but rather to the groups of people who met together for worship in large private houses, or possibly in some cases to those large houses built for other purposes, but where they met for worship.

That same veil: this does not refer to the same piece of cloth that Moses used to hide his face from the people of Israel while speaking to them. Rather, Paul uses this image of concealment in a new context, in which the "same" thing is happening. CEV rightly renders this "something still keeps them from seeing . . . ." Some other possible models are "the thing that keeps them from seeing is still not taken away" or "it is as if something still covers their eyes."

Remains unlifted, because only through Christ is it taken away: the Greek text of this verse may be punctuated in a different way which slightly changes the meaning. If a comma is placed after the word **remains**, the proposition would stop with "that same veil remains." The RSV **unlifted** is more literally "not revealed." The conjunction translated **because** in RSV will be translated "that." The rest of the verse is then translated as "nor is it revealed to them that this covenant has been abolished by Christ." This alternate translation is given in the footnotes of both NJB and NVSR, and in the text of Mft.

Is it taken away: the subject of the verb **taken away** is not explicit in Greek. TEV understands the subject to be "the veil," which is the closest possible noun that could be referred to in the structure of the Greek. This interpretation has the advantage of keeping the same subject as for the verb **remains**. On the other hand the subject of the verb **taken away** in 3.11,13 is the old covenant, and some interpreters consider **the old covenant** to be the implicit subject. The use of the passive form is problematic for many translators. Assuming that it is the veil that is taken away, who actually removes it? Technically it is God in Christ, but since Christ is God's agent, it may be more natural to say with CEV "Only Christ can take away the covering that keeps them from seeing."

Through Christ is literally "in Christ." On the meaning and translation of this expression, see 2.14.

3.15	RSV	TEV

Yes, to this day whenever Moses is read a veil lies over their minds;	Even today, whenever they read the Law of Moses, the veil still covers their minds.

Yes: in the Greek the same conjunction is used here as in the beginning of verse 14, where RSV renders it "But." NEB had translated it "But" in this context, but REB correctly revises to say "Indeed" (likewise NRSV). The purpose of the conjunction in this context is to introduce a further, more intensive statement of what has already been said.

On **to this day** see comments on 3.14.

As elsewhere in the New Testament (Acts 15.21; 21.21), **Moses** refers to the "Law of Moses" (TEV, REB).

Is read: here again the passive form may have to be rendered actively as "when they hear someone read . . . ." To translate "they read" as in TEV risks giving the impression of private reading, which is not intended here (see comments on "when they read" in verse 14).

Their minds is literally "their hearts." See comment on the word "heart" in 1.22. "Hearts" is synonymous in meaning to "minds" or "thoughts" in 3.14.

but when a man turns to the Lord the veil is removed.	But it can be removed, as the scripture says about Moses: "His veil was removed when he turned to the Lord."[c]

[c] *Verse 16 may be translated:* But the veil is removed whenever someone turns to the Lord.

This verse is difficult to translate. The text of the ancient Greek translation, the Septuagint, of Exo 34.34 says "And whenever Moses used to go before the Lord to speak with him, he would remove the veil until he went out." Is Paul alluding to the Septuagint text of Exo 34.34, or is he quoting it? TEV takes the position that Paul is quoting, and adds "as the scripture says about Moses" (so also TNT and REB).

However, the text of this verse is not a literal quotation of Exo 34.34, and the subject of the verb **turns** is not explicit in what Paul wrote. (In the Septuagint Moses is the subject, but the verb is "used to go in [before the Lord].") As RSV and the reading in the footnote of TEV indicate, the subject of the verb may be "anyone." This interpretation is followed by a wide variety of versions, including NIV, TOB, NRSV, and CEV. TOB has the interesting rendering "It is only by conversion to the Lord that the veil falls away."

The Lord may be the Lord Jesus or the Lord God. Since the passage in Exo 34.34 refers to the Lord God, most likely that is the intended meaning here.

The veil is removed: in the Septuagint Moses removed the veil. Here the verb may be interpreted as stressing the agent, with "the Lord" as the subject (so Barrett, "he takes away the veil"). Or the verb may be passive as in RSV. The implied agent of the passive verb is "the Lord." In any case, if the passive idea is accepted, it will have to be rendered actively in many languages. Translators may consider saying "the Lord removes the veil," or more dynamically and without explicitly stating the agent, "the veil disappears." And some languages may require a reminder that this is the figurative veil "over their minds (or, hearts)" mentioned in verses 14-15, and not the literal one over Moses' face (verse 13).

3.17 RSV TEV

Now the Lord is the Spirit, and where the Spirit of the Lord is, there is freedom.	Now, "the Lord" in this passage is the Spirit; and where the Spirit of the Lord is present, there is freedom.

Now: the connecting word here is used to show that Paul intends to comment on what has just been said in the previous verse. But in some languages no overt transition word will be required at this point. The word **Now** is not a reference to the present time. It is rather a kind of logical connector.

The words **the Lord is the Spirit** are Paul's exegesis or interpretation of the word "Lord," from the preceding verse. TEV, which translates 3.16 as a direct quotation from Exo 34.34, adds "in this passage" and puts quotation marks around the words "the Lord." Rather than rely on quotation marks only, which hearers cannot see, translators may want to add "the word," as in FRCL: "Now, the word 'Lord' means here . . . ." The REB translation is similar to TEV, "Now the Lord of whom this passage speaks is the Spirit." Some languages have a kind of pronoun that points back to a previous word. Here they can perhaps use the equivalent of "that 'Lord.' "

Spirit of the Lord: some languages specify "Lord God" or "Lord Jesus," since the word for "lord" is the same as that used for a human master or chief. Here **Lord** may refer to God (3.3) or to Christ (Rom 8.9-10).

The Greek text contains no verb in the second half of this verse. Literally the text says "and where the Spirit of the Lord, freedom." Translators may need to supply the verb **is** or "is present," as in RSV and TEV. Or a more dynamic rendering may be required. Translators may consider one of the following: "freedom comes from the Spirit of the Lord," or "it is the Spirit of the Lord who always gives freedom," or "the Lord's Spirit sets us free" (CEV).

3.18 RSV	TEV
And we all, with unveiled face, beholding[d] the glory of the Lord, are being changed into his likeness from one degree of glory to another; for this comes from the Lord who is the Spirit.	All of us, then, reflect the glory of the Lord with uncovered faces; and that same glory, coming from the Lord, who is the Spirit, transforms us into his likeness in an ever greater degree of glory.

[d] Or *reflecting*

And: some translators may feel that a different kind of transition word is required here. Note that TEV has "then," and CEV begins with "so . . . ." It is less likely that the contrastive "but" (Phps) is appropriate in this case.

We is intended to include all Christians, not just the writers of 2 Corinthians or the apostles.

The participle **beholding** is from a relatively rare verb whose meaning is not certain. It is understood by some interpreters to mean "beholding as in a mirror" (so AB and Knox). RSV and NAB take the participle in the weakened meaning of "beholding." Other interpreters understand this word to mean "reflecting as a mirror does" (so TEV, NIV). Perhaps the AB translation is to be preferred, especially since the contrast seems to be between the Israelites, who could not gaze upon God's glory, and the Christians, who now can. Where there is no specific verb meaning "reflect," this idea may have to be translated "other people can see in us . . ." or "we show . . . ."

The glory of the Lord in this context refers to brightness. See comments on this term in verse 7 above.

Being changed into his likeness: **his likeness** is literally "the same likeness (image)." The passive **being changed** will have to be made active in many languages. One may consider "the Spirit of the Lord is changing us to become more and more like him" or "we are becoming more and more like him."

From one degree of glory to another is literally "from glory to glory." The sense is that Christians are being transformed into higher degrees of glory. Some translators may have to say something like "we are becoming brighter and brighter" or "our glory is constantly becoming greater."

The words **from the Lord who is the Spirit** translate three Greek words which may also be translated "of the Spirit of the Lord" (FRCL, NJB footnote). If the interpretation of FRCL is followed, the meaning is "this is the working of the Spirit of the Lord."

4.1-15

RSV

TEV

Spiritual Treasure in Clay Pots

1 Therefore, having this ministry by the mercy of God, we do not lose heart. 2 We have renounced disgraceful, underhanded ways; we refuse to practice cunning or to tamper with God's word, but by the open statement of the truth we would commend ourselves to every man's conscience in the sight of God. 3 And even if our gospel is veiled, it is veiled only to those who are perishing. 4 In their case the god of this world has blinded the minds of the unbelievers, to keep them from seeing the light of the gospel of the glory of Christ, who is the likeness of God. 5 For what we preach is not ourselves, but Jesus Christ as Lord, with ourselves as your servants for Jesus' sake. 6 For it is the God who said, "Let light shine out of darkness," who has shone in our hearts to give the light of the knowledge of the glory of God in the face of Christ.

7 But we have this treasure in earthen vessels, to show that the transcendent power belongs to God and not to us. 8 We are afflicted in every way, but not crushed; perplexed, but not driven to despair; 9 persecuted, but not forsaken; struck down, but not destroyed; 10 always carrying in the body the death of Jesus, so that the life of Jesus may also be manifested in our bodies. 11 For while we live we are always being given up to death for Jesus' sake, so that the life of Jesus may be manifested in our mortal flesh. 12 So death is at work in us, but life in you.

1 God in his mercy has given us this work to do, and so we do not become discouraged. 2 We put aside all secret and shameful deeds; we do not act with deceit, nor do we falsify the word of God. In the full light of truth we live in God's sight and try to commend ourselves to everyone's good conscience. 3 For if the gospel we preach is hidden, it is hidden only from those who are being lost. 4 They do not believe, because their minds have been kept in the dark by the evil god of this world. He keeps them from seeing the light shining on them, the light that comes from the Good News about the glory of Christ, who is the exact likeness of God. 5 For it is not ourselves that we preach; we preach Jesus Christ as Lord, and ourselves as your servants for Jesus' sake. 6 The God who said, "Out of darkness the light shall shine!" is the same God who made his light shine in our hearts, to bring us the knowledge of God's glory shining in the face of Christ.

7 Yet we who have this spiritual treasure are like common clay pots, in order to show that the supreme power belongs to God, not to us. 8 We are often troubled, but not crushed; sometimes in doubt, but never in despair; 9 there are many enemies, but we are never without a friend; and though badly hurt at times, we are not destroyed. 10 At all times we carry in our mortal bodies the death of Jesus, so that his life also may be seen in our

13 Since we have the same spirit of faith as he had who wrote, "I believed, and so I spoke," we too believe, and so we speak, 14 knowing that he who raised the Lord Jesus will raise us also with Jesus and bring us with you into his presence. 15 For it is all for your sake, so that as grace extends to more and more people it may increase thanksgiving, to the glory of God.

bodies. 11 Throughout our lives we are always in danger of death for Jesus' sake, in order that his life may be seen in this mortal body of ours. 12 This means that death is at work in us, but life is at work in you.

13 The scripture says, "I spoke because I believed." In the same spirit of faith we also speak because we believe. 14 We know that God, who raised the Lord Jesus to life, will also raise us up with Jesus and take us, together with you, into his presence. 15 All this is for your sake; and as God's grace reaches more and more people, they will offer to the glory of God more prayers of thanksgiving.

SECTION HEADING: TEV "Spiritual Treasure in Clay Pots." In this section Paul continues speaking about his ministry as an apostle. The first person plural pronouns in this section are exclusive, that is, they do not include the readers. Some translations use the first person singular throughout, understanding Paul to be talking about himself (so Mft and AT, but not ITCL). The TEV section heading reflects the figurative language of verse 7 in this passage. In some languages, however, it may be appropriate to use more direct language in the section heading. One may say something like "Things of great value in ordinary containers" or, leaving the image of the text altogether in order to focus on the overall content of the passage, "Faithfulness in preaching the Good News."

4.1   RSV   TEV

    Therefore, having this ministry by the mercy of God,[e] we do not lose heart.

    God in his mercy has given us this work to do, and so we do not become discouraged.

[e] Greek *as we have received mercy*

On the pronouns **we** in this entire section, see comments under the section heading.

Therefore: this word, which can also be translated as "For this reason," returns to the thought of 3.12 and introduces a renewed discussion of that point. The sense is "Since we have such hope . . . we do not lose heart." TEV restructures the order of the clauses in this verse and does not maintain the connection between chapters 3 and 4. Most English versions, however, retain the transition word, and this should probably also be done in the receptor language.

    The Greek word translated as **ministry** in RSV is the same word translated "dispensation" in 3.7-9, *diakonia*. **This ministry** is the "ministry of the Spirit" (3.8) and "the ministry of righteousness" (3.9). Others have translated it "service" (Brc) or "work" (the Good News for the World translation [GNW] as well as TEV).

By the mercy of God is literally a passive verb, "we have been mercied." God is not explicitly identified in the Greek as the agent of the verb "to have mercy." Most translations add the word **God** and thus make explicit the agent of this verb, though some do not. NAB says "Since we have this ministry through the mercy shown us," though note that the first edition of NAB says "Because we possess this ministry through God's mercy." Like NAB, AB does not make the agent explicit: "as recipients of mercy." Or one may be able to say "as those who have been pardoned." However, in most cases it will probably be better to make explicit in some manner the fact that it is God who is merciful. CEV says "God has been kind enough to trust us with this work."

Lose heart: the Greek word may mean "to become weary" (as it is translated in 2 Thes 3.13) or "to lose heart," that is, "to become discouraged" (TEV) or "to show fear." In the present context the meaning "to show fear" is also possible, since this verse connects with 3.12, in which Paul says "we are very bold." Knox follows this interpretation, translating "we do not play the coward." The same verb is used again in verse 16 of this chapter.

In some languages it may be more natural to restructure the verse further, saying something like "So we do not give up in doing this work, because it is God who kindly gave it to us" or "Therefore we can never be discouraged, since it is the merciful God who sent us to do this work."

<table>
<tr><td>**4.2**</td><td>RSV</td><td>TEV</td></tr>
</table>

RSV	TEV
We have renounced disgraceful, underhanded ways; we refuse to practice cunning or to tamper with God's word, but by the open statement of the truth we would commend ourselves to every man's conscience in the sight of God.	We put aside all secret and shameful deeds; we do not act with deceit, nor do we falsify the word of God. In the full light of truth we live in God's sight and try to commend ourselves to everyone's good conscience.

This verse begins in Greek with the word "rather" (so NIV). Instead of "losing heart" Paul and his associates do the things mentioned in verse 2. So a strong contrastive conjunction may be appropriate in the receptor language, showing that what follows is in contrast with the idea of "showing fear" or "giving up" in the previous verse.

We have renounced: the Greek verb probably is more emphatic than either RSV or TEV indicates. Barrett brings out the sense of the original: "As far as we are concerned" (so also AB, "we for our part have renounced . . ."). Paul is probably implying that there were people who acted in this way (see 2.17). This verb is also in the past tense. Is Paul referring to the time of his conversion? More likely he is referring to an earlier time in his Christian life, when he rejected practices such as those which follow. Translators should avoid giving the impression that Paul at one time did **practice cunning or . . . tamper with God's word**. The word **renounced** (RSV) as well as "put aside" (TEV) seem to suggest incorrectly that Paul did do these things at one time. It may be better to use a verb like "decided" in an expression such as "we decided never to . . . ," or possibly "we refused to . . . ."

Disgraceful, underhanded ways is literally "the hidden things of shame." The words "of shame" characterize those things that are hidden; they are "secret and shameful deeds." More specifically, does Paul mean that the people who do such deeds are, in fact, ashamed of their deeds? (REB "the deeds that people hide for very shame.") Or does he mean that they should be ashamed and are not? Either is possible, but the majority opinion seems to be that the practices were "so shameful that they have to be kept hidden" (Brc).

We refuse to practice cunning is literally "not walking in deceitfulness." The verb "to walk" is an Old Testament expression that means "to conduct oneself" or "to behave in a certain manner." **Cunning** is the unscrupulous or crafty manner of getting what one wants by deceiving people. NIV says "we do not use deception."

To tamper with God's word: the verb translates a Greek word that means "to water down," as of the watering down or dilution of wine, or "to falsify" (TEV and many other versions). Some other renderings are "distort" (TNT) and "change" (GNW). Other languages may use a verb like "twist," as in CEV. The expression **God's word** here does not refer to the Scriptures of the Old Testament but to the message from God about Christ (see 2.17).

On **God's word** see the comments at 2.17.

But: the same Greek word as at the beginning of this verse. TEV leaves this word untranslated. The conjunction usually marks contrast, and it may be appropriate to include it in the receptor language translation.

By the open statement of the truth: TEV takes the Greek noun "manifestation" in an abstract sense and understands the sense to be that Paul and his associates proclaim the gospel in the realm of truth, "in the full light of truth." More likely the sense is that they openly proclaim the truth of the gospel. REB says "It is by declaring the truth openly." This stands in contrast with the shameful practices that must be hidden, which are mentioned in this context.

We would commend ourselves . . . in the sight of God: on **commend ourselves** see 3.1. **To every man's conscience**: the context seems to include women as well as men. Languages in which "men" or "man" will exclude women may need to use a gender-inclusive word such as "everyone" (TEV, NRSV, LPD).

Normally in the New Testament the word **conscience** refers to one's ability to know that one has done something wrong (see comments on 1.12). Here and in 5.11 **conscience** is used of one's ability to decide on the rightness or wrongness of someone else's behavior. On **in the sight of God**, see the similar phrase in 2.17. Some possible models for translating this idea are "this is how they can know in their hearts what kind of people we are before God" (NCV) or "God is our witness that we speak only the truth, so others will be sure that we can be trusted" (CEV).

4.3   RSV   TEV

And even if our gospel is veiled, it is veiled only to those who are perishing.	For if the gospel we preach is hidden, it is hidden only from those who are being lost.

And even if: despite Paul's intentions to proclaim the gospel openly (4.2), he concedes that it may be hidden from some people.

Our gospel is the good news about Jesus Christ that Paul and his companions preach. Although Paul says **our gospel**, this does not mean that their gospel is different from the gospel of other people. Rather the word **our** shows their personal involvement and commitment to the gospel. Some possible models for translators are "our message" (CEV), "the good news" (Brc), and "the Good News that we preach" (NCV). In those languages that must choose between inclusive and exclusive forms of the first person plural pronoun, the word **our** here should probably be understood as focusing on Paul and his associates as preachers of the Good News.

Veiled: elsewhere in RSV this verb is translated "is hidden" (Matt 10.26) and "cover" (Luke 8.16). The idea is that of something concealed from view. This verb in Greek is related to the noun "veil" in 3.13,14,15,16. But it is used here in a figurative sense. For this reason some translate more dynamically: "our gospel is a mystery" (Knox), or "if the good news which we tell is not clear . . ." (GNW). Another way of avoiding the passive form may be to say "if some people do not understand the Good News we preach"—although this will almost certainly require a restructuring of the rest of the verse.

Those who are perishing: **perishing** refers to spiritual death, that is, the destruction of the whole person, body and soul. The participle used here is present and is the same as in 2.15. CEV "someone who is lost" is therefore perhaps less satisfactory than "those who are on the way to being lost" (TNT) or "those who are on the road to perdition" (Knox).

4.4   RSV   TEV

In their case the god of this world has blinded the minds of the unbelievers, to keep them from seeing the light of the gospel of the glory of Christ, who is the likeness of God.	They do not believe, because their minds have been kept in the dark by the evil god of this world. He keeps them from seeing the light shining on them, the light that comes from the Good News about the glory of Christ, who is the exact likeness of God.

The god of this world: or more literally "the god of this age" (so NIV; similarly NAB and REB). Though God is said to cause spiritual blindness in Isa 44.18, here the words **the god of this world** should not be understood as God but as Satan. TEV adds the word "evil" to make clear that Paul is not here talking about God. The reference is to the Devil. Translators may want to make clear the sense in which Satan is **the god of this world**: "the god who rules this world" (CEV). NCV says more explicitly "the devil who rules this world." ITCL says "Satan, the god of this world."

The two parts of this verse are connected in Greek by words that may indicate either purpose or result. If the former is the correct interpretation, the sense is that the devil blinds unbelievers "in order that" they will not see (so RSV, NRSV, NAB). If the latter interpretation is correct, the sense is that the devil blinds them, and *the result is that* they do not see (so REB). Barrett translates "in order that" but acknowledges that the words could equally well be translated "with the result that." The AB translator has chosen to maintain the ambiguity of the Greek, with the translation "so that," but for many languages it may be necessary to decide between the two alternatives. Perhaps "in order that" is the better choice, but translators may choose either interpretation with equally good reason. It is quite clear that the images of blinding and seeing are figurative and should not be translated in such a way as to be taken literally.

The last part of this verse contains a series of nouns linked by the word **of** in English. Translators may need to restructure to make the relationships clear among these words. **The light of the gospel** is the light that comes from the gospel, or possibly **light** is another way of talking about the gospel. **The gospel of the glory of Christ** is the gospel about the glory of Christ. **The glory of Christ** is a way of talking about the saving presence of Christ (see 3.7-11). The central word in this series of four nouns seems to be **light**. This light is then described in detail as the Good News about the glory of Christ. This is all captured well by AB: "the enlightenment coming from the gospel of the splendor of Christ." But it is rendered in more popular language by CEV: "they cannot see the light, which is the good news about our glorious Christ."

The likeness of God: the English word "image" comes from the Greek noun translated here as **likeness**. Some languages will find it helpful to use a verbal expression such as "who is like God." Some other models are "who shows us what God is like" (CEV) or "who is exactly like God" (Brc).

4.5	RSV	TEV
	For what we preach is not ourselves, but Jesus Christ as Lord, with ourselves as your servants^f for Jesus' sake.	For it is not ourselves that we preach; we preach Jesus Christ as Lord, and ourselves as your servants for Jesus' sake.

^{f} Or *slaves*

For: the transition word here serves to tie the following statement to what is said in the previous verse. Although Paul has spoken of "our gospel" in verse 3, it is clearly the gospel about the glory of Christ (verse 4).

What we preach is not ourselves: the word **ourselves** is in an emphatic position in Greek. To give similar emphasis in English, TEV places the pronoun "ourselves" before the verb. In some languages it is unnatural to use the verb "to preach" with a noun or pronoun object as occurs here. One has to say "preach *about* [something or someone]." Hence "we are not preaching about ourselves" (CEV). Note also that the verb tense here is the present, but it does not indicate something that Paul was doing while writing. Rather it affirms an action that he did on a regular basis. For this reason the habitual verb form will be used in languages where such forms exist.

The Greek grammar clearly suggests that Paul's gospel has two parts: that Jesus Christ is Lord, and that the apostles are the servants of the Christian churches. However, the intended sense may possibly be "we preach Jesus Christ as Lord, and in doing so we are your servants."

Jesus Christ: some versions follow manuscript evidence that reverses these two terms (KJV, NASB, and LB, for example). But translators are advised to follow the order in RSV and TEV in this case.

Jesus Christ as Lord: some languages require a possessive pronoun with the word **Lord**, or a noun phrase indicating the subjects of lordship. A possible translation is "we proclaim that Jesus Christ is our Lord." To claim that Jesus is Lord is to declare that he is sovereign and is Lord over all. The focus of the translation should be on his sovereign lordship and not on those who have accepted his rule. It may be necessary, therefore, to say "Jesus Christ as Lord of all people" or something similar.

Servants: as indicated in the RSV footnote, this word may be rendered as "slaves" (AB and NRSV) or "bond-servants" (NASB). However, in many languages the word "slave" carries such repulsive connotations that it is better to use a more general term. In some languages, however, a clear distinction is made between a person who works for a definite salary and one whose needs are taken care of by his master but who does not receive a regular, fixed wage. The term used by Paul here is more closely related to the latter. Perhaps the idea of a permanent binding relationship rather than an optional or voluntary association is the most important component of meaning of this word in the present context.

4.6	RSV	TEV
	For it is the God who said, "Let light shine out of darkness," who has shone in our hearts to give the light of the knowledge of the glory of God in the face of Christ.	The God who said, "Out of darkness the light shall shine!" is the same God who made his light shine in our hearts, to bring us the knowledge of God's glory shining in the face of Christ.

For: the transition word so rendered in RSV is often translated "Because" (as in AB). Here it introduces the basis for the content of the previous verse. It is because God made his light to shine in the hearts of Paul and his associates that they do not preach about themselves but about Jesus Christ.

Let light shine out of darkness is a freely-worded quotation of Gen 1.3. Translators may wish to indicate that Paul is quoting the Hebrew scriptures. CEV makes this clear: "The Scriptures say, 'God commanded light to shine in the dark.' " Note also that it will be better in some cases to follow the CEV model in making this a separate sentence and starting anew with God as subject in the next part of the verse.

Who has shone: the subject of this clause is God. If this verse is divided into two sentences as suggested above, one may begin the second sentence here with "It is this same God who . . . ."

In our hearts: for the translation of **hearts** see comments at 1.22 as well as the use of the term in 3.15. The pronoun **our** may refer to Paul and his associates only, or to all Christians in contrast to unbelievers (verse 4). While the focus here is probably on Paul and those with him, the receptor language should not give the impression that the light of the gospel had not shone in the hearts of the Corinthian believers.

The light of the knowledge of the glory of God in the face of Christ: the use of several nouns linked by the word **of** is similar in form and content to the end of verse 4. The **light** comes from the **knowledge**, though it is possible to understand **knowledge** as in apposition to **light**, that is, "that illumination that consists in the knowledge" (so Barrett). The word for **knowledge** in this context refers to essentially the same thing as "gospel" (see verse 4).

The glory of God is the content of the **knowledge**. So it may be better in many languages to say "knowledge about the glory of God." The word for **glory** here is the same as in 1.20 and is also found six times in chapter 3 as well as in verse 4 above.

In the face of Christ is contrasted with Moses's face in 3.7. As TEV makes explicit, God's glory is "shining" in the face of Christ.

The editors of the UBS *Greek New Testament* follow manuscripts that say "in the face of Jesus Christ" (so NRSV and REB); but since many good manuscripts omit the name "Jesus," the editors place the name Jesus in brackets. Neither RSV nor TEV follows the reading of the UBS *Greek New Testament* here. The evidence is so evenly divided that translators may follow either RSV or NRSV. The meaning is the same regardless of whether the name "Jesus" is included or omitted.

4.7	RSV	TEV

But we have this treasure in earthen vessels, to show that the transcendent power belongs to God and not to us.	Yet we who have this spiritual treasure are like common clay pots, in order to show that the supreme power belongs to God, not to us.

Verses 7-10 form one long sentence in Greek. RSV and TEV both begin a new sentence with verse 8.

But indicates a contrast with the previous verse. Unlike the glory of God, the Christian messengers are "common clay pots."

We have: though what Paul says is true of all Christians, including the Corinthian readers, in the context of chapter 4, the pronoun **we** does not include the readers (see 4.5,12,14 for the contrast between "we" and "you").

The words **this treasure** refer to the gospel and the task of proclaiming the good news about Jesus Christ. TEV makes explicit the nature of **this treasure** by adding the word "spiritual."

Earthen vessels: this is figurative language in which the human body in its weakness and human limitations is compared to fragile "clay pots." As TEV makes clear, "we . . . are like common clay pots." The word translated **earthen** is found also in 2 Tim 2.20 in the description of ordinary containers as contrasted with those made of precious metals. In the Greek translation of the Old Testament (Lev 6.28; 14.50), this same expression is used to describe the containers that the priests used in offering certain kinds of sacrifices. These containers were regarded as immediately dispensable, if for some reason they became ritually unclean.

The first part of this verse is sometimes recast as follows: "This is something of great value, but we have it in pots made of earth" (GNW) or "We have this treasure from God. But we are only like clay jars that hold the treasure" (NCV).

To show . . . belong: literally "in order that . . . might be." This indicates the purpose of entrusting the valuable treasure of the gospel to ordinary containers, that is, in weak, fragile human beings. The idea may be expressed in a separate sentence beginning with "This fact demonstrates that . . . ."

The transcendent power: the Greek word translated as **transcendent** in RSV emphasizes the great quality or extent of something. AB says "the power which is beyond any comparison." While GNW does not clearly show the relationship to the preceding section, it does capture the idea of this phrase with "this power is greater than any other power." But since such a phrase may be too awkward in this context, some have translated simply "the real power" (CEV), "the splendid power" (Phps), or "the supreme power" (TNT).

In view of the above discussion, the second half of this verse may possibly be worded as follows: "This happens in order to show that the truly great power comes from God and not from us" or, as Knox puts it, "it must be God, and not anything in ourselves, that gives it its sovereign power."

4.8	RSV	TEV

We are afflicted in every way, but not crushed; perplexed, but not driven to despair;	We are often troubled, but not crushed; sometimes in doubt, but never in despair;

We: this pronoun refers to Paul and possibly to others with him, but it does not include the Corinthians. In keeping with their usual practice, Mft and AT take it as an epistolary "we" and translate using first person singular pronouns; but this is less probable and is not recommended here.

As indicated in the NJB note, the images of the four sentences in verses 8 and 9 are taken from the contests of gladiators in the ancient Greek world. There are four sets of participles in which the second of each set is preceded by a negation. There are many passive ideas in these four sentences that will have to be rendered actively in many languages. Frequently the best way to do this is to use an indefinite third person plural form, such as "They [habitually] afflict us . . ." for **We are afflicted**, for example.

The position of **in every way** in the Greek sentence gives emphasis to these words. **In every way** indicates the extent of the suffering: "We are afflicted with all kinds of hardships." TEV inserts the words "often" and "sometimes" in order to indicate that such troubles are not always present everywhere. The word "always" in verse 10 refers to the continuance of the afflictions in one form or another.

On **afflicted** see 1.6, where the same Greek word occurs.

But not crushed: the term so translated has the idea of restriction or narrow confinement. It has been rendered "never cornered" (REB and similarly TNT), while Mft has "not hemmed in." Knox has "yet still have room to breathe," and Brc has "never without a way out."

The words **perplexed** and **driven to despair** come from the same root word in Greek, with the second participle in Greek having a form that indicates "intensely perplexed." The root verb means "to be uncertain of how to act." CEV says "Even when we don't know what to do, we never give up." In an attempt to preserve the relationship between the two verbs, one may possibly translate something like TOB, "sometimes at an impasse, but we manage to pass," or "despairing, but not utterly desperate" (AB), or possibly even "sometimes feeling lost, but never completely lost."

4.9	RSV	TEV
	persecuted, but not forsaken; struck down, but not destroyed;	there are many enemies, but we are never without a friend; and though badly hurt at times, we are not destroyed.

Persecuted, but not forsaken: the exact sense of these verbs is not clear. The imagery may be that from the sports arena: "We are pursued but not overtaken." NJB says "we are pursued but never cut off." Most interpreters understand the first Greek verb here in the specific sense of being **persecuted**. As in the previous verse, the passive idea may have to be translated actively: "they persecute us . . ." or "people torment us . . . ."

But not forsaken: the Greek does not indicate the agent of this passive verb. Who does not forsake them? The "friend" of TEV may be either a human friend or God. This verb in the Septuagint is often used to claim that God will not forsake or abandon his people. The implicit agent of this verb is no doubt "God." CEV says "In times of trouble, God is with us." Or translators may consider saying something like "people cause us to suffer, but God does not abandon us."

The words **struck down** and **destroyed** translate two Greek verbs based on the same root word. Phps preserves the play on words: "knocked down, but not knocked out" (similarly also Brc).

Struck down: the Greek word has a wide range of possible meanings: struck down physically by a blow or a weapon, abused or bullied, rejected, stricken with an illness. All of these make sense in the context. It is not clear whether the words are to be understood in a literal physical sense or in an emotional sense. If the receptor language has a general term which can be understood in a wide variety of ways, it is probably the most suitable one to use here.

Destroyed: as with the preceding verb, it is not clear whether Paul is referring to literal death (REB "never killed"), or whether the sense is that the opponents are not able to destroy the work of Paul's apostolic ministry.

The passive idea of the four verbs in this verse will have to be rendered actively in some languages. Here is a possible model: "we have many enemies, but we also have friends; they [indefinite] make us suffer, but they do not kill us." However, if God is understood as the agent, this will have to be reworded something like this: "we have many enemies, but God is our friend; our enemies make us suffer, but they do not kill us." Another language says "they [indefinite] persecute us, but God does not abandon us; they cause us to fall, but we do not die."

4.10   RSV   TEV

always carrying in the body the death of | At all times we carry in our mortal bod-
Jesus, so that the life of Jesus may also | ies the death of Jesus, so that his life
be manifested in our bodies. | also may be seen in our bodies.

The position of the word **always** in the Greek sentence gives emphasis (see also 4.8). Note that REB renders this "wherever we go . . . ," while NAB has "continually," and Phps reads "every day."

Carrying: some experts see in the use of this verb a possible reference to the missionary travels of Paul. But the use of this verb may be awkward in some languages in such a context. It may not be possible to have **death** as the grammatical object of the verb "carry." The idea is expressed by Phps as "we experience something of the death of Jesus." Two other possible models are "never free from the danger of being put to death like Jesus" (AT) and "wherever I go, I am being killed in the body as Jesus was" (Mft).

The Greek is literally **the body** as in RSV, but "our . . . bodies" (TEV) is more natural English. Some languages require a possessive pronoun with the noun **body**. If the pronoun "our" must be used in a receptor language having inclusive and exclusive forms of the first person plural pronoun, the exclusive form should be used here. If translators agree with Mft that Paul here uses **our** when referring to himself only, it may be necessary to say "my body."

The death of Jesus . . . the life of Jesus: REB says "the death that Jesus died . . . the life that Jesus lives."

So that: this indicates the purpose of the believers' experiencing the death of Jesus. It was to lead to true life.

The life of Jesus here and in verse 11 refers not to the earthly life of Jesus but rather to the power of his resurrection life (see 4.14).

Be manifested: this passive verb will have to be rendered actively in a number of languages. One possible model is "other people may be able to see the life of Jesus in our bodies."

4.11 RSV TEV

For while we live we are always being given up to death for Jesus' sake, so that the life of Jesus may be manifested in our mortal flesh.

Throughout our lives we are always in danger of death for Jesus' sake, in order that his life may be seen in this mortal body of ours.

For: this word indicates that verse 11 supports what Paul has just written in verse 10. Verse 11 basically repeats the thought of the preceding verse. The two verses are so similar that CEV combines them.

While we live we are always is literally "For always we the living." **Always** is in emphatic position in Greek. See comments on verses 8 ("in every way") and 10 ("always").

While we live: literally "we the living." This is understood in a temporal sense by many interpreters. That is, these words indicate *when* they are being given up to death. But the Greek participle "living" has the definite article and more likely indicates "who" rather than "when." Barrett understands Paul to be referring to those Christians who are alive and will be alive when Christ returns: "For we living men are continually being handed over to death." NAB and NIV are similar: "For we who live" and "For we who are alive."

Being given up to death: who is the agent of this passive verb? Paul understands his sufferings as a part of the ministry that God has given him (Phil 1.29-30). The sense may be "God is always giving us up to death." Another way of saying this without making the agent explicit is "we suffer the pains of death . . ." or "we are always being exposed to death for Jesus' sake" (Phps).

Be manifested: the passive verb may have to be made active in verse 10 above.

Mortal flesh is a literal translation of the Greek. **Flesh** here is basically a synonym of "body" in verse 10. A more natural translation in English is "mortal body" (TEV, REB, FRCL). The word **mortal** is used six times in Paul's writings and is related to the noun for death. It bears the meaning "liable to die" and modifies the noun "body" in Rom 6.12; 8.3. In 1 Cor 15.53,54 it is used in much the same way. It appears also in 5.4 of this letter. It may also be translated "temporary," "[bodies] which do not last," or "which [eventually] die."

4.12   RSV   TEV

So death is at work in us, but life in   This means that death is at work in us,
you.   but life is at work in you.

So translates a Greek word which indicates that verse 12 is the consequence of verse 11. TEV captures this meaning with the words "This means
that" (likewise CEV). Others have rendered this transition word "then" (Mft)
and "thus" (REB), showing the logical connection.

Death is at work in us: Paul and his co-workers suffer and are in danger
of dying or of being put to death. The Greek verb **is at work** may be translated
as an active verb with **death** as the subject (so nearly all interpreters). This
verb may, however, be passive in both form and meaning (as are the verbs in
verses 10-11), so that the sense will be that the power of God (4.7) is at work
bringing life and death. This is the interpretation behind the AB translation:
"death is made active [by the power of God] in us." On the basis of grammar
and context, either interpretation is possible. However, as already noted, most
translations have chosen the active meaning of the verb rather than the
passive. One African language has worded this verse as follows: "we have
agreed to struggle with death so that you might find life." Phps provides
another good model: "We are always facing physical death, [so that you may
know spiritual life]."

Though the Greek does not make explicit the relationship of the two
parts of this verse, the sense is that Paul and his co-workers suffer and risk
death, with the result that the Corinthians have spiritual life (4.15). In view
of this contrast between life and death, the conjunction **but** will be crucial in
most languages. However, as indicated above, it may be possible to show the
cause and effect relationship explicitly.

4.13   RSV   TEV

    Since we have the same spirit of   The scripture says, "I spoke be-
faith as he had who wrote, "I believed,   cause I believed." In the same spirit of
and so I spoke," we too believe, and so   faith we also speak because we believe.
we speak,

Verses 13-14 form one long complex sentence in Greek. TEV changes the
order of the phrases in verse 13 and makes two sentences of the one Greek
sentence, making the verse easier to follow in English.

The first part of this verse is literally "having the same spirit of faith
according to what is written." Though it is possible to understand the
comparison to be between Paul and the Corinthians, who have the same spirit
of faith, RSV is probably correct in making the comparison between Paul and
the psalmist.

Translators are ill advised, in some languages, to translate literally the TEV rendering "The scripture says . . . ." It will be much better to say "Someone has said in scripture" or "In scripture someone has written . . . ."

The same spirit of faith: most translations spell "spirit" with a small letter "s" (RSV, NRSV, TEV, NJB, and NIV). According to this interpretation "spirit" refers not to the Holy Spirit but to the human attitude or disposition reflecting the way one thinks about something. It is possible, though, that Paul is referring to the Holy Spirit, who creates faith: "But since we have the same Spirit of faith" (Barrett, so also AB).

As he had who wrote introduces a quotation from the ancient Greek translation of the Old Testament in Psa 116.10. In this passage the immediately preceding verses speak of the psalmist's deliverance from suffering and death, words with which Paul identified. TEV makes explicit that this quotation is from "the scripture" (also REB). Some translations (LPD, ITCL, GNC, NJB) place direct citations from the Old Testament in bold font or in italics to indicate to the reader that Paul's thought and expression are influenced by the Scriptures.

I believed . . . we too believe: the Greek has no object for these verbs. Languages that require an object may add the noun "God" or the noun phrase "God's promises."

So: this connecting word occurs twice in RSV to show the relationship between belief and speaking. NIV uses "therefore." And it has been translated in FRCL and TOB as "this is why . . . ."

4.14   RSV   TEV

knowing that he who raised the Lord   We know that God, who raised the
Jesus will raise us also with Jesus and   Lord Jesus to life, will also raise us up
bring us with you into his presence.   with Jesus and take us, together with
                                            you, into his presence.

The participle **knowing** links verse 14 to the preceding verse by expressing the reason that Paul acts as he does. It may be best rendered as beginning a new sentence, as in TEV, Brc, and several other modern versions.

TEV (also FRCL) makes explicit that "God" is **he who raised the Lord Jesus**. TEV also makes explicit that God raised Jesus from death "to life."

Lord Jesus: some manuscripts omit the word **Lord**. Though the UBS *Greek New Testament* includes this word, the editors were divided over whether Paul wrote "Lord Jesus" or whether a later scribe added the word "Lord." NBE and Knox omit the word "Lord," but most versions include it.

Will raise: is Paul referring to an event in the near future or in the more distant future? Since he apparently expected to be alive at the time of Christ's second coming (1 Thes 4.17; 1 Cor 7.29), the near future seems more likely. **Raise** does not necessarily mean "from death," but in some cases it may mean only "raise up to meet the Lord in the air" (1 Thes 4.17), referring to people who will still be alive at the second coming of Christ.

With Jesus: since Jesus had already been raised from the dead when Paul wrote, the words **with Jesus** do not mean "at the same time as Jesus." The sense is either "will raise us in the same way that Jesus was raised," or "will raise us to be with Jesus," or "will raise us in virtue of our union with Jesus." The last one mentioned is more probable. The more probable meaning may have to be rendered in some languages as "will raise us up because we are united with Jesus." The KJV rendering "by Jesus" seems to refer to Jesus as the means by which they will be raised. This, however, is not what is intended.

The verb translated **bring** in RSV means "to present [someone]" or "to make [someone] stand." Since Paul was not with Jesus at the time he was writing, the English word "take" (TEV) correctly expresses the movement involved. Some other possibilities are "present" (AB and NIV) or "summon" (Knox).

The pronouns **us** are exclusive, since the readers (**you**) are mentioned separately.

4.15   RSV   TEV

For it is all for your sake, so that as grace extends to more and more people it may increase thanksgiving, to the glory of God.	All this is for your sake; and as God's grace reaches more and more people, they will offer to the glory of God more prayers of thanksgiving.

It is all for your sake: Paul's experiences of suffering referred to in 4.8-12 are endured for the sake of the Corinthians. CEV begins this verse with "All of this has been done for you . . . ." In some languages it may be necessary to be even more explicit by saying "all these affairs" or "all of this suffering . . . ."

For your sake: some languages have special verb forms (called benefactive) that indicate that the action of the verb is done for someone else. Such a form would be appropriate here. In other cases translators may say something like "for your welfare," "in your interest," or simply "for you."

Grace: the reference is to grace that comes from God, as TEV makes explicit. Compare 6.1; 8.1; 9.14, where God is clearly named by Paul as the originator of grace. See also 1.2,12 for comments on **grace**.

To more and more people: the Greek is literally "through the majority." In 2.6 this word refers to the majority of the church members. Is Paul thinking that God's grace will extend in greater depth to more and more members of the Corinthian church ("the majority," so Barrett)? Or is he referring to the geographical spread of God's grace, so that more and more people are converted to the Christian faith? Either interpretation is possible, but the latter seems more probable in the context.

Thanksgiving: by those to whom God's grace extended. The subject of the verbal expression **increase thanksgiving** in RSV is the pronoun **it**, referring to the extension of God's grace to a greater number of people. Another way of saying this is "grace . . . may cause thanksgiving to overflow to the glory of God" (AB).

To the glory of God: see comments on 1.20.

The complex form of this verse may be made more understandable by breaking it down into the component parts. It may be stated in four separate sentences: "All this is happening for you. It is taking place so that God's grace will reach more and more people. Then more people will thank God. And this will bring more glory to God."

4.16–5.10

RSV	TEV
	Living by Faith

16 So we do not lose heart. Though our outer nature is wasting away, our inner nature is being renewed every day. 17 For this slight momentary affliction is preparing for us an eternal weight of glory beyond all comparison, 18 because we look not to the things that are seen but to the things that are unseen; for the things that are seen are transient, but the things that are unseen are eternal.
Chapter 5:
1 For we know that if the earthly tent we live in is destroyed, we have a building from God, a house not made with hands, eternal in the heavens. 2 Here indeed we groan, and long to put on our heavenly dwelling, 3 so that by putting it on we may not be found naked. 4 For while we are still in this tent, we sigh with anxiety; not that we would be unclothed, but that we would be further clothed, so that what is mortal may be swallowed up by life. 5 He who has prepared us for this very thing is God, who has given us the Spirit as a guarantee.

6 So we are always of good courage; we know that while we are at home in the body we are away from the Lord, 7 for we walk by faith, not by sight. 8 We are of good courage, and we would rather be away from the body and at home with the Lord. 9 So whether we are at home or away, we make it our aim to please him. 10 For we must all appear before the judgment seat of Christ, so that each one may receive good or evil, according to what he has done in the body.

16 For this reason we never become discouraged. Even though our physical being is gradually decaying, yet our spiritual being is renewed day after day. 17 And this small and temporary trouble we suffer will bring us a tremendous and eternal glory, much greater than the trouble. 18 For we fix our attention, not on things that are seen, but on things that are unseen. What can be seen lasts only for a time, but what cannot be seen lasts forever.
Chapter 5:
1 For we know that when this tent we live in—our body here on earth—is torn down, God will have a house in heaven for us to live in, a home he himself has made, which will last forever. 2 And now we sigh, so great is our desire that our home which comes from heaven should be put on over us; 3 by being clothed with it we shall not be without a body. 4 While we live in this earthly tent, we groan with a feeling of oppression; it is not that we want to get rid of our earthly body, but that we want to have the heavenly one put on over us, so that what is mortal will be transformed by life. 5 God is the one who has prepared us for this change, and he gave us his Spirit as the guarantee of all that he has in store for us.

6 So we are always full of courage. We know that as long as we are at home in the body we are away from the Lord's home. 7 For our life is a matter of faith, not of sight. 8 We are full of courage and would much prefer to leave our home in the body and be at home with the Lord. 9 More than anything else, however, we want to please him, whether in our home here or there. 10 For all of us must appear before Christ, to be judged by him. Each one will receive what he deserves, according to everything he has done, good or bad, in his bodily life.

SECTION HEADING: TEV "Living by Faith." Verse 16 returns to the thought of 4.1, "We do not lose heart." The same verb is used in both cases. The reason that the writers of this letter do not lose heart is explained in terms of the contrasts between the momentary and insignificant sufferings of this life compared with the hope of eternal glory. Paul then contrasts life here on earth with the future life by using a series of images, and then returns in verses 9 and 10 of chapter 5 to the defense of his apostolic ministry.

Some translations begin the new section with 5.1 instead of at 4.16 and use a heading such as "Our Heavenly Dwelling" (NIV), "Longing for the Heavenly Home" (Lu), or "Our Future Destiny" (NAB). However, it is best to avoid breaking the flow of the text between 4.18 and 5.1.

4.16 RSV	TEV
So we do not lose heart. Though our outer nature is wasting away, our inner nature is being renewed every day.	For this reason we never become discouraged. Even though our physical being is gradually decaying, yet our spiritual being is renewed day after day.

So: the transition word used here is a rather strong one linking the following declaration to what has just been said. It is rendered "thus" (AB), "no wonder . . . !" (REB), "that is why . . ." (NJB), and "hence" (Mft). It is probably not wise to leave it untranslated as in CEV and NAB.

We do not lose heart: this is linked to 4.1, where the same verb is used, but it is also linked in thought to the previous verse: the apostles are encouraged by the extension of God's grace. It is not clear whether all of the first person plural pronouns in this section include the readers, or whether the readers are included only in verse 10. If the pronouns are exclusive, neither is it clear whether Paul includes his companions or only himself (so Mft).

The second part of this verse is similar in thought to 3.18.

Outer nature: this refers to the physical part of human existence. Paul does not use this expression elsewhere, but in Rom 6.6 he does talk about "the old person" with much the same sense (likewise Col 3.9 and Eph 4.22). Some possible translation models here are "our body (or, bodies)" (NAB, CEV), "the physical part of us" (Brc), and "the outward part of our nature" (Knox).

Wasting away: the verb used here may be rendered "is gradually decaying" (TEV), "wearing out," or "gradually dying" (CEV).

Inner nature: the reference is to the nonphysical, spiritual part of one's being and stands in contrast with the **outer nature**. The same expression is translated by RSV as "my inmost self" in Rom 7.22 and may be seen as practically synonymous with the "new creature" in 5.17 and Gal 6.15. It has been translated here as "we ourselves" (CEV), "our inner being" (NAB), "our spirit inside us" (NCV), and "our inner life" (Knox).

Being renewed: this verb stands in contrast with **wasting away** and has been rendered "is refreshed" (Knox), "receives fresh strength" (Phps), "are being made stronger" (CEV).

Note that NIV uses the adverbs "outwardly" and "inwardly" to translate the two difficult terms in this verse, and that NAB reverses the order of the two contrasting parts, speaking first of renewal "even though our body is being destroyed."

4.17   RSV   TEV

For this slight momentary affliction is preparing for us an eternal weight of glory beyond all comparison,	**And this small and temporary trouble we suffer will bring us a tremendous and eternal glory, much greater than the trouble.**

The word **For** at the beginning of verse 17 provides the basis for not losing heart (verse 16). Verse 18 is a parenthetic explanation, and 5.1 also is connected to verse 16 by the same transition word, **For**.

This slight momentary affliction: Paul sees his sufferings here on earth as temporary in comparison with eternity. Though the Greek noun is singular, that is, **affliction**, the sense is all of his sufferings as a whole. REB says "Our troubles are slight and short-lived." Other languages may need to use a plural noun to avoid the impression that Paul is talking about one specific incident in which he suffered. Two words are used to emphasize the relative unimportance of the sufferings experienced in this life. The first is an adjective which indicates that they do not last long or are "transitory" (Phps). And the second is formally a noun but serves to underline their pettiness or insignificance. It gives the idea of "lightness" or lack of "weight." Some languages may require that a separate sentence be made of this part of the verse: "The troubles we experience are small and they do not last long."

An eternal weight of glory: the affliction is **slight** or "light" in contrast with the glory, which is "heavy" or "weighty." The words **weight** and **glory** are closely related in Hebrew, since they are spelled with the same consonants. Paul's choice of the Greek words **weight of glory** probably reflects the underlying play on words in Hebrew. In many languages the words **weight of glory** will have no clear meaning. TEV's "a tremendous glory" attempts to capture the sense. Christians are being prepared for **glory**, which has two characteristics opposed to those mentioned for **affliction**: it is "eternal" (as contrasted with the "transitory") and "weighty." In some languages one may render the last term as "abundance" (AB), or in a verbal expression such as "loading us [with everlasting glory]" (Knox).

Beyond all comparison: the comparison is with the short-lived and light-weight suffering of this world. This may have to be made more explicit in the receptor language. That is, one may have to say something like "cannot be compared with the suffering" or "is nothing like the suffering."

The meaning of this verse may be expressed as follows: "These little troubles are getting us ready for an eternal glory that will make all our troubles seem like nothing" (CEV) or "we have our troubles, but they are transitory and unimportant, and all the time they are producing for us a superlative and eternal glory, which will far outweigh all the troubles" (Brc).

4.18 RSV	TEV
because we look not to the things that are seen but to the things that are unseen; for the things that are seen are transient, but the things that are unseen are eternal.	For we fix our attention, not on things that are seen, but on things that are unseen. What can be seen lasts only for a time, but what cannot be seen lasts forever.

Because: it is probably better to begin a new sentence here, since this verse is something of a digression and does not stand in a causal relationship with the preceding verse. It is better translated "so" (NIV) or not at all (NAB).

The pronoun **we** in this verse is inclusive of all people, and of the Corinthians, who look beyond what is immediately evident in this world. It is not limited to Paul and those with him.

Look: this is a rather weak translation of the verb used here. It carries the idea of "focus one's attention on" or "keep one's eye on." This explains the rendering of TEV. CEV goes a step further, clearly showing that mere physical vision is not intended here: "we keep our minds on . . . ." This is especially appropriate, since one cannot "look" at "things that are not seen."

For Paul the **things that are seen** are, in this context, the sufferings and afflictions experienced in this temporary existence on earth. The **things that are unseen** are the glory of eternity with God (4.17). Because these two verbs are passive in form, in many languages the two expressions may have to be rendered more dynamically as "the things that we can (or, cannot) see with our eyes . . ." and "the things that people can (cannot) see . . . ." The words **transient** and **eternal** stand in sharp contrast and in some languages may be translated "passing" and "permanent," or by verbal expressions such as "do not last long" and "last (or, endure) forever."

Although a new chapter begins at this point, translators should note that this section begins at 4.16. The discourse of Paul continues through verse 5 of chapter 5. As in TEV, several modern versions begin a new paragraph at 5.1 (NRSV, NJB), but others have a continuous paragraph beginning at 4.16 and continuing to 5.3 (CEV), or 5.5 (REB), or 5.10 (Mft). Apart from the influence of the traditional chapter divisions, which were added centuries after Paul wrote, the most logical thing to do at this point is probably to continue without a paragraph break. Certainly translators are not well advised to place a section heading here, as has been done in NIV.

For we know that if the earthly
tent we live in is destroyed, we have a
building from God, a house not made
with hands, eternal in the heavens.

For we know that when this tent
we live in—our body here on earth—is
torn down, God will have a house in
heaven for us to live in, a home he himself has made, which will last forever.

For: the transition word used here links the following verses closely to
4.17-18. But if no new paragraph break is used here, it may be possible in
some languages to leave it untranslated, as in REB and CEV.

We: on the first person plural pronouns, see the comments on 4.16.

If the earthly tent we live in is literally "if the house of our earthly tent."
The word **if** does not indicate doubt as to the reality of death, but rather the
uncertainty of when this will happen. TEV makes this meaning clear by saying
"when" rather than "if" (so also GNC). Some languages may need to say
"whenever it happens that . . . ." Of course it is possible that Paul wrote **if** with
the thought in mind that he might still be alive when Christ returned (see
1 Thes 4.13-17).

The figurative use of **tent** points to the fact that life on earth is not
permanent. In some languages it may be necessary to translate **tent** as
"temporary dwelling." TEV makes explicit that the **earthly tent** is a metaphor
for "our body here on earth." A different structure that may be more easily
adaptable as a model for other languages may be CEV, which makes a separate
sentence of this: "Our bodies are like tents that we live in here on earth."

Destroyed: most likely Paul is thinking of the moment of death, but
perhaps the present suffering that leads to the ruin of the physical body is
more the point of meaning. The Greek verb here is used of dismantling a tent.
Some translations preserve the imagery of taking down a tent: Martin,
"dismantled"; NJB, "folded up." Since the verb in this case is passive, some
languages may use the verb "to die" actively in this context. Or it may be
possible to talk about the earthly tent coming to an end.

We have a building from God: the present tense is used in Greek ("we
have"). Paul is so certain of this future reality that he speaks of it as a present
reality. Some English translations maintain the present tense, while others,
like TEV, use a future tense: "God will have a house." In other languages it will
be more natural to turn the sentence around and say "God will give us a house
. . ." or, where the habitual form is appropriate in such a context, "God gives
us houses . . . ."

Although the words for **building** and **house** in this verse are not
identical, they are used synonymously, and there is no reason for translators
to be concerned if different terms cannot be found in the receptor language.

A house not made with hands: this expression points to the spiritual
nature of the house. TEV says "a home which he [God] himself has made."
Some other possible models are "human beings did not build this house" or "it
was not people who erected this structure, but God did it."

Eternal in the heavens: the word **eternal** here links this image to the discussion in 4.18, where the same term is used. And the words **in the heavens** contrasts with **earthly** earlier in this verse.

The structure of RSV in this verse is rather complex, and it may be unwise to try to imitate it in the receptor language. It will probably have to be broken down into shorter, simpler sentences in many languages. One possibility is as follows: "For we know that our bodies here on earth are like tents. And if they die, God will give us a house in his place, which is not made by human beings. Rather it is made by God himself, and it will last forever."

5.2	RSV	TEV
	Here indeed we groan, and long to put on our heavenly dwelling,	And now we sigh, so great is our desire that our home which comes from heaven should be put on over us;

The word **Here** is more literally "In this" and means "In this present body" (REB), "While we are here on earth" (CEV). Some may prefer to say "In this life."

Indeed: this single English word translates two Greek words that may also be translated as "for also" or "for even." Here they introduce a further point or elaboration on the previous verse. Many modern translations leave these Greek words untranslated (so TEV, NRSV, REV, NIV).

We groan, and long: the words **and long** translate a participle which is literally "longing." Paul means either "we groan while we long to put on" or "we groan because we long to put on" (FRCL). In this context the verb translated **groan** should not be taken to mean the kind of noise one makes when in pain or severe doubt. It is rather the sighing that occurs when a person earnestly desires and hopes for something good. In verse 4 below, as in Mark 7.34, the same verb is translated "sigh." Here TNT reads "we . . . cry out for . . . ."

To put on our heavenly dwelling: the verb **to put on** means to put on an item of clothing over what one is already wearing. Paul mixes metaphors, referring to the spiritual body first as a building (5.1) and then as clothing to be put on. The form of the Greek verb **to put on** may be understood as active voice as in RSV or as passive voice as in TEV ("be put on"). If translators accept the verb as passive in meaning, it may be necessary to make the agent explicit: "that God should put on us our home that comes from heaven." Knox has "the shelter of that home," while NAB speaks of having "our heavenly habitation envelop us." Because of the mixed metaphors in this verse, some translators have felt it necessary to change the image of putting on clothing to being hidden in a house, or covered by a house.

5.3 RSV TEV

so that by putting it on we may not be found naked. | by being clothed with it we shall not be without a body.

Verse 3 explains why they long to put on the heavenly body.

So that: this indicates the purpose of being protected by the heavenly dwelling. In some languages it will be more natural to begin a new sentence here saying something like "We want to do this so that . . ." or "We long to put on this God-given body in order that . . . ."

On the verb **putting . . . on**, see comments on 5.2. Instead of the word for **putting on**, a few manuscripts have the verb for **taking off**. The two verbs differ in spelling by one letter only. The editors of the UBS *Greek New Testament* chose the reading "taking off" but indicate that the correct reading is very uncertain. RSV and TEV both accept the reading **putting on**: "by being clothed with it [the home which comes from heaven]." NAB, on the other hand, follows the reading **taking off**: "if indeed, when we have taken it [the earthly body] off, we shall not be found naked." Either way the message that results is basically the same. Paul longs to put on the heavenly dwelling in order not to be found "without a body."

The verb **be found naked** has no explicit agent in the Greek. REB takes the verb as reflexive: "we shall not find ourselves naked." Both the passive and the reflexive may present problems in other languages, but it may be possible to say simply "be naked" or "not have any covering." And in languages where the metaphor is changed in the previous verse, this verse may be rendered "therefore, when we are hidden there, we are not homeless."

5.4 RSV TEV

For while we are still in this tent, we sigh with anxiety; not that we would be unclothed, but that we would be further clothed, so that what is mortal may be swallowed up by life. | While we live in this earthly tent, we groan with a feeling of oppression; it is not that we want to get rid of our earthly body, but that we want to have the heavenly one put on over us, so that what is mortal will be transformed by life.

Verse 4 is a restatement and expansion of what Paul had written in verse 2. In some languages it may be possible to use a transition word that indicates this clearly. Knox tries to indicate this by beginning the sentence with "Yes, ..." Others may say "Indeed" (AB) or something similar.

This tent refers to the mortal human body (see 5.1). TEV adds the word "earthly." In order to show more clearly that each person has his or her own individual body, CEV has translated using the plural "these tents."

Not that we would be unclothed: Paul does not want to die before the return of Jesus. Some translators may need to say something like "we are not sighing because we want to die and leave these earthly bodies."

But that we should be further clothed: Paul's desire is not to die but rather that the spiritual body be put on him while he is still alive in his physical body. Paul wishes that Christ will return and so transform his physical body before he dies.

What is mortal: a reference to the physical body which will eventually die. In some languages the most natural meaningful equivalent will be simply "this body" or something similar.

Be swallowed up: the verb so translated here is rendered "overwhelmed" in 2.7 and "drowned" in Heb 11.29 (in the context of the Egyptians in the Red Sea). In this context it has the idea of being totally consumed or transformed. NAB and Phps use the verb "absorbed," while Brc has "engulfed." But the passive idea will have to be translated actively in many cases. The meaning is clearly expressed in CEV: "It is because we want to change them for bodies that will never die."

Life is "life immortal" in REB. In other languages one may say "eternal life" or "true life."

There are four possible types of model for this verse as a whole. The first drops the image of clothing altogether:

> Indeed, we humans have bodies that are like tents [temporary dwellings]. We cry because of the burden of pain which we carry. We don't want to get rid of this body of ours on earth. But we feel the need to get the body that God has prepared for us, because this body that will die will be changed into one that is forever.

The second kind of model drops the image of the tent but keeps the clothing figure:

> Our bodies on this earth will someday die. We complain because of the aches and pains that we have to bear now. It is not that we want to get rid of the body, but we want to have a new body like a new set of clothes. We want to throw away our old clothes and have the new ones put on us, so that what is liable to death will be covered up by life itself.

The third type of model renders both figures of speech in a nonfigurative way:

> Our earthly bodies will not last forever. We cry because of the suffering which they must bear. It is not true that we want to die, but we do want God to change us and give us a new body that will live forever. That is, we want our earthly bodies to be changed into one that will be permanent.

Finally, it may be possible to retain both the tent and the clothing images by selecting the appropriate parts of the above models.

5.5   RSV   TEV

He who has prepared us for this very thing is God, who has given us the Spirit as a guarantee.

God is the one who has prepared us for this change, and he gave us his Spirit as the guarantee of all that he has in store for us.

RSV preserves the order of the Greek sentence, which has the word **God** at the end of the sentence rather than as the subject of the sentence. The Greek sentence structure gives emphasis to the word **God**. But in some languages this will be done more naturally by beginning the sentence with the word **God**, followed by an emphatic pronoun, "God himself . . . ."

This very thing: this refers to the change of which Paul writes in the previous verse. RSV reflects the emphasis of the Greek construction, as do NRSV and NIV. The Greek means "just this (and nothing else)." Other translations such as TEV, REB, TOB, and SPCL drop the emphasis and say simply "this" rather than "this very."

Who has given us the Spirit: the Spirit is God's Spirit (see TEV), or the Holy Spirit. It may be more natural in some cases to make this a separate sentence: "He [God] has given us his Spirit . . . ."

On **a guarantee**, see 1.22.

5.6   RSV   TEV

So we are always of good courage; we know that while we are at home in the body we are away from the Lord,

So we are always full of courage. We know that as long as we are at home in the body we are away from the Lord's home.

So: this verse begins in Greek with the word "Therefore" (so NAB and NIV), which ties this verse to 4.16a and to 4.1, as well as to the immediately preceding verses.

Good courage translates a word that here carries the idea of quiet confidence. REB, for example, has "we are always confident." Some other renderings are: "this makes us confident" (Phps); "we continue to be confident" (NAB); and "we always have courage" (TNT).

At home in the body means "alive here on earth." Some other models may be "as long as we remain in this human body" or "as long as this body is our home" (Brc).

We are away from the Lord: the Lord here is "the Lord Jesus Christ." Paul is not stating that while we live on earth we have no spiritual relationship with the Lord. AB inserts several words to make the sense clear: "while

we are at home in the body we are away from our home with the Lord" (so also
TEV). Another way of saying this may be "while we are in this human body, we
remain a long way from being in the presence of the Lord."

5.7   RSV   TEV

for we walk by faith, not by sight.   **For our life is a matter of faith, not of**
sight.

The word **for** links verse 7 to verse 6 by clarifying what it means to be
"away from the Lord's home."

Here, as in 4.2, the verb **walk** is used figuratively and should probably
be translated "live" (Brc), or, making **faith** the subject, one may say "faith leads
(or, guides) us, what we see does not."

The nouns **faith** and **sight** refer not so much to the acts of believing and
seeing as they do to "that which is believed" and "that which is seen." The
thought is parallel to that of 4.18.

Two interesting models for translating this brief verse are: "faith is our
guide, not sight" (REB) and "we live by what we believe, not by what we can
see" (NCV).

5.8   RSV   TEV

We are of good courage, and we would   **We are full of courage and would much**
rather be away from the body and at   **prefer to leave our home in the body**
home with the Lord.   **and be at home with the Lord.**

Neither RSV nor TEV translates the Greek word marking the logical
relation of verse 8 to its context. This Greek word often means "but," though
in the present context it indicates that Paul is returning to his earlier thought
regarding "good courage" in 5.6. REB indicates the force of this connecting word
by translating it with the words "I say": "We are confident, I say, . . ." (so also
NIV). And NAB begins this verse with the words "I repeat . . . ."

Be away from the body: Paul would rather die and be with the Lord
Jesus. One African translation has said "it is fitting that we leave this human
body in order to arrive at the place of the Lord."

5.9   RSV   TEV

So whether we are at home or away, we   **More than anything else, however, we**
make it our aim to please him.   **want to please him, whether in our**
home here or there.

The precise reference for the words **at home** and **away** is not clear. TEV takes them to mean "at home here [in our earthly existence]" as in 5.6; but it is just as possible that the sense is "at home with the Lord or away from him" as in 5.8 (so CEV). In either case the meaning is essentially the same, namely, "whether in this life or in the life to come." In some languages **away** will be translated by the negative of **at home**, that is, "not at home."

Note that TEV has restructured this verse so that it speaks first of Paul's strong desire to please the Lord. This may be a helpful model for other languages.

We make it our aim: the verb used here is found elsewhere only in Rom 15.20 and 1 Thes 4.11. It indicates a very strong desire to do something. TEV attempts to reflect this by beginning the sentence with "More than anything else . . . ." Some other possible renderings are: "we make it our ambition . . ." (NJB and AB); "we are eager . . ." (Mft); "we try our best . . ." (CEV).

To please him: the pronoun **him** refers to the Lord Jesus. The verb in this expression may have to be translated in other languages by a causative form such as "cause to be pleased" or "make happy."

5.10	RSV	TEV

For we must all appear before the judgment seat of Christ, so that each one may receive good or evil, according to what he has done in the body.	For all of us must appear before Christ, to be judged by him. Each one will receive what he deserves, according to everything he has done, good or bad, in his bodily life.

For: the transition word used here introduces an additional argument for Christians seeking to live lives pleasing to Christ. In other languages this transition may be conveyed by "Indeed," or "Truly," or possibly "After all" (CEV).

The judgment seat of Christ: the judgment seat was the judicial bench of a city court in the Roman Empire. Paul uses this imagery to refer to the judging activity of Christ. In Rom 14.10b it refers to the "judgment seat of God." It is used of Pilate in Matt 27.19 and John 19.13. The same Greek word is often translated "tribunal" in Acts. In some languages it is a mistake to focus on the word **seat**. The idea may be contained in a verbal expression such as "we must all be judged in the presence of Christ" or "Christ will sit in judgment over every one of us."

The second part of this verse is literally "in order that each one may receive the things through the body according to that which he did, whether good or evil." The words "through the body" apparently go with the words **according to what he has done** and not with the words **one may receive**. The sense is that people will be judged according to the things that they did while living here on earth, that is, **in the body**.

Receive: in some languages the same verb is not appropriate for both receiving punishment and receiving commendation or blessing. In such cases it may be necessary to translate this term by two different words in the receptor language. Some may have to say "be punished" and "be blessed," or use active forms of these two verbs with God as subject.

The words "whether good or evil" occur at the end of the sentence in Greek and may go with the word **receive** (RSV), with **has done** (TEV), or with both of these verbs (NIV and REB). Each interpretation makes good sense in the context, and each is grammatically possible.

5.11–6.13

RSV

TEV

Friendship with God through Christ

11 Therefore, knowing the fear of the Lord, we persuade men; but what we are is known to God, and I hope it is known also to your conscience. 12 We are not commending ourselves to you again but giving you cause to be proud of us, so that you may be able to answer those who pride themselves on a man's position and not on his heart. 13 For if we are beside ourselves, it is for God; if we are in our right mind, it is for you. 14 For the love of Christ controls us, because we are convinced that one has died for all; therefore all have died. 15 And he died for all, that those who live might live no longer for themselves but for him who for their sake died and was raised.

16 From now on, therefore, we regard no one from a human point of view; even though we once regarded Christ from a human point of view, we regard him thus no longer. 17 Therefore, if any one is in Christ, he is a new creation; the old has passed away, behold, the new has come. 18 All this is from God, who through Christ reconciled us to himself and gave us the ministry of reconciliation; 19 that is, in Christ God was reconciling the world to himself, not counting their trespasses against them, and entrusting to us the message of reconciliation. 20 So we are ambassadors for Christ, God making his appeal through us. We beseech you on behalf of Christ, be reconciled to God. 21 For our sake he made him to be sin who knew no sin, so that in him we might become the righteousness of God.

Chapter 6:

1 Working together with him, then, we entreat you not to accept the grace of God in vain. 2 For he says,

"At the acceptable time I have listened to you,
and helped you on the day of salvation."

11 We know what it means to fear the Lord, and so we try to persuade others. God knows us completely, and I hope that in your hearts you know me as well. 12 We are not trying again to recommend ourselves to you; rather, we are trying to give you a good reason to be proud of us, so that you will be able to answer those who boast about a man's appearance and not about his character. 13 Are we really insane? It is for God's sake. Or are we sane? Then it is for your sake. 14 We are ruled by the love of Christ, now that we recognize that one man died for everyone, which means that they all share in his death. 15 He died for all, so that those who live should no longer live for themselves, but only for him who died and was raised to life for their sake.

16 No longer, then, do we judge anyone by human standards. Even if at one time we judged Christ according to human standards, we no longer do so. 17 When anyone is joined to Christ, he is a new being; the old is gone, the new has come. 18 All this is done by God, who through Christ changed us from enemies into his friends and gave us the task of making others his friends also. 19 Our message is that God was making all mankind his friends through Christ. God did not keep an account of their sins, and he has given us the message which tells how he makes them his friends.

20 Here we are, then, speaking for Christ, as though God himself were making his appeal through us. We plead on Christ's behalf: let God change you from enemies into his friends! 21 Christ was without sin, but for our sake God made him share our sin in order that in union with him we might share the righteousness of God.

Chapter 6:

1 In our work together with God, then, we beg you who have received God's grace not

Behold, now is the acceptable time; behold, now is the day of salvation. 3 We put no obstacle in any one's way, so that no fault may be found with our ministry, 4 but as servants of God we commend ourselves in every way: through great endurance, in afflictions, hardships, calamities, 5 beatings, imprisonments, tumults, labors, watching, hunger; 6 by purity, knowledge, forbearance, kindness, the Holy Spirit, genuine love, 7 truthful speech, and the power of God; with the weapons of righteousness for the right hand and for the left; 8 in honor and dishonor, in ill repute and good repute. We are treated as impostors, and yet are true; 9 as unknown, and yet well known; as dying, and behold we live; as punished, and yet not killed; 10 as sorrowful, yet always rejoicing; as poor, yet making many rich; as having nothing, and yet possessing everything.

11 Our mouth is open to you, Corinthians; our heart is wide. 12 You are not restricted by us, but you are restricted in your own affections. 13 In return—I speak as to children—widen your hearts also.

to let it be wasted. 2 Hear what God says:
"When the time came for me to show
    you favor,
I heard you;
when the day arrived for me to save
    you,
I helped you."
Listen! This is the hour to receive God's favor; today is the day to be saved!

3 We do not want anyone to find fault with our work, so we try not to put obstacles in anyone's way. 4 Instead, in everything we do we show that we are God's servants by patiently enduring troubles, hardships, and difficulties. 5 We have been beaten, jailed, and mobbed; we have been overworked and have gone without sleep or food. 6 By our purity, knowledge, patience, and kindness we have shown ourselves to be God's servants—by the Holy Spirit, by our true love, 7 by our message of truth, and by the power of God. We have righteousness as our weapon, both to attack and to defend ourselves. 8 We are honored and disgraced; we are insulted and praised. We are treated as liars, yet we speak the truth; 9 as unknown, yet we are known by all; as though we were dead, but, as you see, we live on. Although punished, we are not killed; 10 although saddened, we are always glad; we seem poor, but we make many people rich; we seem to have nothing, yet we really possess everything.

11 Dear friends in Corinth! We have spoken frankly to you; we have opened our hearts wide. 12 It is not we who have closed our hearts to you; it is you who have closed your hearts to us. 13 I speak now as though you were my children: show us the same feelings that we have for you. Open your hearts wide!

SECTION HEADING: TEV "Friendship with God through Christ." TEV places all of 5.11–6.13 together under one section heading. Translators may find it better to use a verb rather than the abstract noun "friendship" and say something like "God makes people his friends through Christ." Other section headings such as "The ministry of reconciliation" (NIV) or "The message of reconciliation" (REB) focus more on the role of the apostles in announcing God's initiative to restore friendship with people.

5.11	RSV	TEV
	Therefore, knowing the fear of the Lord, we persuade men; but what	We know what it means to fear the Lord, and so we try to persuade

we are is known to God, and I hope it is known also to your conscience.	others. God knows us completely, and I hope that in your hearts you know me as well.

Therefore: this transition word has been left untranslated in TEV, but it should somehow be made apparent in the receptor language that, while a new detail of the argument is beginning here, it is nevertheless closely related to what has just been said.

Fear of the Lord: this expression is found frequently in the Old Testament, but also in Acts 9.31. As TEV makes clear, the meaning is the fear directed toward the Lord. As elsewhere in the Bible, "fear of God" does not mean primarily fright, but rather an attitude of respect, reverence, and awe. It is not clear whether **the Lord** here refers to God or to Jesus. Since these words follow immediately after the words "the judgment seat of Christ" in verse 10, many interpreters understand **the Lord** to refer to Christ. Other interpreters emphasize the use of the expression **fear of the Lord** in the Greek Old Testament as referring to God. The two interpretations are equally possible, and unless translators are forced by their language to say one or the other, it will be better to leave the ambiguity as in Greek.

The verb **knowing** here has the idea of experiencing or being aware of something. It is more than merely knowing about something. It includes an awareness of responsibility. Mft has "with the fear of the Lord before my mind," while NAB reads "standing in awe of the Lord."

Though the Greek says literally **we persuade men**, Paul is no doubt using the word **men** inclusively here, including women also. TEV says "others," and REB says "we address our appeal to men and women." NJB has "we try to win people over." The word **persuade** is to be understood as a present tense that here expresses the idea of incompleteness, or something attempted but not necessarily achieved. This is why TEV has "we try to persuade" (so also NAB). REB says "we address our appeal." The Greek does not make explicit what Paul tries to persuade people to do. Translators may want to follow the model of CEV: "we encourage everyone to turn to him [the Lord]."

Your conscience: on **conscience** see comments on 4.2.

The first person plural pronouns in verses 11-15 clearly do not include the readers. Some interpreters understand all the first person plural pronouns in this section to be referring to Paul alone, except in verse 5.21 (so Mft and AT, which use first person singular pronouns).

5.12	RSV	TEV

We are not commending ourselves to you again but giving you cause to be proud of us, so that you may be able to answer those who pride themselves on a man's position and not on his heart.	We are not trying again to recommend ourselves to you; rather, we are trying to give you a good reason to be proud of us, so that you will be able to answer those who boast about a man's appearance and not about his character.

We: the context here clearly indicates that the pronoun is exclusive. That is, it does not include the Corinthian Christians.

Commending ourselves: see comments on 3.1.

But: the conjunction used here is a rather strong one underlining the contrast between the denial of self-commendation and the affirmation that follows.

Giving you cause: the word translated **cause** has the basic meaning of "a starting point or base of operations for an expedition." But it is used figuratively in the New Testament to indicate a basis or justification for doing something. Elsewhere it is translated "opportunity" in RSV (Rom 7.8,11; Gal 5.13). This may also be a good rendering here. AB has "a suitable basis," while Knox translates the whole clause "we are shewing you how to find material for boasting of us."

To be proud of us: literally "boast of us." The Greek suggests not simply inward pride but rather active "boasting." While some good manuscripts read "of you" in place of **of us**, it is better to translate as in RSV and TEV.

Be able to answer: literally the word **answer** is not in the Greek text. The idea is not that of responding to questions, but rather to "have something to say [to those who are boasting]" (AB, and similarly NAB).

Those who pride themselves in the context of this letter clearly refers to Paul's opponents in Corinth (see 11.12). The root verb used here is the same as in the expression **to be proud of us**. Therefore the idea of outward boasting, rather than a mere inward feeling of pride, should be conveyed in translation. However, the context indicates that there are negative connotations involved here, while the previous reference is positive.

A man's position and not on his heart: literally "in face and not in heart." Since Paul seems to be speaking generally here and not exclusively of men, translators may wish to use inclusive language, such as in REB ("whose pride is all in outward show and not in inward worth") or NRSV ("in outward appearance and not in the heart"). The TEV translation "a man's appearance" should not be understood as referring to a person's physical appearance. The sense is that Paul's opponents boast about external things such as their abilities and status (see 11.22-23).

The CEV is a good model translation for the last part of this verse: "But we want you to be proud of us, when you are with those who are not sincere and brag about what others think of them."

5.13	RSV	TEV

For if we are beside ourselves, it is for God; if we are in our right mind, it is for you.

Are we really insane? It is for God's sake. Or are we sane? Then it is for your sake.

For: the transition word may be important in the receptor language. The content of this verse is tied closely to the previous verse, showing the continuation of Paul's argument.

The first half of this verse probably reflects a criticism made of Paul by his opponents in Corinth. Paul is not claiming that he himself is unsure whether or not he is insane. Rather he is repeating the criticism that has been made of him and is refuting it. Similarly, in the second half of the verse, the word **if** does not mean that Paul had doubts about whether or not he was really sane. CEV exposes the fact that Paul is reflecting the thinking of his readers by translating "If we seem to be out of our minds . . . ." One African translation has rendered this as a separate sentence: "Indeed, they say that we are crazy people."

The contrast between **beside ourselves** (compare Mark 3.21) and **in our right mind** may be expressed in a variety of ways in different languages. Some examples from English versions are: "mad . . . sane" (TNT); "out of our mind . . . in our right mind" (NIV); "unreasonable . . . reasonable" (NJB). Certain languages may use very different kinds of idiomatic expressions to contrast these two mental states.

It is for God: this should not be translated in such a way as to give the impression that Paul's madness would somehow benefit God. The idea seems rather to be that if he were mad, it would be a matter between him and God. Mft says "Well, that is between myself and God," while CEV says "it is between God and us." REB translates "If these are mad words, take them as addressed to God; if sound sense, as addressed to you." Knox earlier handled this passage in much the same way.

5.14   RSV   TEV

For the love of Christ controls us, be-   We are ruled by the love of Christ, now
cause we are convinced that one has   that we recognize that one man died for
died for all; therefore all have died.   everyone, which means that they all
                                            share in his death.

Basic to understanding the thought of verses 14 and 15 is Paul's idea of the union of the believer with Christ. Though Paul does not state here in these two verses that believers are "in Christ" in the sense of being "in union with Christ," this concept lies behind the thought expressed in these two verses.

The love of Christ: grammatically this may be either Christ's love for us or our love for Christ. Nearly all interpreters, however, choose the first option, "Christ's love" (so NIV, GNC, Knox, and AB). CEV is even more specific: "Christ's love for us."

The verb translated **controls** has a wide range of meanings in Greek, but the basic meanings may be grouped under the idea of restraint or compulsion (NIV "compels"), or general control (RSV, TEV, REB, FRCL). NEB translates this verb "leaves us no choice." Note that several English translations turn the sentence around to make it passive, as in TEV. But this will not be possible in languages where passive forms present a problem.

Because we are convinced: literally "having judged this . . . ." The causal element is not as strong as RSV makes it appear. The verb form of the

Greek seems to point to a conclusion reached in the past. AB renders this "our decision having been this . . . ." REB translates naturally "once we have reached the conclusion . . . ."

The conclusion reached by Paul is stated in a concise theological summary: **one** person, Jesus Christ, **died for all** human beings, and the consequence of this is that all human beings are in some sense dead.

Died for all: the meaning of the word **for** is much debated. Is the basic sense that Christ died "for the benefit of" or "on behalf of" (so GNC), or is it "in place of" or "instead of"? Interpreters are divided on the meaning of the preposition **for**, and the translator's theology of atonement often seems to affect the translation.

The word **therefore** introduces the consequence of Christ's death for everyone. This connecting word is important and should be conveyed in the receptor language.

All have died: the TEV rendering of this seems weak. The meaning is rather "in a sense, they all died" (Phps). The problem is in understanding in what sense all have died. But it is probably better if translators render the phrase literally and leave this question for the theologians. Implicitly the word **all** means "all of us" (CEV), understanding the pronoun as inclusive of Paul's readers.

5.15	RSV	TEV
	And he died for all, that those who live might live no longer for themselves but for him who for their sake died and was raised.	He died for all, so that those who live should no longer live for themselves, but only for him who died and was raised to life for their sake.

As RSV shows, verse 15 in Greek begins with the word **And**. This connecting word serves to introduce an elaboration of the final words of verse 14. In some languages one may have to introduce this verse with "that is to say . . ." or something similar. Note that Barclay begins the verse with "So . . . ."

The words translated **for** in **he died for all** and **who for their sake died** later in this verse are the same as in the previous verse. See comments on 5.14.

In the expression **those who live**, the verb "to live" may refer to physical life only, but **those** refers to those who have the newness of spiritual life.

Live . . . for themselves . . . for him: the ideas of living for oneself and living for another person may present special problems in some languages. It may be necessary to say something "live to please themselves" and "live to please him." Or another possible model says "that their lives may not belong to themselves, but to him."

Who for their sake died: literally "who for them died." See comments on 5.14.

Was raised: though the Greek has no agent for this passive verb, Paul elsewhere says that God raised Jesus (Rom 4.24; 8.11; 1 Cor 6.14; 15.15). In languages that do not naturally use the passive form in such a context, it will be possible to translate actively "who rose again," without indicating the agent, or "whom God raised . . . ," making the agent explicit. In some cases it may be necessary to translate actively "he rose," although this may represent a slight change in focus.

5.16   RSV   TEV

From now on, therefore, we re-   No longer, then, do we judge any-
gard no one from a human point of   one by human standards. Even if at one
view; even though we once regarded   time we judged Christ according to
Christ from a human point of view, we human standards, we no longer do so.
regard him thus no longer.

While most versions begin a new paragraph at this point, it is perhaps worth noting that this is not the case in REB.

Interpreters are divided on whether the first person plural pronouns in this verse refer to all Christians, only to Paul and his companions, or only to Paul himself.

From now on: this indicates a new point of departure with regard to the way in which people are judged. It is clear from what Paul says elsewhere (Rom 5.9, 11; 8.1; 11.30) that the word **now** refers to the time when salvation comes through faith. For this reason some have translated "from that time on" (AT).

Therefore: in many languages this transition word may fit better at the beginning of the verse. Barclay begins the sentence "the consequence of all this is . . . ," while NAB has "because of this . . . ." Both of these models clearly show the relationship with what has just been said in Paul's argument.

We regard: literally "we know," but here used in the sense of "estimate" or "evaluate." The pronoun **we** is an emphatic form and is placed in a position ahead of the adverbial phrase in the Greek sentence to show emphasis. These markers of emphasis are probably intended to show that, no matter how others may consider Christ, those represented by the pronoun (whether inclusive or exclusive) now have a different way of looking at him.

From a human point of view means "according to human standards" (TEV), or by "worldly standards" (REB), or "by what they seem to be" (CEV), or "in terms of mere human judgment" (NAB). The Greek is literally "according to flesh" (see comments on "like a worldly man" in 1.17).

We once regarded Christ from a human point of view: literally "we knew according to flesh Christ." As both RSV and TEV make clear, the words "according to flesh" go with the verb "we knew" and not with the noun "Christ." The English word **once** clearly refers to a period of time in the past and not merely a single moment in time.

We regard him thus no longer: the word **thus** refers back to looking at Christ from a human point of view, and this will be clear in many languages. However, another possible model for this part of the verse may be "we no longer look at him in that way," or more specifically "we no longer judge him by human standards."

5.17	RSV	TEV

Therefore, if any one is in Christ, he is a new creation;^g the old has passed away, behold, the new has come.

When anyone is joined to Christ, he is a new being; the old is gone, the new has come.

^g Or *creature*

The precise function of the word **Therefore** which begins this verse is not clear. Is Paul drawing out the consequences of what he has said in verse 16, or does the word **Therefore** go back to verses 14 and 15? If, as seems most likely, verses 16 and 17 are parallel in thought, then both verses draw out the consequences of what Paul has written in verses 14 and 15. Some translations such as TEV and REB fail to translate the connecting word **Therefore** and simply leave unexpressed the precise relationship of verse 17 to what precedes.

On the meaning and translation of **in Christ**, see comments on 1.21; 2.14.

He is a new creation: the pronoun **he** may have to be made more explicit in some languages, since some readers may think it refers to Christ. In those cases translators may have to say "that person is a new being." **New creation** is literally "new *ktisis*." The Greek word *ktisis* nearly always means "creation" in Paul's letters, rather than "creature"; "creature" would make it refer to an individual person. The Greek has no pronoun and no verb, so the verb phrase that translators supply ("he is" or "there is") depends in part on the meaning of the noun *ktisis*. According to TEV and many other versions, the individual person "is a new being." But according to Mft, AB, NJB, and NRSV, "there is a new creation," meaning not just that the individual person has been made new but also that a new situation has been created. The majority of English versions, however, seem to prefer the individual interpretation reflected in RSV and TEV. Translators may choose to place the alternative translation in a footnote, as RSV does.

The old refers to things that characterized the pre-Christian life. REB says "the old order."

Has passed away: this may be rendered "has disappeared" (Knox), "has come to an end" (AB), or "finished and gone" (Phps). This stands in contrast with **has come** at the end of the verse.

Behold: this particle is often left untranslated in modern versions (TEV and REB) or is represented only by an exclamation mark at the end of the sentence (NAB and NIV). NRSV attempts to render it using the less archaic "see . . . !" If the receptor language has a particle that naturally calls attention to what follows, it may be used here.

Some manuscripts have the word "all" both at the end of verse 17 and at the beginning of verse 18. This reading of 17b is found in older translations such as Segond (SE), RVR, and KJV ("all things are become new"), but the editors of the UBS *Greek New Testament* consider it more likely that a scribe later added the word to the end of verse 17.

5.18	RSV	TEV

RSV	TEV
All this is from God, who through Christ reconciled us to himself and gave us the ministry of reconciliation;	All this is done by God, who through Christ changed us from enemies into his friends and gave us the task of making others his friends also.

All this may refer to what Paul has written in verses 14, 16, and 17, but more likely refers to verse 17 only, that is, to God's work in the new creation.

From God is a literal translation. TEV gives the correct sense, "done by God." In languages where the passive form is difficult or unnatural, translators will probably want to turn the sentence around to say "it is God who has done all this." But this may also require that it be a separate sentence, or it may require the use of a colon to introduce the following statement.

Us: as in verse 16, it is not clear whether Paul is referring to all Christians, to himself and his companions, or to himself only (so Mft and AT, but not ITCL) in verses 18-19. Since "we" and "you" are distinguished in verse 20, it seems best to assume that Paul is not including the readers in verses 18b-19. But it is difficult to imagine that Paul would have wanted to exclude his readers from the first **us** having to do with being reconciled with God.

Who through Christ reconciled us to himself: Christ is the means through which God reconciled sinners to himself. Though Paul does not here say explicitly "through the death of Christ," the context (verses 14-15) and parallel passages (Rom 5.10) show that **through Christ** means "through his death."

Paul does not use the verb "to reconcile" or the noun "reconciliation" very often in his letters, but see Rom 5.10. These words are metaphors from the realm of personal relations in which enemies have become friends again. In 1 Cor 7.11 it is used of reconciliation between husband and wife. Implicit in the idea of reconciliation is that the people who are reconciled were previously enemies. TEV makes this explicit: "changed us from enemies into his friends." For Paul it is not God who was our enemy; rather we were the ones who were opposed to God (see Rom 5.10-11). Note that Barclay uses the term "friendship" throughout this section, while CEV draws on the image of "peace."

Ministry of reconciliation: the word rendered **ministry** may also be translated "work" or "service" (*diakonia*; see comments on 3.7; 4.1). CEV fills out the meaning with "the work of making peace between himself and others." The same idea may be expressed "the work of bringing other people back to God" (GNW) or "the task of helping others to accept that friendship" (Brc).

5.19 RSV	TEV
that is, in Christ God was reconciling[h] the world to himself, not counting their trespasses against them, and entrusting to us the message of reconciliation. [h] Or *God was in Christ reconciling*	Our message is that God was making all mankind his friends through Christ.[d] God did not keep an account of their sins, and he has given us the message which tells how he makes them his friends. [d] God was making all mankind his friends through Christ; *or* God was in Christ making all mankind his friends.

That is: these words are variously interpreted: (1) Some interpreters take the two Greek words as equivalent to the word "because" and understand verse 19 as providing the cause or basis for what is said in verse 18. (2) Others understand these words to mean "that is to say" (so RSV), in which case verse 19 is a restatement of verse 18. CEV says "What we mean is that . . . ," and NAB says "namely." (3) Some interpreters think that the words **in Christ God was reconciling the world to himself, not counting their trespasses against them** are traditional material used in the worship of the church, and which Paul quotes here. On this interpretation the first Greek word is transitional, and the second word is the equivalent of quotation marks. AB says "As it is said, God, in Christ, was reconciling . . . ."

The second interpretation (that of RSV, CEV, and NAB) seems to be more probable. Some translations leave this relationship between verses 18 and 19 unexpressed (so TEV, REB).

A major difficulty in translating this verse is knowing whether the words **in Christ** are connected most closely to the word **God** or to the verb **was reconciling**. In the first interpretation Paul would be making a statement concerning the incarnation, that is, that God was in Christ (so SE, KJV, REB, RSV footnote, and TEV footnote). In the latter interpretation Paul would be saying that through Christ God was reconciling the world to himself (so RSV, NRSV, TEV, and REB footnote). The interpretation followed by RSV and TEV seems preferable, though both interpretations fit Paul's theology.

On the translation of **reconciling** see comments on verse 18.

The world: though it is possible that **the world** here means not only human beings but also the entire universe (see Rom 8.19-23), most likely Paul is thinking of people only, "mankind" (so TEV).

Not counting their trespasses against them: the word translated **trespasses** is different from the more usual word for "sin" and possibly focuses on unintentional violation of God's will in some contexts. But here it is virtually synonymous with "sin." The verbal expression "to count against . . ." is one involving the keeping of records of commercial accounts, but it may also have the meaning "to keep a mental record of" in other contexts. The meaning here is that God does not keep an account of human failings but rather forgives them. Some model translations are: "not holding anyone's faults against them" (NJB); "he does not keep against men an account of their offenses" (TNT); "instead of holding men to account for their sins" (Knox).

Entrusting to us the message of reconciliation: the expression **message of reconciliation** focuses more on the verbal aspect of bringing people to God, while the "ministry of reconciliation" (verse 18) has to do more with the actual work. The idea here is that of giving responsibility to proclaim this message to other people. Some possible models are "he gave us the work of telling the news of this friendship" or "he charged us to preach this message of peace."

5.20	RSV	TEV

RSV	TEV
So we are ambassadors for Christ, God making his appeal through us. We beseech you on behalf of Christ, be reconciled to God.	Here we are, then, speaking for Christ, as though God himself were making his appeal through us. We plead on Christ's behalf: let God change you from enemies into his friends!

So: this transition word connects what has just been said about reconciliation to the plea to be reconciled, which follows. It has been rendered "therefore" by NIV, REB, and many others. NAB attempts to convey the same idea by beginning this verse "This makes us ambassadors . . . ."

The pronouns **we** and **us** do not include the readers.

Ambassadors for Christ: ambassadors were persons who represented someone else and who carried a message from the person whom they represented. Mft uses the term "envoy." TEV translates **ambassadors** as "speaking for." CEV maintains the aspect of being sent: "We were sent to speak for Christ." Some languages have a special term that is well known and commonly used for the spokesperson of a chief. Such a term may be appropriate here. Others may use a verbal expression like that of CEV. If a borrowed term for modern ambassadors is widely used and clearly understood in the receptor language, such a term may be helpful here.

The verb **making his appeal** has no object in the Greek. The specific implied object here is the Corinthians; so REB "as if God were appealing to you."

The word **beseech** is archaic or "church" English, and most recent translations use a word such as "beg," "appeal," "plead" (TEV), or "entreat" (NRSV). Though the Greek has no object after the verb **beseech**, the context seems to justify adding **you** (RSV, NRSV).

On behalf of Christ: the idea of doing something on behalf of someone else may have to be expressed in a radically different way in some languages. In some cases there exist benefactive verb forms that will easily represent this idea. In other cases it may be necessary to say something like "in the name of Christ."

On the translation of **be reconciled**, see comments on 5.18. But note that here the form of the verb is passive imperative. This may have to be rendered actively as "let God reconcile you to himself" or "allow God to reestablish friendship between you and himself."

CEV provides a possible model for the last half of this verse: "We speak for Christ and sincerely ask you to make peace with God."

5.21	RSV	TEV

RSV	TEV
For our sake he made him to be sin who knew no sin, so that in him we might become the righteousness of God.	Christ was without sin, but for our sake God made him share our sin in order that in union with him we might share the righteousness of God.

The first person plural pronouns **our** and **we** are inclusive here.

It will be noted that the elements of this verse have been transposed in TEV to make it read more naturally in English. Such restructuring may be necessary in a number of other languages. It will also be necessary to make it clear which persons are referred to by the third person singular masculine pronouns, since they refer to different persons. The pronoun **he** refers to God, and the pronoun **him** refers to "Christ" (TEV, REB).

To be sin: this expression has led to much discussion among interpreters of 2 Corinthians. What does it mean to say that a person (Christ) became an object (sin)? Is Paul using the abstract noun **sin** for the concrete noun "sinner"? Surely Paul is not saying that Christ became a sinner, for that contradicts the very next words in this verse. Some understand Paul to be saying that God made Christ to be a "sin offering" (Martin, NIV footnote; see also Lev 4.25-29). Perhaps the most likely explanation is that Paul is saying that Christ identified in some way with sinful humanity. REB says "made him one with human sinfulness" (similarly GNC). Barclay says "God identified Christ . . . with human sin." One African language has "God caused him to enter the ranks of sinners in our place . . . ." Another has "God laid the blame for people's sin on Christ." Whatever decision seems best for the translator should, if possible, be coordinated with the way in which the other difficult expression is translated, **become the righteousness**.

The words **who knew no sin** are a Hebraic expression which means "to have no personal experience with sin." Paul is stating that Jesus did not sin; he "was without sin" (TEV). Some languages may use a verbal form: "Christ never sinned" (CEV).

The words **in him** usually are understood to mean "in union with him" (TEV), that is, as expressing *where* we share the righteousness of God. It is also possible to understand the preposition as indicating *the means by which* God makes us share his righteousness: "by means of [the death of] Christ."

We might become the righteousness of God: as with the claim that Christ became sin, it seems strange to say that people become an object (righteousness of God). What do these words mean? TEV's translation expresses the meaning that God makes Christians righteous with a righteousness that is his own. Some other possible models are "God caused us to enter the ranks of the righteous . . . ." CEV translates "so that Christ could make us acceptable to God."

As is true of the beginning of chapter 5, the beginning of chapter 6 continues without a section break or section heading.

6.1	RSV	TEV
	Working together with him, then, we entreat you not to accept the grace of God in vain.	**In our work together with God, then, we beg you who have received God's grace not to let it be wasted.**

In the verses that follow, the first person plural pronouns do not include the readers. Possibly these pronouns are examples of the "epistolary plural" (so Mft, AT, and ITCL, who use the first person singular in this section).

Although many versions begin a new paragraph at this point, some more recent translations do not make a paragraph break here. See, for example, AB, REB, and NRSV (similarly Mft). The connecting word **then**, as well as some of the vocabulary used, ties the content of this verse closely to that of the previous section.

Working together with has no object in the Greek. RSV supplies the pronoun object **him**, but the precise reference of this pronoun is unclear. Though several objects are possible—Christ, the Corinthians (NAB), Paul's fellow workers—the most probable object is "God" (TEV, NIV, and REB), as the pronoun **him** suggests in RSV. This is based on the fact that 5.20 speaks explicitly of God making his appeal through Paul (and others).

We entreat you: the verb used here is the same as the one translated "making his appeal" in 5.20. The connection between the two verses is obscured in both RSV and TEV, which use different verbs for the two occurrences. AB attempts to show the relationship between them by translating here "we are also appealing to you . . . ."

The infinitive translated as **not to accept** can refer to the present time (RSV, NRSV) or to past time (TEV, REB). Probably the sense is that they have already accepted or received God's grace, and now they should respond to what God has done. The words **in vain** mean "without result" or "without living the way that Christians should live." It is possible to translate the sense here with a positive rather than a negative appeal. CEV has "we beg you to make good use of God's kindness to you." Or one may use two separate sentences as Barclay does: "You have received the grace of God. We therefore urge you not to let it all go for nothing."

The expression **grace of God** occurs also in 1.12; 8.1; 9.14. On the translation of this phrase, see comments at 1.2,12.

Some editions of the Greek text have a dash at the end of verse 1 and again at the end of verse 2, suggesting that the material in verse 2 is somehow parenthetical. Most versions, however, rightly ignore these marks, and the fourth revised edition of the UBS *Greek New Testament* also omits them.

6.2 RSV TEV

For he says,
  "At the acceptable time I have
    listened to you,
  and helped you on the day of
    salvation."
Behold, now is the acceptable time;
behold, now is the day of salvation.

Hear what God says:
  "When the time came for me to
    show you favor,
  I heard you;
  when the day arrived for me to
    save you,
  I helped you."
Listen! This is the hour to receive God's
favor; today is the day to be saved!

The pronoun **he** refers to God (verse 1). TEV substitutes the noun "God" for the pronoun (so also FRCL and Brc).

This quotation comes from the Septuagint Greek translation of Isa 49.8, not from the original Hebrew. In the Old Testament context the verse refers to God's help to the people of Israel. Paul uses this text to emphasize the urgent nature of his appeal to the Corinthians.

He says: Paul applies these words to the present time as if God were speaking these words directly to the Corinthians. REB's "He has said" indicates that Paul is quoting from words that God had already spoken. The present tense of this verb in Greek indicates the permanent validity of Scripture. Helen Barrett Montgomery's *The New Testament in Modern English* has "For he said," which fails to show the continuing validity of what God said. Translators may wish to make explicit where God has said these words: "in the Scriptures" (so FRCL and CEV).

The acceptable time: though some interpreters understand this to mean "acceptable by human beings," most understand this to be the time acceptable by God to show his favor to his people (so TEV, FRCL, GECL).

The Greek contains a play on words that RSV keeps but TEV does not. In 6.1 Paul says "*to accept* the grace of God"; and in 6.2 he speaks of *the acceptable* **time**. TEV brings in from verse 1 the idea that **the acceptable time** is the time for God's grace to be shown. While Paul uses two related words, both of which are translated **acceptable**, experts in the Greek language make no distinction in meaning, and translators should not feel that they have to look for two different words in their own language.

I have listened to you: God heard the people's prayers. The sense is not merely that God listened impassively to their prayers, but that he answered them favorably. Both NJB and REB use the verb "answered" here.

The second person pronouns in this quotation are singular in Greek, and in the Old Testament they are taken as referring to the Servant of the Lord. This passage may have come to Paul's mind because of a similarity with his own situation. But in the appeal that follows, the application is broadened to include the Corinthians. Nevertheless the receptor language rendering should reflect the singular pronouns of the original quotation.

The day of salvation: God is the implicit agent of the noun **salvation**. The meaning is that God helped his people "when the day arrived for me to save you" (TEV).

The structure of the Old Testament quotation will have to be changed in some languages to make it more natural. It may read "I heard you at the right time; yes, I helped you on the day of salvation." The translation should not give the impression of two separate and distinct events. Rather, this is an example of parallelism where the two elements refer to a single event.

The last sentence in this verse is Paul's comment on the passage from Isaiah. Translators should take care to insure that this is not taken as a part of the Old Testament quotation. This may be very difficult in those languages that do not use quotation marks. Translators in some languages will naturally say something like "That is what he said" at the end of a quotation. In those languages it will be clear for those who hear this verse read that the last part of the verse is not a part of the quotation.

Behold: as in 5.17 (as well as 6.9), this particle serves to call special attention to what follows. TEV attempts to render this with "Listen!" but does not repeat it in the second instance. Other versions use only the exclamation mark (NAB).

6.3   RSV   TEV

We put no obstacle in any one's way, so   We do not want anyone to find
that no fault may be found with our   fault with our work, so we try not to
ministry,   put obstacles in anyone's way.

Note that TEV has reversed the order of the two main clauses in this verse in order to make it read more naturally in English. This may serve as a good model for certain other languages as well.

On the translation of the first person plural pronouns in this verse and through the rest of this section, see the first paragraph of comments on 6.1.

We put no obstacle: literally "not . . . giving obstacle." In accordance with possible Greek verb usage, some interpreters understand the verb translated **We put** (literally "giving") in this context to be expressing intention rather than actual fact. So TEV says "we try not to put obstacles" (so also Barrett). The noun translated **obstacle** occurs only here in the New Testament, but the related verb is found several times. This verb is usually rendered "stumble." So the obstacle involved here is a cause for stumbling or a basis for taking offense. It may be translated "offense" (NAB), "stumbling-block" (TNT), or "discredit" (REB).

In any one's way: these words translate two words in Greek, a preposition and a pronoun. The Greek pronoun may be either masculine ("anyone," as in RSV and TEV) or neuter ("anything," as in REB, which reads "we avoid giving any offense in anything"). The latter interpretation is supported by the use of "in everything" in verse 4, which seems to state the opposite side of Paul's claim. Even if one follows the interpretation of REB, it still remains implicit that Paul does not want to give offense "to anyone."

No fault may be found: the Greek does not express the agent of the verb "to find fault." The context suggests to some interpreters that Paul is here concerned that people (TEV "anyone") not find fault. People, not God, are the implied agent of the verb. On the other hand, some interpreters understand Paul to be referring here to God's judgment at the end time (see 1 Cor 4.2-5). In those languages where the use of the passive form is difficult or impossible, it is probably best to translate something like "we do not want other people to criticize the work . . . ." Translators who follow the interpretation reflected in TEV, that Paul is concerned that people may find fault, may wish to include the following translation as an alternative in a footnote: *Or* "We do not want God to find fault with our work, so . . . ."

Our ministry: the pronoun **our** has been supplied by RSV but is not explicitly stated in the best manuscripts of the original, "the *diakonia*." There is, however, little question that Paul is referring to his own work and that of his associates. Some translators may prefer to say "this ministry."

6.4	RSV	TEV

but as servants of God we commend ourselves in every way: through great endurance, in afflictions, hardships, calamities,	Instead, in everything we do we show that we are God's servants by patiently enduring troubles, hardships, and difficulties.

The list of hardships in 6.4-5 is similar to the list in 11.23-27.

But introduces a contrast with verse 3, which states that they put no obstacle in any one's way. Verse 4 states what they do "instead" (TEV). NIV attempts to reflect the same conjunction with "rather . . . ."

As servants of God we commend ourselves: Greek grammar favors RSV over TEV on the translation of these words. It is not that they were proving that they are servants of God (TEV); but rather, because they are servants of God, they are able to put their lives forward as examples to be followed.

We does not include the readers here.

We commend ourselves: some interpreters understand this verb to be expressing intention (see comments on verse 3). So REB says "we try to recommend ourselves." On the idea of "commending" compare 3.1 and 4.2.

REB punctuates with a colon after "endurance" instead of after "every way." "We try to recommend ourselves in all circumstances by our steadfast endurance: in affliction . . ." (REB). According to this interpretation **great endurance** is not parallel to **afflictions, hardships, calamities** as one of the circumstances in which Paul commends himself, but is rather the manner in which he commends himself in all of the circumstances listed. CEV follows the same interpretation as REB but uses a simpler structure: "We have always been patient, though we have had a lot of trouble, suffering and hard times."

The translation in TEV (also FRCL) seems based on the same punctuation found in REB. That is, **through great endurance** is the manner in which Paul shows that he is God's servant when he experiences troubles, hardships, and difficulties. Nothing in the Greek indicates clearly whether the break should be made after the words **every way** as in RSV, or after **endurance** as in REB. Translators should feel free to choose either interpretation.

Endurance: this word suggests the ability to bear up or endure under difficult circumstances. The same word is used in 1.6 and again in 12.12, where it is rendered "patience."

The three words that follow (**afflictions, hardships,** and **calamities**) are used as synonyms here, and translators need not try to find a corresponding word in the receptor language for each Greek word. On **afflictions** see comment on this word in 1.4. **Hardships** refers to general distress and trouble, and the Greek for **calamities** refers to difficult circumstances in which one is restricted in some way.

6.5   RSV   TEV

beatings, imprisonments, tumults, labors, watching, hunger;	We have been beaten, jailed, and mobbed; we have been overworked and have gone without sleep or food.

The six nouns in this verse continue Paul's list of specific sufferings that they have endured. TEV twice adds "We have been" in order to keep the subject from verse 4 in focus and to make a separate sentence of this verse.

Beatings: there is nothing in the word used here that indicates exactly what kind of beating is involved or what kinds of instruments may have been used, but it certainly involved a rather brutal striking of the body which resulted in noticeable wounds.

Tumults: this refers to violent opposition that involves mob action, hence TEV's "mobbed." CEV says "hurt in riots." The same word is translated "confusion" in 1 Cor 14.33 and "disorder" in 2 Cor 12.20.

Labors: the Greek word suggests labor to the point of fatigue or exhaustion, hence the translation "overworked" (TEV, REB).

Watching is literally "sleeplessness" (so TEV, REB).

In certain languages it may be necessary to go a step further than TEV and make separate verb phrases out of each noun. And since there are many passive ideas involved, some languages will require an active formulation: "they [indefinite] beat us; they threw us into prison; they caused us harm in riots; they made us work very hard, and we did not have enough food to eat or enough time to sleep."

6.6 RSV TEV

by purity, knowledge, forbearance, kindness, the Holy Spirit, genuine love,

By our purity, knowledge, patience, and kindness we have shown ourselves to be God's servants—by the Holy Spirit, by our true love,

Having mentioned in verses 4 and 5 the difficulties encountered in his ministry, he now turns to a list of positive characteristics.

TEV adds the word "our" to the list of qualities that follow, since Paul is referring to himself and his colleagues.

Purity: this refers to moral virtue. The adjectival form of this word is found in 7.11, where it entails moral integrity, and in 11.2, where it involves the chastity of a bride. Languages use various expressions to represent this virtue. One language speaks of a "clean heart," while another says "we do nothing that brings shame."

Knowledge: what is involved here is the understanding that God gives, not just the knowledge of facts.

Forbearance: the basic sense of this word is "patience" (TEV), without complaining. In the context here, **forbearance** includes the idea of being patient with the weaknesses and criticisms of other people. **Kindness** differs from **forbearance** in the aspect of actively showing goodwill by helping others.

In a list of human virtues it is strange that Paul includes **the Holy Spirit**. For this reason some interpreters take this to be the human spirit. Barrett says "in a holy spirit," and NRSV says "holiness of spirit." If the reference is to the Holy Spirit, the sense is "by being imbued with the Holy Spirit" (GNC) or "with gifts of the Spirit" (NEB and NBE). Though either **the Holy Spirit** or the human spirit seems equally possible, translators should probably choose **the Holy Spirit**, because it is the most common translation in many languages (RSV, REB, TEV, NIV, NJB, GECL, FRCL, TOB, SPCL). Translators may find it helpful to expand these words as in SPCL, "by the presence of the Holy Spirit in us," or ITCL "showing . . . the presence of the Holy Spirit . . . ."

Genuine love: some other renderings are "sincere love" (NIV), "unaffected love" (REB), and "authentic love" (AB). CEV says "our love has been real." In some languages this may be stated in a negative way somewhat similar in meaning to the REB rendering: "love that is not deceitful."

TEV repeats the words "we have shown ourselves to be God's servants" from verse 4 in order to help the reader remember the purpose of this long list in verses 4-10. But see the comment on the TEV translation of 6.4a. In some languages it will be more natural to put this at the beginning of the verse.

6.7 RSV TEV

truthful speech, and the power of God; with the weapons of righteousness for

by our message of truth, and by the power of God. We have righteousness as

the right hand and for the left;   our weapon, both to attack and to de-
                                                fend ourselves.

Truthful speech is literally "in a word of truth." The sense may be that
what Paul says is honest and trustworthy, that is, his speech is **truthful** (RSV,
NRSV). But it is also possible to understand these words as parallel to **the
power of God,** in which case "the word of truth" refers to the gospel message
(so TEV). In support of the TEV translation, see Col 1.5, where "the word of the
truth" is called "the gospel." In languages that require separate sentences for
each item in Paul's list, one may wish to say here "we proclaim the true
message" or something similar.

By the power of God: this may be rendered "we act by the power of God"
or "God's power works in us."

Weapons of righteousness: there are three possible interpretations of
these words: (1) "weapons for the defense of righteousness," where **righteousness** is a synonym for "the gospel"; (2) "weapons that we have because we have
been made righteous"; the sense is then that Christians have been given the
moral qualities that come as a result of having been made righteous by God;
and (3) "righteousness as our weapon" (TEV, and apparently most translations).
Most interpreters favor this third interpretation.

For the right hand and for the left: the precise sense of these words is
debated. According to a widely accepted view, the right hand represents the
hand used for offense, that is, for attacking with a sword or spear; and the left
hand represents the hand used for defense, that is, for protecting oneself with
a shield (so TEV, FRCL, NJB, ITCL, LPD). Another view sees the mention of both
hands as a more general way of emphasizing the idea of being completely
equipped.

If the interpretation followed by TEV is accepted, translators should
recognize that this is figurative language. Paul is not talking about attacking
and defending oneself in a physical sense. Brc captures the sense well:
"Goodness has been our armour both to commend and to defend the faith." NCV
says "We use our right living to defend ourselves against everything."

6.8   RSV   TEV

in honor and dishonor, in ill repute and   We are honored and disgraced; we are
good repute. We are treated as impos-   insulted and praised. We are treated as
tors, and yet are true;   liars, yet we speak the truth;

TEV continues to break down the long, complex sentence of the original
by making separate sentences here. This will probably serve as a good model
for the receptor language in most cases. The words **honor, dishonor, ill repute,**
and **good repute** form a stylistic construction known as chiasmus. In such a
construction the two center words are paired together, and the two outer words
are paired together in the form a-b-b'-a'. In both cases the paired words are
basically synonyms. In some languages it may be more natural to put the

positive element first in each of the two pairs, but in others the negative element may come first in each case. Naturalness in the receptor language should be the determining factor in the arrangement of these four expressions.

In honor and dishonor: the word translated as **honor** is the Greek word often translated as "glory" (see 1.20 and 3.7-18). In this context it means "in good reputation," making it virtually synonymous with the following statement **good repute**. The term **dishonor** is elsewhere translated "menial" (Rom 9.21), "degrading" (1 Cor 11.14), "shame" (2 Cor 11.21) and "ignoble" (2 Tim 2.20). This noun is made up of a negative prefix and the stem of a verb meaning "honor," "revere" or "value." It seems to refer to the same sort of activities that result in **ill repute** which follows. Here it may be translated as "by shameful treatment" or "someone esteems me, someone else treats me with contempt" (ITCL).

In ill repute and good repute: the two Greek terms refer to having a bad reputation and a good reputation. The first two pairs of words may be translated "sometimes people respect us and sometimes they shame us. Sometimes they mock us and sometimes they praise us." This will also solve the problem of translating passive meanings where this is a problem.

We are treated as impostors and yet are true: treated by whom? Christians? Non-Christians? Literally the Greek says "as deceivers and true." RSV and TEV correctly translate the last two words of this verse as opposed to what precedes. Though they are treated as deceivers, they speak the truth. The meaning is clearly expressed in CEV: "We always told the truth about ourselves. But some people said we did not." Another possible model avoiding the passive form is "people accuse us of being liars, but we always tell the truth."

6.9	RSV	TEV
	as unknown, and yet well known; as dying, and behold we live; as punished, and yet not killed;	as unknown, yet we are known by all; as though we were dead, but, as you see, we live on. Although punished, we are not killed;

Unknown, and yet well known: the sense may be that they are unknown in the sense that most people do not know them, or, more specifically, the sense is probably that their apostolic authority is "unrecognized" by some Christians (so Barrett). The Greek does not state who knows Paul and his associates. According to TEV it is other Christians ("by all"). REB says "whom all men know," and CEV says "but well known to you." Possibly Paul means that, even though certain Christians do not recognize his authority, yet God does, that is, "we are known by God." Or perhaps Paul is thinking of both people and God. The passive ideas will have to be made active in many languages. Some suggested models are: "people do not accept us, but God accepts us" or, following the other interpretation, "people say they don't know us, but they are always watching us." Brc reads "no one knows us and everyone knows us." However, it is probably more likely that different agents are intended for the words "known" and "unknown." The probable meaning is "some Christians do not recognize our apostolic authority, yet our authority as apostles is well known to Christians everywhere."

As dying, and behold we live: Paul was constantly in danger of losing his life, and that seems to be the sense of the words **as dying**. On the word **behold** see 5.17 and 6.2. A possible model for this part of the verse: "they say that we are dying, but look! we are still alive." Or "people think we are dying, yet we live on!"

As punished, and yet not killed: punished by whom? The parallel of Psa 118.17-18 to 6.9b,c suggests that God is the implicit subject of the verb **punished**. In agreement with the Old Testament teaching that God's punishment is intended to lead to correction (see, for example, Psa 94.12; 119.67), Paul may have interpreted his sufferings as God's disciplinary action. On the other hand, the events of Paul's life as we know them from Acts and from his own letters give support to the view that Paul has in mind here punishment by other human beings. In languages without appropriate passive forms, one may wish to say "they [indefinite] persecute us, but they do not kill us" or "we suffer greatly, but we do not die."

6.10   RSV   TEV

as sorrowful, yet always rejoicing; as poor, yet making many rich; as having nothing, and yet possessing everything.

although saddened, we are always glad; we seem poor, but we make many people rich; we seem to have nothing, yet we really possess everything.

Sorrowful . . . rejoicing: once again Paul uses a pair of contradictory terms and maintains that both are true. It may be more natural in some languages to reverse the order: "we are always happy, even in times of suffering" (CEV).

As poor . . . as having nothing: the words **poor** and **having nothing** should probably be taken in a literal sense.

Making many rich: this is figurative language, as are the words **yet possessing everything**. **Possessing everything** should be understood in the same sense as Paul's words in 1 Cor 3.21-23. Christians belong to Christ, and to have Christ is to have all that matters. Through his apostolic ministry Paul was able to bring God's blessings to many people. Knox translates "beggars, that bring riches to many; disinherited, and the world is ours."

6.11   RSV   TEV

Our mouth is open to you, Corinthians; our heart is wide.

Dear friends in Corinth! We have spoken frankly to you; we have opened our hearts wide.

116

Our mouth is open refers to what he has just said; this is figurative language meaning that he has "spoken frankly" (TEV, NRSV) without holding anything back. REB has "we have spoken very frankly," while Mft translates "I am keeping nothing back from you," and Phps reads "we are hiding nothing from you."

The term of address, **Corinthians,** will fit more naturally at the beginning of the verse in many languages. Note that TEV fills it out by saying "Dear friends in Corinth," and NJB has "people of Corinth," since a more literal translation may sound too harsh.

Our heart is wide is also figurative language. The meaning is not so much that Paul and his associates have told the Corinthians everything that they were thinking. A broadened heart is rather the sign of great affection (see 7.3). In view of this some possible models are "we love you with all our hearts" (GNW) or "there is room in our hearts for you" (CEV).

6.12	RSV	TEV
	You are not restricted by us, but you are restricted in your own affections.	It is not we who have closed our hearts to you; it is you who have closed your hearts to us.

A literal translation of this verse is "You are not squeezed (crushed) by us, but you are squeezed (crushed) by your bowels." All of this verse is metaphorical language, and it continues to deal with the figure of space in verse 11, "our heart is wide." In biblical Greek the bowels are the seat of emotions, hence **affections** (RSV) and "hearts" (TEV). Paul says that he is not squeezing the Corinthians into a small place where there is little room for affection. Any restriction of space for affection is on their side. TEV captures the sense of the original, as does CEV: "We are not holding back on our love for you, but you are holding back on your love for us." Knox provides another possible model: "it is not our fault, it is the fault of your own affections, that you feel constraint with us." Or some translators may prefer "We have not stopped loving you, but it is your love for us that has grown weak (or, cold)." Note how several of these modern versions have had to abandon the figure of space, since local expressions of affection do not deal with such figures of speech, or else use other figures such as warm and cold, strong and weak.

6.13	RSV	TEV
	In return—I speak as to children—widen your hearts also.	I speak now as though you were my children: show us the same feelings that we have for you. Open your hearts wide!

In return is literally "the same recompense." The sense is clear. Paul asks the Corinthians to open their hearts to him and his colleagues just as he and his associates have opened theirs to the Corinthians. That is, in return for the love that Paul and his associates have for the Corinthians, they want to be repaid by experiencing love from the people they love.

That Paul compares the Corinthians to children does not mean that they are immature (as in 1 Cor 3.1-2); rather in this context the word **children** is an expression of affection (see 1 Cor 4.14; Gal 4.19). REB says "If I may speak to you like a father."

The Greek has no pronoun before **children**. Some languages will require a possessive pronoun here. Though the pronoun "our" (Paul and his co-workers) would be appropriate, in light of the first person singular **I speak**, the pronoun "my" (TEV, FRCL) seems more appropriate. Translators should avoid suggesting that Paul actually has children.

Widen your hearts also: see comments on 6.11. TEV keeps the metaphorical language ("Open your hearts wide!") while translating the meaning also ("show us the same feelings that we have for you"). Depending on how verse 11 has been rendered, translators may want to consider one of the following models: "love us with all your hearts also" or "make room in your hearts for us also."

The whole verse may possibly be rendered "since we still love you, I am asking that you rekindle your love for us (I am talking to you now as if you were my children)."

B-4. Warnings against pagan influences
6.14–7.1

RSV

14 Do not be mismated with unbelievers. For what partnership have righteousness and iniquity? Or what fellowship has light with darkness? 15 What accord has Christ with Belial? Or what has a believer in common with an unbeliever? 16 What agreement has the temple of God with idols? For we are the temple of the living God; as God said,
"I will live in them and move among them,
and I will be their God,
and they shall be my people.
17   Therefore come out from them,
and be separate from them, says the Lord,
and touch nothing unclean;
then I will welcome you,
18   and I will be a father to you,
and you shall be my sons and daughters,
says the Lord Almighty."

TEV

Warning against Pagan Influences

14 Do not try to work together as equals with unbelievers, for it cannot be done. How can right and wrong be partners? How can light and darkness live together? 15 How can Christ and the Devil agree? What does a believer have in common with an unbeliever? 16 How can God's temple come to terms with pagan idols? For we are the temple of the living God! As God himself has said,
"I will make my home with my people
and live among them;
I will be their God,
and they shall be my people."
17 And so the Lord says,
"You must leave them
and separate yourselves from them.
Have nothing to do with what is unclean,
and I will accept you.
18   I will be your father,

Chapter 7:

1 Since we have these promises, beloved, let us cleanse ourselves from every defilement of body and spirit, and make holiness perfect in the fear of God.

and you shall be my sons and
daughters,
says the Lord Almighty."

Chapter 7:

1 All these promises are made to us, my dear friends. So then, let us purify ourselves from everything that makes body or soul unclean, and let us be completely holy by living in awe of God.

SECTION HEADING: TEV "Warning against Pagan Influences." Interpreters are puzzled by the presence of these verses (6.14–7.1) at this location in 2 Corinthians. They seem to interrupt the connection between 6.13 and 7.2. In addition to that, these verses contain parallels to writings from the first century Jewish Qumran community, and some scholars think that these few verses were originally from a Qumran document. Whether or not a later editor inserted here verses not written by Paul, or whether Paul himself later inserted these verses here, need not be discussed now. Translators will translate the text of 2 Corinthians as it now exists, regardless of whether the present form of the text is identical to the original form.

In this section Paul may be primarily warning the Corinthians against siding with his opponents; or, more likely, he is truly talking about nonbelievers, that is, pagans. Some other models for the section heading are "You are the true temple of the living God," or "Getting rid of all bad influences," or "Do not get involved with people who do not know God."

The first person plural pronouns in this section include all Christians.

6.14 RSV TEV

Do not be mismated with unbelievers. For what partnership have righteousness and iniquity? Or what fellowship has light with darkness?

Do not try to work together as equals with unbelievers, for it cannot be done. How can right and wrong be partners? How can light and darkness live together?

Mismated translates a word meaning "yoked with another of a different kind." Paul may have had in mind the admonition of Deut 22.10, which forbids plowing with an ox and a donkey yoked together. In what way the Christians are not to be yoked together is not stated. TEV interprets this as working together. Possibly it refers to marriage, but this meaning is probably too limited in this context. The verb occurs only here in all the New Testament. But a related word is found in Phil 4.3, where it is translated "yokefellow." Other translations of the verb here have rendered it "harness yourselves in an uneven team with" (NJB) and "consent to be yokefellows" (Knox). The verb and the negation are together translated in CEV as "stay away from . . . ," by Mft as "keep out of all incongruous ties with . . . ," and elsewhere as "refuse to be united with . . . ."

Unbelievers refers to persons who are not Christians. More specifically, in the context between appeals to the Corinthians to be reconciled to Paul, he possibly has in mind his opponents in the church at Corinth, who have rejected his apostolic authority. In areas where Islam is strong, translators must pay careful attention to the meaning of the word for **unbelievers,** since it is very likely to carry the meaning of "non-Muslim." In such cases it is better to use an expression like "people who do not believe in Christ."

Partnership . . . fellowship: these two words are different in Greek but virtually synonymous in meaning in this context. The first is used only here in the New Testament and comes from an expression for having something together with someone else. The related verb form occurs in 1 Cor 9.10,12; 10.21. The second occurs frequently—especially to describe the close association believers have with each other (Acts 2.42 and Gal 2.9) or the fellowship of believers with Christ (1 Cor 1.9). Its basic meaning is that several people share a common feature or common activity, and this binds them in a special unity.

Righteousness: in Paul's writings the word **righteousness** usually refers to being put right with God, but here the sense seems to be that of right conduct. See also the comments on this term at 3.9 and 5.21.

Iniquity: this same term is translated elsewhere in RSV as "wickedness" (Matt 24.12) and "lawlessness" (2 Thes 2.7; Heb 1.9; 1 John 3.4). It carries the basic meaning of illegality or violation of God's laws and stands in radical opposition to **righteousness** both here and in Rom 6.19. Since these two terms are abstract, some languages will require that they be personified by talking about "a righteous person" or "righteous people" on the one hand and "an evil person" or "evil people" on the other.

Light and **darkness,** as with **righteousness** and **iniquity,** express opposites. Here **light** and **darkness** are used metaphorically to refer to moral qualities or to belief and unbelief (see Rom 13.12; Eph 5.11-14; 1 Thes 5.5). In some languages it may be necessary to use the words for "daylight" and "night" to express these two figures of speech.

The two questions in this verse are rhetorical questions. The implicit reply to both questions is that there is certainly no partnership, no fellowship. GNC retains the question form but adds the word "why?" to the first question; such an addition in English clearly suggests that a negative response is implied: "Why, what kinship is there between righteousness and lawlessness?" In languages where the rhetorical nature of these questions may not be recognized, translators may need to restructure and express these two questions as emphatic statements. Others will possibly express the idea as follows: "a righteous person and an evil person cannot agree with each other, and light cannot unite with darkness. Is this not true?"

6.15	RSV	TEV
	What accord has Christ with Belial?[i] Or what has a believer in common with an unbeliever?	How can Christ and the Devil agree? What does a believer have in common with an unbeliever?

[i] Greek *Beliar*

As in the previous verse, these two questions are rhetorical, with a strong negative response being understood. Some languages will perhaps need to express these two questions as negative statements which affirm emphatically that there is no **accord** and nothing **in common**.

The two verbal expressions in this verse translate two Greek nouns. The Greek has no verbs in verse 15. The first noun involves agreement or "harmony" (Mft and NIV). The Greek term is actually the source of the English word "symphony." The second noun means a "share" or a "common lot" (NAB). The Greek is literally "But what accord Christ with Beliar, or what part faith with unbelief?" But it is wise to transform these into verbal expressions, as most English versions do. This is done as follows in existing English versions: "agree . . . join with" (REB); "agree . . . have in common with" (AT) and "come to an agreement with . . . share" (NJB); "What harmony is there . . . ? What does a believer have in common . . . ?" (NIV); or "How can . . . have any agreement? What can a believer have together with . . . ?" (NCV).

Belial comes from Hebrew and means "wickedness" or "worthlessness." RSV translates this word in the Old Testament as "base fellows" or "worthless fellows" (Judges 20.13; 1 Sam 10.27). "Beliar," a variant form of the name, is used in the Greek text (see RSV footnote). It occurs in several Jewish writings of the intertestamental period, and the name **Belial** occurs in the Qumran writings. In these intertestamental writings **Belial** is the name given to Satan. Since the name **Belial** is unknown to most readers, TEV (also FRCL, GECL, NBE) uses the more widely understood term, "the Devil." Other translations say "Satan" (CEV, *La Biblia Interconfesional* [LBI]).

On the terms for **believer** and **unbeliever**, see comments on the previous verse.

6.16 RSV	TEV
What agreement has the temple of God with idols? For we are the temple of the living God; as God said, "I will live in them and move among them, and I will be their God, and they shall be my people.	How can God's temple come to terms with pagan idols? For we are the temple of the living God! As God himself has said, "I will make my home with my people and live among them; I will be their God, and they shall be my people."

As in verses 14 and 15, the question at the beginning of verse 16 is rhetorical (see comments on verses 14-15). And as in the previous verses, the verb **has** is understood. The noun translated **agreement** does not occur elsewhere in the New Testament. It is used outside the Bible for mental assent to philosophical insights. But most English versions have translated the idea of a contractual agreement or coming to terms, with: "compromise with" (NJB); "what bargain can . . . make" (AT); "what compact can there be" (Mft). Some other languages have attempted to render the idea here by using the verbal expression "to exist together" or "to be in the same place."

As TEV makes explicit, **idols** refers to the gods worshiped by pagans. NJB says "false gods." The meaning is clearly translated in CEV: "Do idols belong in the temple of God?"

Though good manuscript support exists for the reading "you are the temple of the living God" (so RVR, KJV, NRSV footnote) instead of **we are the temple,** the editors of the UBS *Greek New Testament* think it is more likely that a scribe changed the pronoun "we" to "you" in light of 1 Cor 3.16 and in light of the second person plural pronouns in the verses before and after verse 16.

The temple of the living God: using metaphorical language, Paul calls the Christian believers **the temple of . . . God.** In 1 Cor 6.19 Paul declares that the physical body of each believer is the temple where God dwells, but here in 6.16 the sense is that the community as a whole is the temple where God dwells (see 1 Cor 3.16; Eph 2.21). Just as **the temple of . . . God** is metaphorical language, perhaps the word **idols** is to be understood as metaphorical and not literal. If Paul's words are metaphorical, the sense is "What agreement has the Christian community with things contrary to God?" Translators, however, should make every effort to keep the image of **temple** and **idols.**

On the phrase **the living God**, see comments on 3.3.

The quotation in verse 16 is a combination of two verses from the Old Testament, Lev 26.12 and Ezek 37.27. Just as God may be said to live in a temple, so here he lives "in" the Christian community, which is said to be God's temple. Since the point in this context is that God lives "among" the people in the community as a whole rather than living in the heart of each believer, the preposition **in** of RSV may be incorrectly understood to mean "in the individual's heart." NJB captures the sense better: "I shall fix my home among them and live among them" (so also GNC "I will live in their midst and move among them").

I will live and move among them: the second of the two verbs **live and move** (see Acts 17.28) literally gives the idea of "walking about" among the people, but they actually speak of the same event rather than two separate and distinct happenings. The quotation is intended to emphasize the fact that God will actually be present with his people.

I will be their God and they shall be my people: this statement is virtually identical with Jer 31.33 and Ezek 37.27 and is repeated in Heb 8.10. It is a dual reminder of the relationship between God and his people. In some languages it may be necessary to say something like "They will worship me as [the only] God, and I will care for them as my people."

6.17 RSV	TEV
Therefore come out from them, and be separate from them, says	And so the Lord says, "You must leave them

the Lord, and touch nothing unclean; then I will welcome you,	and separate yourselves from them. Have nothing to do with what is unclean, and I will accept you.

Verse 17 continues to quote from words of God in the Old Testament, Isa 52.11 (6.17abc) and Ezek 20.34,41 in the Septuagint (6.17d). Since the quotation does not continue from the same place in the Old Testament as the quotation in verse 16, GNC adds the words "as we also find in scripture" at the beginning of verse 17. By transposing the words inserted by Paul, "And so the Lord says," TEV likewise indicates that the quotation in verse 17 does not follow directly the quotation in verse 16. Paul also adds the logical connector **Therefore**, which is not found in the Old Testament text but is important to the New Testament argument. In Paul's thinking it is because of what he cited in verse 16 that the appeal of verse 17 can be made. The TEV rendering seems weak. One may prefer to translate "Therefore the Lord also says . . . ."

In the Old Testament context the Israelite people are called upon to leave the city of Babylon, where they have been living in captivity. As Paul applies these quotations to the church, believers are to separate themselves from the immoral behavior and influence of nonbelievers (**from them**). In some languages it will be necessary to render the pronoun explicitly as "those who do not believe."

The Lord in this verse is clearly "the Lord God" and not "the Lord Jesus."

Unclean had a cultic sense in the passage from Isaiah, "not fit for use in worship." For Paul the word **unclean** has primarily an ethical sense, "dirty because of sin."

Then I will welcome you: God's acceptance of his people depends upon their becoming separate from unbelievers. RSV expresses this connection with the word **then**. Similarly NJB and Mft. In the Septuagint text of Ezek 20.34,41, God's promise to **welcome** his people refers to welcoming or receiving them back from exile to the land that he had given them. For Paul, the meaning is that God will "accept" his people.

6.18   RSV   TEV

and I will be a father to you, and you shall be my sons and daughters, says the Lord Almighty."	I will be your father, and you shall be my sons and daughters, says the Lord Almighty."

The quotation in this verse comes from 2 Sam 7.14 or 1 Chr 17.13, where it is the formal statement by which the Lord adopts King David as his son. Paul has changed the pronoun from the third person singular ("him," referring to King David) to the second person plural (**you**) and has inserted the words

and daughters in order to apply this verse more directly to the entire
community of believers.

The Lord Almighty: this is the only instance in Paul's letters of this
expression, but it is used nine times in the book of Revelation (see Rev 1.8). In
the Septuagint this phrase translates the Hebrew words "Yahweh Sabaoth"
("LORD of hosts" in RSV). GNC translates these words as "the Lord, the ruler of
all." FRCL has "the Lord all-powerful." If in the receptor language there is the
possibility that the readers will think this refers to Jesus, it will be necessary
to say something like "the Lord God, who has all power."

The break between chapters 6 and 7 is unfortunate and disrupts the
continuity of Paul's argument. Translators should be careful not to give the
impression that a new section is beginning at this point.

7.1	RSV	TEV
	Since we have these promises, be-loved, let us cleanse ourselves from every defilement of body and spirit, and make holiness perfect in the fear of God.	All these promises are made to us, my dear friends. So then, let us purify ourselves from everything that makes body or soul unclean, and let us be completely holy by living in awe of God.

On the translation of **we**, see comments on the section heading above at
6.14.

These promises refers to God's promises in verses 6.16-18 and shows the
continuity of Paul's argument. Knox begins this verse "Such are the promises
. . . ." Others may wish to make clear the origin of these promises: "God has
made these promises" (CEV).

Beloved: see also 12.19. The Corinthians are loved by Paul. TEV says "my
dear friends," though "our dear friends" is also possible. In many languages
this affectionate term of address will fit more naturally at the beginning of the
verse, as in CEV, "My friends, God has made these promises." The same form
of address is also used by Paul in Rom 12.19.

Let us cleanse ourselves: most versions maintain the image of ritual
purification: "wash ourselves clean" (NJB); "purify ourselves" (NAB and Brc). But
CEV attempts to convey the idea without the precise imagery of the Old
Testament: "So we should stay away from everything that keeps our bodies
and spirits from being clean." Another translation has "let us not do anything
that would make our bodies or spirits unclean."

Only here in his letters does Paul use the Greek noun translated as
defilement, although the related verb is found in 1 Cor 8.7. A **defilement** is
something that makes a person ritually unclean or impure so as to be unfit for
participating in Temple worship.

Body and spirit is literally "flesh and spirit." Here the reference is to the
body and the human spirit. Taken together, **body** and **spirit** refer to the whole
human being, the outward and inward aspects of one's being. The use of these

two terms makes it perfectly clear that Paul has in mind something more than mere ritual purity, which is so prominent in the Old Testament.

Holiness in this context refers to holy living, that is, the kind of behavior that God requires of people. The idea of **holiness** is difficult to convey in many languages. In some cases translators speak of "giving one's self to God," since the root meaning of **holiness** is to be set apart for God.

Make . . . perfect: the idea of perfection may be even more difficult to express than holiness in some languages. Sometimes an adverb meaning "completely" or "totally" can be used with a verb phrase, to get close to this meaning; for example, "give ourselves totally to God's way of living."

On **the fear of God** see comments on 5.11.

Some possible models for the very difficult last part of this verse are "Therefore let us respect God and give ourselves entirely to him" or "We should honor God and try to become completely like him" (CEV).

B-5. Paul's joy

7.2-16

RSV

TEV

Paul's Joy

2 Open your hearts to us; we have wronged no one, we have corrupted no one, we have taken advantage of no one. 3 I do not say this to condemn you, for I said before that you are in our hearts, to die together and to live together. 4 I have great confidence in you; I have great pride in you; I am filled with comfort. With all our affliction, I am overjoyed.

5 For even when we came into Macedonia, our bodies had no rest but we were afflicted at every turn—fighting without and fear within. 6 But God, who comforts the downcast, comforted us by the coming of Titus, 7 and not only by his coming but also by the comfort with which he was comforted in you, as he told us of your longing, your mourning, your zeal for me, so that I rejoiced still more. 8 For even if I made you sorry with my letter, I do not regret it (though I did regret it), for I see that that letter grieved you, though only for a while. 9 As it is, I rejoice, not because you were grieved, but because you were grieved into repenting; for you felt a godly grief, so that you suffered no loss through us. 10 For godly grief produces a repentance that leads to salvation and brings no regret, but worldly grief produces death. 11 For see what earnestness this godly grief has produced in you, what eagerness to clear yourselves, what indignation, what alarm, what longing, what zeal, what punishment! At every point you have proved yourselves guiltless in the matter.

2 Make room for us in your hearts. We have wronged no one; we have ruined no one, nor tried to take advantage of anyone. 3 I do not say this to condemn you; for, as I have said before, you are so dear to us that we are always together, whether we live or die. 4 I am so sure of you; I take such pride in you! In all our troubles I am still full of courage; I am running over with joy.

5 Even after we arrived in Macedonia, we did not have any rest. There were troubles everywhere, quarrels with others, fears in our hearts. 6 But God, who encourages the downhearted, encouraged us with the coming of Titus. 7 It was not only his coming that cheered us, but also his report of how you encouraged him. He told us how much you want to see me, how sorry you are, how ready you are to defend me; and so I am even happier now.

8 For even if that letter of mine made you sad, I am not sorry I wrote it. I could have been sorry when I saw that it made you sad for a while. 9 But now I am happy—not because I made you sad, but because your sadness made you change your ways. That sadness was used by God, and so we caused you no harm. 10 For the sadness that is used by God brings a change of heart that leads to salvation—and there is no regret in that! But sadness that is merely human causes death. 11 See what God did with this sadness of

12 So although I wrote to you, it was not on account of the one who did the wrong, nor on account of the one who suffered the wrong, but in order that your zeal for us might be revealed to you in the sight of God. 13 Therefore we are comforted.

And besides our own comfort we rejoiced still more at the joy of Titus, because his mind has been set at rest by you all. 14 For if I have expressed to him some pride in you, I was not put to shame; but just as everything we said to you was true, so our boasting before Titus has proved true. 15 And his heart goes out all the more to you, as he remembers the obedience of you all, and the fear and trembling with which you received him. 16 I rejoice, because I have perfect confidence in you.

yours: how earnest it has made you, how eager to prove your innocence! Such indignation, such alarm, such feelings, such devotion, such readiness to punish wrongdoing! You have shown yourselves to be without fault in the whole matter.

12 So, even though I wrote that letter, it was not because of the one who did wrong or the one who was wronged. Instead, I wrote it to make plain to you, in God's sight, how deep your devotion to us really is. 13 That is why we were encouraged.

Not only were we encouraged; how happy Titus made us with his happiness over the way in which all of you helped to cheer him up! 14 I did boast of you to him, and you have not disappointed me. We have always spoken the truth to you, and in the same way the boast we made to Titus has proved true. 15 And so his love for you grows stronger, as he remembers how all of you were ready to obey his instructions, how you welcomed him with fear and trembling. 16 How happy I am that I can depend on you completely!

SECTION HEADING: TEV "Paul's Joy." In this section Paul declares his joy that the Corinthians have repented of the wrongs which had led him to write a harsh letter to them. Paul also expresses his joy over the way in which the Corinthians had received Titus on his recent visit to them. In some languages it may be necessary to indicate more specifically in the section heading what causes the joy that Paul felt. CEV has "The Church Makes Paul Happy," while NAB reads "Joy over Repentance."

The first person plural pronouns in this section do not include the readers. Some interpreters take all of the pronouns to be "epistolary plurals" (so Mft, AT, and ITCL translate with the pronouns "I" and "me").

7.2   RSV   TEV

Open your hearts to us; we have wronged no one, we have corrupted no one, we have taken advantage of no one.

Make room for us in your hearts. We have wronged no one; we have ruined no one, nor tried to take advantage of anyone.

Verse 2 returns to the thought of 6.13 ("Widen your hearts also"). The expression **open your hearts to us** is the opposite of the verb translated "restricted" in 6.12. See comments on 6.11 and 13. In contemporary English idiom, "to open one's heart to someone" means "to expose one's inner private feelings." For this reason "Make room for us in your hearts" (TEV, NRSV, and many other modern versions) is better than the RSV translation.

The AB translation of verse 2 preserves the emphasis on the pronouns **no one** in the Greek text: "No one did we wrong, no one did we corrupt, no one did we defraud." The use of the emphatic forms for **no one** will serve the same purpose in many languages. In other cases the emphasis may be maintained by saying something like "no one at all" in each case.

The threefold denial in this verse is primarily for rhetorical effect; no great distinction of meaning is intended among the three denials. **Wronged** is perhaps more general than the two verbs that follow. **Corrupted** may also be translated as "bribed." **Taken advantage of** may be translated as "cheated" (CEV), "defrauded," or "exploited." The order of the three verbs is not important and may be altered for the sake of naturalness in the receptor language.

Though Paul's threefold denial of wrongdoing would be true as a general statement, the context suggests that he is responding to charges of wrongdoing at Corinth by certain persons among the Corinthian Christians (see 12.17-18).

7.3	RSV	TEV
	I do not say this to condemn you, for I said before that you are in our hearts, to die together and to live together.	I do not say this to condemn you; for, as I have said before, you are so dear to us that we are always together, whether we live or die.

The word **this** refers to what Paul has written in the preceding verse. Paul's denials in verse 2 were not stated in order to criticize the Corinthians (or his opponents in Corinth). He simply states the facts without accusing them of wrongdoing. In some languages it may be more natural to recast the sentence to say "When I speak in this manner, I am not condemning you . . . ." The word **condemn** is translated in RSV as a verb, but Greek has the same noun found in 3.9. Coupled with the verb "to say," the idea in this context is that of passing negative judgment on someone. Other languages may say something like "criticize," "denounce," or "accuse of wrong."

For: this transition word introduces Paul's explanation why the Corinthian readers should not take his words as a condemnation.

I said before: probably referring to statements earlier in this letter (see 1.4-7; 3.2; 4.10 and following; 5.14; 6.9,11-12), but possibly referring to a previous visit to Corinth or to an earlier letter. This may be rendered "I have already said," but in some languages the verb form itself will make it unnecessary to add an adverb like "before" or "already."

You are in our hearts: the expression **in our hearts** is used in 1.22 and 4.6, but the context is different in those cases. Here Paul indicates that the Corinthians are in his heart (and the hearts of his associates). This is an indication of deep affection and may be better not translated literally in a number of languages. Both TNT and TEV render it "you are so dear to us." In other languages one may wish to say "we love you so very much" or something similar.

To die together and to live together: many scholars interpret this expression as a well-known formula used to indicate lasting friendship. And this sense seems to fit the context here. Combined with the preceding affirmation, the meaning seems to be that "we love you and will keep on loving you no matter what happens." One translation says "we will not be separated whether we live or die."

7.4 RSV	TEV
I have great confidence in you; I have great pride in you; I am filled with comfort. With all our affliction, I am overjoyed.	I am so sure of you; I take such pride in you! In all our troubles I am still full of courage; I am running over with joy.

As the RSV translation indicates, verse 4 in Greek consists of four short phrases followed by the words **with all our affliction**. There are two different ways in which the words **with all our affliction** may be connected to the preceding words. TEV, REB, GECL, and FRCL connect the words **with all our affliction** with the final two clauses, **I am filled with comfort** and **I am overjoyed**. REB says "In all our many troubles my cup is full of consolation and overflows with joy." Other translations such as NRSV, NIV, and TOB, however, agree with RSV in connecting the words **with all our affliction** with the last clause only, that is, with **I am overjoyed**. Though both interpretations are possible, perhaps the grammatical construction favors the RSV translation more than the TEV.

The translation **I have great confidence in you** does not seem to capture the meaning of the Greek. The word **confidence** in RSV is the same word translated as "bold" in 3.12. As indicated in the comments on that verse, this Greek word often means "boldness in speech." Paul's relationship of trust with the Corinthians permits him to speak boldly to them. It may be translated "I have great confidence before you . . . ." AB expresses the meaning clearly: "I feel I can speak quite candidly to you." REB similarly says "I am speaking to you with great frankness." NAB and Phps translate similarly, speaking of "utter frankness."

I have great pride in you: in some languages the idea of taking pride in someone else is expressed by saying "I am very happy about you" or "you make my heart rejoice."

I am filled with comfort: while comfort and encouragement are closely related, the latter seems more appropriate in this context. Paul states that he is encouraged by the Corinthians. The passive may be avoided by saying "I have received great comfort," or by making the Corinthians the subject of the verb, "you give me much encouragement . . . ."

The pronoun **our** in **all our affliction** probably does not include the readers.

I am overjoyed: literally "I overflow with joy." The sense is that, in spite of all his trouble, Paul is nevertheless extremely happy.

7.5 RSV TEV

For even when we came into Macedonia, our bodies had no rest but we were afflicted at every turn—fighting without and fear within.

Even after we arrived in Macedonia, we did not have any rest. There were troubles everywhere, quarrels with others, fears in our hearts.

With verse 5 Paul returns to the subject of his travel plans which he left in 2.13. See the comments at the section heading for 2.14-17. It will be important to make a paragraph break at this point in the receptor language, as in most English versions.

On **Macedonia** see 2.13. Paul is writing from Macedonia (see 9.1-4), so the verb **we came** probably refers to a recent arrival.

Our bodies had no rest is literally "our flesh had no rest." Here "flesh" refers to the entire person, with the additional sense that human beings are subject to frailty. The natural translation of this thought into English is expressed in the TEV's pronoun "we," though perhaps TEV lacks the idea expressed by "flesh," that the body is subject to weariness and pain. In some languages it may be perfectly natural to say "we did not let our bodies rest," retaining the notion of "body" but using the more natural subject "we." Others may say "we were physically exhausted."

We were afflicted: this passive verb will have to be translated actively in many cases. However, there is no direct evidence as to the cause of the affliction. It may be possible to say simply "we suffered" or "there was trouble [for us]." Other languages will have to use the indefinite third person plural, "they caused us suffering."

At every turn: literally "in all," that is, in every way. Barclay translates this element by his choice of verb: "we were surrounded by troubles."

Fighting without and fear within: the word **fighting** is not to be taken literally as referring to physical battle, but rather in the figurative sense of "quarrels" (TEV) with other people who were **without**, meaning "outside the church." These other people were perhaps Christian opponents, non-Christians, or both. **Fear within**: refers to concerns and anxieties within their own "hearts." One possible model may be "while we struggled with other people, we also had to struggle with the fears in our minds (or, hearts)."

7.6 RSV TEV

But God, who comforts the downcast, comforted us by the coming of Titus,

But God, who encourages the downhearted, encouraged us with the coming of Titus.

But: Paul uses the strong adversative conjunction here to mark the contrast between the affliction of the previous verse and the encouragement that God gave him in it.

On the translation of the verb **comforts**, see the comments on 1.4. As in chapter 1, RSV understands the primary meaning of the Greek word here to be "consolation." TEV understands the primary meaning to be "encouragement."

The downcast: that is, those people who, like Paul and his associates, are worried by various kinds of external troubles or internal distress. The term has been rendered "low in spirit" (NAB); "distressed" (NJB); "depressed" (Phps); "dejected" (Mft).

Comforted us by the coming of Titus: Titus had apparently just recently arrived when Paul wrote this letter. The use of the perfect tense in English in REB ("has comforted") is better than the simple past tense of RSV and TEV, if the very recent past is referred to.

The coming of Titus: Titus had come to Macedonia (see 7.5). Since it was God's doing that Titus came to Paul in Macedonia, some translators may wish to follow the model of CEV here: "when he sent Titus to us."

7.7   RSV   TEV

and not only by his coming but also by the comfort with which he was comforted in you, as he told us of your longing, your mourning, your zeal for me, so that I rejoiced still more.	It was not only his coming that cheered us, but also his report of how you encouraged him. He told us how much you want to see me, how sorry you are, how ready you are to defend me; and so I am even happier now.

The fact of Titus' arrival in Macedonia was a source of comfort for Paul, but the good news that Titus brought regarding the Corinthians was also a source of comfort. On the interpretation and translation of **comfort**, see comments on 1.4 and 7.6.

Comfort with which he was comforted: the related noun and verb are used together similarly in 1.4,6. Because a passive form occurs here, some languages will require that an active formulation be used. Some may say "the comfort which he received [from you]" or "the way in which you comforted him."

The Corinthians were **longing** to see Paul and to reassure him of their love for him. They were **mourning** because of the strained relationship between themselves and Paul that occurred because of their failure to deal with the divisive issue (see 2.5-11). And they had a **zeal** for Paul. How their **zeal** was expressed is not stated, but it probably took the form of being eager to restore the broken relationship with Paul and to support and defend him. Following the form of the Greek, many translations do not state how they showed their zeal. Other translations such as TEV and FRCL "how ready you are to defend me" do imply that the Corinthians wished to restore the broken relationship.

The Greek is literally "your longing, your mourning, your zeal for me." Though only the last noun, **zeal**, has the words **for me**, Paul is most likely the implied object for the first two nouns also. It is also possible, however, that the implied object is the pronoun "us," that is, Paul and his co-workers.

The meaning of these three nouns will have to be elaborated in some receptor languages. It may be necessary to say something like the following: "how you sincerely wanted to see me, how sorry you were about what had happened, and how eager you were to support me."

7.8 RSV	TEV
For even if I made you sorry with my letter, I do not regret it (though I did regret it), for I see that that letter grieved you, though only for a while.	For even if that letter of mine made you sad, I am not sorry I wrote it. I could have been sorry when I saw that it made you sad for a while.

The Greek syntax is broken in this verse, and scribes made various attempts to improve the grammar of this verse, but the meaning is clear: Paul had second thoughts about having written the letter, when he learned that it caused the Corinthians some temporary grief, but now he was glad that he wrote it.

The logical sequence of thoughts may be explained as follows: **For** in the Greek does not express reason but introduces a further statement of the previous clause "I rejoiced still more," that is, **I do not regret** [writing the letter]. Then he introduces his own mixed feelings on the subject, for in fact **I did regret it**, since, after all, the letter made the people in Corinth feel sad **for a while**, and he didn't really feel happy about that. But in general, **even if I made you sorry . . . I do not regret it**. Most translators may have to rearrange this sequence of thoughts in a logical order that will be clear to those who hear it read in the receptor language.

Even if: some interpreters do not think that there is any doubt about whether or not Paul had grieved the Corinthians by his previous letter. For this reason NJB translates "though I did distress you . . . ," and CEV has "even though my letter hurt your feelings" (and similarly AB).

Made you sorry may be translated as "hurt your feelings" (CEV), although it may be unwise or even impossible to render this English idiom directly in other languages. Other models are "upset you" (Phps) or "caused you distress."

With my letter is literally "with the letter." KJV incorrectly says "with a letter." Since the Greek has the definite article, it is clear that Paul is referring to a specific letter that he wrote (see 2.3). So RSV appropriately adds the word **my**, and TEV correctly says "that letter of mine." REB makes explicit that this letter was "sent" to the Corinthians: "by the letter I sent."

The verb translated **made . . . sorry** at the beginning of this verse and **grieved** toward the end are actually the same in Greek and are thus translated identically in TEV, "made you sad." The verb rendered **regret** (positively and negatively) in RSV has to do with a general feeling of remorse and is clearly distinguished from the stronger verb translated "repent" in the following verse. It involves sorrow for having committed some act. In Matt 27.3 Judas is said to feel regret (using this verb) but not repentance.

7.9   RSV   TEV

As it is, I rejoice, not because you were grieved, but because you were grieved into repenting; for you felt a godly grief, so that you suffered no loss through us.

But now I am happy—not because I made you sad, but because your sadness made you change your ways. That sadness was used by God, and so we caused you no harm.

This verse begins in Greek with the word "now," implying a contrast between how he had felt and how he now feels. Though he was sad for a while because of the effect his letter had on the Corinthians, "now" he is happy.

Grieved: this is the same verb as translated "made . . . sorry" and "grieved" in the previous verse. See comments there.

The word **repenting** contains two aspects of meaning: admission and regret of doing wrong, and a resolve to change one's behavior. And note that TEV has brought out the idea of change by translating "change your ways." Brc attempts to reflect the same thing with "change of mind." See comments on "regret" in the previous verse regarding the distinction between "regret" and "repent."

The words **godly grief** are difficult to interpret and translate, as the different translations of these words by TEV and REB indicate: TEV "that sadness was used by God;" REB "You bore the pain as God would have you bear it." Verse 10 contrasts "godly grief" with "worldly grief." **Godly grief** appears to be grief that is sincere and is approved by God, not merely a grief or remorse that is shown in order to impress human beings.

So that you suffered no loss through us: the words **so that** translate a single Greek word that may express either purpose or result. TEV, NIV, NJB, and REB translate it as expressing result ("and so"), that is, "with the result that we caused you no harm." It seems better, however, to understand the Greek word as expressing purpose (so Barrett, Martin, AB). It was God's purpose for them to experience grief "in order that" they would not suffer loss. AB says "For you were grieved as God willed, that you might not sustain a loss in any way because of us."

Loss: Paul does not state the nature of the loss. Loss of a future visit by Paul, loss of their salvation, and loss of their positive Christian attitudes have all been suggested by commentators. But the presence of the words "in nothing" in the Greek suggests that Paul was not limiting the idea of a loss to any particular loss. NCV includes a separate sentence at the end of the verse to translate **you suffered no loss through us**: "So you were not hurt by us in any way." In languages where the passive form is a problem, translators may wish to say "So we did not harm you in any way."

Through us means "because of what we did" (REB "from what we did"). Though it is possible to understand RSV as implying that the Corinthians experienced loss because of what others did, such an understanding reads too much into Paul's words.

7.10 RSV TEV

For godly grief produces a repentance that leads to salvation and brings no regret, but worldly grief produces death.	For the sadness that is used by God brings a change of heart that leads to salvation—and there is no regret in that! But sadness that is merely human causes death.

Paul uses three "event" nouns followed by an adjective in the first half of this verse: **grief, repentance, salvation**, and **no regret**. Most likely the Corinthians are the ones who experienced grief, who repented, who will be saved, and who had no regrets. But it is also possible to understand that Paul was the one who had no regrets, that is, "For the sadness that God causes you brings about a change in your hearts that leads to your salvation, and I do not regret that." See verse 8: "I do not regret it (though I did regret it)."

NCV translates this verse, not as a particular reference to the Corinthians, but as a general statement regarding repentance: "Being sorry in the way God wants makes a person change his heart and life. This leads to salvation, and we cannot be sorry for that . . . ." The pronoun "we" in NCV includes Paul along with all Christians.

In many languages it will be necessary to make explicit the agents of these "event" nouns and the adjective. The context favors understanding the reference to be to the Corinthians specifically and not to Christians in general. And the structure of the sentence in Greek favors having the same agent, that is, the Corinthians rather than Paul, as the one having **no regret**.

Produces: twice in this verse and once in the next verse, Paul uses verbs translated as **produces** in RSV. The sense of these verbs is "to bring about," "to give rise to," or "to create." The two Greek verbs come from the same stem and are synonyms here.

On the meaning of **repentance** see comments on 7.9, where the same Greek word is translated as "repenting" in RSV.

Worldly grief is contrasted with **godly grief**. **Worldly** here means "merely human" (TEV). Some possible models for these two expressions may be "when God makes you feel sorry . . . when this world makes you feel sorry" (CEV); "distress, accepted as God means it to be accepted . . . distress, regarded from the world's point of view" (Brc).

Salvation and **death**: on the term **salvation** see 1.6 and 6.2, where the same term is used. It is possible that **salvation** here refers to the spiritual well-being of the church community at Corinth as in 1.6. More likely, however, Paul is thinking here of the future salvation of individual Christians. Since **death** stands in contrast to **salvation** in this verse, **death** is not primarily physical death but rather spiritual death.

7.11   RSV   TEV

For see what earnestness this godly grief has produced in you, what eagerness to clear yourselves, what indignation, what alarm, what longing, what zeal, what punishment! At every point you have proved yourselves guiltless in the matter.

See what God did with this sadness of yours: how earnest it has made you, how eager to prove your innocence! Such indignation, such alarm, such feelings, such devotion, such readiness to punish wrongdoing! You have shown yourselves to be without fault in the whole matter.

In this verse Paul lists several nouns that involve strong emotions. The nouns appear as a disconnected list, yet every one of them is related to events in the experience of the Corinthians that Titus had reported to Paul (see verses 6 and 7).

The style of this verse in Greek is difficult to capture in translation. A more literal translation than RSV may express something of the force and style of the first sentence of verse 11: "For behold this very being made sorrowful by God how great an earnestness it has produced in you—not only that but also eagerness to defend yourselves, not only that but also such indignation, not only that but also such alarm, not only that but such longing, not only that but such zeal, not only that but such punishment!"

For see . . . : the word translated **see** is the same one rendered "behold" in 5.17 and 6.2,9. It is used here to highlight the fact that God used remorse to bring about positive change. The receptor language may have a very different way of focusing on an important notion such as this. But translators should look for the most natural way of doing this.

Earnestness: this noun is rendered by Knox as "devotion." AB speaks of "your concern [to defend yourselves]." The same word is translated "zeal" in Rom 12.8 and 11. It involves enthusiasm and intensity in carrying out any activity. In this context the enthusiasm is for self defense.

The terms in this verse should be understood against the background of 2.1-11. **Eagerness to clear yourselves**: literally "defense." The context indicates that the sense is "eagerness to clear themselves of siding with the offender against Paul. Indeed, they showed **indignation**, anger, at what the offender had done.

The word **alarm** is the word usually translated as "fear." They took very seriously the problem caused by the offender.

On **longing** and **zeal**, see comments on 7.7.

The Greek does not state what the object of their **longing** was, nor does TEV. The object is probably "Paul," that is, their desire to see him again. REB reads "your longing for me," while Phps has "you long for my presence."

The noun **punishment** carries an implicit subject and object. Who punished whom? TEV states the object to be "wrongdoing." If, as seems probable, Paul is thinking of the situation discussed in 2.1-11, the one to be punished may be "the wrongdoer" (see 7.12). REB says "your eagerness to see justice done!" Indeed RSV, **what punishment**, probably gives a false impression that Paul enjoyed hearing about the kind of punishment that the church exercised.

At every point: literally "in all" as in verse 5 above. TEV attempts to convey this, using the word "whole" in describing **the matter**. It is also possible to translate "in every way" (Mft, NJB, and TNT).

If Paul is writing about the situation mentioned in 2.1-11, then **the matter** refers to that incident. However, **the matter** is probably left vague by Paul because he wants to forget about the case and move on to more important matters.

It may be difficult in some languages to find adequate synonyms for the string of nouns which Paul uses in this verse. In some languages they will have to be translated by a series of verbal expressions such as "it made you very serious. It made you want to prove that you were not wrong. It made you angry and afraid. It made you want to see me. It made you care. It made you want the right thing to be done" (NCV).

7.12	RSV	TEV

RSV	TEV
So although I wrote to you, it was not on account of the one who did the wrong, nor on account of the one who suffered the wrong, but in order that your zeal for us might be revealed to you in the sight of God.	So, even though I wrote that letter, it was not because of the one who did wrong or the one who was wronged. Instead, I wrote it to make plain to you, in God's sight, how deep your devotion to us really is.

So: although some see this transition word as connecting this verse with 5-7, it is more likely that it joins what follows with the entire preceding passage, including 8-11.

On **I wrote** see comments on the "letter" in 7.8.

The one who did the wrong refers to the person mentioned in 2.5-8. The masculine singular participle in Greek shows that the **one who did the wrong** was a male. Some translators may wish to say "that man who acted wrongly" or "the person who committed the bad deed."

Paul does not identify **the one who suffered the wrong**, but he probably is alluding indirectly to himself (see 2.5). However, it is not wise to make this explicit in translation. It will be better to leave the rendering indefinite, as does the original: "the injured party" (Mft); "the one who was hurt" (CEV).

The Greek word translated as **zeal** in RSV is the same word translated as "eagerness" by RSV in 7.11 and is not the same as the Greek word translated as "zeal" in 7.11. Nevertheless, here it seems to be synonymous with the Greek word translated as "zeal" in verse 11. GNC says "your earnest concern for us."

In order that your zeal for us might be revealed to you: Paul here states positively the purpose of his writing after indicating two possible reasons that he did not have in mind. That is, it was not for the sake of the offender nor for the person who had been wronged. Rather it was to bring about an understanding of how much the Corinthians cared for Paul and his associates. Since

Paul is attempting to get the readers of his letter to become aware of something within themselves, some languages may require special grammatical forms or idiomatic expressions here. Although this is stated using a passive verb in RSV, an active formulation will be required in many languages. One may consider saying something like "Rather I wrote to you so that you might see how much you care for us" or ". . . in order that you might come to understand how much you really do love us." CEV makes God the implied agent in the verb "reveal" by translating "so that God would show you how much you do care for us." On the other hand Furnish thinks that the implied agent is the Corinthian congregation itself, though this is less probable.

The phrase **in the sight of God** occurs also at 4.2. See the comments on the similar phrase in 2.17.

7.13   RSV   TEV

Therefore we are comforted.   That is why we were encouraged.
    And besides our own comfort we   Not only were we encouraged;
rejoiced still more at the joy of Titus,   how happy Titus made us with his
because his mind has been set at rest by   happiness over the way in which all of
you all.   you helped to cheer him up!

Therefore: verse 13a states the result of verse 12, and most translations retain 13a with the preceding paragraph (for example, RSV, NRSV, TEV, NJB, NAB).

The pronoun **we** does not include the Corinthian readers.

On the meaning of the word translated as **comforted** in RSV and "encouraged" in TEV, see 1.4. One African translation renders this "our sadness came to an end."

Besides our own comfort: in addition to the fact that Paul and his associates were encouraged, they were even happier about the fact that Titus was cheered up.

His mind has been set at rest is literally "his spirit was set at rest." In this context "spirit" refers to one's inner life of feelings and will. This provides the reason for Titus' happiness. It was because the Corinthians put his mind at ease that he found joy.

Beginning at the paragraph break, this part of the verse may be reworded as one language has done: "Indeed, our sadness came to an end, but we had even greater joy when we heard how you made Titus happy and how you all caused his heart to lie down."

7.14   RSV   TEV

For if I have expressed to him some   I did boast of you to him, and you have
pride in you, I was not put to shame;   not disappointed me. We have always
but just as everything we said to you   spoken the truth to you, and in the

was true, so our boasting before Titus
has proved true.

same way the boast we made to Titus
has proved true.

For: this word introduces a statement about why Paul was pleased that
Titus was so happy.

In Greek this verse begins with the word **if**. It is clear in the context that
Paul is not really expressing doubt about whether he expressed pride in the
Corinthians. To avoid a misunderstanding by English readers, TEV and many
other versions do not use the "if" construction.

The verb **put to shame** is in the passive in Greek. TEV uses the active
voice and makes the subject explicit: "you have not disappointed me." Martin
says "you did not embarrass me." Some languages speak of "seeing shame" and
so translate "you did not cause me to see shame."

A few Greek manuscripts have the word "always" rather than **everything**.
The two words are similar in spelling. RSV follows the preferred manuscript
reading. It is not clear whether TEV (also TOB, NBE) is following the Greek
reading "always" here or whether the TEV translator understands **everything
we said** to mean "we have always spoken."

The tense in Greek (**we said**) may point to a specific time in the past
(RSV, NAB, REB) or to the past as a whole (TEV, TOB, NBE). Also possible but less
likely is that the verb is an epistolary aorist (see comments on 8.17), in which
a verb in the past tense is used for the present. If the last interpretation is
accepted, then Paul is referring to what he has written earlier in this letter
(see 1.12-14 and 4.2).

The exact meaning of the words **before Titus** is not clear. The fact that
some Greek manuscripts have the word "to" instead of "before" indicates that
some scribes thought the word "before" was ambiguous. Though TEV (and NRSV)
may be correct in translating these words as "to Titus," the Greek is ambiguous and may be translated as "before" in the sense of "in the presence of Titus"
(REB).

Proved true: more literally "became true." AB renders this "turned out to
be true." Or possibly one may translate "people can see that what we boasted
to Titus is true (not a lie)."

7.15   RSV   TEV

And his heart goes out all the more to
you, as he remembers the obedience of
you all, and the fear and trembling with
which you received him.

And so his love for you grows stronger,
as he remembers how all of you were
ready to obey his instructions, how you
welcomed him with fear and trembling.

Heart translates the Greek word "bowels" (see comments on 6.12). Even
KJV, which is normally quite literal, here translates "inward affection." The
whole expression **his heart goes out . . . to you** is more literally "his bowels
are abundantly toward you." This simply means that his love for the
Christians at Corinth has grown stronger. NAB reads "His heart embraces you

with an expanding love." And CEV conveys the same idea with the common language equivalent "Titus loves all of you very much."

The word **obedience** is a noun in Greek. Some languages may need to use a verb and make explicit who obeyed whom, as does TEV (REB: "how ready you all were to do what he asked").

Paul uses the words **fear and trembling** in 1 Cor 2.3; Eph 6.5; and Phil 2.12. Pointing to passages such as Exo 15.16 and Psa 2.11, where human beings respond with "fear and trembling" in awareness of God's presence, some interpreters think Paul means here "with fear and trembling in the sight of God" (see 7.1,12). More likely Titus was the object of their **fear and trembling**.

In some languages it may be more natural to restructure the ideas of this verse along the following lines: "Therefore, when he thinks of the way all of you obeyed him and how you received him with great respect, his love for you increases."

7.16   RSV   TEV

I rejoice, because I have perfect confi-   How happy I am that I can depend on
dence in you.   you completely!

Paul's expression of joy and confidence is implicitly in contrast with the concern and anxiety he had concerning the Corinthian church prior to Titus' coming. REB makes this contrast explicit by inserting the word "now": "How happy I am now."

Confidence translates the same Greek word translated in RSV as "having courage" in 5.6,8. The context here favors the meaning "confidence." The adjective **perfect** is literally "all." For this reason TEV uses the adverb "completely." Other versions read "I can repose such full confidence in you" (Knox); "I can trust you fully" (NCV); "I trust you utterly" (NAB). Some languages may have to say "I put my heart in you in all things."

C. The Collection for the Jewish Christians in Jerusalem

(8.1–9.15)

C-1. Christian giving

8.1-15

RSV

1 We want you to know, brethren, about the grace of God which has been shown in the churches of Macedonia, 2 for in a severe test of affliction, their abundance of joy and their extreme poverty have overflowed in a wealth of liberality on their part. 3 For they gave according to their means, as I can testify, and beyond their means, of their own free will, 4 begging us earnestly for the favor of taking part in the relief of the saints— 5 and this, not as we expected, but first they gave themselves to the Lord and to us by the will of God. 6 Accordingly we have urged Titus that as he had already made a beginning, he should also complete among you this gracious work. 7 Now as you excel in everything—in faith, in utterance, in knowledge, in all earnestness, and in your love for us—see that you excel in this gracious work also.

8 I say this not as a command, but to prove by the earnestness of others that your love also is genuine. 9 For you know the grace of our Lord Jesus Christ, that though he was rich, yet for your sake he became poor, so that by his poverty you might become rich. 10 And in this matter I give my advice: it is best for you now to complete what a year ago you began not only to do but to desire, 11 so that your readiness in desiring it may be matched by your completing it out of what you have. 12 For if the readiness is there, it is acceptable according to what a man has, not according to what he has not. 13 I do not mean that others should be eased and you burdened, 14 but that as a matter of equality your abundance at the present time should supply their want, so that their abundance may supply your want, that

TEV

Christian Giving

1 Our brothers, we want you to know what God's grace has accomplished in the churches in Macedonia. 2 They have been severely tested by the troubles they went through; but their joy was so great that they were extremely generous in their giving, even though they are very poor. 3 I can assure you that they gave as much as they could, and even more than they could. Of their own free will 4 they begged us and pleaded for the privilege of having a part in helping God's people in Judea. 5 It was more than we could have hoped for! First they gave themselves to the Lord; and then, by God's will they gave themselves to us as well. 6 So we urged Titus, who began this work, to continue it and help you complete this special service of love. 7 You are so rich in all you have: in faith, speech, and knowledge, in your eagerness to help and in your love for us. And so we want you to be generous also in this service of love.

8 I am not laying down any rules. But by showing how eager others are to help, I am trying to find out how real your own love is. 9 You know the grace of our Lord Jesus Christ; rich as he was, he made himself poor for your sake, in order to make you rich by means of his poverty.

10 My opinion is that it is better for you to finish now what you began last year. You were the first, not only to act, but also to be willing to act. 11 On with it, then, and finish the job! Be as eager to finish it as you were to plan it, and do it with what you now have. 12 If you are eager to give, God will accept your gift on the basis of what you have to give, not on what you don't have.

there may be equality. 15 As it is written, "He who gathered much had nothing over, and he who gathered little had no lack."

13-14 I am not trying to relieve others by putting a burden on you; but since you have plenty at this time, it is only fair that you should help those who are in need. Then, when you are in need and they have plenty, they will help you. In this way both are treated equally. 15 As the scripture says, "The one who gathered much did not have too much, and the one who gathered little did not have too little."

SECTION HEADING: TEV "Christian Giving." Some interpreters consider chapters 8 and 9 to have been originally parts of separate letters (see "Translating 2 Corinthians," page 5). But in the form of 2 Corinthians as it now exists, these two chapters together form a major section of the letter. Some translations (NJB, NAB, LPD, REB) group these two chapters together under a major section heading such as "The collection for the church [or the Christians] in Jerusalem" (REB, LPD, NVSR). Other translations such as RSV and NRSV, which do not use section headings, indicate by leaving extra space before and after this section that these two chapters belong together.

Within this larger unit most translations group verses 1-15 together as a section with a title similar to that in TEV, "Christian Giving." Perhaps more precise are the section headings in LPD and NVSR, which group 8.1-5 together and 8.6-15 together; this makes verses 1-5 and verses 6-15 two separate sections. The first is entitled "An example of generosity" in LPD, while NVSR has "The example of the churches in Macedonia." The section heading for verses 6-15 is then "An appeal to the generosity of the Corinthians."

8.1   RSV   TEV

We want you to know, brethren, about the grace of God which has been shown in the churches of Macedonia,

Our brothers, we want you to know what God's grace has accomplished in the churches in Macedonia.

The pronoun **We** here is clearly contrasted with **you** (plural) and so does not include the readers of the letter.

We want you to know: in some languages it will be more natural to say "We want to inform you" or "Let us tell you."

Brethren: on the translation of this as "brothers and sisters" (NRSV) and "friends" (REB), see the comments on 1.8. For languages that require a possessive pronoun with kinship terms such as "brother," the pronoun "our" may be added, as in TEV. Since Paul writes in the first person singular in verses 3, 8, and 10, it is possible that "my brothers" (GNC) reflects Paul's thought here. In any case it will probably be more natural in most languages to place the term of address at the beginning of the sentence, as in TEV, rather than in the middle, even though the RSV structure reflects the Greek.

The grace of God which has been shown: here and in 9.14 **grace** refers to God's action in the lives of the Christians that causes them to be generous toward others. On **grace** see also the comments on 1.2,12. Some languages will find it unnatural to say that grace was **shown**. A more natural translation may be similar to that of REB, "about the grace that God has given." Or another way to avoid the passive form may be to say "about the way in which God has shown his grace . . . ."

The churches: on translating **churches** see comment on 1.1. Note, however, that here and throughout the rest of this letter (8.18,19,23,24; 11.8,28; 12.13), the word is plural, referring to local assemblies of believers.

Macedonia was a Roman province that included the cities of Philippi, Thessalonica, and Beroea. See comments on 1.16. It may be wise to add the classifier term "province" in many languages.

8.2	RSV	TEV
	for in a severe test of affliction, their abundance of joy and their extreme poverty have overflowed in a wealth of liberality on their part.	They have been severely tested by the troubles they went through; but their joy was so great that they were extremely generous in their giving, even though they are very poor.

For: according to RSV, verse 2 provides the reason that Paul wants the Corinthians to know about the grace which God has shown to the Macedonian churches. The Greek word translated as **for** in RSV may also be translated as "that." Verse 2 then states the thing that Paul wants them to know rather than the reason that he wants them to know: "We want you to know, concerning the grace of God which has been shown in the churches of Macedonia, that . . . ."

The **severe test of affliction** refers to the persecution that the Christians in Macedonia experienced (see 1 Thes 1.6; 2.14; Acts 16.20; 17.50). While the passive model of TEV may be helpful in some languages, this expression will be better rendered by an active verb phrase in other languages: "they saw [experienced] much suffering" or "they were going through hard times" (CEV).

Their abundance of joy: in some languages it will be more natural to use a verb rather than a noun to translate these words: "they have been so exuberantly happy" (REB). A more common language model would be something like "their joy did not end" or "they were always happy."

Their extreme poverty: these words also may be more naturally translated with a verb in some languages: "they are very poor" (TEV). As TEV makes explicit by adding "even though," there is a contrast implied between the fact that they were very poor and the fact that they gave generously. The structure of RSV reflects the Greek, but it will be more natural in some languages to put this expression about poverty together with the one about suffering, since they are both seen as negative. Some translations begin the verse with "although they experienced much suffering, and although they themselves were in great need . . . ."

Overflowed in a wealth of liberality on their part: with the previous phrases this is literally "abundance of joy of them and deep poverty of them overflowed to [yield] riches of liberality." Logically this is contradictory since it is difficult to see how extreme poverty could result in riches even when accompanied by great joy. But Paul is not trying to be logical here. What he is talking about goes beyond reasoning. As the following verses indicate, Paul is referring to the fact that the Macedonian Christians were "extremely generous in their giving" (TEV) to the collection being raised for the Christians in Jerusalem. The word translated **wealth** and **liberality**, combined with the verb **overflowed**, build up a picture of extravagant charity. It is not essential to find three different words in the receptor language to translate this expression, but the cumulative effect is striking and should be reflected, if it is possible to do so naturally. The verb **overflowed** makes use of an image that may not be meaningful in some receptor languages. Together with the context it is sometimes rendered "caused them to give abundantly" or ". . . to be generous beyond measure" (so TNT).

8.3	RSV	TEV
	For they gave according to their means, as I can testify, and beyond their means, of their own free will,	I can assure you that they gave as much as they could, and even more than they could. Of their own free will

For introduces the description of how the Macedonians gave so generously.

They gave: these words are not actually in the Greek text of verse 3; they are introduced from verse 5. But in most languages it will be essential to have such a verb at this point.

According to their means: literally "according to power." TEV correctly translates the sense "as much as they could." This expression stands in parallel with **beyond their means**, which follows. Together they are translated by CEV "as much as they could afford and even more." In some languages the second expression may be translated "they went beyond the limit . . . ."

As I can testify means that Paul serves as a witness; that is, he has personal knowledge of the situation and can therefore speak reliably regarding the Macedonian Christians. Note that TEV shifts this forward to the beginning of the verse, translating "I can assure you . . . ." This may be a good model to follow in other languages.

Of their own free will: these words may be considered a part of the sentence which precedes, that is, the Macedonians gave of their own free will (so RSV, NRSV, NJB, SPCL), or to the sentence which follows in verse 4, that is, of their own free will they begged to take part in the collection (so TEV, NIV, REB, NJB, TNT, FRCL). The latter interpretation follows the punctuation of the UBS *Greek New Testament* and is probably more likely.

8.4   RSV   TEV

begging us earnestly for the favor of taking part in the relief of the saints—	they begged us and pleaded for the privilege of having a part in helping God's people in Judea.

Begging us earnestly: literally "with much appealing begging us." This has been rendered "They begged us insistently" (NAB) and "imploring us most urgently" (AB). In some languages one may say "they would not stop begging us" or "they urged us time after to time [to allow them] . . . ."

The favor of taking part in the relief is literally "the grace (*charis*) and the fellowship (*koinōnia*) of the service (*diakonia*)." As in Acts 11.29, the word translated **relief** in RSV, *diakonia,* is more frequently rendered "service" or "ministry" (see 4.1; 5.18; 6.3), although RSV has "dispensation" in 3.7-9. The opportunity of contributing to help fellow Christians was considered an advantage or a privilege instead of a responsibility or a burden. The NRSV translation retains the sense that the help is seen as a form of ministry or service: "the privilege of sharing in this ministry." Similarly REB retains the idea of service: "to share in this generous service."

The relief of the saints refers specifically to the collection that Paul was gathering for Jewish Christians in Jerusalem (see 1 Cor 16.1-4; Gal 2.10; Rom 15.25-28). TEV makes this reference clear with the translation "helping God's people in Judea." Since Paul elsewhere states that the collection is for saints in Jerusalem (Rom 15.25,31; 1 Cor 16.3), translators may wish to follow the model of LPD and ITCL by adding the words "in Jerusalem" rather than "in Judea," as in TEV. On the translation of the word **saints**, see comments on 1.1 above.

8.5   RSV   TEV

and this, not as we expected, but first they gave themselves to the Lord and to us by the will of God.	It was more than we could have hoped for! First they gave themselves to the Lord; and then, by God's will they gave themselves to us as well.

This: the reference is back to the act of giving on the part of the Macedonians, explained in verses 3 and 4. NCV makes this more explicit by repeating the verb: "and they gave [in a way that we did not expect]."

Not as we expected: more literally "not according as we had hoped." This element may fit more naturally into the structure of the receptor language at the end of the verse than at the beginning. Having stated what the churches of Macedonia did, one may say in a separate sentence something like "That was not at all what we had expected" or "We did not think that they could give like that."

The word **first** may have temporal significance, meaning that the first thing they did was to give themselves to the Lord (so TEV, FRCL). But the meaning can be that the most important thing they did was to give themselves to the Lord. REB reflects the second interpretation: "for first of all they gave themselves to the Lord and, under God, to us" (also NAB).

They gave themselves to the Lord and to us: the Macedonian Christians submitted their will to that of the Lord and to the apostles. **The Lord** is most likely Christ, not God the Father.

By the will of God: the sense is that they did that which God wished. These words are frequently used in the introductions to Paul's letters to explain how he became an apostle (see 1.1). In this context one may wish to translate using a verbal expression such as "because God desired it" or "just as God wanted them to" (CEV).

8.6	RSV	TEV

Accordingly we have urged Titus that as he had already made a beginning, he should also complete among you this gracious work.	So we urged Titus, who began this work, to continue it and help you complete this special service of love.

Note that CEV and Phps begin a new paragraph at this point, but most English versions follow the UBS *Greek New Testament,* which has no break here.

Accordingly translates a Greek construction that introduces in verse 6 the result of the Macedonian churches' example in the preceding verses. REB begins verse 6 with the words "the upshot is that."

Titus: see comments on 2.13.

As he had already made a beginning probably means that Titus had earlier begun to organize the collection in Corinth (see 8.10). Since this is information about something that happened before the events Paul is now relating, it may be better to place it at the beginning of the verse, possibly in a separate sentence: "Titus was the one who got you started doing this good thing . . ." (CEV). In other languages it may fit better at the end of the verse as in TNT: "he was in charge of it at the beginning."

He should complete among you: Titus was assigned the responsibility to help the Corinthians complete the raising of the collection.

This gracious work is literally "this grace," using the same word as in verse 4, where it is translated "favor." Perhaps Paul was thinking of God's undeserved favor in giving to the Corinthians the desire to give generously (see 8.1).

8.7	RSV	TEV

Now as you excel in everything—in faith, in utterance, in knowledge, in all earnestness, and in your love for us—	You are so rich in all you have: in faith, speech, and knowledge, in your eagerness to help and in your love for us.[e]

see that you excel in this gracious work also.	And so we want you to be generous also in this service of love.

^e your love for us; *some manuscripts have* our love for you.

The Greek word translated as **Now** in RSV may be understood to indicate a contrast with what precedes, "But." Paul's appeal is based not only on the example of the Macedonian Christians, but also on an appeal to the spiritual resources of the Corinthian Christians.

You excel in everything: the verb used here has the meaning "to have more than enough" or "to be present in abundance," and by extension, "to be extremely rich." This is the same Greek verb translated by RSV as "have overflowed" in 8.2. Just as the churches of Macedonia had "overflowed," now the church in Corinth is "overflowing" **in everything**. However, the comparative idea of CEV ("You do everything better than anyone else") should probably be avoided. Translators may rather consider "you are rich in every respect" (NAB) or "you are outstanding in every sphere" (Brc).

Faith here can refer to "faith that saves" or, more likely, to "faith that performs miracles" (see 1 Cor 12.9,10).

In utterance is literally "in word." Here Paul is referring to the ability to speak eloquently (see 1 Cor 1.5). NJB, GNC, and LPD translate this as "eloquence," REB as "discourse."

In knowledge refers to knowledge about spiritual realities. In 1 Corinthians Paul speaks frequently about **knowledge**. Jesus Christ is said to be its source (1.5). But it is passing (13.8) and without love it is useless (13.2) and can actually cause pride (8.1) and the destruction of others (8.11). See also the use of this term in 2 Cor 6.6.

In all earnestness is translated as "concern for everything" (NJB) and "the utmost zeal" (GNC). The Corinthians have a zeal for the Christian cause. See 7.11 and 12.

In some languages it will be more natural to translate the nouns **faith**, **utterance**, **knowledge**, and **earnestness** as verbal expressions. A possible model using verbal expressions may be "you have strong faith, you preach well, you are very wise, and you do not give up."

The Greek manuscripts provide strong support for two different readings in this verse. The editors of the UBS *Greek New Testament* have followed the more difficult reading, "in our love for you" (literally "the from us in you [plural] love"). This reading is followed by NRSV: "in our love for you" (so also revised NAB, AB; footnotes of TEV and NIV). TOB, ITCL, and Martin also follow the text of the UBS *Greek New Testament* but with different interpretations from that in NRSV and from each other. TOB says "and the love that you have received from us," meaning that the love originating with Paul and his companions is now dwelling within the Corinthians. ITCL says "and among you there is that love that I have taught you to have." Martin translates "in the love that we have aroused in you," and explains this as referring to the readers' attitude to Paul. According to Martin, the sense is that Paul's love has aroused the Corinthians to love Paul in return. This understanding agrees in part with the translation in RSV, which is based on a different reading in the Greek text.

The other reading, **in your love for us** (RSV, TEV, NIV), seems more appropriate in the context of this verse; but precisely because the other reading is more difficult, a scribe may have changed the text to read "in your love for us." The editors of the UBS *Greek New Testament* give a "C" evaluation to this reading, meaning that translators should feel free to choose either reading.

The above discussion shows that, even when translators have decided which Greek reading to translate, they still have the difficult task of determining the exact meaning of the words. If the text of the UBS *Greek New Testament* is followed, then TOB and ITCL seem to capture more faithfully the correct meaning. It is probably going to far to specify that the love the Corinthians have is for Paul. In line with the ITCL translation, one may say "and there is among you that love that we [I] taught you to have [for all people]."

See that you excel in this gracious work also: literally "in order that in this grace you might overflow also," repeating with imperative meaning the same verb used in the indicative earlier in this verse. RSV correctly translates these words as a command. **Also** indicates that as they have excelled in the items mentioned in 8.7, they must likewise excel in their contribution to the poor in Jerusalem.

The structure of this verse will require special attention in many languages, since the words set off by dashes in RSV constitute a sort of parenthetical statement and contain considerable implicit information. One possible structure for the whole verse is the following:

> You have great faith. You know how to preach well. You have much knowledge and are so sincere. And you love us very much. In fact, you do everything so extremely well. So we really want you to do especially well also in this matter of giving generously.

8.8   RSV   TEV

I say this not as a command, but to prove by the earnestness of others that your love also is genuine.

I am not laying down any rules. But by showing how eager others are to help, I am trying to find out how real your own love is.

The words **I say this not as a command** point back to what Paul has just written in the preceding verses. Some other possible models, in addition to TEV, are "I am not saying that you must do it" (GNW) or "I am not issuing any orders" (Mft).

But to prove: the conjunction marks contrast between what Paul is not doing (issuing orders) and what he really hopes to do. In some languages it will be necessary to add the implied information following the conjunction: "but what I want to do is to prove . . . ." AB has "I intend to verify the reality of your love."

The earnestness of others refers to the generosity of the Macedonian Christians. The generosity of the Macedonian Christians becomes the standard by which Paul measures the love of the Corinthians. Martin says "but I am seeking to try out the reality of your love also by using the eagerness of others [as a standard]."

Your love has no stated object. Probably Paul is thinking primarily of their love for fellow Christians, and perhaps also for him (see 8.24). In those languages where an object is required, one may say simply "for other people."

Genuine: the word so translated is rendered "true" in Phil 4.3; 1 Tim 1.2; Titus 1.4. It is the opposite of fake, counterfeit or false. In some languages it may be translated negatively by saying something like "not a lie" or something similar. Others may have specific terms used in commerce to distinguish quality goods from inferior imitations. If such a term is used figuratively, it would be appropriate here.

8.9	RSV	TEV
	For you know the grace of our Lord Jesus Christ, that though he was rich, yet for your sake he became poor, so that by his poverty you might become rich.	You know the grace of our Lord Jesus Christ; rich as he was, he made himself poor for your sake, in order to make you rich by means of his poverty.

Verse 9 is somewhat parenthetical in nature, interrupting the flow of Paul's argument to ground his appeal in the example of Christ. Though some interpreters understand this verse as referring to the conditions of Jesus' earthly life, more likely Paul is alluding to the incarnation. The **grace** to which Paul refers, *charis,* is explained as the fact that Christ, who was rich, became poor for the sake of the Corinthians. REB translates **grace** here as "the generosity." *Charis* is also found in verse 4, where it is translated **favor**, and in verse 6, where RSV renders it **gracious work**.

He was rich and **he became poor** are not to be understood in terms of financial wealth. **Rich** refers to Christ's divine existence prior to the incarnation. **Became poor** refers to the incarnation, that is, to his birth as a human being. In some languages this may be better translated "he abandoned his wealth."

Your sake: a few manuscripts read "our sake" instead of **your sake**. The editors of the UBS *Greek New Testament* give a "B" evaluation to the reading of the text, indicating that the pronoun "your" is almost certain to be the correct reading, but that there is some degree of doubt. The pronoun "our" is not at all contrary to Paul's theology, and it is easy to understand why a scribe would change pronouns to include Paul as well as the readers. The context and the best manuscripts, however, strongly favor the reading in the UBS *Greek New Testament*.

By his poverty: literally "by the poverty of that one." This expression indicates that the means of the Corinthians becoming spiritually rich was the voluntary impoverishment of Christ.

Become rich: while this is clearly not intended to refer to material wealth, readers in many languages will easily understand the figurative sense in this context. If, however, there is any danger of this expression being taken literally, it may be necessary to clarify the meaning by saying something like "rich in the eyes of God."

8.10

RSV	TEV
And in this matter I give my advice: it is best for you now to complete what a year ago you began not only to do but to desire,	My opinion is that it is better for you to finish now what you began last year. You were the first, not only to act, but also to be willing to act.

While there is no new paragraph here in RSV, it will probably be better to follow TEV, CEV, REB, and others in making a break at this point.

In this matter is simply "in this" in Greek. These words may look back to what Paul has just written about the reality of their love, or it may look ahead to his comments about the collection. The latter seems probable, though Paul's comments about their "love" and about "the collection" are closely related. If it seems necessary to clarify the meaning, translators may consider the following models: "I will tell you what I think about the collection . . ." or "Now about the matter of gathering money, I want you to know how I feel . . . ."

It is best for you . . . : literally "for this is fitting for you who were the kind of people not only to do . . . ." The Greek pronoun is not the simple relative pronoun "who." It is difficult in translation to capture the sense of the pronoun "who were the kind of people," and neither RSV nor TEV do so. GNC attempts to preserve the force of this Greek pronoun: "I am simply offering an opinion, that being the proper course to take with people like you who led the way . . . ." Martin also attempts to maintain the force of the Greek pronoun: "for this advice befits you, you who last year were those who . . . ."

A year ago is literally "from last year." The period covered can be from a couple of months ago to twenty-three months ago. The Greek does not necessarily mean "twelve months ago." Both **a year ago** and "last year" are possible translations. The RSV translation suggests an interval of twelve months, which is more precise than what we can really know.

You began: the Greek word translated as **you began** in RSV is ambiguous. Literally the word is "you began beforehand," and RSV does not fully capture the sense of this verb. Probably it means that the Corinthians began "first" (TEV), that is, before the Macedonians (so also Martin, see 9.2). Although less likely, it is possible that this means that they began "before Titus had come to Corinth."

Not only to do but to desire: the logical order is that one first desires something and then one acts on that desire. Paul has reversed the order here, however, to give emphasis to their desire. For Paul it was important that the Corinthians began to collect money for the Christians in Jerusalem, but it was even more important that they had the desire to do so.

A possible model for this verse as a whole is provided by Knox: "I am only giving you my advice, then, in this matter: you can claim that as your due, since it was you who led the way, not only in acting, but in proposing to act, as early as last year." Providing a different model, CEV restructures the verse as follows: "A year ago you were the first ones to give, and you gave because you wanted to. So listen to my advice. [11] I think you should finish what you started." It should be noted, however, that the RSV words **to complete now** occur as a part of this verse; yet CEV translates them as the first part of verse 11, which is where the idea of completion is found in Greek. The problem is that RSV has expressed the idea of completing in this verse and then repeated it in the following verse, but CEV has chosen to translate this idea only once.

8.11 RSV	TEV
so that your readiness in desiring it may be matched by your completing it out of what you have.	On with it, then, and finish the job! Be as eager to finish it as you were to plan it, and do it with what you now have.

So that: RSV continues the sentence started at the beginning of verse 10, but this connection is misleading. The Greek of this verse actually begins "but now . . . ." This contrasts the present time with "last year" in verse 10. Having reminded his readers that they had initiated the idea of a collection during the previous year, Paul now urges them to see to it that the task is completed.

Readiness: this word is repeated in verses 12 and 19 of this chapter as well as in 9.2. In Acts 17.11 it is translated "eagerness." It has to do with a willingness or predisposition to do something.

Desiring . . . completing: here Paul uses two infinitives preceded by definite articles, literally "the to will . . . the to complete." That is, the verbs are used as nouns. This may be translated "you eagerly wanted to do it, so now do it," or in some cases reversing the order to these two elements, "be as eager to complete . . . as to plan."

May be matched: this may be translated "be as eager to X as to Y," as indicated above. Such a structure will avoid the difficult passive form of RSV.

Out of what you have: obviously whatever the Corinthians would give would have to come out of what they had. The sense seems to be that they were to give, not by concerning themselves with how much the Macedonians had given, but rather by considering how much they were able to give out of what resources they had. Barrett translates "as far as your resources permit."

A literal translation of this verse reads as follows: "But now also finish the doing just as the readiness to desire so also the finishing from the having." Possible models for the verse as a whole are: "I think you should finish what you started. If you give according to what you have, you will prove that you are as eager to give as you were to think about giving" (CEV), "It is now time to complete what you started, using what you have now. Prove that you can finish the job as eagerly as you started it," or "So now finish the job. By giving as much as you can, you will show people that you are eager to act as well as to plan for action."

8.12   RSV   TEV

For if the readiness is there, it is accept-   If you are eager to give, God will accept
able according to what a man has, not   your gift on the basis of what you have
according to what he has not.   to give, not on what you don't have.

If the readiness is there: this, of course, refers to the willingness of the Corinthians to give to those in need. In most languages it will be more natural to fill in what is implied here: "if you really want to give . . . ."

It is acceptable: the Greek does not specify to whom the gift will be acceptable. TEV no doubt correctly makes God the subject of the verb: "God will accept your gift." Less likely, the Christians in Jerusalem could be the subject, since in Rom 16.31 Paul expresses concern that the Jerusalem Christians might accept the collection.

The Greek verbs are in the third person singular, which RSV makes apply to a hypothetical **man**. Since the context makes it clear that these words are spoken concerning the situation of the Corinthians, TEV changes to second person pronouns. These, of course, are to be understood as second person plurals and should be so translated in most receptor languages. Some, however, may prefer a general statement more like the Greek: "God accepts gifts on the basis of what people are able to give, not on the basis of what they cannot give."

8.13-14   RSV   TEV

13 I do not mean that others should be   13-14 I am not trying to relieve
eased and you burdened, 14 but that as   others by putting a burden on you; but
a matter of equality your abundance at   since you have plenty at this time, it is
the present time should supply their   only fair that you should help those who
want, so that their abundance may sup-   are in need. Then, when you are in need
ply your want, that there may be equal-   and they have plenty, they will help
ity.   you. In this way both are treated equal-
          ly.

The verse division in the UBS *Greek New Testament* is different from that in RSV. In the Greek verse 14 begins with the words **your abundance at the present time**. For this reason TEV combines verses 13 and 14.

That others should be eased: or, more literally, "that others should have relief" (AB). The word "relief" is the same as used in 2.13 and 7.5, where it is rendered "rest" in RSV. In the context of Acts 24.23 this word is translated "liberty." In some languages one may translate this phrase "I do not mean to place a heavy load on you so that other people can carry a light load . . . ."

Equality: the two phrases containing this term may be translated by a single sentence in some languages. It may be possible to say "I want things to be equal for everyone involved."

Your abundance . . . their abundance: the idea here is more like superabundance, that is, what is left over when all normal needs are taken care of. The same word is used of the "pieces left over" in the feeding of the four thousand in Mark 8.8. Here AB translates "your surplus . . . their surplus."

At the present time: though the same words are found in Rom 8.18 and refer to the time of suffering before God's glory is revealed, it is not likely that such a theological meaning is intended here. In this context Paul seems to be referring only to the time when the Jerusalem Christians have needs and the Corinthian Christians have resources enough to help meet those needs.

Their want is literally "the needs of others." Note that NRSV has changed the word **want** to "need," and most other modern versions translate this way. Paul is referring to the needs of the Jerusalem Christians. Some interpreters think that Paul is referring to the needs of the Macedonian Christians, but translators who retain the pronoun **their** or a similar expression will not have to decide this issue.

So that their abundance may supply your want: at the time when Paul was writing, the Jerusalem Christians did not have an abundance. TEV adds the word "when" to indicate that Paul is referring to a future time when the situations of the two groups of Christians might be reversed. LPD says "so that one day their abundance might supply your needs."

Their want and **your want**: the meaning is not "that which is desired or wanted" but rather "what is lacking and needed." It stands in contrast with **your abundance** and **their abundance**.

8.15	RSV	TEV
	As it is written, "He who gathered much had nothing over, and he who gathered little had no lack."	As the scripture says, "The one who gathered much did not have too much, and the one who gathered little did not have too little."

As it is written: TEV and REB make explicit that this quotation is written in the "scripture." The citation comes from Exo 16.18, concerning the gathering of the manna in the wilderness. For Paul this verse illustrated the point concerning equality, though in Exodus the equality was not due to voluntary sharing of resources. In languages that require an object for the verb "to gather," the word "manna" should be supplied. Barclay says "As scripture said about the manna."

He who gathered: since many people were involved in gathering manna, some languages may require that plurals be used in both cases where this expression is found: "the people who gathered much . . . and the people who gathered little." Similarly CEV.

Had nothing over . . . no lack: various English renderings may suggest other ways of saying this in the receptor language: "had nothing extra . . . no shortage" (AB); "had not too much . . . not too little" (TNT); "had nothing left . . . had all they needed" (CEV).

C-2. Titus and his companions
8.16-24

RSV	TEV
	Titus and His Companions
16 But thanks be to God who puts the same earnest care for you into the heart of Titus. 17 For he not only accepted our appeal, but being himself very earnest he is going to you of his own accord. 18 With him we are sending the brother who is famous among all the churches for his preaching of the gospel; 19 and not only that, but he has been appointed by the churches to travel with us in this gracious work which we are carrying on, for the glory of the Lord and to show our good will. 20 We intend that no one should blame us about this liberal gift which we are administering, 21 for we aim at what is honorable not only in the Lord's sight but also in the sight of men. 22 And with them we are sending our brother whom we have often tested and found earnest in many matters, but who is now more earnest than ever because of his great confidence in you. 23 As for Titus, he is my partner and fellow worker in your service; and as for our brethren, they are messengers of the churches, the glory of Christ. 24 So give proof, before the churches, of your love and of our boasting about you to these men.	16 How we thank God for making Titus as eager as we are to help you! 17 Not only did he welcome our request; he was so eager to help that of his own free will he decided to go to you. 18 With him we are sending the brother who is highly respected in all the churches for his work in preaching the gospel. 19 And besides that, he has been chosen and appointed by the churches to travel with us as we carry out this service of love for the sake of the Lord's glory and in order to show that we want to help. 20 We are being careful not to stir up any complaints about the way we handle this generous gift. 21 Our purpose is to do what is right, not only in the sight of the Lord, but also in the sight of man. 22 So we are sending our brother with them; we have tested him many times and found him always very eager to help. And now that he has so much confidence in you, he is all the more eager to help. 23 As for Titus, he is my partner and works with me to help you; as for the other brothers who are going with him, they represent the churches and bring glory to Christ. 24 Show your love to them, so that all the churches will be sure of it and know that we are right in boasting about you.

SECTION HEADING: TEV "Titus and His Companions." Paul informs the Corinthians that Titus and two other Christian colleagues are being sent to Corinth to receive the collection from the Christians there (see 8.6). He emphasizes the trustworthiness of these individuals and the fact that they are messengers chosen by the churches. Only Titus is identified by name. For this reason the heading in NIV reads "Titus Sent to Corinth." Other versions attempt to reflect the fact that more than one person was involved. The NJB section heading here is "The delegates recommended to the Corinthians."

8.16   RSV   TEV

But thanks be to God who puts the same earnest care for you into the heart of Titus.	**How we thank God for making Titus as eager as we are to help you!**

The Greek noun **thanks** has no explicit subject (see also 9.15). TEV uses a verb ("thank") with the exclusive pronoun "we" as the subject. REB makes Paul alone the subject of the verb: "I thank God." The expression **thanks be to God** is typically Pauline, occurring also in Rom 6.17; 7.25; 1 Cor 15.57; 2 Cor 2.14; 9.15, although the word order in Greek varies in two cases.

The same . . . : Paul does not state the complete comparison when he writes that Titus has the same concern. To whom is Titus' concern compared? Probably to the concern that Paul himself has for the Corinthians (see verse 17). TEV and REB make this comparison explicit: "as eager as we are." NRSV makes Paul alone the point of comparison: "the same eagerness for you that I myself have." It is also possible, but less likely in light of verse 17, that the comparison is between Titus' zeal and the zeal of the Corinthians (7.11; 8.7) and of the Macedonians (8.8).

Earnest care translates the same Greek word translated in RSV as "earnestness" in 7.11; 8.7,8; and "zeal" in 7.12.

On the **heart** as the center of one's will, rational activity, and moral choice, see comments on 1.22;3.3,15. In this context the idea of God's putting concern into the heart of Titus may be expressed by a causative verb form in some languages. In others translators may wish to say something like "I thank God because he gave Titus the same love for you that I have" (NCV) or "I am grateful that God made Titus care as much about you as we do" (CEV).

8.17   RSV   TEV

For he not only accepted our appeal, but being himself very earnest he is going to you of his own accord.	**Not only did he welcome our request; he was so eager to help that of his own free will he decided to go to you.**

The word **For** introduces the statement that indicates why Paul is able to speak of Titus as he does in verse 16. In some languages it may be left implicit, as in TEV.

Our appeal: that is, "our urging" (NJB) or "what we asked him to do" (NCV). Note that Mft, AT, and ITCL take the plural pronoun here as referring only to Paul, and thus translate using the singular "my." The expression

accepted our appeal may be better rendered "he agreed to do what we asked him to do."

Being himself very earnest: as TEV makes explicit, Titus was eager "to help" with the collection.

He is going to you is literally "he went to you." This use of the past tense, in which the writer expresses himself from the time perspective of the readers as they read the letter, is called an epistolary aorist (see 7.14; 9.5). 8.24 seems to indicate that Paul's letter was to arrive in Corinth at the same time as Titus and the two other companions. The present tense, **he is going**, correctly expresses the sense in English.

Of his own accord: this comment seems to contradict Paul's earlier statement in this same verse that he had urged Titus to go to Corinth. The sense must be that Titus was already wishing to make the trip even before Paul urged him to go.

A good model for this verse as a whole is found in TNT, which reads "We asked him to come to you and he agreed, but he was all ready to come to you of his own free will." Or "When we begged Titus to visit, he said he would. He wanted to because he cared so much for you" (CEV).

8.18	RSV	TEV
	With him we are sending the brother who is famous among all the churches for his preaching of the gospel;	With him we are sending the brother who is highly respected in all the churches for his work in preaching the gospel.

We are sending is literally "we sent." Paul has again used the past tense when writing about a future event; this is an epistolary aorist (see 8.17). The three individuals had not already been sent when Paul was writing; rather, they were about to be sent, probably taking this letter with them.

The brother will require a possessive pronoun in some languages. Possibly this person was Titus' own brother. More likely Paul means simply "a fellow Christian." Since this "brother" was known to Paul and his companions but may not yet have been known to the Corinthians, the exclusive first person plural pronoun may be used: "our brother." See the comments below on the words **all the churches**.

This **brother** is said to be **famous** for his **preaching of the gospel**. The Greek is literally "of whom the praise in the gospel in all the churches." What exactly does "in the gospel" mean? Most interpreters take it to mean that he preached (RSV, TEV, NAB). Since the Greek is not specific, some translations use a general expression such as "for his service to the gospel" (NIV; also REB, TOB, Lu, LPD). The choice of a verb to translate the idea of fame or praise may require a slight change in the subject of the verb. In some languages this clause may have to be rephrased as follows: "the brother whom the people in all the churches respect for his work in proclaiming the Good News."

All the churches: on the word **churches** see comments on verse 1 of this chapter. The term is used again in verse 19. It is not clear how inclusive the words **all the churches** are here. If Paul refers only to the churches in Macedonia, as in 8.1, then the Corinthian readers probably did not know **the brother** mentioned in this verse. If **all the churches** includes the Corinthians, then they would have known this man whom Paul was sending with Titus.

8.19	RSV	TEV

and not only that, but he has been ap-pointed by the churches to travel with us in this gracious work which we are carrying on, for the glory of the Lord and to show our good will.	And besides that, he has been chosen and appointed by the churches to travel with us as we carry out this service of love for the sake of the Lord's glory and in order to show that we want to help.

And not only that: this element seems to be omitted by NAB and CEV. However, the wording found here is often used to compare something important with something even more important and should probably be represented in the receptor language. The use of the word "too" in Knox is an attempt to get at this ("he too is a man whom the churches have appointed"). REB has "moreover," and NJB renders it "what is more."

He has been appointed: the passive formulation here will have to be made active in many languages. But since the agent is specified in the original, this should present no major problems. The meaning is "the churches selected him . . . ." However, in some cases the expression used for "churches" may not fit logically with verbs such as "choose" or "appoint." If this is the case one may have to say "the people of the churches chose . . . ."

By the churches: probably refers to the churches in Macedonia (8.1-6), or possibly by the churches of Asia Minor, or even by the churches in Judea. Since the churches were just mentioned in the previous verse, REB uses a pronoun here: "they have duly appointed him . . . ."

To travel with us: Paul is not speaking about traveling around in general. Rather the brother mentioned in verse 18 is to travel with Paul on this specific trip regarding the collection, probably all the way to Jerusalem. ITCL says "Moreover, the churches have appointed him to accompany me in the trip that I'm making in order to carry to the end this generous pledge."

This gracious work: "this *charis*"; literally "this grace" as in verse 6 above. No doubt Paul has in mind the specific task of sharing with those in need. CEV translates "while we carry this gift," while Mft has "on the business of administering this fund."

The relationship of the final clause, that is, **for the glory . . . our good will**, to what precedes is not clear. With most translations TEV connects this clause with "we carry out this service." It is also possible, however, to connect this clause with the words **he has been appointed by the churches to travel with us** (so AB).

On **the glory of the Lord**, see comments on 1.20; see also 4.15. The **Lord** here is probably God. The UBS *Greek New Testament* prints the pronoun "himself" in square brackets, and the editors express considerable doubt about the correct reading by giving a "C" evaluation to the decision to include the pronoun in the text. If translators follow the UBS *Greek New Testament* (so NRSV, REB, NIV, TOB, AB), the translation will say "for the glory of the Lord himself."

To show our good will: the sense is probably that found in TEV "to show that we want to help," and NAB "for the expression of our eagerness." However, if these words connect to the words **appointed by the churches**, then the sense may be that Paul has shown his good will by agreeing to have this Christian travel with them for the purpose of proving that Paul is not being irresponsible or dishonest in his handling of the money (see verse 20).

8.20 RSV	TEV
We intend that no one should blame us about this liberal gift which we are administering,	We are being careful not to stir up any complaints about the way we handle this generous gift.

We intend: the verb used here has the idea of "We avoid" or "We guard" against something undesirable. Paul is not concerned about being criticized for having raised large sums of money. He is concerned lest people think that he is taking the money for his own use and profit. Mft says "for I want to take precautions against any risk of suspicion in connection with the administration of this charity." And Phps has "naturally we want to avoid the slightest breath of criticism in the distribution of their gifts."

Blame: this verb is found only here and in 6.3, where it is translated by the idea of "finding fault." However, the noun meaning "blot" or "blemish" is found in 2 Peter 2.13, and its opposite "blameless" or "without blemish" occurs more frequently (see, for example, Eph 1.4 and 1 Thes 3.13). Here it is clearly a matter of Paul's wishing to avoid any hint of dishonesty or incompetence in handling money that did not belong to him.

The **liberal gift** translates a word that indicates "abundance." In the specific context of this chapter, the reference is to the large amount of money collected for the church in Jerusalem. REB translates this word as "these large sums."

Administering: the idea of the management of funds belonging to other people may be difficult to express in some languages. Several modern English versions use the verb "handle." But in some languages it may be necessary to use two different verbs showing both aspects of this money management. Translators may speak of "collecting and distributing funds." Since Paul probably did not intend to distribute the funds himself, it may be better to say "overseeing the collection and distribution."

8.21 RSV TEV

for we aim at what is honorable not only in the Lord's sight but also in the sight of men.

Our purpose is to do what is right, not only in the sight of the Lord, but also in the sight of man.

Paul's words in this verse reflect the language and thought of Pro 3.4 in the Septuagint, the Greek translation of the Hebrew scriptures.

We aim at: "we think of beforehand," "we have in mind"; or "we pay attention to" (AB); "we are concerned" (NAB). This may be seen as a more positive and more general statement about what has already been said negatively and more specifically in the previous verse.

What is honorable: that is, what is accepted as proper behavior. Some other ways of saying this are: "being above reproach" (Mft); "what is good" (TNT); "what pleases [the Lord]" (CEV).

In the sight of: that is, "in front of" or "in the presence of," implying the opinion or judgment of the persons viewing. Compare 2.17; 4.2; 7.12.

The Lord in this context is God, the Father, as in 8.19.

Though the Greek is literally "in the sight of men," the sense is clearly "in the sight of human beings" (AB) or "in the sight of people" (NJB). Paul is concerned not merely with pleasing God but also with avoiding the appearance of evil in the eyes of his fellow human beings.

8.22 RSV TEV

And with them we are sending our brother whom we have often tested and found earnest in many matters, but who is now more earnest than ever because of his great confidence in you.

So we are sending our brother with them; we have tested him many times and found him always very eager to help. And now that he has so much confidence in you, he is all the more eager to help.

With them, that is, with Titus (8.17) and the unnamed brother (8.18). In some languages it may be better to say "with these two men . . . ." CEV goes even further, making a separate sentence of this: "we are also sending someone else with Titus and the other follower."

We are sending is literally "we sent" (see comments on the verb tense in 8.17).

Our brother is not to be taken in the literal, biological sense. This brother apparently is a Christian who has worked with Paul, so the pronoun **our** probably does not include the readers. The individual is not identified. Translators need to be clear that this brother is not the same as the person mentioned in verses 18-19. REB says "We are sending with them another of our company." ITCL says "I am sending with them another of our brothers," and Brazil's Portuguese common language version (BRCL) says "With them we are sending another brother." It may be advisable to add the word "another [brother]."

Though Paul does not state how the brother was **tested**, it was probably by having always done the tasks that were assigned to him.

Earnest: some languages may speak of "enthusiasm," "eagerness" or "fervor." See comments on 8.16.

In the specific context the brother's **great confidence** probably refers primarily to his confidence that the Corinthians will contribute generously and willingly to the collection for the Christians in Jerusalem.

8.23 RSV	TEV
As for Titus, he is my partner and fellow worker in your service; and as for our brethren, they are messengers of the churches, the glory of Christ.	As for Titus, he is my partner and works with me to help you; as for the other brothers who are going with him, they represent the churches and bring glory to Christ.

My partner: the term *koinōnos* used here is very close in meaning to **fellow-worker**, which follows. It refers to someone with whom one shares intimately, as a close associate. The term is used in 1.7, where RSV translates using the verb "share," and it is also related to *koinōnia,* translated "taking part" in 8.4. Some other possible translations in this context are "my companion" (NAB) or "my colleague" (Mft).

The words **fellow worker in your service** contain a slight ambiguity (see comments on 1.24 and 6.1). Most likely Titus is Paul's fellow worker to help the Corinthians (TEV, NJB). REB says "my fellow worker in dealings with you." But it is also possible to understand the Greek to mean "your fellow-worker" (as in Schonfield's *The Original New Testament*), though this is unlikely in the context.

Our brethren refers to the other persons who are traveling with Titus (so TEV). TEV avoids the problem of inclusive–exclusive pronouns by saying "the other brothers." Some languages, however, must use a possessive pronoun here; the pronoun **our** probably does not include the readers. This refers to the other two men who had been chosen to accompany Titus. CEV states specifically "the other two followers."

Messengers of the churches: literally "apostles" or "sent ones" of the churches. Paul is not referring to the twelve apostles, however. The precise identity of **the churches** is not known to us (see comment on 8.19). But this expression clearly refers to local congregations or assemblies of believers in the place from which Paul is writing.

The glory of Christ seems to refer to **the churches** in RSV. NJB correctly says "they are emissaries of the churches and the glory of Christ." To say that someone is the glory of someone else makes little sense in English. Some translations therefore attempt to express the meaning of **glory of Christ**: "an honor to Christ" (NIV), "bring glory to Christ" (TEV).

8.24 RSV TEV

So give proof, before the churches, of your love and of our boasting about you to these men.	Show your love to them, so that all the churches will be sure of it and know that we are right in boasting about you.

So: this represents the conjunction often translated "Therefore" (NRSV). It introduces the logical conclusion of Paul's argument on this point.

Give proof . . . of our boasting: the sense is "give proof of the truthfulness of our boasting." TEV expresses this sense with "show" and by adding the words "will be sure of it and know that we are right."

Our boasting about you: different forms of the word "boast" appear nearly thirty times in this letter. The references are sometimes positive (as in this case) and sometimes negative. In this context translators may say something like CEV's "why we bragged about you," or possibly "the expression of our happiness with you." See also 1.12.

Before the churches is literally "in the face of the churches." Paul wants Christians in other churches to see or be made aware of the love that the Corinthians have. **The churches** may refer to all the local assemblies. TEV inserts the word "all" (so also NJB and Martin). Perhaps, though, Paul is referring only to the churches that are mentioned in verses 19 and 23, that is, the churches which appointed these men to represent them. So NBE says "before their churches." In view of the difference of opinion among scholars on the meaning of **churches** here, it is probably better not to add the word "all" as TEV has done.

As in 8.8, the Greek does not specify the object of **your love**. TEV says "your love to them [Titus and the brothers]," but this could be either their love for Titus and the brothers, which some translations make explicit (FRCL, SPCL, BRCL), or their love for Paul. In light of 8.7, it is unlikely that this refers to Christian love in general.

C-3. Help for fellow Christians
9.1-15

RSV TEV
Help for Fellow Christians

1 Now it is superfluous for me to write to you about the offering for the saints, 2 for I know your readiness, of which I boast about you to the people of Macedonia, saying that Achaia has been ready since last year; and your zeal has stirred up most of them. 3 But I am sending the brethren so that our boasting about you may not prove vain in this case, so that you may be ready, as I said you would be; 4 lest if some Macedonians come with me and find that you are not ready, we be humiliated—to say nothing of you—for being so confident. 5 So I thought it necessary to urge the	1 There is really no need for me to write you about the help being sent to God's people in Judea. 2 I know that you are willing to help, and I have boasted of you to the people in Macedonia. "The brothers in Achaia," I said, "have been ready to help since last year." Your eagerness has stirred up most of them. 3 Now I am sending these brothers, so that our boasting about you in this matter may not turn out to be empty words. But, just as I said, you will be ready with your help. 4 However, if the people from Macedonia should come with me and find out that you are not ready, how

brethren to go on to you before me, and arrange in advance for this gift you have promised, so that it may be ready not as an exaction but as a willing gift.

6 The point is this: he who sows sparingly will also reap sparingly, and he who sows bountifully will also reap bountifully. 7 Each one must do as he has made up his mind, not reluctantly or under compulsion, for God loves a cheerful giver. 8 And God is able to provide you with every blessing in abundance, so that you may always have enough of everything and may provide in abundance for every good work. 9 As it is written,

"He scatters abroad, he gives to the poor;

his righteousness endures for ever."

10 He who supplies seed to the sower and bread for food will supply and multiply your resources and increase the harvest of your righteousness. 11 You will be enriched in every way for great generosity, which through us will produce thanksgiving to God; 12 for the rendering of this service not only supplies the wants of the saints but also overflows in many thanksgivings to God. 13 Under the test of this service, you will glorify God by your obedience in acknowledging the gospel of Christ, and by the generosity of your contribution for them and for all others; 14 while they long for you and pray for you, because of the surpassing grace of God in you. 15 Thanks be to God for his inexpressible gift!

ashamed we would be—not to speak of your shame—for feeling so sure of you! 5 So I thought it was necessary to urge these brothers to go to you ahead of me and get ready in advance the gift you promised to make. Then it will be ready when I arrive, and it will show that you give because you want to, not because you have to.

6 Remember that the person who plants few seeds will have a small crop; the one who plants many seeds will have a large crop. 7 Each one should give, then, as he has decided, not with regret or out of a sense of duty; for God loves the one who gives gladly. 8 And God is able to give you more than you need, so that you will always have all you need for yourselves and more than enough for every good cause. 9 As the scripture says,

"He gives generously to the needy;

his kindness lasts forever."

10 And God, who supplies seed for the sower and bread to eat, will also supply you with all the seed you need and will make it grow and produce a rich harvest from your generosity. 11 He will always make you rich enough to be generous at all times, so that many will thank God for your gifts which they receive from us. 12 For this service you perform not only meets the needs of God's people, but also produces an outpouring of gratitude to God. 13 And because of the proof which this service of yours brings, many will give glory to God for your loyalty to the gospel of Christ, which you profess, and for your generosity in sharing with them and everyone else. 14 And so with deep affection they will pray for you because of the extraordinary grace God has shown you. 15 Let us thank God for his priceless gift!

SECTION HEADING: TEV "Help for Fellow Christians." In chapter 8 Paul related how the Macedonian Christians had voluntarily and generously contributed to the collection, and he held them up as an example to motivate the Corinthians to do likewise. Now in chapter 9 he tells how he used the Corinthians as an example to motivate the Macedonian Christians in their giving, and he asks the Corinthians not to embarrass him by failing to complete what they had begun. Paul bases the reason for giving in the hope that God will be glorified.

Though TEV includes all of chapter 9 together under one section heading, some interpreters group verses 1-5 together as "A new appeal to generosity" (LPD) or "Once more: concerning the collection for Jerusalem" (GECL), and then group verses 6-15 together under the title "Blessings to be expected from the collection" (LPD, NJB, NVSR) or "God gives so that we can give" (GECL).

9.1   RSV   TEV

Now it is superfluous for me to   There is really no need for me to
write to you about the offering for the write you about the help being sent to
saints,   God's people in Judea.

The word **Now** in RSV should not be understood as primarily temporal,
expressing the idea of "now and not some other time." The word **Now** is used
here to indicate a transition in subject matter. AB translates this transition
word "So," showing its logical rather than temporal character. Mft begins this
verse with the word "Indeed."

It is superfluous: the root of the noun used here has to do with surplus
or overabundance (see 8.2,7). It would be something more than necessary for
Paul to write about the money the Corinthians planned to give. NRSV changes
this expression into a negative statement, "it is not necessary." Another way
to say this may be "I can see no reason to   ." or "there is no purpose for me
to . . . ."

The pronoun **you** is plural here and throughout chapter 9. It refers to the
Corinthian readers in general.

The offering for the saints translates the Greek "ministry (*diakonia*) for
the saints." Paul is writing specifically about the collection for the Jewish
Christians in Jerusalem. Translators may need to make clear the identification
of the "saints." TEV's "God's people in Judea" is an attempt to make the
identification explicit, but this translation is not very precise. "God's people"
may be misunderstood to mean "the Jewish people" or "Christians in general"
(including Gentile Christians). Translators may need to be more precise: "the
Jewish Christians." Since Paul states specifically in Rom 15.26 that the
collection is for the poor among the saints in Jerusalem, translators may want
to add the name "Jerusalem" (LPD, ITCL) instead of "Judea" (TEV).

9.2   RSV   TEV

for I know your readiness, of which I   I know that you are willing to help, and
boast about you to the people of Mace-   I have boasted of you to the people in
donia, saying that Achaia has been   Macedonia. "The brothers in Achaia,"
ready since last year; and your zeal has I said, "have been ready to help since
stirred up most of them.   last year." Your eagerness has stirred
                                          up most of them.

For: verse 2 states why Paul considers it not necessary to write to the
Corinthians about the collection. He knows that they are already prepared "to
give" (CEV).

Readiness: this is the same word as in 8.11, 12 and 19. See comments
at that point.

Macedonia . . . Achaia were Roman provinces. (See map, page vi.) On
Macedonia see comments on 1.16; 2.13. On **Achaia** see comments on 1.1. It is

important for readers to understand that Corinth was a part of the province of Achaia (see 1.1). Readers of the receptor language translation should know that "the brothers in Achaia" included the Corinthians, who "are willing to help." Translators may include this information in the text as CEV does: "And I have proudly told the Lord's followers in Macedonia that you people in Achaia have been ready for a whole year." Or, alternatively, a footnote may be used to provide this information.

The Greek says literally "Achaia has been ready." TEV indicates that it is the Christians ("brothers") there who have been ready. Since Paul no doubt means both men and women, translators will want to avoid a word that implies men only. It may be possible to say "the Christians in Achaia" or "you believers in Achaia." And readers may need to be reminded explicitly that Achaia is a province, not a city, since they may not recall the classifier term used at the beginning of this letter.

For comments on **since last year**, see 8.10, "a year ago."

The report of what Paul said to the believers in Macedonia is translated as an indirect quote in most versions, but it will be more natural in some languages to present it as direct speech and to set it off with quotation marks: "I said to them, 'Our fellow believers in Achaia have been ready to give since last year.' "

Your zeal has stirred up most of them: in the context **your zeal** means specifically the eagerness of the Corinthians to contribute to the collection. The word for **zeal** is the same as in 7.7,11, as well as in 11.2 and 1 Cor 3.3, where it is translated "jealousy" in a different context. The verbal expression **stirred up** has the result that the Macedonians are eager to contribute also. CEV says "Now your desire to give has made them want to give."

9.3 RSV TEV

RSV	TEV
But I am sending the brethren so that our boasting about you may not prove vain in this case, so that you may be ready, as I said you would be;	Now I am sending these brothers, so that our boasting about you in this matter may not turn out to be empty words. But, just as I said, you will be ready with your help.

As noted in "Translating 2 Corinthians," page 5, and at the beginning of chapter 8, some interpreters regard both chapters 8 and 9 to have been parts of separate letters that were later pieced together to form part of 2 Corinthians as we now have it. One's decision on this issue has important implications for the translation of this verse, as the following comments will indicate.

The word **But** indicates a contrast: Paul has the feeling that there is no need to write (9.1), since he knows that the Corinthians are ready to give (9.2); yet he is sending co-workers on ahead of himself to be sure that the money is ready when he will arrive later.

I am sending is in the past tense in Greek, "I sent" (so KJV, RVR). NASB has "I have sent." If chapter 9 was originally a separate letter written after chapter 8, then perhaps Paul had already sent these co-workers on to Corinth. If, however, chapters 8 and 9 were originally written as part of the same letter, then the verb "I sent" is probably an epistolary aorist and should be translated in the present tense (see explanations at 8.17 and 9.5). Since we now have the letter in the form of a single, whole letter, the latter explanation should probably be adopted by modern translators.

The brethren translates the Greek word for "brothers." Though this word sometimes seems to include Christian women also, in this verse it probably does refer to men only. Paul is referring to the three persons already mentioned in 8.16-24. The words "these brothers" (TEV, FRCL, and Mft) or "these friends" (REB) indicate that Paul is referring to brothers who have already been mentioned. Though **the brethren** may possibly refer only to the two unnamed men of 8.16-24, Titus is probably included (see 8.18). Translators may want to make explicit the identity of "these brothers": "I am sending Titus and the two others" (CEV). Or one may prefer to say simply "these three men."

If chapter 9 was a separate letter written later than chapter 8, then possibly **the brethren** do not refer to Titus and the two brothers of chapter 8 but rather to other Christians whom Paul had sent. The translations of TEV and CEV cited in the previous paragraph assume that these two chapters originally were part of the same letter as they now exist.

So that our boasting about you might not prove vain: this explains not why Paul is sending the delegation, but why he expects the Corinthians to be ready with their offering when they arrive. It may be better in some languages to make this a separate sentence as in CEV: "This will prove that we were not wrong to brag about you."

This case means in the matter of their being ready to contribute to the collection. Another way of saying this would be "in this matter" (Brc). And note that CEV leaves this part of the verse implicit.

Ready: in many languages it will be necessary to state clearly what is only implied in this word: "ready to help" or "ready to give."

As I said you would: or "just as I promised others you would be ready [to give]."

9.4	RSV	TEV
	lest if some Macedonians come with me and find that you are not ready, we be humiliated—to say nothing of you—for being so confident.	However, if the people from Macedonia should come with me and find out that you are not ready, how ashamed we would be—not to speak of your shame—for feeling so sure of you!

Verse 4 expresses the reason that Paul is sending these brothers on ahead to Corinth (verse 3). He wanted to determine whether they were really prepared, in order to avoid mutual embarrassment.

Lest: while RSV and certain other versions follow the Greek in continuing the sentence started at the beginning of verse 3, it will be better in most languages to start a new sentence here with a word like "Otherwise" (FRCL) or "However" (TEV).

To whom do the words **some Macedonians** refer? The Greek is literally "Macedonians." By adding the definite article "the" before the word "people," TEV suggests a specific group of people. It seems that after sending Titus and the two unnamed brothers, Paul himself will go to Corinth and may take with him some Christians from the province of Macedonia. The translations **some** (RSV, NRSV, NJB) people from Macedonia or "if any Macedonians" (NAB, NIV) are preferable to "*the* people from Macedonia" (TEV), since Paul does not appear to be referring to a specific group of people. The REB translation, "men from Macedonia," is more specific than the Greek requires; women may have been included also.

Paul was concerned that the Corinthians may **not** be **ready**, that is, that they may not have their part of the contribution ready (see 1 Cor 16.1-2). CEV says "I want them to find that you have the money ready."

The context clearly shows that the **we** in this case excludes the Corinthian readers, since it contrasts with **you** later in the same sentence.

Be humiliated: in those languages where passive expressions are problematic, it will be necessary to indicate who the agent is in the process of humiliation. In this case it is clearly the Corinthians if they are unprepared for the offering. One may say more directly "you will cause us to feel shame." But in some languages it will be possible to say simply "we will feel shame."

To say nothing of you: literally "lest I say you." This rather cryptic parenthetical statement may have to be translated in some languages as a separate sentence at the end of the verse. One may say "I won't even mention the shame you might feel."

For being so confident: it is doubtful whether the meaning "confidence" can be established for the Greek word translated as **confident** in RSV. TEV and most other English versions, however, follow the same meaning as RSV. The Greek word is better translated as "plan," "project," or "undertaking." The end of this verse should therefore be translated as "we would be humiliated—to say nothing of you—in this undertaking" (NRSV and AB).

At the end of this verse, some manuscripts add the words "of this boasting" (so REB footnote). The UBS *Greek New Testament* does not include these words, and the editors give a "B" evaluation to the printed text, suggesting that the printed text is almost certainly correct. KJV is based on the manuscripts that have this addition: "should be ashamed in this same confident boasting." With the additional words the sense is clearly that Paul would be humiliated for having confidently boasted about the Corinthians (see 7.14 and 9.3). Some translations such as RSV and TEV have followed manuscripts that do not have these additional words; but the translators understand the sense to be the same, even without the addition.

As already stated, however, the Greek word translated **confident** in RSV is more accurately translated "undertaking." The humiliation that Paul fears is not that he may have boasted in vain. Rather he will be humiliated if the undertaking of the fund-raising for the Christians in Jerusalem should fail. The following translation may serve as a model for this verse:

However, if some people from Macedonia should come with me to Corinth and find out that you are not ready, how ashamed we [exclusive] would be if this project of collecting money should fail. And I will not even talk about your shame in this matter.

9.5 RSV	TEV
So I thought it necessary to urge the brethren to go on to you before me, and arrange in advance for this gift you have promised, so that it may be ready not as an exaction but as a willing gift.	So I thought it was necessary to urge these brothers to go to you ahead of me and get ready in advance the gift you promised to make. Then it will be ready when I arrive, and it will show that you give because you want to, not because you have to.

So: this logical transition word may also be rendered "Therefore" (AB and Brc) or "That is why" (Mft and Knox).

The past tense used at the beginning of this verse (**I thought**) is called by scholars an "epistolary" aorist (see 7.14; 8.17). This means that the writer uses the past tense, in the perspective of the readers for whom the time of Paul's actions will be in the past when they read his letter. If the past tense in the receptor language will indicate that Paul had already sent the brothers on to Corinth before writing these words, the use of the present tense may be better: "So I think it is necessary . . .." (though see comments on verse 3). It is true, of course, that Paul continues to have this opinion. However, if in the receptor language the writer of a letter takes the point of view of the readers, the past tense may be preferred.

As in verse 3, TEV says "these brothers," since Paul is referring to persons whom he has already mentioned in chapter 8 (though see comments on verse 3).

Arrange in advance: the verb so translated is found only in this verse but comes from a more frequently occurring verb that involves repairing, arranging, or putting things in order. An added prefix here indicates that the verbal action is done beforehand or in advance. Titus and his companions were to go ahead of Paul and make sure that the money promised was actually collected. GNC translates "making things straight well in advance," and NCV has "finish getting in order."

This gift you have promised is literally "your promised blessing." Though the Greek does not indicate to whom the promise was made, the context seems to indicate that they promised Paul.

An exaction: the verb that comes from the same root as this noun occurs in 2.11 and 7.2, where RSV translates as "gaining an advantage over" someone and "take advantage of" someone. The NIV translation "grudgingly given" perhaps fails to capture an important aspect of meaning. Paul wants the Corinthians to have the money ready before he arrives, lest it appear that he uses force or other inappropriate methods to obtain money from them. Perhaps a better translation is "an extortion" (NRSV, REB), or "because I have forced you to give," or "not as money wrung [squeezed] out of you" (Mft).

9.6   RSV   TEV

The point is this: he who sows sparingly will also reap sparingly, and he who sows bountifully will also reap bountifully.

Remember that the person who plants few seeds will have a small crop; the one who plants many seeds will have a large crop.

Many translations begin a new paragraph with verse 6. And NJB has a section heading at this point. It reads "Blessings to be expected from the collection." Verses 6-11 provide one motive for giving, that is, God will bless the giver; and verses 12-15 provide a second motive, God will be glorified.

The point is this: literally "but this." The Greek words indicate that what follows is a summary of what he has already written concerning the matter of giving. Some may wish to translate "What I am trying to say is this . . . ." CEV highlights the fact that what follows seems to have been a well-known adage that was perhaps frequently quoted in Paul's day: "remember this saying . . . ." The words are set off in poetic format and enclosed in quotation marks. However, we do not know the source of the saying.

He who sows . . . he who sows: these two participles are masculine in Greek, but since Paul does not seem to be referring exclusively to men, translators may wish to use inclusive terms as in TEV or NRSV ("the one who sows"). CEV says "A few seeds make a small harvest, but a lot of seeds make a big harvest." In some languages it will be more natural to make the subject both human and plural: "people who plant only a few seeds will gather in only a little food, but those people who plant many seeds will gather in much food."

9.7   RSV   TEV

Each one must do as he has made up his mind, not reluctantly or under compulsion, for God loves a cheerful giver.

Each one should give, then, as he has decided, not with regret or out of a sense of duty; for God loves the one who gives gladly.

Though the word **Each one** is masculine in Greek, Paul is almost certainly addressing both men and women among the Corinthian Christians. NRSV accordingly says "Each of you must give as you have made up your mind," and AB says "Let each person contribute as each has decided."

The first part of this verse is literally "each as he has made up his mind." Most translations add a verb to specify the action decided upon. RSV adds **must do**, and TEV adds "should give."

His mind is literally "the heart," without the possessive pronoun. On the heart as the center of one's will, see comments on 3.3 In many languages it will be quite natural to say "as each person has decided in his or her (or, the) heart . . . ." And in some the addition of the possessive pronoun may be unnecessary. In many languages the absence of a pronoun in such a context would mean "the heart of a person," as is apparently the case in Greek.

The words **reluctantly** (literally "from sorrow" or "from pain") and **under compulsion** refer to attitudes of grief or regret upon doing something that one does not want to do, and of being forced either by inner moral conviction or by outer pressure from other people to do something that one does not want to do. These words may be rendered "with no regrets and no coercion" or, using full verb phrases, "be happy to give and do not give simply because someone is pushing you to do so."

For God loves a cheerful giver: the word order is reversed in Greek: "a cheerful giver God loves." Knox therefore attempts to preserve the emphasis by translating "it is the cheerful giver that God loves" (similarly TNT). However, the emphasis in this sentence is not a contrast between whom God loves and whom he does not love. The contrast is between the cheerful giver who gives out of a desire to do so, and the giver who gives reluctantly or because he is required to give. These words are a loose quotation from Pro 22.8a in the Septuagint. Here, as frequently in the Old Testament wisdom books, the words **God loves** mean "God approves" (NBE) or "God values." The opposite is not that God hates the person who gives grudgingly, but rather that he disapproves. Note that CEV translates "God loves people who love to give." The adjective **cheerful** is found only here in all the New Testament, although it is used in the Greek translation of Pro 22.9. It stands in contrast with grumbling or acting only out of a sense of responsibility. Some languages will say simply "with joy" or "in an attitude of happiness."

9.8	RSV	TEV

And God is able to provide you with every blessing in abundance, so that you may always have enough of everything and may provide in abundance for every good work.

And God is able to give you more than you need, so that you will always have all you need for yourselves and more than enough for every good cause.

As noted at 9.1, the pronoun **you** is plural here, as throughout chapter 9.

God is able: this may also be rendered "God has the power" (AB) or "God can . . ." (Brc and CEV).

Every blessing is literally "every grace." NAB says "God is able to make every grace abundant for you" (so also NIV). Here "grace" does not refer to God's saving grace but rather to the benefits that he freely gives to the Corinthians.

The second half of this verse states that the givers will have enough for their own needs (**enough of everything**) and enough to give to the needs of others also (**provide in abundance**). The word translated **enough** is found elsewhere only in 1 Tim 6.6, where it is translated "contentment." It carries the idea of self-sufficiency.

For every good work: note that TEV, like Brc and Phps, speaks of "every good cause." Some languages may have to say something like "[to help] all those who are in need."

Here Paul seems to be intentionally piling up words indicating totality, completeness, and abundance. In this short verse the Greek word for "all (or, every)" occurs four times, "always" once, and the verb "to be abundant" appears twice. The cumulative effect is to emphasize the fact that God takes complete care of all his people at all times. But a literal rendering may sound heavy or unnatural in some languages.

9.9

RSV	TEV

As it is written,
    "He scatters abroad, he gives to
        the poor;
    his righteousness^k endures for
        ever."
	As the scripture says,
	    "He gives generously to the
	        needy;
	    his kindness lasts forever."

^k Or *benevolence*

As it is written: TEV, ITCL, GECL, and REB make explicit that this quotation comes from the "scripture" (see also 3.16; 8.15; 10.17; 13.1). Paul is quoting directly from the Septuagint translation of Psa 112.9. But since the quotation is not from the Hebrew original, the receptor language translation of this verse need not look exactly like the rendering of the verse in the Psalms.

He . . . his: the referent of these two pronouns is debated by scholars. Though some understand the reference to be to God (CEV "God freely gives . . ."), it is unlikely that God is the intended subject of the verb **scatters**, or that the later reference is to God's **righteousness**. It is more likely that, as is clearly the case in Psalm 112, the righteousness is that of a person who fears the Lord (see verse 1 of that Psalm).

Scatters abroad . . . gives to the poor: these two verbs are rendered by a single verb in several English translations (TEV and CEV, for example). The first is the opposite of "gathering in" but does not necessarily imply the sowing of seed. Here it probably means "be liberal or generous." For this reason it may be translated by an adverb such as "generously" (TEV) or "freely" (TNT). REB includes this idea in the verb: "he lavishes his gifts on the needy." Perhaps a more difficult problem is to decide whether the verb tenses should be present (RSV, TEV, REB, CEV) or past (NIV, NAB, NJB, AB). Though the verbs **he scatters** and **he gives** are past tense in Greek, they may be translated in the present tense or by habitual verb forms in many languages. Greek often used past tense verbs in axioms and proverbial statements.

Here in Hebrew parallelism **righteousness** perhaps means "acts of almsgiving." In Hebrew the word for **righteousness** came to mean "almsgiving" in some contexts. REB translates as "his benevolence lasts for ever." Since this verse contains Hebrew parallelism, it is not likely that **righteousness** here has the sense of upright character in general, as it sometimes has in other contexts.

9.10	RSV	TEV

He who supplies seed to the sower and bread for food will supply and multiply your resources^l and increase the harvest of your righteousness.^k

And God, who supplies seed for the sower and bread to eat, will also supply you with all the seed you need and will make it grow and produce a rich harvest from your generosity.

^l Greek *sowing*
^k Or *benevolence*

In verse 10 Paul does not quote directly from the Old Testament, but the words **seed to the sower and bread for food** are no doubt influenced by the words of Isa 55.10. The words **the harvest of your righteousness** are influenced by the words of Hos 10.12. Some translations (LPD, GNC, NJB) place these and other direct citations from the Old Testament in bold font or in italics to indicate to the reader that Paul's thought and expression are influenced by the Scriptures.

He: though the pronoun "he" in verse 9 probably refers to a human being, here in verse 10 it refers to God, as TEV makes quite clear by using the noun "God" in place of the pronoun (also FRCL, GECL, Brc, and CEV).

Sower: in some languages this may have to be translated "farmer" or "the person who plants [seeds]."

Bread for food: God's provision is not limited to bread, and the word for bread is often used in the Bible for food in general. In some languages, therefore, it may be more natural here to say "food to eat" or "food for people to eat."

Supply: this verb may be rendered "furnish" or "provide," and in some cases "give."

Multiply your resources: as indicated in the RSV note, the Greek may be translated "multiply your sowing," or more literally "multiply your seed." But seed is intended to be understood figuratively here, continuing the figure from the first clause in the verse. If the figurative language will be understood in this context, the more literal rendering is acceptable.

As in verse 9, **righteousness** here seems to refer specifically to acts of "generosity" (TEV).

Increase the harvest of your righteousness: God will not allow their generosity to lack results, as the following verses make clear. In some languages it will not be advisable to retain the figure of speech using the idea of harvest. A possible model in this case is "He will increase what you have, so that you can give even more to those in need" (CEV). If the image of the harvest is retained in translation, a possible model may be "he will cause it to become much, so that you may act as people of righteousness indeed."

As noted on 9.1, the pronoun **your** is plural here and throughout chapter 9.

9.11

RSV	TEV
You will be enriched in every way for great generosity, which through us will produce thanksgiving to God;	He will always make you rich enough to be generous at all times, so that many will thank God for your gifts which they receive from us.

The Greek verb translated **will be enriched** is passive. Some languages must make explicit the subject of the verb. Continuing the thought of verse 10, God is the one who makes a person "rich enough to be generous." One language has avoided the passive by translating the first part of this verse as follows: "He [God] will give you abundance in all things so that you will be able to share freely with other people."

In every way for great generosity: literally "in all unto every generosity." "In all" seems to mean "in every aspect of life." The Greek adjective "each (or, every)" may mean "every single form of generosity" or, as in RSV, "generosity to the highest degree." TEV takes "all generosity" to imply that the readers will be able to be generous "at all times." Similarly Martin: "so that you can always be generous." The English translations of RSV and TEV are not really as different in meaning as they first appear to be. Note that the word translated **generosity** is also found in 1.12; 8.2; 9.13; 11.3.

Which through us will produce thanksgiving to God: the meaning in the context is that the Jerusalem Christians will thank God for the gifts that are the result of the ministry of Paul and his fellow-workers. Though TEV says "which they receive from us," translators should avoid suggesting that the gifts are already being received. CEV shows that the gift has not yet been delivered: "Then many people will thank God when we deliver your gift." The second half of this verse shows the result of the Corinthians becoming rich and sharing their wealth with others: "this will make others thankful to God for what we have done" (TNT).

9.12

RSV	TEV
for the rendering of this service not only supplies the wants of the saints but also overflows in many thanksgivings to God.	For this service you perform not only meets the needs of God's people, but also produces an outpouring of gratitude to God.

For: the transition word here indicates the logical continuation of Paul's argument. It is, however, sometimes not overtly represented in translation.

The rendering of this service . . . supplies: literally "the ministry (*diakonia*) of this service . . . provides fully." In a number of languages such a noun phrase does not fit well as the subject of the verb that follows. So it may be necessary to say "when you perform this service, you provide . . ." or "when you serve in this way, you supply . . . ."

This service refers to the offering that the Gentile churches are raising for the poor Christians in Jerusalem. The Greek word translated here as **service**, *leitourgia,* sometimes has a religious sense. LPD accordingly focuses on the spiritual aspect of this word in its translation: "this holy service." The Greek word, however, often means "public service" in a secular sense.

The wants: the Greek word refers to that which one needs but does not have. The reference is not to something that is simply desired but to something that is essential and needed. NRSV shifts from **wants** to "needs." Similarly some other translations speak of "providing for people who are in need," "helping God's people who lack," or "meeting the needs of fellow Christians."

As in 9.1, **the saints** refers specifically to the Jerusalem Jewish Christians. In the context of the collection, it is important that readers recognize that Gentile Christians are making a contribution for poor Jewish Christians (see Rom 15.27). The TEV translation "God's people" may be too vague (see comment on 9.1). Translators may wish to add the words "in Jerusalem" following the word "saints" (so Martin).

On the word **overflows**, see 8.2 above.

Many thanksgivings to God: the sense may be that the Jerusalem Christians will give **many thanksgivings** to God. Alternatively the sense may be "through the thanksgiving of many people." If the latter is correct, then Paul may have been referring to thanksgivings by his Gentile converts also.

9.13 RSV	TEV
Under the test of this service, you^m will glorify God by your obedience in acknowledging the gospel of Christ, and by the generosity of your contribution for them and for all others;	And because of the proof which this service of yours brings, many will give glory to God for your loyalty to the gospel of Christ, which you profess, and for your generosity in sharing with them and everyone else.

^m Or *they*

Under the test of this service: or, more literally, "through the testing of this ministry." Paul indicates here that the Corinthians would prove themselves by their obedience to the Good News of Christ. Some languages may say "this matter will demonstrate that you are true . . . ."

You will glorify God by your obedience: the Greek does not state the subject of the word **glorify**. The Greek is literally "glorifying God." It may be the Corinthians themselves who glorify God (so RSV, NRSV) or, more likely, the

Christians in Jerusalem (so NVSR, LPD; REB "those who receive it will give honour to God"). Thus the reading in the RSV footnote is probably the better one to follow in the receptor language. Curiously NRSV omits this footnote. TEV, however, adopts this understanding in translating "many," leaving the referent less specific than REB.

The words **the generosity of your contribution** (RSV, NRSV) may be translated in various ways. **Generosity** may also be translated as "sincerity," and **contribution** as "fellowship" (*koinōnia*). While the demonstration of fellowship took the form of a contribution, for Paul the contribution was a sign of fellowship. Several interpretations and translations are possible: "the sincerity of your fellowship with them"; "the generosity of your fellowship with them" (NVSR, TEV,); "the generosity with which you are united with them" (LPD, NBE).

The pronoun **them** refers to the "saints" in Jerusalem. **All others** refers to Christians in other places.

9.14	RSV	TEV

while they long for you and pray for you, because of the surpassing grace of God in you.	And so with deep affection they will pray for you because of the extraordinary grace God has shown you.

They long for you: the Greek participle "longing" may mean "to have a great affection or love" (so TEV, NJB, NIV, NVSR, SPCL, RVR). On the other hand it is often used by Paul to indicate his desire to see his converts face to face. If this meaning is present here also, then the sense is that the Jerusalem Christians long to see the Gentile Christians who are giving financial help to them. CEV adopts this second interpretation, translating "[they] want to see you."

The surpassing grace: on the meaning of **grace** here, see comments on 8.1. **Surpassing** indicates that this grace is far beyond the ordinary. Compare 3.10, where the same verb is used.

The grace of God in you is better translated in some languages as the grace that God has "given you" (REB, NRSV, NIV) or "shown you" (TEV).

9.15	RSV	TEV

Thanks be to God for his inexpressible gift!	Let us thank God for his priceless gift!

Thanks be to God: the Greek does not indicate who is to give thanks to God (see 2.14 and 8.16). The implied agent is "we" (TEV, LPD).

The **inexpressible gift**, or "present," may be the grace that God has given to the Corinthians, and the resulting unity of Jews and Gentiles in one universal Church. Or it may be his son Jesus Christ. Whatever the precise meaning, Paul says that this is a gift so wonderful that it cannot be described in words. The TEV rendering seems to focus more on value rather than on the fact that the gift cannot be described by human speech. However, most versions retain the meaning "indescribable" (NAB and NRSV): "beyond all telling" (NJB); "which no words can describe" (TNT); "too wonderful for words!" (CEV).

D. Paul's defense of his apostolic authority

(10.1–13.10)

D-1. Paul defends his ministry

10.1-18

RSV

TEV
Paul Defends His Ministry

1 I, Paul, myself entreat you, by the meekness and gentleness of Christ—I who am humble when face to face with you, but bold to you when I am away!—2 I beg of you that when I am present I may not have to show boldness with such confidence as I count on showing against some who suspect us of acting in worldly fashion. 3 For though we live in the world we are not carrying on a worldly war, 4 for the weapons of our warfare are not worldly but have divine power to destroy strongholds. 5 We destroy arguments and every proud obstacle to the knowledge of God, and take every thought captive to obey Christ, 6 being ready to punish every disobedience, when your obedience is complete.

7 Look at what is before your eyes. If any one is confident that he is Christ's, let him remind himself that as he is Christ's, so are we. 8 For even if I boast a little too much of our authority, which the Lord gave for building you up and not for destroying you, I shall not be put to shame. 9 I would not seem to be frightening you with letters. 10 For they say, "His letters are weighty and strong, but his bodily presence is weak, and his speech of no account." 11 Let such people understand that what we say by letter when absent, we do when present. 12 Not that we venture to class or compare ourselves with some of those who commend themselves. But when they measure themselves by one another, and compare themselves with one another, they are without understanding.

13 But we will not boast beyond limit,

1 I, Paul, make a personal appeal to you—I who am said to be meek and mild when I am with you, but harsh with you when I am away. By the gentleness and kindness of Christ I beg you 2 not to force me to be harsh when I come; for I am sure I can deal harshly with those who say that we act from worldly motives. 3 It is true that we live in the world, but we do not fight from worldly motives. 4 The weapons we use in our fight are not the world's weapons but God's powerful weapons, which we use to destroy strongholds. We destroy false arguments; 5 we pull down every proud obstacle that is raised against the knowledge of God; we take every thought captive and make it obey Christ. 6 And after you have proved your complete loyalty, we will be ready to punish any act of disloyalty.

7 You are looking at the outward appearance of things. Is there someone there who reckons himself to belong to Christ? Well, let him think again about himself, because we belong to Christ just as much as he does. 8 For I am not ashamed, even if I have boasted somewhat too much about the authority that the Lord has given us—authority to build you up, not to tear you down. 9 I do not want it to appear that I am trying to frighten you with my letters. 10 Someone will say, "Paul's letters are severe and strong, but when he is with us in person, he is weak, and his words are nothing!" 11 Such a person must understand that there is no difference between what we write in our letters when we are away and what we will do when we are there with you.

but will keep to the limits God has apportioned us, to reach even to you. 14 For we are not overextending ourselves, as though we did not reach you; we were the first to come all the way to you with the gospel of Christ. 15 We do not boast beyond limit, in other men's labors; but our hope is that as your faith increases, our field among you may be greatly enlarged, 16 so that we may preach the gospel in lands beyond you, without boasting of work already done in another's field. 17 "Let him who boasts, boast of the Lord." 18 For it is not the man who commends himself that is accepted, but the man whom the Lord commends.

12 Of course we would not dare classify ourselves or compare ourselves with those who rate themselves so highly. How stupid they are! They make up their own standards to measure themselves by, and they judge themselves by their own standards! 13 As for us, however, our boasting will not go beyond certain limits; it will stay within the limits of the work which God has set for us, and this includes our work among you. 14 And since you are within those limits, we were not going beyond them when we came to you, bringing the Good News about Christ. 15 So we do not boast about the work that others have done beyond the limits God set for us. Instead, we hope that your faith may grow and that we may be able to do a much greater work among you, always within the limits that God has set. 16 Then we can preach the Good News in other countries beyond you and shall not have to boast about work already done in another man's field.

17 But as the scripture says, "Whoever wants to boast must boast about what the Lord has done." 18 For it is when the Lord thinks well of a person that he is really approved, and not when he thinks well of himself.

SECTION HEADING: TEV "Paul Defends His Ministry." Chapters 10–13 form a unit within 2 Corinthians. Numerous interpreters consider these four chapters to have been originally part of a separate letter written to Corinth, either earlier than chapters 1–9 or some time later than the first nine chapters. Some translations group chapters 10–13 together under a major section heading such as "Paul's Defense of His Ministry" (NAB, similarly NJB) or "Paul's Self-Defense" (LPD). Translators may follow the model of TEV and use one section heading such as "Paul Defends His Ministry" (also FRCL) for all of chapter 10. Or they may divide the chapter into two sections: 10.1-11 (NJB and LPD: "Paul's reply to accusations of weakness") and 10.12-18 (NJB and LPD: "His [Paul's] reply to charges of ambition").

10.1   RSV   TEV

I, Paul, myself entreat you, by the meekness and gentleness of Christ—I who am humble when face to face with you, but bold to you when I am away!—

I, Paul, make a personal appeal to you—I who am said to be meek and mild when I am with you, but harsh with you when I am away. By the gentleness and kindness of Christ I beg you

I, Paul, myself: the use of the personal pronoun, proper name and the intensive pronoun combine to emphasize as strongly as possible the apostle's personal involvement in the appeal that follows. This strong emphasis should be reflected in the receptor language, using forms that are natural in such circumstances. Compare Rom 7.25; 9.3; 15.14; also 2 Cor 12.13.

Entreat: the same Greek verb is used earlier in this letter of Paul's appeals to the Corinthians (2.8; 5.20; 6.1), although it is translated by different English words ("beg," "beseech," "entreat").

The meekness and gentleness of Christ: the Greek word translated **meekness** suggests a gentleness of attitude and behavior, a lack of harshness. The word translated **gentleness** suggests the quality of gracious forbearing. The words **meekness** and **gentleness** often occurred together in ancient Greek writings and are synonyms. The idea of begging someone **by** these attributes of Christ may be difficult to convey in some languages. It may be more natural to say something like "I beg you in the name of Christ, who is meek and gentle."

Paul's language in this verse is sarcastic. The words **who am humble when face to face with you but bold to you when I am away** almost certainly reflect a charge made against Paul, either by the Corinthians themselves or by opponents who have come to Corinth. TEV adds the words "am said to be" to indicate that Paul is echoing a charge made against himself, but which he does not accept (similarly FRCL). Some languages do not express sarcasm in this manner, and a literal translation may wrongly suggest that Paul is simply giving his own description of himself in the second half of this verse. REB also adds words to show that this is not Paul's own self-evaluation: "I who am so timid (you say) when face to face with you."

Humble . . . bold: the word rendered **humble** here is similar in significance to **meekness and gentleness**, but here almost has the meaning "weak," "afraid," or "timid" (REB). It contrasts with **bold**, which may have to be translated "strong" or "brave" in some cases.

As in chapter 9, the pronouns **you** are all plural in chapter 10.

Some languages may find it more natural to reverse the order of the two main elements in this verse by beginning with the false accusation:

> Some people among you keep saying that I am weak when I am with you and become strong only when we are far apart. But I myself, Paul, I beg you in the name of Christ, who was kind and gentle, not to push me into being strong when I see you face to face.

10.2   RSV   TEV

I beg of you that when I am present I may not have to show boldness with such confidence as I count on showing against some who suspect us of acting in worldly fashion.

not to force me to be harsh when I come; for I am sure I can deal harshly with those who say that we act from worldly motives.

It will be noted that the words "I beg you" are found at the end of verse 1 in TEV as part of its restructuring of that verse. The meaning is essentially the same as **I . . . entreat you** at the beginning of verse 1, even though the verb is different here. The structure used in the receptor language translation may require that only one verb be used, not two verbs.

When I am present should not be understood as a timeless statement meaning "anytime that I am present with you." Paul is referring specifically to his next visit to Corinth, whenever that may be. Accordingly TEV says "when I come" (also REB, NBE). Some languages require that the translation indicate that this is not Paul's first visit to Corinth; for example, it may be rendered "when I come again" (see also 10.11). Or other languages may prefer to say "the next time I am present with you" or "the next time we meet."

Show boldness with such confidence . . . : the verb **show boldness** (used also in 5.6,8; 7.16; 10.1) and the noun **confidence** (found in 1.15; 3.4; 8.22) reinforce each other, and together they constitute a very strong statement. While the two may have to be translated as a single verb in some languages, translators should look for a very emphatic way of saying "to be very firm" or "to be severe (strict, harsh)."

I count on showing: even though he does not wish it, Paul indicates by these words that he feels it will be necessary to show that he is strong when he faces his accusers. Note that the verb translated **count on** is the same in Greek as the one translated **suspect** in the following clause. NCV says "I plan to be very strict . . . ." In some languages it may be better to say "I have decided I will have to show" or "I know that I will have to demonstrate."

Suspect: the word so translated in RSV actually means "reason" or "reckon." The verb is actually the same as the one translated "count on." NJB shows the relationship by translating the two verbs with the same English word, "reckon." It says ". . . as I **reckon** to use when I am challenging those who **reckon** that we are guided by human motives." In this case AB says "who **reason** that we are conducting ourselves according to worldly standards," while REB has "those who **assume** my behavior to be dictated by human weakness." But the context makes it clear that what was involved in this case was not a mere suspicion that Paul's enemies kept to themselves, but that they were telling others about it. For this reason, it is at least possible to translate "say" (TEV) rather than "think" (NRSV, NIV).

Acting in a worldly fashion: literally "walking according to the flesh." The use of the verb "walk" reflects a common Hebrew idiom referring to a person's "behavior" or "conduct" (see comments at 4.2 on "practice"). The word "flesh" is often used in Scripture for "human nature." In this context the idea is one of "behaving in a manner that is controlled by natural human desires." In Rom 8.4 the same expression contrasts with "walking according to the Spirit." Some possible models here are "living for the things of this world" (GNW), "act like the people of this world" (CEV) or "our activities are on a purely human level" (Phps).

The logical connections between the various parts of verses 1 and 2 may be difficult, but translators should make every effort to make them clear to readers and hearers. The following is a possible model showing these relationships:

> 1-2 I, Paul myself, appeal to you with the gentleness and kindness of Christ to listen to me. I am making this request because some people accuse us of doing things just to please ourselves. They say we are weak when we are with you, but very bold when we are far away [from you]. But this is my appeal to you: I beg you not to force me to be bold when I come to visit you. However, I am sure that I can be bold with those who accuse me.

Another possible model is that of CEV:

> 1 Do you think I am a coward when I am with you and brave when I am far away? Well, I ask you to listen, because Christ himself was humble and gentle. 2 Some people have said that we act like people of this world. So when I arrive, I expect I will have to be firm and forceful in what I say to them. Please don't make me treat you that way.

10.3   RSV   TEV

| **For though we live in the world we are not carrying on a worldly war,** | **It is true that we live in the world, but we do not fight from worldly motives.** |

Paul uses terms drawn from the realm of the military in verses 3-6. In the following notes on these verses, attention will be drawn to this technical terminology, and renderings that preserve this imagery in English will be suggested.

A literal translation of this verse is "For though we walk in the flesh, we do not fight [as soldiers] according to the flesh" (compare KJV and NASB). Thus Paul uses words from the accusation in the previous verse to defend himself. Paul acknowledges that Christians live in the world, that is, in their fleshly bodies, but "worldly motives" do not guide their life. One rather dynamic rendering of this in an African language is "It is true that we are only human, but we do not fight in a human way."

Though what Paul says in verses 3-5 is true for all Christians, in the immediate context of chapter 10 the first person pronoun **we** should be translated as exclusive here, as well as in all of chapter 10—that is, the readers are not included. Very likely the first person plural pronouns and verbs in 10.3-16 are epistolary plurals. Mft, AT, and ITCL use first person singular forms in these verses.

The verb translated as **carrying on a . . . war** in RSV is a military term in Greek. A comparable term in English is to "wage war" (AB and NIV) or "make war" (Mft). Knox attempts to maintain the image while showing the figurative sense, by translating "fight our battles" (so also REB). This military metaphor continues through verse 6. In languages that require a direct object for the verb "make war," it will be possible to say "make war against other people." In other languages translators may be able to change the structure to say something like ". . . as in a normal war."

10.4 RSV	TEV
for the weapons of our warfare are not worldly but have divine power to destroy strongholds.	The weapons we use in our fight are not the world's weapons but God's powerful weapons, which we use to destroy strongholds. We destroy false arguments;

For: this indicates the logical continuation of Paul's argument. In some cases it may be rendered "indeed   ." But it is possible to leave the logical connection implicit.

On the pronoun **we** or **our**, see verse 3.

The weapons . . . are not worldly is literally "the weapons . . . are not fleshly," that is, not strictly human. On "flesh" see verse 2 above.

Warfare translates a military term meaning "military campaign." But it may have to be translated "struggle" or "battle" in some languages.

Divine power: that is, power from God.

To destroy strongholds is literally "for the demolition of strongholds" (AB), or "fortresses." This continues the use of military terminology. Where the idea of fortified military installations are unknown, it is reasonable to say "put an end to the strength of the enemy" or "tear down defenses that are difficult to destroy."

10.5 RSV	TEV
We destroy arguments and every proud obstacle to the knowledge of God, and take every thought captive to obey Christ,	we pull down every proud obstacle that is raised against the knowledge of God; we take every thought captive and make it obey Christ.

The Greek text followed by TEV includes the words **We destroy arguments** at the end of verse 4 rather than at the beginning of verse 5. While either verse division is possible, translators should probably follow the most widely used major language translation in their area. These words continue the military imagery and may be translated as "we demolish" (AB) arguments or "put an end to arguments." The word translated **arguments** is more literally "reasoning." It has been rendered "theories" (Mft), "sophistries" (REB), and "ideas" (NJB).

As the contrast with **your** at the end of verse 6 indicates, the pronoun **we** does not include the readers.

Every proud obstacle to continues the military imagery. AB says "every great height raised up in opposition to." Paul apparently had in mind the high bulwarks that were built up to protect a city from attack. In some languages the adjective **proud** does not naturally fit with a noun like **obstacle**, so a more literal rendering of "great height" or "high thing" may be appropriate.

The knowledge of God is not knowledge that God has but rather human knowledge about God. **The knowledge of God** may be thought of as a synonym for "the gospel." Note, however, that CEV translates "every bit of pride that keeps anyone from knowing God."

Paul does not explicitly state whose thoughts are to be taken captive, but the meaning is that the thoughts of those who were opposed to Christ will be taken captive.

To obey Christ is literally "unto the obedience of Christ." It may not be acceptable in a given language to make the noun **thought** the direct object of the verb "take captive" or the subject of the verb "obey." In this context the idea is that people will come to obey Christ in the way that they think. In order to maintain the imagery of the military, it may be wise to use a simile in some languages. One may say something like "the thoughts of people are like enemies that we capture. We take every one of them prisoner and make them obey Christ."

10.6   RSV   TEV

being ready to punish every disobedience, when your obedience is complete.	And after you have proved your complete loyalty, we will be ready to punish any act of disloyalty.

At this point Paul switches from "capturing" people in general for Christ to a discussion of the Corinthian Christians being captured for Christ. Once they are captured and become obedient to Christ, strict measures must be followed to discipline anyone who reverts to a life of disobedience and disloyalty.

Being ready is an expression used of military troops standing ready for battle. AB says "We stand at the ready."

Every disobedience, that is, of those in Corinth who continue to disobey. It is not actually the disobedience that is punished. What is meant here is that "we will be ready to punish any person who acts disobediently" or "we will be prepared to exercise discipline whenever someone is insubordinate."

The object of **obedience** is probably Christ (see verse 5). So it may be advisable in some languages to translate "when we see that you are obeying Christ completely."

TEV changes the order of the two main statements of this verse in order to place the thought in chronological order. This will be a good model for many other languages as well.

10.7 RSV TEV

Look at what is before your eyes. If any one is confident that he is Christ's, let him remind himself that as he is Christ's, so are we.

You are looking at the outward appearance of things. Is there someone there who reckons himself to belong to Christ? Well, let him think again about himself, because we belong to Christ just as much as he does.

A major question of interpretation in verses 7-11 is whether Paul is referring to a specific person or whether he is speaking hypothetically, that is, speaking as if such a person may exist. The words **If any one** may refer to a particular person. If they do, then the verb translated as **they say** in verse 10 may refer to this particular individual (the Greek verb is singular). And the words "Let such people" in verse 11 may also be referring to the particular person first mentioned in verse 7 (the Greek is singular, "such a person"). See comments on 11.20 and 21, where the same pronoun is used and refers to Paul's opponents in Corinth.

Look at what is before your eyes: these words may be translated as a command as in RSV (also NRSV, REB, LPD, NVSR), as a statement of fact as in TEV (also NAB, NIV, CEV and FRCL), or as a question (KJV). If this expression is taken as a command, the readers are being asked to consider what is self-evident, but if it is a statement, they are apparently considering only outward appearance. Most translations choose one of the first two possibilities, but the context does not decisively favor one interpretation over the others. This being the case, it may be better simply to follow the exegetical choice of the major language translation most likely to be consulted by readers of the receptor language. However, it is very unlikely that this should be translated as a question.

Christ's: literally "of Christ," that is, "belongs to Christ."

Let him remind himself: this rather awkward English command in the third person may be more naturally stated as "that person should remember" or "let him reflect further" (Knox).

As he is Christ's, so are we: there may be many different ways of wording this statement. The point is that the person Paul has in mind should realize that Paul and his associates are as much Christians as he is. Mft, taking the plural as referring to Paul alone, translates "I 'belong to Christ' as much as he does." Or as Knox puts it, "we belong to Christ's cause no less than himself."

The pronoun **we** does not include the readers.

10.8 RSV TEV

For even if I boast a little too much of our authority, which the Lord gave for

For I am not ashamed, even if I have boasted somewhat too much about the

building you up and not for destroying you, I shall not be put to shame.

authority that the Lord has given us—authority to build you up, not to tear you down.

Boast: see 5.12; 7.14; 9.2, where the same verb is used. It is repeated many times in the remainder of the next two chapters.

A little too much: the idea is that of slight overstatement or exaggeration. Mft speaks of boasting "somewhat freely." Some languages have unusual ways of communicating this thought. For example, the use of a verb meaning "surpass" or "excel" will convey the idea in certain cases. In this context one may say "to excel in boasting" or something similar.

The Lord here and in 13.10 is probably Christ rather than God, since Paul claims to be speaking for Christ (12.19; 13.3).

For building you up means in this context "to build your faith" (REB). **For destroying you** is not to be taken in a literal physical sense but in the sense of destroying their faith. See 13.10, where the same words occur.

Be put to shame: this notion is very frequent in the Old Testament (especially in the Psalms) and also occurs elsewhere in Paul's writings (Rom 9.33; 10.11). Since it is passive in form, many languages will require an active formulation. NRSV retranslates "I will not be ashamed of it" referring back to the idea of boasting earlier in the verse. NAB has "this will not embarrass me in the least." Some may need to restructure the whole verse along the lines of TEV or in some other way. The following is another possible model: "Even though I have been boasting too much about the authority that the Lord gave us, I feel no shame [about it]. The reason he gave me this authority is not to destroy you but so that you could be strengthened."

10.9   RSV   TEV

I would not seem to be frightening you with letters.

I do not want it to appear that I am trying to frighten you with my letters.

I would not seem to be frightening you: as the TEV rendering indicates, this is no tentative observation on the part of Paul. Rather it shows clearly that he wanted to avoid any appearance of trying to cause fear in the Corinthians by writing letters. NRSV says "I do not want to seem as though I am trying to frighten you with my letters." Another model is "I do not want you to get the idea that I am the kind of person who would try to scare you . . ." (Brc).

As verse 10 makes clear, **letters** are letters from Paul sent to the Corinthians. Translators may want to make this clear by adding the word "my" (TEV, NRSV, FRCL, LPD).

10.10 RSV TEV

For they say, "His letters are weighty and strong, but his bodily presence is weak, and his speech of no account."

Someone will say, "Paul's letters are severe and strong, but when he is with us in person, he is weak, and his words are nothing!"

For they say is only one word in Greek that introduces a quotation without indicating who said it. It introduces what seems to be a criticism of Paul that was circulating in Corinth, either by an individual or by his opponents there. TEV makes this more hypothetical rather than actual by translating "Someone will say," but RSV is probably to be preferred. AB avoids the question of whether this is to be understood as referring to a single individual or more than one person by translating "it is said." However, the passive formulation will not be helpful in some languages. Mft has "my opponent says . . ."; NJB "someone said." RSV is correct in taking this as a real situation rather than a hypothetical one (TEV). Though the third person singular verb in Greek may be understood impersonally in the sense of "it is said" or **they say** (RSV), it is perhaps better to use a third person singular subject and verb in translation, as in NJB: "Someone said, 'His letters . . . .'" TEV uses a singular subject and verb, "someone will say," but TEV also gives the impression that Paul is speaking about a hypothetical situation. NJB is probably correct in showing that Paul is referring to a real situation in which an unnamed person has criticized him.

His letters . . . his presence . . . his speech: it should be made clear in the receptor language that the third person singular pronouns here refer to Paul. If the accusation is changed from direct to indirect speech, one must translate using first person singular pronouns: ". . . that my letters are hard, but I am weak when I am with you and my words are worthless."

Weighty and strong are not to be understood in a physical sense but figuratively as meaning "strict and stern" or "severe and forceful" (NAB).

His bodily presence: the Greek is quite literally "the presence of his body," but the idea is that of nearness or physical presence as opposed to distance or total absence, during which time Paul wrote letters to maintain contact. The contrast may be heightened by saying "when he is not here" when talking about **his letters**, and "when he is here" or "when he is with us" in this case.

His speech refers specifically to his style of speaking in public, rather than to the content of his speech. Paul does not speak with the highly popular oratorical style of some of the Greek philosophers. See also 11.6.

Of no account: these words reflect a passive verb form that is usually translated "despised." The meaning is quite strong and means more than merely "a poor orator" (Knox). AB and NRSV use the word "contemptible," while Mft and REB have "beneath contempt."

10.11 RSV	TEV
Let such people understand that what we say by letter when absent, we do when present.	Such a person must understand that there is no difference between what we write in our letters when we are away and what we will do when we are there with you.

Let such people understand: such people is literally "such a one." See comment on verse 7, and note that it will be important to translate here in a way that will refer to the person mentioned in verse 7. The verb form used here expresses Paul's wish that the person or persons involved would realize and admit the fact that Paul is consistent in his dealing with the Corinthians. In some languages it may be better to use the first person singular pronoun as the subject of the sentence, as in NJB, "I should like that sort of person to take note . . . ."

What we say by letter: it will be more natural in many languages to translate as in TEV, "what we write in our letters."

Absent and **present** mean "away from you [in Corinth]" and "there with you [in Corinth]" (TEV, FRCL).

When present may also be expressed "when I come" (REB). Some translations need to indicate that this will not be Paul's first visit: "when I come again" or "when I return to you" (see also 10.2).

10.12 RSV	TEV
Not that we venture to class or compare ourselves with some of those who commend themselves. But when they measure themselves by one another, and compare themselves with one another, they are without understanding.	Of course we would not dare classify ourselves or compare ourselves with those who rate themselves so highly. How stupid they are! They make up their own standards to measure themselves by, and they judge themselves by their own standards!

Paul is speaking with a bit of irony or sarcasm as he states that he and his co-workers would not dare to consider themselves as equals to those who commend themselves. Paul is referring, of course, to his opponents in Corinth.

Venture: the same verb is used in verse 2 above and translated "showing," but implies showing boldness. Here, however, the context is slightly different. This verb is also found in Rom 5.7 and 15.18. The idea is to "dare" (NRSV, CEV) or "to be so bold as to" (compare NAB).

To class or compare ourselves: the two words used here are very similar in form and meaning. They form a kind of play on words in Greek. One commentator suggests the English words "to pair and compare" as similar. But it will probably be impossible to reflect the original word-play in most languages. Languages have different ways of talking about sorting things into groups or classes. Some speak of putting things (or people) in the same row or line, while others may use another image such as "the same basket" or "the same bag."

Who commend themselves: this is the same expression used frequently throughout this letter. See comments at 3.1; 4.2; 5.12; 6.4; and 7.11.

But: the conjunction here introduces and underlines the contrast with those who "commend themselves." AB has "indeed." Paul now begins to speak directly and harshly, no longer with sarcasm.

Measure . . . compare: the first verb here is the usual one for measuring anything. The second is the same as the verb translated similarly above. Paul's enemies are themselves their own standard of measurement. The idea of **compare** is expressed in some languages as "look at along side of" or "examine together with."

Some manuscripts do not have the last two words of this verse (**they are without understanding**) and the first two words of verse 13 (**But we**). The editors of the UBS *Greek New Testament* explain the absence of these words in a few manuscripts as the result of an accidental omission. Nearly all translations agree in retaining these words, though a few (Mft) follow those manuscripts that omit them. Some other ways of expressing **they are without understanding** are as follows: "they lack knowledge," "their discernment fails," or "they need insight from others."

10.13 RSV	TEV
But we will not boast beyond limit, but will keep to the limits God has apportioned us, to reach even to you.	As for us, however, our boasting will not go beyond certain limits; it will stay within the limits of the work which God has set for us, and this includes our work among you.

The RSV translation is rather literal and incomprehensible in English. This is a difficult verse to translate, but the general meaning is clear. Unlike the "false apostles" in Corinth who claim an authority in Corinth that they have no right to claim, Paul will not lay claim to any authority that is beyond the area which God has given him to work in. That area includes Corinth, where he himself founded the church. The point of verses 13-14 is that Paul is not going beyond what God commissioned him to do when he exercises his apostolic authority in the church at Corinth.

The words **But we** are emphatic in Greek. "As for us, however" (TEV) or "by contrast we" (NJB) better preserve the emphasis of the Greek than does the RSV translation. Paul is contrasting himself and his co-workers with his opponents whom he has ridiculed in verse 12.

Will not boast beyond limit: Paul continues the theme of "boasting" (see 9.2,3; 10.8). His words here have a double meaning: there is a limit to the amount of his talk or boasting and a limit to the geographic area of his authority. Paul's boasting won't go out of control, because God controls him and his work, which includes his work with the Corinthians.

To reach even you: this is a rather cryptic way of saying that Paul's work among the Corinthians is well within the bounds of what God had called him to do, even if the scope of his work is seen as limited.

The meaning of verse 13 is clearly expressed in CEV: "We won't brag about something we don't have a right to brag about. We will only brag about the work that God has sent us to do, and you are part of that work." NCV provides another possible model: "But we will not brag about things outside the work that was given us to do. We will limit our bragging to the work that God gave us. And this work includes our work with you."

10.14 RSV	TEV
For we are not overextending ourselves, as though we did not reach you; we were the first to come all the way to you with the gospel of Christ.	And since you are within those limits, we were not going beyond them when we came to you, bringing the Good News about Christ.

The first part of verse 14 justifies the claim that Paul makes in the preceding verse. Paul was within the limits of the work God had assigned to him when he preached the gospel in Corinth.

We are not overextending ourselves: these words translate a present tense verb, but this is rendered as past by TEV and NRSV: "we were not overstepping our limits." Probably Paul's words have a double sense. (1) He has not gone too far by encroaching on territory not included in his calling (so TEV). REB speaks of "not overstretching our commission." (2) But in addition, he also means that he is not extending himself by writing them this letter (so RSV); writing this letter is within the realm of his apostolic authority. NIV says "we are not going too far in our boasting" (similarly CEV and NCV). Use of the past tense as in TEV eliminates the second meaning. Translators should therefore use a verb tense which allows for both meanings, if possible.

As though we did not reach you: the present participle represented by these words may indicate that Paul was thinking about his continuing responsibilities toward the Corinthian believers as well as his past activity in founding the church there. But it is probably better to translate something like "as would be the case if we had not come to you" (NIV).

We were the first to come: the Greek verb may be translated as "to come before [someone else]" as in RSV (also NRSV, REB, NAB, TOB, SPCL, NBE), or simply "to come" as in TEV (also FRCL, GNC). If one follows the interpretation of RSV, then Paul is explicitly stating that he had preached the gospel in Corinth before his opponents ever arrived there. Both meanings of this verb are found elsewhere in Paul's other letters. Either seems to fit equally well here. Since there is no sure way to know which meaning Paul intended here, translators must simply decide to follow either RSV or TEV.

All the way to you: this repeats the same phrase found in verse 13 above, where it is translated "even to you."

The gospel of Christ refers to "the gospel about Christ."

10.15	RSV	TEV

We do not boast beyond limit, in other men's labors; but our hope is that as your faith increases, our field among you may be greatly enlarged,	So we do not boast about the work that others have done beyond the limits God set for us. Instead, we hope that your faith may grow and that we may be able to do a much greater work among you, always within the limits that God has set.

Verse 15 contains an implicit criticism of Paul's opponents, that they have exceeded their rights to boast because they have based their claims on someone else's (Paul's) work.

The first half of verse 15 is basically a restatement of 10.13a. If Paul were to boast and take credit for the missionary work of other evangelists, he would be taking credit for work he had not done.

In other men's labors may be understood to include the work of women as well as men. TEV, NRSV, and REB all use a more inclusive word, "others." REB translates 10.15a as follows: "And we do not boast of work done where others have laboured, work beyond our proper sphere."

But: this seems to mark the contrast between what Paul does not do (**boast beyond limit**) and what he does do (**hope**). TEV introduces the change with "instead."

The Greek grammar of 10.15b is rather difficult, but the point seems to be that, as the Corinthians' faith grows, Paul and his co-workers will be able to have an even greater ministry among the Christians there. REB says "Our hope is rather that, as your faith grows, we may attain a position among you greater than ever before, but still within the limits of our sphere."

Our field among you may be greatly enlarged: is literally only "among you to be magnified." The subject of the passive verb "magnified," translated **enlarged**, is not actually specified, but most scholars seem to feel that the implied subject is the "area of activity" (NIV) or **field** (RSV) of Paul and his associates. While the meaning of the verb is thought to be **enlarged**, "magnified" can also mean "praised," as it probably does here. In this case the implied subject is Paul and his colleagues themselves rather than their **field** of service. Of the eight occurrences of this verb in the New Testament, six of them have to do with praise. For example, it is translated by the verb "extol" (Acts 10.46; 19.17) and "honor" (Phil 1.20), or "hold in high honor" (Acts 5.13). AB therefore translates "[our hope is that as your faith grows] we may be abundantly praised among you." If this interpretation is followed, the passive construction may be avoided by saying something like "that you may give us abundant praise" or "that you may abundantly praise our work." REB seems to follow this same basic interpretation when it says "that our influence may also grow among you and overflow." This meaning may be more simply worded as in the footnote alternative of CEV: "you will praise us even more because of our work among you."

In addition to taking "magnified" as "praised," AB also includes the final clause "in accord with our jurisdiction" and notes that, by repeating a part of the phrase in verse 13, Paul is clarifying the idea of being praised on the basis of the principle presented in that verse.

10.16 RSV	TEV
so that we may preach the gospel in lands beyond you, without boasting of work already done in another's field.	Then we can preach the Good News in other countries beyond you and shall not have to boast about work already done in another man's field.

Gospel: that is, the Good News about Jesus Christ.

In lands beyond you probably refers to new territory to the west, as far as Spain (see Rom 15.24,28). The word translated **lands beyond** is a noun created from an adverb meaning "beyond." It is used only here in all the New Testament. Some versions supply the noun "lands" (REB as well as RSV), others have "regions" (NIV) or "areas" (Barrett). There is no particular focus on political entities, as TEV might suggest. So it is probably better to use a more general geographical term such as "regions." Since Spain is to the west of Corinth, it can be legitimate to translate "in areas to the west of you."

Without boasting of work already done in another's field repeats the thought of verse 15a. Some may prefer to translate this as a separate sentence: "[By going into places where no one has preached the Good News] we will not praise ourselves for work that other people have already done in those places where God gave them work to do."

10.17 RSV	TEV
"Let him who boasts, boast of the Lord."	But as the scripture says, "Whoever wants to boast must boast about what the Lord has done."

Verse 17 is a freely-worded quotation from Jer 9.24, the second time that Paul has quoted this verse in his letters to the Corinthians (see 1 Cor 1.31). The quotation marks in RSV, NRSV, and NAB indicate that Paul is quoting these words, without identifying the source. Other translations print this verse in italics to show that it is a quotation from scripture, and cite the source from Jeremiah in a note (NBE, NJB, LPD). TEV, CEV, and FRCL make explicit that Paul is quoting from the scripture by adding "as the scripture says." (See comments on 13.1). ITCL introduces the quotation by adding "The scripture says" and also uses italics for the quotation.

Boast of the Lord: NAB, NIV, and NRSV have "boast in the Lord." TEV correctly takes this to mean "about what the Lord has done." **The Lord** in verses 17 and 18 is probably Christ rather than God, though either is possible (in the passage in Jeremiah itself, of course, "the LORD" is God), and the translator should leave the matter open. But if the language forces a decision, it will probably be better to say "the Lord Christ."

10.18 RSV	TEV
For it is not the man who commends himself that is accepted, but the man whom the Lord commends.	For it is when the Lord thinks well of a person that he is really approved, and not when he thinks well of himself.

The translation **the man** is misleading. The meaning is rather "the person." Though the Greek uses masculine pronouns, Paul no doubt includes both women and men. To avoid giving the impression in English that only men are referred to, NRSV uses the plural pronouns "those" and "themselves."

Is accepted: the Greek does not state who accepts the person whom the Lord commends. Does Paul mean "The Lord does not approve of the person who commends himself" or "Other human beings do not accept the person who commends himself"? Either interpretation is possible, though perhaps divine approval fits better in the context. In those languages where the use of a passive verb is impossible in this context, one should probably translate "that the Lord accepts" rather than "that other people accept."

The whole structure of this verse may be changed as in TEV for some languages. Another possible alternative is "For the person who praises himself does not really have praise (or, honor). The one whom the Lord approves, that is the one who has true praise."

D-2. Paul and the false apostles

11.1-15

RSV	TEV
	Paul and the False Apostles
1 I wish you would bear with me in a little foolishness. Do bear with me! 2 I feel a divine jealousy for you, for I betrothed you to Christ to present you as a pure bride to her one husband. 3 But I am afraid that as the serpent deceived Eve by his cunning, your thoughts will be led astray from a sincere and pure devotion to Christ. 4 For if some one comes and preaches another Jesus than the one we preached, or if you receive a different spirit from the one you received, or if you	1 I wish you would tolerate me, even when I am a bit foolish. Please do! 2 I am jealous for you, just as God is; you are like a pure virgin whom I have promised in marriage to one man only, Christ himself. 3 I am afraid that your minds will be corrupted and that you will abandon your full and pure devotion to Christ—in the same way that Eve was deceived by the snake's clever lies. 4 For you gladly tolerate anyone who comes to you and preaches a different Jesus, not the one we

accept a different gospel from the one you accepted, you submit to it readily enough. 5 I think that I am not in the least inferior to these superlative apostles. 6 Even if I am unskilled in speaking, I am not in knowledge; in every way we have made this plain to you in all things.

7 Did I commit a sin in abasing myself so that you might be exalted, because I preached God's gospel without cost to you? 8 I robbed other churches by accepting support from them in order to serve you. 9 And when I was with you and was in want, I did not burden any one, for my needs were supplied by the brethren who came from Macedonia. So I refrained and will refrain from burdening you in any way. 10 As the truth of Christ is in me, this boast of mine shall not be silenced in the regions of Achaia. 11 And why? Because I do not love you? God knows I do!

12 And what I do I will continue to do, in order to undermine the claim of those who would like to claim that in their boasted mission they work on the same terms as we do. 13 For such men are false apostles, deceitful workmen, disguising themselves as apostles of Christ. 14 And no wonder, for even Satan disguises himself as an angel of light. 15 So it is not strange if his servants also disguise themselves as servants of righteousness. Their end will correspond to their deeds.

preached; and you accept a spirit and a gospel completely different from the Spirit and the gospel you received from us!

5 I do not think that I am the least bit inferior to those very special so-called "apostles" of yours! 6 Perhaps I am an amateur in speaking, but certainly not in knowledge; we have made this clear to you at all times and in all conditions.

7 I did not charge you a thing when I preached the Good News of God to you; I humbled myself in order to make you important. Was that wrong of me? 8 While I was working among you, I was paid by other churches. I was robbing them, so to speak, in order to help you. 9 And during the time I was with you I did not bother you for help when I needed money; the brothers who came from Macedonia brought me everything I needed. As in the past, so in the future: I will never be a burden to you! 10 By Christ's truth in me, I promise that this boast of mine will not be silenced anywhere in all of Achaia. 11 Do I say this because I don't love you? God knows I love you!

12 I will go on doing what I am doing now, in order to keep those other "apostles" from having any reason for boasting and saying that they work in the same way that we do. 13 Those men are not true apostles— they are false apostles, who lie about their work and disguise themselves to look like real apostles of Christ. 14 Well, no wonder! Even Satan can disguise himself to look like an angel of light! 15 So it is no great thing if his servants disguise themselves to look like servants of righteousness. In the end they will get exactly what their actions deserve.

SECTION HEADING: TEV "Paul and the False Apostles." In verses 1-15 Paul argues that he is in no way inferior to rival apostles, whom he sarcastically calls "superapostles," apostles whose authority the church at Corinth is accepting while rejecting that of Paul. Various translations have a section heading similar to that in TEV (so NIV, NVSR, FRCL, GECL, Lu, SPCL). Interpreters do not agree on who these "superapostles" were, but fortunately for translation purposes it is not necessary to identify them. In some languages it may be better to leave the name of Paul out of the section heading altogether— partly because the way of expressing "False Apostles" will be so long. Some translators may wish to indicate that this section is about "People who pretend to be apostles" or "Liars who say they are Apostles."

Other interpreters group 11.1–12.13 together. Some translations close this section at the end of 12.10 (REB), while others continue to the end of 12.18 (NJB). Various titles have been given to this division (REB "Paul speaks as a fool," or NJB "Paul is driven to sound his own praises"). According to this longer division of the text (11.1–12.13), Paul interrupts his appeal for obedience from the Corinthians to make a "fool's" speech. In 12.14 he resumes his appeal for obedience. Since Paul has to defend his apostolic status and authority, he is forced to boast of his credentials, the very thing for which he criticizes the "superapostles"!

Paul's language in 11.1–12.18 is full of irony and parody. That is, he uses words to say something that is the opposite of the literal meaning of his words, and he deliberately criticizes his opponents in Corinth by imitating their claims to apostolic authority.

11.1   RSV   TEV

> I wish you would bear with me in   I wish you would tolerate me,
> a little foolishness. Do bear with me!   even when I am a bit foolish. Please do!

The pronoun **you** in this verse and throughout chapter 11 is plural, referring to the Christian community at Corinth, or to some group within it.

The verb **bear with**, used twice in this verse, may also be rendered "be patient with," as in TNT. The same Greek word is translated "endure" in 1 Cor 4.12, and later in this chapter (verse 4) it is rendered "submit." The idea of being patient or tolerant with someone or something is rendered in some languages as "close your heart for," "accept," or "support."

The pronoun **me** in Greek may be taken with the verb **bear with** as in RSV and TEV, or with the noun **foolishness** as in NIV ("put up with a little of my foolishness," so also NJB). Probably the pronoun should go with the verb, as it does at the end of the verse, but either way the meaning is essentially the same.

Foolishness: the terms for "fool" and "foolishness" occur more frequently in 2 Corinthians than in any other New Testament book. These terms are derived from the verb meaning "to foam at the mouth," which was thought to be a sign of an insane person. Here, of course, foolishness is used in a figurative sense of not using one's good judgment. The word for "foolishness" is repeated in verses 17 and 21. Related terms are found in verses 16 and 19 of this chapter and in 12.6,11.

The verb in the second sentence of this verse is taken as a command by RSV and TEV, but it is also possible to understand the verb as a statement of fact, as in NIV and TNT for example, since the verb form may be either imperative (command) or indicative (statement). The first two Greek words in this second sentence are left untranslated in RSV and TEV, but they may be understood as expressing emphasis (so AB, "Indeed, do put up with me!") or as expressing a contrast with the first sentence of the verse, as in NIV ("but you are already doing that"). Either interpretation fits the context, but perhaps the context favors taking 11.1b as a command, as in RSV and TEV.

11.2   RSV   TEV

I feel a divine jealousy for you, for I betrothed you to Christ to present you as a pure bride to her one husband.	I am jealous for you, just as God is; you are like a pure virgin whom I have promised in marriage to one man only, Christ himself.

Paul considers himself to be like a father to the Christians of Corinth (see 1 Cor 4.15), a father who keeps a watchful eye on his daughter who has been promised in marriage.

Verse 2 is connected to the preceding verse in Greek with the word "for." RSV and TEV leave this word untranslated, but translators in other languages may choose to translate this word, which expresses the reason for Paul's wish and command in verse 1.

I feel a divine jealousy is literally "I have zeal (or, jealousy) with a zeal of God." A formal equivalent for the English adjective **divine** may be very difficult to find in some languages. It may be more natural to be closer to the Greek in this case: "I am jealous for you, and this jealousy comes from God." Others may reflect the fact that this "jealousy" is not to be understood in a negative sense, by saying "I love you as God loves you" or "I care deeply for you . . ." (AB). The word **jealousy** in English is usually used for the strong, angry feelings of people who are worried that they will lose the affection of a spouse or of someone else whom they love. Therefore it will be important to use a term that is suitable for this context, namely, that of a parent, for example, who is deeply concerned for a betrothed child and is therefore constantly watchful, constantly protecting the child.

I betrothed you: NRSV makes the meaning clearer and more natural English with "I promised you in marriage." Or one may prefer "it was I who arranged for your engagement" (Brc). In some languages it may be advisable to make the figurative character of this image more obvious in translation. TEV does this by saying "you are like a pure virgin whom I have promised in marriage." Or one may say "I see you as a young woman who has never known a man, and I have arranged for you to marry one man, that is, Christ."

A pure bride is rendered in REB as "a chaste virgin."

The **one husband**, or "one man," that is, Jesus Christ. Compare 1 Cor 7.2, where Paul indicates that "each man should have his own wife and each woman her own husband."

11.3   RSV   TEV

But I am afraid that as the serpent deceived Eve by his cunning, your thoughts will be led astray from a sincere and pure devotion to Christ.	I am afraid that your minds will be corrupted and that you will abandon your full and pure devotion to Christ—in the same way that Eve was deceived by the snake's clever lies.

Verse 3 is connected to verse 2 with the word **But**, which TEV does not translate. Verse 3 is in contrast to what Paul hopes for on the basis of his actions described in verse 2. In many languages it will be helpful to mark this contrast explicitly, using a conjunction like "but" or "however."

As the serpent deceived Eve: Paul alludes here to the account in Gen 3.1-6,13. Some languages will need to indicate that this incident refers to a time in the remote past. Though Paul does not identify the **serpent** with Satan, he probably understood the passage in Genesis as referring to Satan (see Wisdom of Solomon 2.24).

On the translation of **cunning** see 4.2. In some languages it will be redundant to translate this word explicitly, since the verb used to translate **deceived** will already contain the idea of cunning or trickery.

Your thoughts will be led astray: the verb **led astray** has a root meaning of "ruin," "corrupt," or "spoil." In some languages a word such as "spoil" rather than "lead astray" may tie in better with the following words **sincere and pure**. As the next verse indicates, the implicit agent of the verb **be led astray** is "someone who preaches a different gospel from the one that Paul preaches." In those languages where a passive verb cannot naturally be used here, one may have to say "someone will trick you and make you abandon [your faith in Christ]," or possibly even "by their cunning those false apostles will cause you to go away from [Christ]." Since Paul more than likely had specific persons in mind, it is not a good idea to make Satan the primary subject of the verb "to lead astray" in the receptor language. Languages often have rather unusual ways of talking about deceiving or leading other people astray. Some may say things like "to lead by the ears" or "to treat like an animal."

The word **sincere** (literally "sincerity") is translated in RSV as "liberality" in 8.2 and "generosity" in 9.11,13. Here the sense is "singleness of purpose," that is, a "full" or "total" (AB) devotion.

Pure is literally "purity." Some manuscripts omit the word **pure** after sincere (followed by NJB, TOB, and REB), but the editors of the UBS *Greek New Testament* kept the word "pure" in brackets, thinking it is more likely that a scribe accidentally omitted the word. But since the meaning of the two words is very similar in this context, they may possibly be rendered by a single term in the receptor language.

Both RSV and TEV restructure according to the implied meaning of the Greek, adding **devotion** to show that the "sincerity" and "purity" are qualities demonstrating a relationship with Christ. The Greek phrase may also be rendered "sincerity and purity [maintained] toward [or, for the sake of] Christ." For normal English, of course, RSV and TEV do well to restructure as they do.

One possible restructuring of this verse may be as follows: "You remember the old story about the snake tricking Eve. I am afraid that you will be like that. Someone will trick you and then you will abandon your true and complete love for Christ."

For if some one comes and preaches another Jesus than the one we preached, or if you receive a different spirit from the one you received, or if you accept a different gospel from the one you accepted, you submit to it readily enough.	For you gladly tolerate anyone who comes to you and preaches a different Jesus, not the one we preached; and you accept a spirit and a gospel completely different from the Spirit and the gospel you received from us!

The word **For** connects verse 4 both to verse 3, indicating why Paul is concerned, and to verse 1, indicating why he expects that they should bear with him also, since they are willing to tolerate those who preach a gospel contrary to what Paul preaches. NAB shows the connection more clearly by beginning this verse "I say this because . . . ."

The words **if some one comes** should not be understood to mean that Paul is talking about a hypothetical situation, that is, about an event only imagined, but one which could indeed happen at any time. Verses 11.19-20 make clear that he is dealing with a problem already present in Corinth. To avoid suggesting that Paul is speaking hypothetically, TEV omits the word **if**. And other English versions use "when" or "whenever." The words **some one** may refer to a group or possibly to a representative person. Though the relationship with verse 5 is not entirely clear, Paul is probably referring to a representative from the group he calls the "superlative apostles" in the next verse. (See also 12.11.) Paul appears to be referring to someone from outside the Corinthian church, so REB says "if some newcomer proclaims." Or, to avoid giving the impression that Paul is not referring to a real life situation, one may prefer to say "whenever a newcomer comes and . . . ."

Preaches another Jesus: in many languages it is awkward to talk about "preaching a person." Rather it is more natural to say "preach a message about a person" or "preach the story of a person." Although expressions like "preach Jesus" may have entered into the vocabulary of church members, translators should avoid language that is exclusive to Christians and use what is most natural for all speakers of the language. The idea is clearly that of preaching a message that is not consistent with the facts about Jesus. Some may say "tells you about a different Jesus" or "preaches another message concerning Jesus."

Implicit in the expressions **from the one you received** and **from the one you accepted** is that the Corinthians **received** a spirit and **accepted** a gospel "from us," that is, from Paul and his associates. TEV and FRCL make this information explicit.

You submit to it readily enough: this part of the verse may have to be transposed to a position much earlier in the structure of some languages, as in TEV "you gladly tolerate . . . ." It may also be necessary to break the verse down into two or more sentences:

You seem so eager to accept a new person when he comes and tells you about a different Jesus. That is not the Jesus we told you about. And you happily pay attention when you receive a spirit and a message that are not like the Spirit and the message that we brought to you.

A different sort of restructuring of this verse is found in CEV:

We told you about Jesus, and you received the Holy Spirit and accepted our message. But you let some people tell you about another Jesus. Now you are ready to receive another spirit and accept another message.

11.5   RSV   TEV

I think that I am not in the least infe-   I do not think that I am the least
rior to these superlative apostles.   bit inferior to those very special so-
                                                  called "apostles" of yours!

The term **superlative apostles** may be a straightforward description of Paul's enemies, but given the use of irony in this part of 2 Corinthians, Paul's language is no doubt to be understood as irony. He does not really consider them to be superapostles (see 11.12; 12.11). TEV captures the note of irony with the words "so-called 'apostles' of yours" (see also the use of quotation marks in NIV: "those 'superapostles' "). In some languages there are special particles that express the sense of irony. A literal translation of the words **superlative apostles** may distort Paul's intended criticism. The identity of these super-apostles is much debated, and fortunately one's translation does not depend on the answer that one gives. Translators may need to identify these words as irony by a footnote, as Williams does ("cutting sarcasm"), in order to make clear that Paul does not really regard these persons as superapostles. In those languages where the irony will be misunderstood, it may be necessary to state more directly that these people were "those who pretend to be apostles."

These superlative apostles is literally "the superapostles." The Greek term for **superlative** means "outstanding, extra-special." Almost certainly Paul is referring to the people who have preached a different gospel in Corinth from that which he preached (verse 4). RSV says **these** superlative apostles to indicate that Paul is not introducing a new group but is rather referring to the group mentioned in verse 4. Similarly TEV and FRCL indicate that the super-apostles were accepted in the Corinthian church: "of yours." SPCL makes explicit that these superapostles "came after" Paul to the church in Corinth: "I am not inferior to those superapostles who came later."

Some languages have attempted to get at the meaning by translating "I think that those people you call 'the big apostles' are not really bigger than I am at all" and "I don't think that your special 'apostles' do any better work than I do!"

On the translation of the word for **apostle**, see 1.1. In languages where an expression like "one sent from God" is used, it may be necessary to indicate that Paul did not consider them necessarily sent from God, by saying "those big men who think they have been sent by God" or ". . . who claim that God has sent them."

11.6   RSV   TEV

Even if I am unskilled in speaking, I am not in knowledge; in every way we have made this plain to you in all things.   Perhaps I am an amateur in speaking, but certainly not in knowledge; we have made this clear to you at all times and in all conditions.

Unskilled in speaking: the word **unskilled** means "untrained" (NRSV). Paul was not an expert in this area. **In speaking** refers specifically to "public speaking" (AB). The meaning is clearly expressed in GNC, "Granted that I lack skill as an orator." Or a better model in some languages may be "It is true that I do not speak well before crowds (or, other people)." See comments on 10.10.

Not in knowledge: the translation of these words will depend to some extent on the way the first part of this verse has been rendered. But in many cases a verbal expression will be called for: "I may not speak as well as they do, but I know as much as they do" or "my knowledge is not inferior to theirs, even if my public speaking is."

In every way and **in all things**: according to both RSV and TEV, Paul has made plain his knowledge **in every way** and **in all things** to the Corinthians. Another interpretation is possible, however. The words **in all things** may be masculine, that is, "among all men." If this second interpretation is followed, the sense of 11.6b is that expressed in GNC: "And that is a fact which we have made evident in every way among men, wherever they may be, through what we are in our relations with you."

11.7   RSV   TEV

Did I commit a sin in abasing myself so that you might be exalted, because I preached God's gospel without cost to you?   I did not charge you a thing when I preached the Good News of God to you; I humbled myself in order to make you important. Was that wrong of me?

Verse 7 is a rhetorical question that expects the answer "No." In some languages the sense will be clearer if this is rendered as in TEV, as a clear negative statement followed by the question "Was that the wrong thing to do?" The answer will then be obvious. Or in other cases the most natural rendering will include the explicit answer "No!" after the question has been asked.

In abasing myself: Paul "humbled" himself (TEV, NRSV). The verb used here is related to the noun "humble" in 10.1. One language has translated "I became like a common laborer." Another speaks of "lowering myself [in order to lift you up]."

That you might be exalted: exaltation, or lifting up, is a common theme in both the Old and the New Testaments and in some cases refers to ultimate exaltation to heavenly glory. However, in this case it is simply the opposite of humiliation. Paul endures humiliation in order to show respect for the Corinthian Christians. The passive may be avoided by following the model of CEV, "honor you."

Paul identifies his gospel as **God's gospel**. Unlike the superapostles who preached a "different gospel" (11.4), Paul's gospel comes from God.

Without cost to you means that Paul did not ask for any remuneration from the Corinthian church. Note that TEV transposes this to the beginning of the verse. Some other possible models of this clause are "I did not make you pay me for the Good News that I preached to you" or "I did not ask for money when I told you the Good News."

11.8	RSV	TEV
	I robbed other churches by accepting support from them in order to serve you.	While I was working among you, I was paid by other churches. I was robbing them, so to speak, in order to help you.

Paul does not mean that he literally **robbed other churches**. To show that Paul is using figurative language, TEV adds the words "so to speak." In other languages it may be more natural and less likely to be misunderstood if the figurative meaning is rendered "It was as if I was robbing . . . ."

The **other churches** were not other churches in the city of Corinth, but most likely churches in the region of Macedonia (see verse 9). In some languages it may sound awkward to speak of robbing "churches." The object of the verb is more naturally "people." Consequently one may translate "robbing the people of other churches."

In English the word **support** is rather broad in meaning, including emotional help as well as material help. The Greek word is more limited, meaning "wages," "salary," or "provisions." SPCL translates the Greek word as "money," as does CEV. Brc speaks of "taking pay."

In order to serve you: literally, "for your ministry [*diakonia*]." See comments on *diakonia* at 3.7.

11.9	RSV	TEV
	And when I was with you and was in want, I did not burden any one, for my needs were supplied by the brethren who came from Macedonia. So I re-	And during the time I was with you I did not bother you for help when I needed money; the brothers who came from Macedonia brought me everything

frained and will refrain from burdening you in any way.

I needed. As in the past, so in the future: I will never be a burden to you!

In want refers in this context specifically to material needs such as food, money, and clothing. The term used here is related to the one for **wants** in 9.12, which is also the same word that is rendered **needs** later in this verse. Possibly financial needs are primary here, as TEV makes explicit, "when I needed money." But it may be best to use a more general word as in Greek. See for example NIV, "when I . . . needed something." Another version speaks of "my necessities." And NRSV uses the English idiom "if I ran short." In other languages people may use verbs like "be lacking" or simply "want." Still others may have more unusual expressions like "have an empty sack" or "lose one's purse (money pouch)."

I did not burden any one: that is, Paul did not burden anyone among the Corinthian Christians. The same verb is used again in 12.13 and 14 but nowhere else in the New Testament. This idea may be expressed in a variety of ways: "I never asked you for anything at all," "I was no encumbrance to anybody" (Mft), "I didn't bother you" (CEV).

The brethren who came from Macedonia: some languages will need to use a possessive pronoun with the word **brethren**: either "my brothers" or "our [not including the readers] brothers." It is not clear whether these brothers were Paul's co-workers Timothy and Silas (see Acts 18.5) or, less likely, whether they were Macedonian Christians. If the "brothers" were Christians from the churches in Macedonia, then women were perhaps included. In order not to exclude the possibility that women were included, NRSV and REB say "friends who came from Macedonia" and "friends from Macedonia." Neither NRSV nor REB is satisfactory, however, since neither translation would normally be understood to refer to Paul's co-workers. Perhaps a literal translation "the brothers" is preferable. CEV has "some of the Lord's followers."

On **Macedonia** see 1.16 and 2.13.

11.10

RSV	TEV
As the truth of Christ is in me, this boast of mine shall not be silenced in the regions of Achaia.	By Christ's truth in me, I promise that this boast of mine will not be silenced anywhere in all of Achaia.

As the truth of Christ is in me: this is a formula used to introduce a solemn statement which a person wants hearers or readers to be certain about. It is similar to the oath formula in Rom 9.1. While the word **truth** sometimes refers to the gospel in Paul's writings (4.2 and 6.7, for example), here it is more general in meaning, yet within what is Christian truth. This whole formula may fit better at the end of the verse in some languages.

This boast of mine, that is, his claim in the preceding verses not to have received help from the Corinthian Christians while he was in Corinth.

Will not be silenced: this passive formulation will have to be made active in many languages. What Paul is saying is that it would be impossible for another person to prevent him from speaking about this matter: "no one in all the country of Achaia shall silence this boast of mine" (Knox) or ". . . shall prevent me from boasting about this."

In the regions of Achaia: see comments on Achaia in 1.1 and 9.2. The word translated **regions** is a geographical term usually signifying a fairly small area. It does not refer to a political unit. The use of the plural here is commonly understood as referring to all the **regions** together forming the entire province, which would make this expression the same in meaning as "the whole of Achaia" in 1.1.

11.11 RSV TEV

And why? Because I do not love you? God knows I do!

Do I say this because I don't love you? God knows I love you!

And why? These words refer primarily to 11.9b rather than to verse 10. The meaning is "And why have I made it a rule not to be a burden to you?" rather than "Why will I not be silenced?" The referent of the demonstrative pronoun "this" in TEV is equally ambiguous. It will probably be better in most languages to make the meaning clear by saying "Why do I not burden you?" if the structure of RSV is adopted or, following a more dynamic rendering, "When I say that I will not burden you, is it because I do not love you?"

God knows I do! Literally simply "God knows." RSV supplies the implied information, which is further expanded by TEV.

11.12 RSV TEV

And what I do I will continue to do, in order to undermine the claim of those who would like to claim that in their boasted mission they work on the same terms as we do.

I will go on doing what I am doing now, in order to keep those other "apostles" from having any reason for boasting and saying that they work in the same way that we do.

What I do I will continue to do, that is, he will continue to refuse to accept financial help from the Corinthian Christians. Note that TEV has reversed the order of the two parts of this statement to make it more natural in English.

In order to undermine the claim: literally, "that I may cut off the basis . . . ." This expresses the purpose of Paul's continuing refusal to accept help from the Corinthian Christians. The word translated **claim** is the same as used in 5.12 for the "cause" or basis of the Corinthians pride in Paul. Here Paul wants to remove any ground or basis that might be used to compare his mission with that of the so-called "superapostles." Some possible models to translate this clause may be "I want to stop those people from having a reason [to brag]" (CEV) or "take away their opportunity . . ." (GNC).

Those who would like to claim: **those** refers to the superapostles of verse 5.

Who would like to claim: the RSV translation perhaps suggests that Paul's opponents were not actually making the claim to work on the same terms, but only that they **would like to**. Paul's opponents have in fact already made the claim which he is seeking to show to be false. This may be better translated "who want to have a basis . . . ."

In their boasted mission: NRSV is more like the original when it says "in what they boast about." There is no word corresponding to **mission** in the Greek.

The superapostles, however, really have no basis for claiming to work on the same terms as Paul does, since they have accepted support and continue to accept support from the Corinthians (see 11.20).

11.13	RSV	TEV
	For such men are false apostles, deceitful workmen, disguising themselves as apostles of Christ.	Those men are not true apostles—they are false apostles, who lie about their work and disguise themselves to look like real apostles of Christ.

The masculine plural pronouns, nouns, and participle in verse 13 may refer to males only (RSV, TEV), or they may include women as well as men. To allow for the latter possibility, REB says "Such people," and NRSV says "such boasters." The reference is to the superapostles of 11.5.

False apostles are people who claim to be apostles but really are not. In some languages one may translate the idea here by saying "such people are not apostles at all, even though they claim to be." See comments on the heading for this section.

Deceitful workmen: Paul considers these "false apostles" to be deceitful. Pretending to seek the spiritual well-being of the Corinthian Christians, they really seek their own well-being. Perhaps Paul intends a criticism by calling them **workmen**, that is, they take money from the Corinthians for what they do while Paul did not (11.7-9). REB renders this "confidence tricksters," where NEB has "crooked in all their practices." In some languages these two words may be better rendered by a verbal expression such as "they work at fooling people" or "they deceive people in their work."

Disguising themselves: the idea of disguise will be translated in some languages as "trying to make themselves look like . . ." or "they trick people into thinking they are . . . ."

11.14   RSV   TEV

And no wonder, for even Satan disguises himself as an angel of light.	Well, no wonder! Even Satan can disguise himself to look like an angel of light!

Paul apparently is alluding to Jewish traditions outside the Hebrew scriptures that tell of Satan disguising himself as a shining angel when he deceived Eve in the Garden of Eden. On **Satan** see comments on 2.11.

And no wonder that these false apostles behave in deceptive ways and disguise themselves to be what they are not; even Satan, who is their master (verse 15), behaved in a similar manner. Some languages may require a full verb phrase at this point: "It is no surprise that they do this!" or "we should not be astonished that this happens."

Disguises himself: or, as in the previous verse, "tries to make himself look like . . ." or "tricks people into thinking he is . . . ."

An angel of light: the relationship between the words **angel** and **of light** may be that the **angel** (or, messenger) brings light. But more likely Paul's thought reflects Jewish traditions in which Satan appears in the form of a shining angel in order to deceive people. The words **of light** function as an adjective, that is, "a shining angel" (AT). Most translations keep the form of the Greek, **angel of light**. Some omit the words **of light** (GECL, ITCL), since angels by nature shine with light. Translators should translate the words **of light**. AT is a good model, since it expresses clearly in English the Semitic influence on the Greek grammar here.

11.15   RSV   TEV

So it is not strange if his servants also disguise themselves as servants of righteousness. Their end will correspond to their deeds.	So it is no great thing if his servants disguise themselves to look like servants of righteousness. In the end they will get exactly what their actions deserve.

So: the transition word here indicates the logical inference of what has just been said about Satan. It may also be rendered "Then" (NJB and NIV) or "Therefore" (Brc and AB).

It is not strange: or, more literally, "nothing so great." The meaning here is not very different from the first words in the previous verse, "no wonder." AB has "it is . . . no great surprise." Similarly NJB has "it is nothing extraordinary."

The words **his servants**, that is, the servants of Satan, refer to the false apostles. **Servants** here is *diakonoi,* this time used in a context of evil.

Servants of righteousness: **righteousness** here probably does not have the theological connotation that it frequently has in Paul's writings. The meaning is more general here, that they disguise themselves "as agents of good" (REB) or "servants of uprightness" (NJB).

Their end will correspond to their deeds: literally "the end of whom will be according to their works." The idea of ultimate punishment is clearly implied here. The TEV rendering "In the end" may be easily misunderstood to mean "In the last days." But what is involved here is the end of these servants of Satan. The idea is more like "they will end up getting the punishment which they deserve."

D-3. Paul's sufferings as an apostle
11.16-33

RSV

16 I repeat, let no one think me foolish; but even if you do, accept me as a fool, so that I too may boast a little. 17 (What I am saying I say not with the Lord's authority but as a fool, in this boastful confidence; 18 since many boast of worldly things, I too will boast.) 19 For you gladly bear with fools, being wise yourselves! 20 For you bear it if a man makes slaves of you, or preys upon you, or takes advantage of you, or puts on airs, or strikes you in the face. 21 To my shame, I must say, we were too weak for that!

But whatever any one dares to boast of—I am speaking as a fool—I also dare to boast of that. 22 Are they Hebrews? So am I. Are they Israelites? So am I. Are they descendants of Abraham? So am I. 23 Are they servants of Christ? I am a better one—I am talking like a madman—with far greater labors, far more imprisonments, with countless beatings, and often near death. 24 Five times I have received at the hands of the Jews the forty lashes less one. 25 Three times I have been beaten with rods; once I was stoned. Three times I have been shipwrecked; a night and a day I have been adrift at sea; 26 on frequent journeys, in danger from rivers, danger from robbers, danger from my own people, danger from Gentiles, danger in the city, danger in the wilderness, danger at sea, danger from false brethren; 27 in toil and hardship, through many a sleepless night, in hunger and thirst, often without food, in cold and exposure. 28 And, apart from other things, there is the daily pressure upon me of my anxiety for all the churches. 29 Who is weak, and I am not weak? Who is made to fall, and I am not indignant?

30 If I must boast, I will boast of the things that show my weakness. 31 The God and Father of the Lord Jesus, he who is bless-

TEV

Paul's Sufferings as an Apostle

16 I repeat: no one should think that I am a fool. But if you do, at least accept me as a fool, just so I will have a little to boast of. 17 Of course what I am saying now is not what the Lord would have me say; in this matter of boasting I am really talking like a fool. 18 But since there are so many who boast for merely human reasons, I will do the same. 19 You yourselves are so wise, and so you gladly tolerate fools! 20 You tolerate anyone who orders you around or takes advantage of you or traps you or looks down on you or slaps you in the face. 21 I am ashamed to admit that we were too timid to do those things!

But if anyone dares to boast about something—I am talking like a fool—I will be just as daring. 22 Are they Hebrews? So am I. Are they Israelites? So am I. Are they Abraham's descendants? So am I. 23 Are they Christ's servants? I sound like a madman—but I am a better servant than they are! I have worked much harder, I have been in prison more times, I have been whipped much more, and I have been near death more often. 24 Five times I was given the thirty-nine lashes by the Jews; 25 three times I was whipped by the Romans; and once I was stoned. I have been in three shipwrecks, and once I spent twenty-four hours in the water. 26 In my many travels I have been in danger from floods and from robbers, in danger from fellow Jews and from Gentiles; there have been dangers in the cities, dangers in the wilds, dangers on the high seas, and dangers from false friends. 27 There has been work and toil; often I have gone without sleep; I have been hungry and thirsty; I have often been without enough food, shelter, or clothing. 28 And not to mention other things, every day I am under the pressure of my concern for all the churches. 29 When someone is weak, then

ed for ever, knows that I do not lie. 32 At Damascus, the governor under King Aretas guarded the city of Damascus in order to seize me, 33 but I was let down in a basket through a window in the wall, and escaped his hands.

I feel weak too; when someone is led into sin, I am filled with distress.

30 If I must boast, I will boast about things that show how weak I am. 31 The God and Father of the Lord Jesus—blessed be his name forever!—knows that I am not lying. 32 When I was in Damascus, the governor under King Aretas placed guards at the city gates to arrest me. 33 But I was let down in a basket through an opening in the wall and escaped from him.

SECTION HEADING: TEV "Paul's Sufferings as an Apostle." Numerous translations group verses 16-33 together under a heading similar to that in TEV (FRCL, NVSR, SPCL, NIV, Lu). In these verses Paul boasts of his weakness and sufferings, unlike the "superapostles." Such suffering, Paul argues, is a true sign of apostleship. Some other possible wordings for this section heading are "Paul's Sufferings for Christ" (CEV) and "Paul Tells about His Suffering" (NCV).

11.16	RSV	TEV

I repeat, let no one think me foolish; but even if you do, accept me as a fool, so that I too may boast a little.

I repeat: no one should think that I am a fool. But if you do, at least accept me as a fool, just so I will have a little to boast of.

This verse must be seen in the overall context of Paul's irony. But the logic may still be difficult to follow. Paul says first that he does not want to be taken for a fool and then speaks of actually being taken as a fool. His intention seems to be that, although he does not want to be considered a fool, on second thought to be accepted as a fool would have the advantage of allowing him to act in a foolish way and boast to a certain degree.

I repeat looks back to 11.1. In some languages the verb **repeat** will be out of place because of so much discourse between the first statement and this one. In such cases one may say "As I said earlier . . ." or "I have already said it, but I will say it again."

If you do: that is, if you do think I am foolish. Paul is asking that the Corinthians give him a hearing even if they do think he is being foolish. The idea here is "even if you see me as a fool, accept me . . ." or "at least treat me as you would a fool and tolerate my boasting."

Foolish . . . fool: see comments on verse 1.

The implication of the words **I too** . . . are that Paul's opponents in Corinth, the false apostles, were boasting. TEV fails to preserve this aspect of meaning. REB says "and let me have my little boast like others." See 11.18. In those languages that require some kind of object for the verb **boast**, it may be necessary to say "boast of myself" or something similar.

11.17 RSV	TEV
(What I am saying I say not with the Lord's authority but as a fool, in this boastful confidence;	Of course what I am saying now is not what the Lord would have me say; in this matter of boasting I am really talking like a fool.

Note that RSV encloses verses 17 and 18 in parentheses. But these marks are not used in NRSV. What is said in these two verses is a kind of a side explanation, but it will probably not be necessary to use parentheses in the receptor language.

What I am saying: not in the whole letter, but in this part of the letter in which he is boasting.

With the Lord's authority is literally "not according to the Lord." REB says "not speaking like a Christian." But this seems rather weak. Some other attempts to render the meaning of this expression are as follows: "is not inspired by the Lord" (Mft) and "I speak not as the Lord desires" (NAB). **The Lord** here refers to Jesus Christ (see comments on 2.12).

Instead of saying "not according to the Lord" (the text of the UBS *Greek New Testament*), a few manuscripts say "not according to God." One manuscript says "not according to man." The evidence of the manuscripts is overwhelming in support of the UBS text, and the editors give the reading in the text an "A" evaluation, indicating certainty that the text is the original reading.

The Greek word translated as **confidence** occurs at 9.4, where RSV translates it as "confident" and NRSV as "undertaking." REB says in 11.17 "In boasting so confidently." It is doubtful, however, whether the meaning "confidence" can be established for this Greek word. It seems better therefore to translate as "matter" (TEV) or "business" (AB). See comments on "confident" in 9.4. Some languages have restructured this part of the verse to say "when I am praising myself in that way, I am acting like a fool."

11.18 RSV	TEV
since many boast of worldly things, I too will boast.)	But since there are so many who boast for merely human reasons, I will do the same.

Of worldly things is literally "according to flesh." REB says "of their earthly distinctions" (similarly NAB). AB, on the other hand, translates "in a worldly way," indicating that this expression refers to the manner in which the boasting is done rather than the things of which other people boast. The latter interpretation seems somewhat more likely and is followed by NIV, "in the way the world does."

As in 11.16, Paul says that he **too** will boast, that is, in addition to the **many**. In this context, **many** is an indirect reference to the "superapostles."

11.19   RSV   TEV

For you gladly bear with fools, being wise yourselves!	You yourselves are so wise, and so you gladly tolerate fools!

Paul's language here is full of sarcasm as he refers to his opponents in Corinth as **fools**. He does not really think that the Corinthians "are so wise." Rather Paul thinks that they are very unwise because they gladly tolerate fools. In order to avoid suggesting that Paul's words should be taken literally, translators may wish to follow the model of LPD, which says "you who consider yourselves to be so wise." Alternatively translators may wish to include a note, as Williams does in his translation: "keenest sarcasm; even more sarcastic in next sentence."

On the translation of the verb **bear with**, see verse 1 above.

11.20   RSV   TEV

For you bear it if a man makes slaves of you, or preys upon you, or takes advantage of you, or puts on airs, or strikes you in the face.	You tolerate anyone who orders you around or takes advantage of you or traps you or looks down on you or slaps you in the face.

As elsewhere in 2 Corinthians, **if** is used for the effect that it creates and is not intended to express doubt about the reality of what follows. See comments on 11.4. TEV therefore omits the word **if**.

A man is literally "any one." Paul alludes indirectly to his opponents in Corinth. See also 11.21 and 10.7, where the same pronoun is used with the same referent. In view of the indefinite reference of this term, some languages may prefer to translate it by a plural, "people" or "they."

A major difficulty in translating this verse lies in deciding whether some or all of the verbs are to be taken as metaphorical language. If so, will a literal translation be understood literally by the readers?

The words **makes slaves of you** are used metaphorically. The sense is that Paul's opponents in Corinth are dominating the congregation there, treating the members of the church as if they were slaves. To avoid a literal understanding, some translations drop the metaphorical language (so TEV, GECL, and REB: "If someone tyrannizes over you") or change the metaphor to a simile ("commands you as slaves," FRCL).

Preys upon you is literally "eats you up." This is metaphorical language also, meaning "takes advantage of you" (TEV) or "exploits you" (NIV, REB). Or in a slightly more literal sense, Paul may mean that the opponents are being supported entirely by the Corinthians (so Barrett: "eats you out of house and home"). CEV adopts this same material interpretation in translating "steal from you."

Takes advantage of you: literally "if anyone receives [you]." The same verb is used in 12.16, where it is rendered "got the better of you." Barrett translates "gets you in his power."

Puts on airs: literally "lifts himself up." A direct rendering of the RSV expression will be absurd in most languages. The verb used here is found also in 10.5, where it is translated in RSV by the adjective "proud." Here it can be translated "behaves proudly" or, as AB puts it, "acts presumptuously." NJB speaks of one who "sets himself above you" (NJB).

Strikes you in the face is probably not to be taken literally, though nearly all translations render this phrase literally. Paul's opponents were insulting the Corinthians by the way they treated them. Martin says "even when he deeply insults you!" Knox also seeks to render the figurative sense here while maintaining the image of beating when he translates "browbeats you."

Mft provides a model worth considering for the verse as a whole: "You put up with a man who assumes control over your souls, with a man who spends your money, with a man who dupes you, with a man who gives himself airs, with a man who flies in your face."

11.21   RSV   TEV

To my shame, I must say, we were too weak for that!	I am ashamed to admit that we were too timid to do those things!
But whatever any one dares to boast of—I am speaking as a fool—I also dare to boast of that.	But if anyone dares to boast about something—I am talking like a fool—I will be just as daring.

The first sentence in this verse is strongly sarcastic. Paul means the opposite of what he says.

To my shame is literally "according to shame I speak," without any possessive pronoun. Possibly he means to the shame of the Corinthians (so NJB, "I say it to your shame"), but most likely he means to his own shame (so RSV, TEV, NRSV, NIV, NAB); this interpretation retains the sarcasm.

For that: TEV makes the meaning clearer by saying "to do those things," clearly referring to the series of negative actions described in the previous verse.

The pronoun **any one** refers specifically to Paul's opponents in Corinth. But, as in the previous verse, it may be better translated by a plural. See also 10.7. The structure here is a kind of comparison where Paul is comparing himself with **any one** who may be so bold as to boast. In some languages the idea "whatever someone else dares . . . I also dare" may have to be shifted to say "what others boast of . . . I also boast." And note that the parenthetic **I am speaking as a fool** may have to be shifted to the end of the verse or to a position much earlier rather than breaking up the comparison.

The words between dashes in RSV and TEV may be more easily understood if enclosed in parentheses in the receptor language. Or in some cases this sentence can be placed at the end of this verse without using parentheses. This in fact is what CEV has done by concluding "but it is a foolish thing to do."

| **11.22** | RSV | TEV |

Are they Hebrews? So am I. Are they Israelites? So am I. Are they descendants of Abraham? So am I.

Are they Hebrews? So am I. Are they Israelites? So am I. Are they Abraham's descendants? So am I.

In a series of brief rhetorical questions, Paul makes the point that he is no way inferior to his opponents. Both RSV and TEV are rather literal translations and fail to capture the dynamics of the situation. Paul's opponents were making claims about their own credentials in order to establish their authority in the church at Corinth. Martin expresses well the sense of Paul's questions: "Do they claim to be Hebrews? . . . Do they claim to be Israelites? . . ."

Hebrews were persons who were full-blooded Jews. The term may also imply that they spoke Hebrew or Aramaic. One's ethnic background is prominent in this word.

Israelites were persons who belonged to God's chosen covenant people. One's religious background is prominent in the word **Israelite**.

It is legitimate to highlight in the receptor language the fact that Paul is talking here about race, religion, and lineage in this series of questions. It should also be made clear that these were in fact the claims being made by the false apostles to establish their credibility. One possible model is "Do they claim to belong to the Hebrew race? So do I. Do they claim to belong to the Israelite (Jewish) religion? So do I. Do they say they are members of the family of Abraham? So am I." Another possible structure is "With regard to race, do they say they are Hebrews? So am I. With regard to religion, do they say they are Israelites? So am I. With regard to family (lineage), do they say they are descendants of Abraham? So am I."

| **11.23** | RSV | TEV |

Are they servants of Christ? I am a better one—I am talking like a madman—with far greater labors, far more imprisonments, with countless beatings, and often near death.

Are they Christ's servants? I sound like a madman—but I am a better servant than they are! I have worked much harder, I have been in prison more times, I have been whipped much more, and I have been near death more often.

The answer to the question at the beginning of this verse is slightly different from the ones given in the previous verse. In verse 22 the answer was "also I," but here it is "more so I." In the first case the idea of "more" may have to be translated "better," as in "I am a better servant of Christ" or "I serve Christ better . . . ."

I am talking like a madman: the word translated **madman** here is related to but stronger than "fool" in verse 21 above. If there are not two different degrees of madness in the receptor language, this progression from bad to worse may be reflected by the use of an additional adverb, "now I am *really* talking like a fool," or by some other means. As in verse 21, this parenthetical statement may fit better at the end of the verse rather than following the structure of RSV and TEV.

Far greater labors: this is not intended to indicate the greatness or importance of the work done, but rather the volume of work accomplished or the intensity with which Paul worked. Many modern versions speak of his having "worked harder." Some languages will naturally require that the comparison be made explicit: "I worked harder than they have" (ITCL, BRCL, FRCL, SPCL) or "I surpassed my enemies in work." This is also the case with **far more imprisonments**, which is likewise a comparison with Paul's opponents. ITCL says "I have been in prison more than they have."

The Greek word translated as **countless** in RSV may indicate the number of beatings (RSV, TOB) or the severity of the beatings, that is, beaten "more severely" (NIV, REB). The **beatings** is a rather general term. Two specific kinds of beatings are mentioned in the verses that follow: thirty-nine lashes by the Jews (verse 24), and the whipping by Roman authorities (verse 25).

Often near death: literally "in deaths often." These words follow a series of comparisons in which Paul has claimed that his qualifications are better than those of the "superapostles." Therefore many translations and interpreters understand these words to mean by implication that Paul had "been near death more often" than those to whom he is comparing himself (so TEV, FRCL, ITCL). In some languages **near death** may be understood to mean "near a dead person." But the meaning here is clearly that Paul himself was "nearly dead" or "in serious danger of dying." Some may therefore prefer to translate "I have almost died many times."

As noted above, the Greek does not have a word in this last phrase of verse 23 corresponding to the English word "more" as in TEV. The UBS *Greek New Testament* places a period at the end of verse 23, and all translations follow this punctuation. Ellingworth suggests, however, that a period should be placed after the words **with countless beatings** and a new sentence begin with the words **often near death** (Ellingworth 1992). In other words, these final three Greek words "in deaths often" are the beginning of a new stage in the argument, in which Paul will stress the number of times he has suffered in various ways. If translators follow Ellingworth's suggestion, the translation will look something like this: "many times near death, [24] five times . . . ." Ellingworth's suggested punctuation is certainly possible, and it takes account of the fact that the final words of verse 23 in Greek do not contain the words "more often."

In the context, however, Paul probably intended the words "in deaths often" to imply that he had been near death more often than the "superapostles." TEV therefore remains a good model.

11.24   RSV   TEV

Five times I have received at the hands   Five times I was given the thirty-nine
of the Jews the forty lashes less one.   lashes by the Jews;

The forty lashes less one: according to Deut 25.1-3, the maximum
number of whip strokes that could be given a guilty person when punished by
a Hebrew court was forty. In order that the number not surpass forty by
accidental miscounting and the law be violated, tradition limited the maximum
number to thirty-nine. These whippings were done with leather straps. TEV
and REB say simply the "thirty-nine lashes." Possible restructurings of this
verse are as follows: "I received punishment with the whip at the hands of the
Jews five different times. Each time they gave me thirty-nine strokes" or "Five
times the Jews whipped me, using thirty-nine strokes each time."

11.25   RSV   TEV

Three times I have been beaten with   three times I was whipped by the Ro-
rods; once I was stoned. Three times I   mans; and once I was stoned. I have
have been shipwrecked; a night and a   been in three shipwrecks, and once I
day I have been adrift at sea;   spent twenty-four hours in the water.

Beating with wooden **rods** was a form of punishment used by the
Romans (see Acts 16.37). To make clear that the beatings in verse 25 were by
Romans and not by Jews, TEV adds "by the Romans" (likewise Mft, FRCL, BRCL).
But TEV as it stands risks losing the fact that a different instrument was used
in this beating, especially since "whipped" implies that a flexible whip was
used rather than a rod or stick. This distinction, however, may be easily
preserved by saying something like "the Romans beat me with sticks three
times" (compare CEV).

I was stoned in contemporary American English means that one was
drunk or experiencing the hallucinating effects of drugs. This is clearly not the
meaning of the text. Hence NRSV says "I received a stoning." See Acts 14.19.
The passive formulation will have to be made active in many languages. But
since the agent of this action is not known, one may say "some people threw
stones at me in order to kill me" or "my enemies stoned me" (CEV).

I have been shipwrecked: in an attempt to translate this English passive
verb actively, GNW says "Three times I was in a boat when it broke in the sea."
But this may be misunderstood to mean that the same boat was wrecked each
time. In those languages where the passive presents difficulties, one may say
"I have been in three different ships that broke up in the sea."

A night and a day translates a compound word in Greek consisting of the
words "night" and "day." TEV provides a more natural rendering in English,
"twenty-four hours" (so also REB). However, it may be more natural in the
receptor language to follow the more literal rendering instead of counting the

hours. In some languages there is a specific term that refers to a twenty-four hour period.

I have been adrift at sea: literally "I have done [night and day] in the deep." The idea is that Paul was actually in the water, probably holding on to some piece of the wrecked ship. Some may therefore want to translate "one time I had to spend all day and night in the water."

11.26 RSV	TEV
on frequent journeys, in danger from rivers, danger from robbers, danger from my own people, danger from Gentiles, danger in the city, danger in the wilderness, danger at sea, danger from false brethren;	In my many travels I have been in danger from floods and from robbers, in danger from fellow Jews and from Gentiles; there have been dangers in the cities, dangers in the wilds, dangers on the high seas, and dangers from false friends.

On frequent journeys: this may be understood as the first in the series of hardships, as the wording of RSV (and REB) seems to imply. But it is better to understand this phrase as referring to the time when the hardships of this verse were experienced. The latter is the interpretation followed by TEV, CEV, and many other versions. It was during Paul's many journeys that the following dangers arose.

Danger: the word so translated is found only in this verse and in Rom 8.35, where it is rendered "peril." But it is used eight times in succession here. The repetition serves to reinforce the sense of peril, and this recurrence may be reflected in the receptor language if it is not unnatural. While the list of ways in which Paul experienced danger may seem at first haphazard, it should be noted that there are important pairs or triplets that are apparently intended to be all-inclusive. For example, **my own people** and **Gentiles** as well as **city**, **wilderness** and **sea**.

My own people is literally "from people." The specific mention of the **Gentiles** in the next phrase justifies understanding this to mean the Jews, as TEV and FRCL ("fellow-Jews") make explicit. REB says "from my fellow-countrymen." And NIV translates similarly but without the word "fellow." **Gentiles** may be quite naturally translated "people who are not Jews" in this case.

Danger in the city, danger in the wilderness is literally "danger in city, danger in wilderness." Paul is not referring to one specific city or one specific wilderness, as RSV may suggest by using the definite articles. TEV is the more natural translation of the meaning in English, using plural nouns. **City** and **wilderness** refer to contrasting places—places where many people live, and places that have little or no population. The term **wilderness** may be better translated in some languages as "the open country" (NJB, TNT, and SPCL) or "in uninhabited places" (LPD). Compare Mark 1.3.

Danger at sea: this will be difficult to translate in those languages where there is no word for "sea." Some are forced to use expressions like "the great water" or something similar.

False brethren is not to be taken in the literal biological sense. TEV's "false friends" is perhaps too general. Paul is referring to persons whom he regards as "false Christians" (REB). In some cases it may be necessary to say something like "people who pretend to be Christians" or something similar.

11.27 RSV	TEV
in toil and hardship, through many a sleepless night, in hunger and thirst, often without food, in cold and exposure.	There has been work and toil; often I have gone without sleep; I have been hungry and thirsty; I have often been without enough food, shelter, or clothing.

It will be noted that TEV starts a new sentence at the beginning of this verse, and this may serve as a good model in other languages.

The words translated **toil and hardship** occur also in 1 Thes 2.9, where RSV renders them as "labor and toil." Paul is referring to his hard work as a craftsman. One language has translated these two words by the following sentence: "I saw [experienced] pain in hard work." Another says "I did hard work, and difficult labor wore me out."

Through many a sleepless night translates the same expression as found in 6.5, but here the word for **many** is added. Paul does not mean that he had difficulty falling asleep at night. Rather he would often work late into the night at his trade in order to be free to preach the gospel during the day.

Often without food: It is unlikely that this expression refers to fasting. It is more likely another way of talking about **hunger** just mentioned.

In cold: the term used here is found only twice elsewhere in the New Testament (John 18.18 and Acts 28.2). Here it is taken by TEV as referring to a lack of shelter. This provides the reason for Paul's feeling cold.

Exposure is literally "in nakedness." Though some translations take this quite literally ("naked" NIV, LPD), the word occurs in Greek literature in reference to someone who has only one rough cloak. Knox translates this term "ill-clad," while TNT has "without sufficient clothing." A translation such as "without enough clothing to keep warm" is probably closer to the correct meaning than the word "naked" is. The TEV translation "without enough . . . clothing" fails to preserve the idea that Paul suffered from the cold. Better is CEV, which combines the last two items as follows: "I have been cold from not having enough clothes to keep me warm."

11.28   RSV   TEV

And, apart from other things, there is the daily pressure upon me of my anxiety for all the churches.	And not to mention other things, every day I am under the pressure of my concern for all the churches.

The word translated as **other things** means "besides" or "apart from what is left unmentioned." Both NEB and REB take the Greek word to refer to external things, hence REB translates "Apart from these external things." But it is doubtful that the Greek word ever has the meaning "what is external," so translators should follow RSV and TEV rather than NEB or REB here. One translation attempts to convey the idea here by saying "I refrain from counting the sufferings that remain, but . . . ," and Mft has "and all the rest of it" as the conclusion to the list in verses 26 and 27 rather than an introduction to what is about to be said in this verse.

The daily pressure: while many English versions use the word "pressure," Phps speaks here of "the daily burden of responsibility" which conveys the meaning and will be more easily translated in many languages. Paul's concern for the churches was like a heavy load weighing him down. While "stress" or "tension" may be good modern English equivalents, these will be difficult to translate into certain languages. Some will use the word for "thoughts" or "many thoughts" in such a context to convey the idea of anxiety. Others may use the verb "to worry." Or there may be more unusual idiomatic expressions in the receptor language to convey this idea.

My anxiety is literally "the anxiety" without the possessive pronoun, but the context makes clear that this is the anxiety that Paul has for the churches for which he feels responsible.

All the churches: Paul probably has in mind all the groups of believers that he founded and about which he would be especially concerned. Compare the same expression in 8.18.

11.29   RSV   TEV

Who is weak, and I am not weak? Who is made to fall, and I am not indignant?	When someone is weak, then I feel weak too; when someone is led into sin, I am filled with distress.

These two sentences are rhetorical questions; that is, Paul is not really asking for the names of people who are weak or who are made to fall. To avoid suggesting that Paul is asking for information, TEV changes Paul's rhetorical questions into statements. Even in languages where rhetorical questions are common, the structure here many require a shift to an affirmative statement.

Who is weak: the Greek word translated as **weak** is general and sometimes refers to spiritual weakness and other times to physical weakness. The context is simply too ambiguous here to give clear guidance. In those languages which must use specific terms for different kinds of weaknesses, translators should choose the term that seems most appropriate to them. Some languages speak of weakness in terms of "lacking strength."

Who is made to fall: the verb used here is found frequently in the Gospels and also in Rom 14.21 and 1 Cor 8.13. **To fall** is not to be taken in a literal physical sense. It refers to the moral downfall of someone (REB "If anyone brings about the downfall of another"), that is, to "sin" (TEV). The passive idea of RSV and TEV, however, will have to be made active in some cases: "when someone makes another person fall" or "when someone leads a companion to commit sin."

And am not indignant is literally "and I am not burning." NIV says "and I do not inwardly burn?" Paul uses figurative language here. Some interpreters understand the sense to be that Paul is "burning with indignation" against the people who cause others to fall (so RSV). Others understand the sense to be "burning with sympathy or distress" on behalf of those people who have been made to fall (so TEV, NJB, "I burn in agony myself"). Though both interpretations are possible, most interpreters agree with the former. REB, for example, says "does not my heart burn with anger?"

11.30   RSV   TEV

If I must boast, I will boast of the   If I must boast, I will boast about
things that show my weakness.   things that show how weak I am.

If does not mean that Paul has any doubt. The Greek may be translated as "Since I must boast" or "Since I have to lift myself up (or, show myself)." Or it may be possible to translate "If I am forced to boast . . ." or "Whenever I have to boast . . . ."

The future tense **I will boast** does not mean that Paul only now will begin to boast, but that he plans to boast in the following manner. What follows in this verse is a summary statement of the kinds of things that he plans to boast about whenever he must.

My weakness: the term used here is found in Rom 8.26 and 1 Cor 2.3. It occurs again in this letter at 12.9 and 13.4. In some languages it may be more naturally translated by a verbal expression such as "that I lack strength."

11.31   RSV   TEV

The God and Father of the Lord Jesus,   The God and Father of the Lord Je-
he who is blessed for ever, knows that I   sus—blessed be his name forever!—
do not lie.   knows that I am not lying.

The God and Father of the Lord Jesus: this is a repetition of the same basic formula used at the beginning of this letter (1.3) and elsewhere (Rom 15.6; Eph 1.3; 1 Peter 1.3). It is used here to emphasize the solemnity of what Paul is about to say. See discussion under 1.3.

When Paul says **I do not lie**, he is not speaking in general terms but is referring specifically to what he says in this part of the letter. For that reason the English translation "I am not lying" or "I am speaking the truth" (GNC) is preferable to "I do not lie." Probably he is referring to the previous verses, but some interpreters think he is pointing ahead to story he tells in the next two verses. Either seems equally possible.

Both RSV and TEV are ambiguous as to whether it is God or Jesus **who is blessed for ever**. The Greek is clear: God is blessed for ever. REB removes the ambiguity in English: "He who is blessed for ever, the God and Father of the Lord Jesus." As in 1.3, to "bless" means to praise, honor, or glorify. The passive idea will have to be rendered actively in many languages. So the whole verse may read something like "We always praise the God and Father of our Lord Jesus forever! For he knows that I am telling the truth." Or, transposing the two main elements of the verse, "God, the Father of the Lord Jesus, knows that I am not lying. May his name receive honor forever!"

This whole verse is a rather complicated formula used as an oath to guarantee that what has been said is absolutely true. It serves the same purpose as certain expressions in the Muslim world in which the name of Allah is mentioned to support the truth of something said.

11.32	RSV	TEV
	At Damascus, the governor under King Aretas guarded the city of Damascus in order to seize me,	When I was in Damascus, the governor under King Aretas placed guards at the city gates to arrest me.

Verses 32 and 33 serve to illustrate Paul's humiliation and weakness. Another account of the story is provided by Luke in Acts 9.23-25, but here Paul furnishes some details not found there.

Some languages may require the translator to indicate whether Paul knew the governor and the king, but the Greek text gives no indication, though perhaps it would be surprising if Paul did know these rulers in a city where he did not live.

Damascus was a walled Syrian city ruled by the Romans through Arab governors. It is often mentioned in the Old Testament and in Acts (chapters 9, 22, and 26), and in Gal 1.17.

The governor is literally "the ethnarch" and is so translated by Mft, NAB, and others. The historical evidence is not conclusive, whether this ethnarch ruled over the entire city or only over a particular ethnic group within Damascus. Knox translates "the agent of the King." In the receptor language it will be possible to use a general term meaning "ruler" or "chief," or to use a verbal expression, "the person who ruled in the name of [King Aretas]."

King Aretas: this refers to Aretas IV, who was an Arab king who ruled from 9 B.C. to A.D. 40. The particular Arab group that he ruled was called the Nabateans. The Nabateans lived in the region east and southwest of the Dead

Sea. At the time of Paul's ministry, the Nabateans may have ruled the city of Damascus far to the northeast of the Dead Sea.

The Greek is literally **guarded the city**. Some historians think it is unlikely that the Romans would have allowed the Nabatean king to control an area outside of the city of Damascus. For this reason it is likely that the city was guarded from within rather than from without. Assuming that the guards were not placed outside the city but were rather inside, TEV, FRCL, SPCL, ITCL, and BRCL say "placed guards at the city gates" (so also NBE, "placed guards in the city"). But the Greek is not as specific as TEV, and the translation "put guards round Damascus city" (NJB) is equally defensible. Translators should avoid suggesting that the governor himself guarded the city, as RSV might suggest.

In order to seize me: a number of manuscripts have the words "and wanted to" before the words "seize me." The reading in these manuscripts is followed by KJV and the NRSV footnote. The editors of the UBS *Greek New Testament* consider the words "and wanted to" to be an addition by a scribe who wished to improve the style. Even if they are not original, the addition of these words (only one word in Greek) does not really change the meaning.

11.33	RSV	TEV
	but I was let down in a basket through a window in the wall, and escaped his hands.	But I was let down in a basket through an opening in the wall and escaped from him.

I was let down: in languages where an active formulation is required, one may say "some people let me down" or "my friends lowered me."

The **basket** in which Paul was let down through the wall was apparently large enough to hold an adult man and may have been made out of braided ropes.

The **wall** refers to the wall that surrounded the city of Damascus. Translators should understand that dwellings were built into the city wall so that in some cases the window of a house would look out over the countryside surrounding the city. In this way it was possible to escape from the city without passing through the closely guarded gates. In some languages the word **window** may have to be translated "an opening (or hole) in the wall."

Escaped his hands: the word **hands** is, of course, used figuratively. See TEV "escaped from him." The idea is that Paul escaped from the forces of the governor. Mft, AT, and REB speak of escaping from "his clutches."

D-4. Paul's visions and revelations
12.1-10

RSV	TEV
	Paul's Visions and Revelations

RSV

1 I must boast; there is nothing to be gained by it, but I will go on to visions and revelations of the Lord. 2 I know a man in Christ who fourteen years ago was caught up to the third heaven—whether in the body or out of the body I do not know, God knows. 3 And I know that this man was caught up into Paradise—whether in the body or out of the body I do not know, God knows—4 and he heard things that cannot be told, which man may not utter. 5 On behalf of this man I will boast, but on my own behalf I will not boast, except of my weaknesses. 6 Though if I wish to boast, I shall not be a fool, for I shall be speaking the truth. But I refrain from it, so that no one may think more of me than he sees in me or hears from me. 7 And to keep me from being too elated by the abundance of revelations, a thorn was given me in the flesh, a messenger of Satan, to harass me, to keep me from being too elated. 8 Three times I besought the Lord about this, that it should leave me; 9 but he said to me, "My grace is sufficient for you, for my power is made perfect in weakness." I will all the more gladly boast of my weaknesses, that the power of Christ may rest upon me. 10 For the sake of Christ, then, I am content with weaknesses, insults, hardships, persecutions, and calamities; for when I am weak, then I am strong.

TEV

Paul's Visions and Revelations

1 I have to boast, even though it doesn't do any good. But I will now talk about visions and revelations given me by the Lord. 2 I know a certain Christian man who fourteen years ago was snatched up to the highest heaven (I do not know whether this actually happened or whether he had a vision—only God knows). 3-4 I repeat, I know that this man was snatched to Paradise (again, I do not know whether this actually happened or whether it was a vision—only God knows), and there he heard things which cannot be put into words, things that human lips may not speak. 5 So I will boast about this man—but I will not boast about myself, except the things that show how weak I am. 6 If I wanted to boast, I would not be a fool, because I would be telling the truth. But I will not boast, because I do not want anyone to have a higher opinion of me than he has as a result of what he has seen me do and heard me say.

7 But to keep me from being puffed up with pride because of the many wonderful things I saw, I was given a painful physical ailment, which acts as Satan's messenger to beat me and keep me from being proud. 8 Three times I prayed to the Lord about this and asked him to take it away. 9 But his answer was: "My grace is all you need, for my power is greatest when you are weak." I am most happy, then, to be proud of my weaknesses, in order to feel the protection of Christ's power over me. 10 I am content with weaknesses, insults, hardships, persecutions, and difficulties for Christ's sake. For when I am weak, then I am strong.

SECTION HEADING: TEV "Paul's Visions and Revelations." On the translation of "Visions" and "Revelations" see verse 1. In this section, 12.1-10, Paul argues that he is not inferior to the "superapostles" when it comes to spiritual experiences; but rather than boast of such things, he instead talks about a "thorn" in the flesh that he received to remind him that God's power is made perfect in weakness. The section heading in TEV does not indicate why Paul speaks of his visions and revelations. The heading in LPD says "Paul is not inferior in revelations of the Lord." Some other possible models are "Paul's vision and his sufferings" (compare NIV, "Paul's Vision and His Thorn," which retains the image of the "thorn" in the section heading) and "Matters that the Lord Jesus showed Paul."

12.1   RSV   TEV

I must boast; there is nothing to   I have to boast, even though it
be gained by it, but I will go on to vi-   doesn't do any good. But I will now talk
sions and revelations of the Lord.   about visions and revelations given me
                                              by the Lord.

I must boast: in the best ancient manuscripts the words here are
identical with what follows "If" in 11.30. However, some manuscripts have the
conjunction sometimes rendered "but" in place of **must**, a difference of only one
letter in Greek. Combined with the following words, this yields the translation
found in KJV, "it is not expedient for me doubtless to glory." However, no
modern version adopts this reading, and the editors of the UBS *Greek New
Testament* give an "A" evaluation to the printed text.

There is nothing to be gained by it, that is, to be gained in terms of
building up the Corinthian church. The passive **to be gained** may be rendered
actively by saying "no one gains anything by it" or "no person benefits if I do
so."

I will go on . . . : the idea here seems to be "I will continue to boast . . ."
by adding comments on **visions and revelations** to what has already been said.
The TEV rendering "Now I will talk . . ." seems to weaken this slightly.

Visions and revelations: the precise distinction, if any, which Paul
intended between these two words is not clear. Nearly all interpreters consider
these terms to be synonyms in this verse. Paul does not use the word **vision**
elsewhere in his writings. And the only other New Testament writer to use it
is Luke (1.22 and 24.23). The word for **revelations** is found more frequently,
notably at 1 Cor 1.7 and Rev 1.1. It is repeated in verse 7 of this chapter. The
two terms may have to be translated by a single word or expression in some
languages. But one African language has attempted to retain two separate
items by using two verbal expressions: "matters that the Lord Jesus showed
me as a dream and secrets he made known to me in my heart."

Revelations of the Lord are "revelations granted by the Lord" (REB)
rather than revelations in which the Lord was seen. TEV adds that the
revelations were given to Paul ("given me"). **The Lord**, here and in verse 8, is
most likely Christ and not God.

12.2   RSV   TEV

I know a man in Christ who fourteen   I know a certain Christian man who
years ago was caught up to the third   fourteen years ago was snatched up to
heaven—whether in the body or out of   the highest heaven (I do not know whe-
the body I do not know, God knows.   ther this actually happened or whether
                                              he had a vision—only God knows).

Verse 7 makes clear that Paul is talking about himself in these verses,
but use of the third person contributes to the ironical style in which one

pretends to be less than one really is. The uncertainty regarding details is part of the satirical nature of verses 2-4. In verses 1-6 Paul is using paradoxical language. Ecstatic heavenly visions, which his opponents valued, are treated in satirical fashion as having no value in authenticating one's apostleship. Using a well-known form of rhetoric, Paul speaks here in a way that his readers would have recognized as "tongue in cheek."

I know a man: since Paul later reveals that he was the **man** he is speaking about, some translators have thought that this is just another way of saying "There was a man . . . ." This may be a better rendering for some languages.

A man in Christ refers to "a Christian man" (TEV, REB), but note that CEV renders this as "one of Christ's followers." On the meaning and translation of **in Christ**, see comments in 1.21, and its use in 2.14.

Was caught up: the passive form used here is found also in Acts 8.39 and Rev 12.5 to describe the experience of someone transported into the supernatural realm. If it has to be made active in the receptor language, the most likely agent is God himself. One may consider saying something like "God received him for a time" or "God transferred him."

The third heaven: the concept of various strata or layers of heaven was common in the first century (see Eph 4.10; Heb 4.14). In Jewish writings the number of heavens was most commonly considered to be seven, but other numbers, including three, were also mentioned. Paul probably was thinking of three heavens only rather than seven, since he later equates the third heaven with Paradise (12.3). It does not seem likely that Paul would boast about being caught up only to the third heaven if he thought that more levels existed. TEV is therefore probably correct in saying "the highest heaven" (so also FRCL, BRCL), that is, where God lived.

In the body or out of the body: Paul states that he actually ascended into the highest heaven but that he does not know whether he went in his physical body or whether the experience was in his spirit only. Jewish traditions indicate that Enoch, Abraham, Seth and his mother, and Baruch ascended bodily into the heavens. On the other hand first-century Judaism also knew of ascensions in a bodiless form. The TEV translation—"I do not know whether this actually happened or whether he had a vision" (also FRCL, BRCL)—does not adequately express Paul's thought. Indeed, it did happen; he was caught up to the highest heaven. The question for Paul was whether it was a bodily ascension or "in spirit only" (GECL). The CEV translation correctly communicates the meaning: "I don't know if the man was still in his body when it happened, but God surely knows."

God knows: TEV understands these words to mean that "only God" knows. It may well be, though, that the force of these words is to underline Paul's own indifference to a matter that had such importance for his opponents (see comments on satirical language above on this verse). In that case the sense is "I suppose God knows, but I don't."

A possible model for restructuring this difficult verse may be the following: "Fourteen years ago God lifted up a certain Christian that I know about, and took him to the highest heaven. (I do not really know if his body actually went to heaven or if it was only his spirit; but surely God knows.)"

12.3-4 RSV	TEV
3 And I know that this man was caught up into Paradise—whether in the body or out of the body I do not know, God knows—4 and he heard things that cannot be told, which man may not utter.	3-4 I repeat, I know that this man was snatched to Paradise (again, I do not know whether this actually happened or whether it was a vision—only God knows), and there he heard things which cannot be put into words, things that human lips may not speak.

Since Paul is actually repeating in verse 3 what he has already said, TEV introduces this restatement by saying "I repeat . . ." CEV accomplishes the same thing by beginning "As I said . . . ," and AB starts with "Indeed . . . ."

Note that TEV combines verse numbers 3 and 4, because the verb phrase translated **was snatched up into Paradise** is actually a part of verse 4 in the Greek. RSV, however, moves the verbal expression up into verse 3 without any indication that the transposition has occurred.

Was caught up: see comments on verse 2 above.

Paradise: in the Septuagint **Paradise** is used for the Garden of Eden. In the New Testament period **Paradise** was regarded as the place where righteous people went after death. Translators will face the same term in Luke 23.42 and Rev 2.7. Here Paul uses **Paradise** as a synonym for "the third heaven" (verse 2).

In the body or out of the body: see comments on verse 2 above.

Things that cannot be told: this expression is a play on words, literally "sayings unsayable." REB says "words so secret that human lips may not repeat them." The Greek expression appears to have been a semi-technical term used of divine mysteries which the worshiper was not allowed to reveal to the public. This means that these words are not completely synonymous with the expression **which man may not utter**, which follows, even though the second expression seems to reinforce the first. But where the passive **cannot be told** must be avoided, a single expression may have to be used. Two models are "things that are too wonderful to tell" (CEV) and "so secret that no man dare try to put them into words" (TNT).

12.5 RSV	TEV
On behalf of this man I will boast, but on my own behalf I will not boast, except of my weaknesses.	So I will boast about this man—but I will not boast about myself, except the things that show how weak I am.

Of this man: literally "of such a one." This has been taken by some scholars as meaning "of such an incident." Mft, for example, begins this verse "of an experience like that I am prepared to boast." But most scholars agree in taking this expression as referring to the person who had the experience, as in RSV and TEV.

Except . . .: in Greek the words are literally "if not . . . ." Some languages require that exception clauses be translated by separate sentences. In this case one may consider saying something like "I will boast only that I am weak" or "However I can boast that I lack strength."

In some languages it may be more natural to reorder the elements in this verse slightly: "I will boast about a person like that, but I will not boast about myself unless it is to show how frail I am."

12.6 RSV	TEV
Though if I wish to boast, I shall not be a fool, for I shall be speaking the truth. But I refrain from it, so that no one may think more of me than he sees in me or hears from me.	If I wanted to boast, I would not be a fool, because I would be telling the truth. But I will not boast, because I do not want anyone to have a higher opinion of me than he has as a result of what he has seen me do and heard me say.

I shall not be a fool: Paul is not talking here about actually being a fool, but rather about acting like a fool by boasting. Actually Paul does not think it foolish, since he is telling the truth. TNT reads "that would not be foolish of me." Some languages will require a more natural restructuring such as "I would not be acting like a fool if I decided to boast, because I would be telling the truth." Compare verse 11 below.

I refrain from it: that is, "I refuse to go on boasting"; or, as CEV has it, "I will try not to say too much."

Most translations complete one sentence at the end of verse 6 with the words "hears from me" (RSV, TEV, REB) and begin a new sentence at verse 7. In Greek the first words of verse 7 are "by the abundance of revelations." Other translations, such as NJB and Martin, connect the words "by the abundance of revelations" to the end of verse 6. NJB translates 12.6b-7a as follows: "But I will not go on in case anybody should rate me higher than he sees and hears me to be, because of the exceptional greatness of the revelations" (so also NRSV, NAB, NVSR, and the UBS *Greek New Testament*). According to this second interpretation people would think too highly of Paul because of the abundance of revelations that he has had.

Though the Greek is literally **so that no one**, CEV is surely correct in translating this as "none of you."

12.7 RSV TEV

And to keep me from being too elated by the abundance of revelations, a thorn was given me in the flesh, a messenger of Satan, to harass me, to keep me from being too elated.	But to keep me from being puffed up with pride because of the many wonderful things I saw, I was given a painful physical ailment, which acts as Satan's messenger to beat me and keep me from being proud.

By the abundance of revelations: these words may connect with the end of verse 6 and indicate why others would think highly of Paul (so NJB; see comments on 12.6), or they may indicate the reason that Paul might be tempted to be puffed up with pride (so RSV, TEV, REB). The Greek syntax at the beginning of verse 7 is extremely difficult; either scribes copied incorrectly or else Paul wrote garbled Greek here. The general sense, however, seems clear, depending on whether one begins a new sentence at the beginning of verse 7 or after the first five Greek words in verse 7, as in NRSV, NJB, and the other translations and Greek texts mentioned in verse 6.

A thorn was given me in the flesh: most interpreters agree that the implicit agent of the verb **was given** is probably God. Whether God or Satan is understood as the agent, Paul at least believes that God permitted it, as in the case of Job in the Old Testament. TEV translates this as "I was given a painful physical ailment." Indeed, scholars have proposed all sorts of physical ailments on the slightest of biblical evidence: some kind of eye disease, malaria, epilepsy, severe headaches, defective speech, and so forth. Yet the word **flesh** does not necessarily refer here to the physical body. It may be a synonym for "physical existence in general." Understanding **flesh** in this way, other interpreters have suggested that the **thorn** referred to Paul's opponents. See Num 33.55 in the Septuagint, where Israel's enemies are described as "thorns" in the eyes of the Israelites. Because of the uncertainty regarding the identity of Paul's thorn in the flesh, translators who choose to be as specific as TEV may wish to have a note such as the following:

> The Greek is literally "a thorn in the flesh was given me."
> While many scholars think this refers to a physical problem,
> Paul may have been referring to persecutions and opposition
> from his opponents.

A messenger of Satan: on Satan see 2.11 and 11.14. The word translated **messenger** may also be rendered "angel" (AB, NAB, Knox, and CEV). In 11.15 Paul speaks of Satan's "ministers."

To harass is literally "to strike with a closed fist." But the verb is obviously used more figuratively here. So it may legitimately be translated "abuse" or "torment." Some scholars feel that the persistence indicated by the present tense should be made evident in translation by saying something to show continuous action; for example, "to torment me continually" or "to keep on harassing me."

Some manuscripts omit the words **to keep me from being too elated** at the end of this verse (see NIV). The editors of the UBS *Greek New Testament* think it likely that a scribe omitted these words as an unnecessary repetition from the beginning of the verse, and so it is better to retain them.

Because of the complexities of this verse, it will probably require considerable restructuring in the receptor language. Here is a possible model:

> But I must not become too proud about the wonderful things that God has shown me. That is why he gave me a very difficult problem to deal with. It was as if a person with a message from Satan intended to beat me and keep me from being too proud.

12.8   RSV   TEV

Three times I besought the Lord about this, that it should leave me;	Three times I prayed to the Lord about this and asked him to take it away.

Besought: the verb so translated here is elsewhere in this letter rendered as "beg" (2.8), "entreat" (6.1 and 10.1), and "urge" (8.6 and 9.5). Most English versions seem to prefer "begged" or "appealed" in this context, but since the object is **the Lord**, it may legitimately be translated "prayed" as in TEV.

Though Paul normally prays to God the Father through Christ rather than directly to Christ, **the Lord** in this verse is probably "the Lord Jesus," as in 12.1 (see 1 Cor 1.2; 1 Thes 3.12-13)

About this, that it should leave me: CEV says "Three times I begged the Lord to make this suffering go away." In some languages restructuring will be required to make the translation more natural: "I begged the Lord [Jesus] three times to take this problem away from me."

12.9   RSV   TEV

but he said to me, "My grace is sufficient for you, for my power is made perfect in weakness." I will all the more gladly boast of my weaknesses, that the power of Christ may rest upon me.	But his answer was: "My grace is all you need, for my power is greatest when you are weak." I am most happy, then, to be proud of my weaknesses, in order to feel the protection of Christ's power over me.

Since what is said in this verse is in response to the appeal of the previous verse, it is quite legitimate to translate the verb **said** by "answer" as in TEV. In many languages this will be seen as more natural.

My grace is sufficient for you: in Greek the word order is literally "Sufficient for you my grace," placing emphasis on the words **sufficient for you**. Though the "thorn" was a hindrance or difficulty for Paul, God's unmerited favor, his **grace**, was greater than the difficulty caused by the thorn. Some possible models for this expression are "my kindness is all you need" (CEV) or "my grace is enough, more than enough, for you" (GNC).

For my power is made perfect in weakness: literally "for power is made perfect in weakness." Though many manuscripts read "my power," the editors of the UBS *Greek New Testament* consider the possessive pronoun **my** to be an addition by scribes. NRSV follows the UBS *Greek New Testament:* "for power is made perfect in weakness" (so also REB). Since this "power" is identified as **the power of Christ** at the end of verse 9, and since Christ is the one who speaks in 12.9a (see **Lord** in 12.8), it seems certain that Paul is not talking about power in general but rather about the power of Christ, that is, **"my power."** Therefore it is appropriate to follow RSV here.

Is made perfect: this verb involves two difficult problems for many translators: (1) the form is passive, and (2) it is often difficult to find an equivalent to express the idea of perfection, especially perfection of power. With regard to the passive form, it may be avoided in many languages by using the verb "become." The resulting translation will be something like "my power becomes perfect in weakness." On the second point, there is no notion here of moral perfection; rather it is one of fulfillment or making complete. The power of Christ is made complete when a person is weak and depends on him.

In some languages the direct discourse used here will be better rendered as indirect: "But he answered that his grace would be all that I would ever need, and that his power is complete when a person recognizes that he is weak."

That the power of Christ may rest upon me: the verb **rest upon** has the sense of "enter or take up residence in [a tent]." It is not found elsewhere in the New Testament. But Paul does not mean that his boasting has actually caused the power of Christ to start living in him. Rather he is stressing that boasting of his weaknesses makes the fact of Christ's presence in him apparent to others. While the GNC "may come and enshrine itself in me" is hardly common language, it does attempt to capture the idea of the verb. At a different level of language, NCV says simply "can live in me." CEV restructures the last part of this verse, saying "so if Christ keeps giving me his power, I will gladly brag about how weak I am." But although this structure may be helpful as a model, it considerably weakens the meaning of the verb.

12.10 RSV	TEV
For the sake of Christ, then, I am content with weaknesses, insults, hardships, persecutions, and calamities; for when I am weak, then I am strong.	I am content with weaknesses, insults, hardships, persecutions, and difficulties for Christ's sake. For when I am weak, then I am strong.

For the sake of Christ: in the Greek text these words come at the end of the list of troubles (as in TEV), but the expression actually modifies the verb.

The idea is that, if the problems listed are experienced for the sake of Christ, then Paul is satisfied.

Then: this transition word, often rendered "therefore" (NRSV, NAB, and TNT), is omitted by TEV, but translators will probably want to retain it in most languages, since it shows the logical connection between what has been said and what Paul says in this verse. AB has "so," and NIV translates it "that is why . . . ."

Insults: perhaps the meaning of the Greek word here is "difficulties" which are caused by being mistreated. TNT, in fact, translates the word "ill-treatment," and NAB has "mistreatment."

Hardships: see comment on 6.4.

Persecutions: for Paul the persecutions were for religious reasons. Compare Mark 4.17 and Rom 8.35, where the same word is used.

Calamities: see comment on 6.4.

This series of five nouns may be more naturally rendered as verbal expressions in some languages: "I am happy when I lack strength, when people insult me, when I am in need, when people persecute me, and when I suffer."

For when I am weak, then I am strong: considered superficially, this statement is actually a contradiction in terms. The meaning, of course, is that Paul has real, spiritual strength just when he acknowledges his weakness and dependence on Christ. It will, however, be unwise to make too much explicit in translating this brief but powerful paradox. If readers are likely to misunderstand it, perhaps a footnote is in order.

D-5. Paul's concern for the Corinthians
12.11-21

RSV

TEV
Paul's Concern for the Corinthians

11 I have been a fool! You forced me to it, for I ought to have been commended by you. For I was not at all inferior to these superlative apostles, even though I am nothing. 12 The signs of a true apostle were performed among you in all patience, with signs and wonders and mighty works. 13 For in what were you less favored than the rest of the churches, except that I myself did not burden you? Forgive me this wrong!

14 Here for the third time I am ready to come to you. And I will not be a burden, for I seek not what is yours but you; for children ought not to lay up for their parents, but parents for their children. 15 I will most gladly spend and be spent for your souls. If I love you the more, am I to be loved the less? 16 But granting that I myself did not burden you, I was crafty, you say, and got the better of you by guile. 17 Did I take advantage of you through any of those whom I sent to you? 18 I

11 I am acting like a fool—but you have made me do it. You are the ones who ought to show your approval of me. For even if I am nothing, I am in no way inferior to those very special "apostles" of yours. 12 The many miracles and wonders that prove that I am an apostle were performed among you with much patience. 13 How were you treated any worse than the other churches, except that I did not bother you for financial help? Please forgive me for being so unfair!

14 This is now the third time that I am ready to come to visit you—and I will not make any demands on you. It is you I want, not your money. After all, children should not have to provide for their parents, but parents should provide for their children. 15 I will be glad to spend all I have, and myself as well, in order to help you. Will you love me less because I love you so much?

16 You will agree, then, that I was not

urged Titus to go, and sent the brother with him. Did Titus take advantage of you? Did we not act in the same spirit? Did we not take the same steps?

19 Have you been thinking all along that we have been defending ourselves before you? It is in the sight of God that we have been speaking in Christ, and all for your upbuilding, beloved. 20 For I fear that perhaps I may come and find you not what I wish, and that you may find me not what you wish; that perhaps there may be quarreling, jealousy, anger, selfishness, slander, gossip, conceit, and disorder. 21 I fear that when I come again my God may humble me before you, and I may have to mourn over many of those who sinned before and have not repented of the impurity, immorality, and licentiousness which they have practiced.

a burden to you. But someone will say that I was tricky, and trapped you with lies. 17 How? Did I take advantage of you through any of the messengers I sent? 18 I begged Titus to go, and I sent the other Christian brother with him. Would you say that Titus took advantage of you? Do not he and I act from the very same motives and behave in the same way?

19 Perhaps you think that all along we have been trying to defend ourselves before you. No! We speak as Christ would have us speak in the presence of God, and everything we do, dear friends, is done to help you. 20 I am afraid that when I get there I will find you different from what I would like you to be and you will find me different from what you would like me to be. I am afraid that I will find quarreling and jealousy, hot tempers and selfishness, insults and gossip, pride and disorder. 21 I am afraid that the next time I come my God will humiliate me in your presence, and I shall weep over many who sinned in the past and have not repented of the immoral things they have done—their lust and their sexual sins.

SECTION HEADING: TEV "Paul's Concern for the Corinthians." The section headings in various translations basically agree with that in TEV, that verses 12.11-21 express "Paul's Concern for the Corinthians" (NIV, TOB, FRCL, NBE). Using sarcasm, irony, and genuine expressions of concern for the spiritual well-being of the church in Corinth, Paul hopes that, by the time he makes his third visit, the opposition to him and the problems within the church will have been solved. Since the word "concern" may cause difficulties for some translators, the following alternative models may be considered: "The Corinthians make Paul worry," "Paul has a heavy heart for the Christians in Corinth," and "Paul wants to help the people at Corinth."

12.11 RSV	TEV
I have been a fool! You forced me to it, for I ought to have been commended by you. For I was not at all inferior to these superlative apostles, even though I am nothing.	I am acting like a fool—but you have made me do it. You are the ones who ought to show your approval of me. For even if I am nothing, I am in no way inferior to those very special "apostles" of yours.

The words **I have been a fool** translate a Greek verb which indicates that he continues to be a fool. Paul is referring to what he has just said in the preceding paragraphs, for to boast has he has been doing is the mark of a fool.

As indicated in verse 6 above, it may be better to say "I have been acting like a fool . . ." as in TEV.

You forced me to it: the subject pronoun is emphatic here. The idea is "you are the ones who made me [act like a fool]." One dynamic-equivalent rendering of this is "but it is your fault."

I ought to have been commended by you: since the agent is identified in the text, this passive construction can easily be made active as "you are the people who should have commended me." On the verb **commend**, note that this should reflect the expressions used in the discussion about needing "letters of recommendation" and "commending oneself," as in 3.1; 4.2; and elsewhere.

I was not at all inferior translates a verb in the past tense. In light of verse 12 Paul is probably referring to the time when he was in Corinth and performed miracles and other signs (so RSV, REB, TOB). Some interpreters, however, understand the past tense verb to be a "timeless" past tense and translate with the present tense, as in TEV, NRSV, FRCL, and NAB: "I am in no way inferior."

These superlative apostles: see the comments on 11.5. The Greek is literally "the superlative apostles." The context indicates that these "superlative apostles" were recognized as apostles with authority by at least some of the Corinthians. For that reason TEV adds the words "of yours."

Even though I am nothing: as frequently in chapters 10–13, Paul speaks with sarcasm here in claiming to be **nothing**. The "superapostles" who oppose Paul consider him to be "nothing." "True," Paul says sarcastically, "but I am not inferior to them."

12.12 RSV	TEV
The signs of a true apostle were performed among you in all patience, with signs and wonders and mighty works.	The many miracles and wonders that prove that I am an apostle were performed among you with much patience.

The signs of a true apostle: the Greek word which RSV translates as **signs** occurs twice in this verse. But the first occurrence of this noun appears to have a more general meaning and may be translated as "the marks of a true apostle" (so Martin, NEB), that is, "the signs that mark out a true apostle."

The Greek does not state directly who **performed among** the Corinthians **the signs of a true apostle**, though the context indicates that the subject of the action was Paul himself. TEV does not directly say that Paul himself performed the miracles and wonders that prove he is an apostle, though TEV does show that the **true apostle** refers to Paul himself. REB makes explicit that Paul was the subject of the action: "The signs of an apostle were there in the work I did among you." CEV says "When I was with you, I was patient and worked all the powerful miracles and signs and wonders of a true apostle."

A true apostle is literally only "an apostle." However, nearly all translations insert the word **true**, since the context indicates that Paul is contrasting the work of true apostles with the work of those who are only "false apostles."

On the translation of **apostle**, see 1.1.

In all patience: most interpreters understand these words to be stating the manner in which Paul performed signs of an apostle (so RSV, TEV). It is also possible to understand these words as parallel to and included in the series of signs, wonders, and mighty works, as does NJB: "All the marks . . . have been at work among you: complete perseverance, signs, marvels, demonstrations of power." Though the interpretation reflected in NJB is grammatically possible, most interpreters follow the alternative interpretation found in RSV and TEV. **In all patience**, then, expresses the manner in which the signs of an apostle were performed; and the words **with signs, wonders and mighty works** express the means by which the signs were performed.

With signs and wonders and mighty works: are these three items miracles that were performed along with, that is, in addition to, the signs of a true apostle (RSV)? The Greek does not have the separate word **with**, but the sentence allows for its translation in English. Or are they simply an elaboration or explanation of what the signs of a true apostle are (TEV, NRSV, NJB,)? NIV follows the latter interpretation and says "The things that mark an apostle—signs, wonders and miracles—were done among you." See also Mft, which is similar to NIV.

According to the interpretation reflected in TEV, Paul claims that the miracles he performed prove that he is a true apostle. Perhaps the implication is that the "superapostles" do not perform such miracles and are not, therefore, true apostles. But to claim that miracles are the signs of a true apostle seems to contradict what Paul says in chapters 11–13, so the TEV translation should probably not be followed.

According to RSV the **signs and wonders and mighty works** (12.12b) are not equated with the signs of a true apostle (12.12a); rather such miracles were performed in addition to the signs of a true apostle. The grammatical construction in Greek favors this interpretation. Perhaps the "superapostles" perform miracles, but they do not have the signs of the true apostle as Paul does.

The three terms **signs**, **wonders**, and **mighty works**, should not be pushed to find three different kinds of miracles. Probably these words indicate three different ways of looking at miracles: **signs** refers to the ability of the miracle to increase spiritual understanding by pointing to a spiritual reality; **wonders** refers to the sense of awe which the miracle creates; and **mighty works** refers the fact that these are acts of God. The first two terms occur frequently together (Mark 13.22; John 4.48; Rom 15.9; 1 Thes 2.9; and several times in Acts). And all three terms occur together in Heb 2.4.

12.13	RSV	TEV

For in what were you less favored than the rest of the churches, except that I myself did not burden you? Forgive me this wrong!

How were you treated any worse than the other churches, except that I did not bother you for financial help? Please forgive me for being so unfair!

In what were you less favored: the apostle Paul is the implicit agent of the verb **were less favored**, that is, "In what way did I treat you any worse than the other churches?" This will be a good way to avoid the passive construction of RSV and TEV. Another possibility is "What did I do for the other churches that I have not done for you?"

The rest of the churches refers to other churches in other cities where Paul had been and from which he had received financial support.

I . . . did not burden you: the pronoun is emphatic in Greek as in RSV, **I myself**. Perhaps Paul has in mind the false apostles, who did burden the Corinthian church. In this context the clear meaning is that he did not accept any "financial help" (TEV) from the Corinthians. The verb used here is the same as in 11.9, and it is repeated in the following verse.

Paul is using sarcasm in this verse. His plea that they **forgive me this wrong!** is not really a plea for forgiveness but is sarcasm. RSV and TEV attempt to communicate this sarcasm by the use of an exclamation mark. Languages that do not use sarcasm in this way may need to restructure and find some way to indicate that Paul is saying just the opposite of what he really means. Williams has a note which states that Paul's words here are sarcastic. Though the Greek does not state explicitly against whom the wrong was done, CEV correctly says "Forgive me for doing you wrong."

12.14 RSV	TEV
Here for the third time I am ready to come to you. And I will not be a burden, for I seek not what is yours but you; for children ought not to lay up for their parents, but parents for their children.	This is now the third time that I am ready to come to visit you—and I will not make any demands on you. It is you I want, not your money. After all, children should not have to provide for their parents, but parents should provide for their children.

Here translates the Greek word "behold" (so KJV, RVR, NVSR). This single Greek word is used to emphasize the importance of what Paul is about to say. RSV does not completely capture the force of the Greek, and TEV does not even attempt to translate this Greek word. Many languages will have some way of emphasizing or drawing attention to the importance of what is about to be said.

The words **for the third time I am ready to come to you** do not mean that twice before Paul was ready to come and did not come, as the TEV translation also seems to suggest. Rather, Paul has already gone twice before to Corinth, and now he is ready to make a third trip (see also 13.1 and comments). REB says "I am now getting ready to pay you a third visit." In some languages it may even be necessary to use two separate sentences and say something like "I have already been with you twice. Now I am ready to come to you a third time."

And I will not be a burden: Paul did not accept financial help from the Corinthian Christians during his past visits, and he will continue to refuse material help from them (see 11.9 and 12.13). Some languages may require the addition of the word "still," as in CEV, which says "But I still won't make a burden of myself." And the idea of being a burden may have to be translated more explicitly as "I do not intend to cripple you with expenses" (Knox). In some cases the conjunction "but" may fit better to introduce this clause, since it may be expected that Paul would require some hospitality.

For I seek not what is yours, but you: the words **what is yours** refer to the Corinthian Christians' money (so TEV, REB). What Paul is saying is that he does not want the things that belong to the people in Corinth, but he wants them. However, in many languages it will be awkward or possibly misleading to translate literally either "I want . . . you" or "I seek . . . you." One language finds it necessary to translate "I am coming to help you; I am not trying to get your money."

For children ought not to lay up for their parents, but parents for their children: the implicit point of comparison is that Paul is the spiritual parent to the Corinthian "children" (see 1 Cor 4.15). The verb translated **lay up** gives the idea of setting something aside for future use (see Matt 6.19). It has been translated "make provision for" (REB) and "save up for" (NAB, NJB, AB, and CEV).

12.15 RSV	TEV
I will most gladly spend and be spent for your souls. If I love you the more, am I to be loved the less?	I will be glad to spend all I have, and myself as well, in order to help you. Will you love me less because I love you so much?

Spend and be spent: Paul continues to use terms related to money (see "lay up" in verse 14). Two closely related verbs are used here, but the second is more intense in meaning and is passive in form; literally "be spent out," that is, spent until nothing is left. REB attempts to reflect the intensive nature of the second verb by adding "to the limit." In many languages it will be impossible to retain the biblical image of Paul himself being "spent," using the same term as used for spending money. The idea of "being spent" for someone may have to be translated "to give oneself" or "to commit oneself." CEV translates "I will gladly give all that I have and all that I am."

The word **souls** here refers to the whole person. So it will be more natural in most languages to translate "for you" or "for your lives."

The more . . . the less: many languages require clarification of the comparisons here. More or less than what or whom? While there is a comparison between the way Paul loves the Corinthians and the way they love him, the first term may be translated in an absolute sense. Many versions translate **the more** as "too much." The word used here is, in fact, the same as in 10.8, where RSV renders it "too much." It is also translated "abundant" (2.4), "excessive" (2.7), and "all the more" (7.15). One version says "If I love you beyond limit like that, will you love me so little?"

Am I to be loved the less: the Greek has no explicit agent for the verb **be loved**. TEV correctly makes explicit that the Corinthians are the agent.

12.16   RSV   TEV

But granting that I myself did not bur- den you, I was crafty, you say, and got the better of you by guile.

You will agree, then, that I was not a burden to you. But someone will say that I was tricky, and trapped you with lies.

Even if Paul's opponents were to grant that he had not accepted financial help from the Corinthians, Paul still had to counter the suspicion, or perhaps the accusation, that he had put into his own pocket the collection money that Titus and his companions had collected from Corinth (verses 17-18). One model says "so you know that I did not ask you for anything at all."

But granting: literally, "Let it be so." Barrett translates "All right." Paul is saying, "OK, we have come to this point of agreement, that I didn't burden you, but then you will say that I tricked you." TEV captures the force of the Greek with the words "You will agree, then."

Burden: the verb used here is different from the one in 11.9 and 12.13,14. This is, in fact, the only occurrence of this verb in the New Testament. Possibly it is a bit stronger than the verb so translated earlier. The idea may be "to weigh down." But most English versions make no distinction between the two verbs.

You say: the Greek does not contain the words **you say**. It is not clear whether the Corinthians themselves or the "superapostles" were making these accusations against Paul, but RSV and TEV seem justified in inserting some phrase such as **you say** or "someone will say." Since the charge had probably already been made, the future tense of TEV ("someone will say") seems less satisfactory than the present tense of RSV (so also REB, GNC). TNT attempts to solve the problem by adding "you think . . . ." By failing to insert a phrase such as "you say" or "you think," a translation may give the impression that Paul himself is actually claiming that he tricked the Corinthians, as NJB seems to do: "All right, then; I did not make myself a burden to you, but, trickster that I am, I caught you by trickery."

I was crafty . . . and got the better of you by guile: literally "but being crafty, with deceit I took you." The words translated **crafty** and **guile** are very similar in meaning. The first occurs only here in all the New Testament, but a related word is found in 4.2 and 11.3 which is translated "cunning." It focuses on intelligence used for evil purposes. The second term entails trickery or deceit. The verb "to take" in this context means "to catch" or "to trap" in a figurative sense. The sense is "I got the better of you by roundabout means" (GNC).

A good model translation that captures the imagined dialogue Paul has with the Corinthians is that by Danker (page 202), although it contains certain idioms that may not be easy for second language speakers of English. It reads "Very well, 'You didn't freeload,' you will say to me. But in the same breath, 'Ah, but you were clever and took advantage of us in our naïveté.' "

12.17   RSV   TEV

Did I take advantage of you through   **How? Did I take advantage of you**
any of those whom I sent to you?   **through any of the messengers I sent?**

On the verb **take advantage of**, see comments on 7.2.

The identity of **those whom I sent to you** becomes clear in the next verse. Paul's question is rhetorical. He knows that the correct answer is that he did not take advantage of the Corinthians.

Some translators may wish to recast this verse as follows: "Among those people whom I sent to you, did any of them take advantage of you for me?" or, translating the rhetorical question as a statement, "I certainly did not make any of those people I sent take advantage of you."

12.18   RSV   TEV

I urged Titus to go, and sent the broth-   **I begged Titus to go, and I sent the**
er with him. Did Titus take advantage   **other Christian brother with him.**
of you? Did we not act in the same   **Would you say that Titus took advan-**
spirit? Did we not take the same steps?   **tage of you? Do not he and I act from**
                                                the very same motives and behave in
                                                the same way?

I urged Titus: see the similar expression in 8.6.

To go, that is, "to visit you" (CEV).

I sent: if chapters 10–13 are originally part of the same letter as chapters 1–9, then the verb **I sent** is possibly an epistolary aorist (see 8.17) and may be translated as "I am sending." That is, the trip of 8.17 has not yet begun at the time Paul writes this letter, and 12.18 refers to the same upcoming trip. It is also possible that **I sent** refers to an earlier visit than the one mentioned in 8.17, and should therefore be translated with the past tense as in RSV and TEV. If chapters 10–13 were written later than chapters 1–9 and formed part of a separate letter, then Paul is indeed referring to a past action, and the past tense **I sent** should be used. On the question of whether chapters 10–13 were part of a separate and later letter from chapters 1–9, see "Translating 2 Corinthians," page 3.

Since Paul mentions only one brother here, it may be that 12.18 refers to an early trip by Titus and one other person, and does not refer to the trip that Titus and two brothers are about to make to Corinth (chapter 8). If an earlier trip is being referred to here, then the verb should be translated in the past tense, **I sent**.

The brother does not have a possessive pronoun in Greek. Languages that must have a possessive pronoun may say "our [not including the readers] brother." REB says "I sent our friend," but the English is ambiguous as to whether "our" includes the readers also. The **brother** is not identified, but he may be the brother mentioned in 8.16-19. Surely the Corinthians knew this Christian brother, especially if he had already been sent to Corinth earlier. So ITCL correctly says "that other brother whom you know."

We: in this case the first person plural pronoun refers to Paul and Titus. It is probably better translated "he and I" in this context.

Same spirit: the reference here is probably not to the Holy Spirit (compare Rom 8.4 and Gal 5.16) but to the way of thinking of the two men, as in 7.13, where the word used here is translated "mind."

As in the previous verse, Paul's questions here are all rhetorical. He knows that Titus did not take advantage of them, that he acted in the same spirit as Titus did, and that he behaved in the same way as Titus did. If this series of questions is transformed to emphatic statements, they may read something like this: "Titus certainly did not take advantage of you. He and I acted in the same way and with the same motive." Or it may be possible to provide the answer to the question in translation, as NCV does: "Titus did not cheat you, did he? No, you know that Titus and I did the same thing and with the same spirit."

12.19	RSV	TEV

Have you been thinking all along that we have been defending ourselves before you? It is in the sight of God that we have been speaking in Christ, and all for your upbuilding, beloved.	**Perhaps you think that all along we have been trying to defend ourselves before you. No! We speak as Christ would have us speak in the presence of God, and everything we do, dear friends, is done to help you.**

Paul's reason for writing as he has is not to defend himself but to insure that the church at Corinth will be what it ought to be. The first sentence of verse 19 may be translated as a question as in RSV (so also FRCL, NRSV, NIV, TOB), or as a statement as in TEV (so also NJB, REB).

Some manuscripts have the word "again" (see KJV) in place of **all along**. The two words are quite similar in spelling in Greek, and the editors of the UBS *Greek New Testament* follow the more difficult reading ("all along"), which is also supported by the best manuscripts.

In the sight of God that we have been speaking in Christ: these same words occur in 2.17 (see comments there). REB says "speaking as Christians." On the meaning and translation of **in Christ**, see comments on 1.21.

And all for your upbuilding: the Greek contains no verb in this part of the verse. Should one repeat the verb **have been speaking**, that is, "all that we have been speaking is for your upbuilding"? Or should one supply a different verb such as "we do," as in TEV? The word **all** seems to suggest that Paul is referring not just to what he says (RSV) but also to what he does (TEV).

Your upbuilding: Paul and his companions are the ones who build up or edify the Corinthians. TEV makes this explicit by using a verb with subject ("we") and object ("you").

Beloved: see the comment on 7.1. TEV says "dear friends." Some languages will require a possessive pronoun here. The context permits either "my dear friends" or "our dear friends." In most languages this term of address will probably fit better at the beginning of the sentence rather than at the end (RSV) or the middle (TEV).

12.20 RSV	TEV
For I fear that perhaps I may come and find you not what I wish, and that you may find me not what you wish; that perhaps there may be quarreling, jealousy, anger, selfishness, slander, gossip, conceit, and disorder.	I am afraid that when I get there I will find you different from what I would like you to be and you will find me different from what you would like me to be. I am afraid that I will find quarreling and jealousy, hot tempers and selfishness, insults and gossip, pride and disorder.

Paul is afraid that the Corinthians will be fighting among themselves over rival claims of authority regarding Paul and the "superapostles."

I may find you not what I wish . . . you may find me not what you wish: literally "not as I wish I find you and I be found by you not as you wish." This rather awkward construction has been rendered in one language as "your way of acting will not please me and my way of acting will not please you."

The list of evils that Paul fears he will find is like similar lists elsewhere. The first four items in this verse are found in the same order in Gal 5.20. They are all four fairly common words indicating strife, jealousy, fierce indignation, and factiousness. The one translated **jealousy** may be used in a positive sense (as in 7.7 and 9.2), but here it is clearly negative. Most of the remaining words occur only once or twice in the New Testament.

Quarreling: fighting primarily in the sense of dissension and arguing; **jealousy**: not in terms of a lover's attitude toward a rival, but the desire to have what belongs to someone else; **anger**: more in the sense of outbursts of rage (TEV "hot tempers"); **selfishness**: working for one's own interests, including creation of factions; **slander**: evil speech about others; **gossip**: spreading false rumors; **conceit**: arrogance and wrongful pride; **disorder**: used of political and social disturbances. **Disorder** occurs five times and has to do with instability or "acting like a mob" (CEV). Compare 1 Cor 14.33, where it is translated "confusion."

12.21 RSV	TEV
I fear that when I come again my God may humble me before you, and I may have to mourn over many of those who sinned before and have not repented of the impurity, immorality, and licentiousness which they have practiced.	I am afraid that the next time I come my God will humiliate me in your presence, and I shall weep over many who sinned in the past and have not repented of the immoral things they have done—their lust and their sexual sins.

Again: this word may go with the verb **come** (so RSV, TEV) or with the verb **may humble** (so AB, "that my God may again humiliate me in your presence when I come," and Martin). Grammar and context allow for either interpretation, though the latter seems more likely for at least two reasons: Paul has already indicated that he is coming [again] in verse 20, so to say "when I come again" seems unnecessary. And grammatically, the words **when I come** seem to be parenthetical. On Paul's previous or first humiliation, see 2.1,5.

My God: in a few languages the use of a possessive pronoun with the name of God is problematic. A literal translation may give the false impression that Paul considered himself to have a different God from that of his Corinthian readers. The sense is "the God I serve." Note that the possessive pronoun is omitted by LB, Phps, Brc, and Hughes commentary.

Mourn: this verb may be understood in some cultures as referring to an internal feeling that does not necessarily have any outward manifestation. However, in this context the term used is probably intended to indicate some visible display of sorrow. For this reason TEV translates "weep," and Knox has "shall have tears to shed" (so also Brc).

Many of those who sinned before: the tense of the Greek verb **sinned before** suggests that these people have continued to sin. AB says "many who have continued in their former sinning." Paul is probably referring to sin which has continued since his second visit and his painful letter (2.1-4). The Greek verb indicates that the guilty persons had sinned at an earlier time. The sins "in the past" (TEV) are not sins committed before they became Christians, but rather sins committed as Christians.

Have not repented: while this verb is common in the Gospels, Acts, and Revelation, this is the only time it occurs in the letters of the New Testament. The related noun is, however, found at 7.9-10. It involves a change of heart and a new direction in life.

Impurity, immorality, and licentiousness: these same three words occur in Gal 5.19, though in a different order. The first of these three words, **impurity**, is a general word which came to mean ceremonial or moral uncleanness, with no special emphasis on sexual sins. Paul, however, often uses this word along with other words that refer to sexual immorality, so the sense here is probably sexual uncleanness. **Immorality** is a general word which can be used for any kind of sexual sins or immoral acts. **Licentiousness** refers to sexual excesses that result in public indecent behavior. In Greek a single definite article ("the") is used for all three nouns, which may suggest that Paul is using the three different terms as synonyms.

D-6. Final warnings and greetings
13.1-10

RSV	TEV
	Final Warnings and Greetings

1 This is the third time I am coming to you. Any charge must be sustained by the evidence of two or three witnesses. 2 I warned those who sinned before and all the others, and I warn them now while absent, as I did when present on my second visit, that if I come again I will not spare them—3 since you desire proof that Christ is speaking in me. He is not weak in dealing with you, but is powerful in you. 4 For he was crucified in weakness, but lives by the power of God. For we are weak in him, but in dealing with you we shall live with him by the power of God.

5 Examine yourselves, to see whether you are holding to your faith. Test yourselves. Do you not realize that Jesus Christ is in you?—unless indeed you fail to meet the test! 6 I hope you will find out that we have not failed. 7 But we pray God that you may not do wrong—not that we may appear to have met the test, but that you may do what is right, though we may seem to have failed. 8 For we cannot do anything against the truth, but only for the truth. 9 For we are glad when we are weak and you are strong. What we pray for is your improvement. 10 I write this while I am away from you, in order that when I come I may not have to be severe in my use of the authority which the Lord has given me for building up and not for tearing down.

1 This is now the third time that I am coming to visit you. "Any accusation must be upheld by the evidence of two or more witnesses"—as the scripture says. 2 I want to tell those of you who have sinned in the past, and all the others; I said it before during my second visit to you, but I will say it again now that I am away: the next time I come nobody will escape punishment. 3 You will have all the proof you want that Christ speaks through me. When he deals with you, he is not weak; instead, he shows his power among you. 4 For even though it was in weakness that he was put to death on the cross, it is by God's power that he lives. In union with him we also are weak; but in our relations with you we shall share God's power in his life.

5 Put yourselves to the test and judge yourselves, to find out whether you are living in faith. Surely you know that Christ Jesus is in you?—unless you have completely failed. 6 I trust you will know that we are not failures. 7 We pray to God that you will do no wrong—not in order to show that we are a success, but so that you may do what is right, even though we may seem to be failures. 8 For we cannot do a thing against the truth, but only for it. 9 We are glad when we are weak but you are strong. And so we also pray that you will become perfect. 10 That is why I write this while I am away from you; it is so that when I arrive I will not have to deal harshly with you in using the authority that the Lord has given me—authority to build you up, not to tear you down.

SECTION HEADING: TEV "Final Warnings and Greetings." The title of this section in TEV is similar to that in several other translations (TOB, FRCL, GECL). This Handbook, like some translations, breaks this section into two parts and groups verses 11-13 separately under the heading "Final Greetings" (NIV) or "Recommendations, greetings, final good wishes" (NJB). If this is done in the receptor language, it may be important to omit any reference to "greetings" at this point. One may say simply "Final Warnings." One language has entitled this final chapter simply "Concluding Matters." Earlier in this letter, as well as during his second visit to Corinth, Paul had warned the church there that he would act to restore discipline when he came, if they themselves did not do so. Now he gives his final warnings (verses 1-10), followed by greetings (verses 11-13).

13.1   RSV   TEV

This is the third time I am com-   This is now the third time that I
ing to you. Any charge must be sus- am coming to visit you. "Any accusa-
tained by the evidence of two or three tion must be upheld by the evidence of
witnesses.   two or more witnesses"—as the scrip-
                                     ture says.

The third time: see 12.14 and 13.2. The first visit was when Paul founded the church in Corinth (see Acts 18.1-18), and the second was the painful visit mentioned in 2.1.

I am coming to you: the verb tense may have to be altered in some languages. In order to show that the visit is yet in the future at the time of writing, several English versions have "this will be my third visit" or something similar.

The English words **charge, sustained, evidence**, and **witnesses** all evoke the image of a civil law court. But Paul is thinking more in terms of the religious requirements of the Old Testament, where civil and religious affairs were less distinct than in most cultures today. The statement that **any charge must be sustained by the evidence of two or three witnesses** indicates that Paul intends to follow the teachings of Deut 19.15. Though Paul does not state that he is referring to the teaching of the Old Testament, it is clear that he is; some translations such as TEV and NAB place quotation marks around these words. TEV and REB further add the words "as the scripture says." GNC adds the words "so we read" and uses bold type to highlight the quotation from the Old Testament, but GNC does not indicate where this is read.

As in 10.17, some translations use italics to indicate that Paul is quoting from the Old Testament, and they put the source of the quotation in a note (NBE, LPD, NJB). NRSV places quotation marks around the citation, as in 10.17, but does not directly indicate, as TEV does, that these words are from the Scriptures.

The passive construction **be sustained** will require some restructuring in many languages. Two possible models are "it takes at least two or three witnesses to support any accusation" or "only if two or more witnesses swear that they saw something does that matter show itself to be true."

To avoid the misunderstanding that only two or three witnesses, and no more, were allowed to present evidence, TEV says "two or more witnesses."

Why does Paul quote this rule from Deuteronomy? It is not likely that he means that he will take the Corinthian Christians to court or that he will apply the biblical way of settling a dispute when he comes to the church in Corinth. Rather, Paul compares the number of his visits to Corinth (**This is the**

third time I am coming to you) to the number of witnesses required to convict someone. Paul is telling them that they have had the necessary warnings which the Scriptures require. While it may not be desirable to include this idea in the translation, some translators may wish to include a footnote, as the REB Oxford Study Bible does: "The three witnesses (Deut 19.15) may be the three visits."

13.2 RSV	TEV
I warned those who sinned before and all the others, and I warn them now while absent, as I did when present on my second visit, that if I come again I will not spare them—	I want to tell those of you who have sinned in the past, and all the others; I said it before during my second visit to you, but I will say it again now that I am away: the next time I come nobody will escape punishment.

Those who sinned before refers to people who had sinned prior to Paul's second visit to Corinth and who heard his warning during his second visit. In some languages it may be necessary to say explicitly "those who were doing wrong before my last visit."

All the others refers to any other people who have sinned since his second visit, either by immoral behavior or by supporting the "false apostles." The warning is that Paul "will not be lenient" (NAB) with offenders when he comes for the third time.

Some manuscripts add the words "I write" after the words "being absent now" in Greek, and KJV and RVR follow this reading: "and being absent now I write to them." Though the original Greek almost certainly did not include the word translated "I write," the addition does not change the meaning.

That if I come again, I will not spare them: the word **that** may introduce an indirect quotation as in RSV, or it may be the equivalent of quotation marks: "I said, 'The next time I come, nobody will escape punishment' " (similarly TEV, FRCL, NIV).

If I come again: the Greek probably means nothing more than "when I come again" (see TEV, FRCL, NIV), and more than likely it does not mean that Paul had doubt about whether he would visit the Corinthian church again.

I will not spare them: Paul will not hesitate to exercise strong discipline against the offenders. The verb translated **spare** is the same as in 1.23 as well as 12.6, where it is translated "refrain" in RSV. Here the idea is to refrain from punishing the guilty persons, although there is no expressed object in Greek. The pronoun **them** has been added by RSV. But TNT adds the pronoun "you." NRSV revises to say "I will not be lenient," while NJB reads "I shall have no mercy."

The structure of this verse may have to be simplified in certain languages. The first verb indicates something that Paul did on his previous visit, his second to Corinth. Translators may change the order of the statements as follows:

On my second visit with you I warned those who did wrong and everyone else to stop doing wrong. Now that I am far away from you, I am giving you the same warning. When I come again, no one who does wrong will be able to avoid discipline.

Another possible model, putting the quotation first, may read as follows:

This is what I say: "When I come again, no one who does wrong will escape discipline." On my second visit to you I warned those who did wrong and all others to stop acting that way. Now that I am far from you, I am giving the same warning again.

13.3   RSV   TEV

since you desire proof that Christ is speaking in me. He is not weak in dealing with you, but is powerful in you.	You will have all the proof you want that Christ speaks through me. When he deals with you, he is not weak; instead, he shows his power among you.

The beginning of verse 3 justifies Paul's threat in verse 2, explaining why he is willing to punish the offenders. While RSV continues the rather complex sentence begun in the previous verse, it will probably be better to start a new sentence here, as in TEV. The word **since** introduces the reason why Paul will be strict on his next visit.

You desire proof: the verb used here is the same as in 1 Cor 1.22 and 4.2. The meaning is somewhat stronger than **desire**. In this context it is more like "demand" (AT and AB).

In the phrase **Christ is speaking in me**, the words **in me** are better translated as "through me" (TEV), since the point is that Christ is speaking to the Corinthians by means of Paul, his apostle, his ambassador. Another way of saying this in some languages may be "Christ is speaking by my mouth" or "Christ is causing me to speak."

He is not weak: the reference is to Christ. Some will rephrase this more naturally as "he does not lack strength." It should be noted that this verse (together with verses 4 and 9) constitutes the conclusion of the strength and weakness theme which started in 10.10. Translators should insure that as far as possible the same words are used throughout for these key terms.

The words **in you** (RSV, NRSV, NAB) are better translated as in TEV, "among you" (so also NJB, NIV, REB, and GNC). The focus is not on the spiritual working of Christ within each individual's life ("in you") but rather on his working within the collective life of the Christian community ("among you").

13.4   RSV   TEV

For he was crucified in weakness, but lives by the power of God. For we are weak in him, but in dealing with you we shall live with him by the power of God.	For even though it was in weakness that he was put to death on the cross, it is by God's power that he lives. In union with him we also are weak; but in our relations with you we shall share God's power in his life.

He was crucified: the verb used here does not occur elsewhere in this letter. It is frequent in the Gospels and is found four times in 1 Corinthians (1.13,23; 2.2,8). It involves putting a person to death by nailing him to a cross. The passive form will have to be made active in many languages. Translators may say "people killed him by nailing him to a cross" or, leaving certain information implicit, simply "he died on the cross."

In weakness refers to the weakness of Christ's human nature, that is, he was weak because he was a human being. Some languages may speak of "lacking strength in his body."

Christ **lives by the power of God**, meaning that God showed his power in raising Christ from the dead (see Rom 1.4). The whole first half of this verse may read "It is true that he lacked strength when they attached him to the cross, but he now lives by the power of God."

The sense of the second half of the verse is that, when Paul comes to Corinth, weak as he may appear to be, he will be in fellowship with the risen Christ and will share God's power in his dealings with the Corinthian church.

The pronoun **we** in this verse is exclusive, that is, the readers are not included. Since Paul uses the first person singular pronoun in verses 1-3, it is not clear whether the change to first person plural (**we**) is a stylistic change only or whether he intends to include his co-workers also. If translators decide that Paul is using the epistolary plural (see comments on 1.1 and on page 5), they may wish to use the pronoun "I" instead of "we" (so NBE) here and in verses 6 and 7.

In dealing with you: or, more literally, "toward you," which in Greek stands in contrast with **in him**. AB attempts to reflect this contrast as follows: "we are weak in him, but toward you we shall live with him by the power of God." However, it may be unnatural to try to do this in other languages. The meaning is "we are weak just as Christ was, but you will see that we will live by the power of God, just as Christ does."

The words **we shall live with him** do not here refer to the future life after death but to Paul's present fellowship with the risen Christ. It will perhaps be necessary to say something like "we shall go on living with him."

13.5   RSV   TEV

Examine yourselves, to see whether you are holding to your faith. Test	Put yourselves to the test and judge yourselves, to find out whether

yourselves. **Do you not realize that Jesus Christ is in you?**—unless indeed you fail to meet the test!	you are living in faith. Surely you know that Christ Jesus is in you?—unless you have completely failed.

The words **Examine yourselves** and **Test yourselves** mean essentially the same thing. Some languages have translated these two terms "look [carefully] at yourselves" and "ask yourselves." The pronouns **yourselves** are both in emphatic position. This leads AB to translate "it is yourselves that you must test . . . it is yourselves that you must put to the proof." Though they demand proof from Paul that he is speaking for Christ (13.3), he exhorts them to examine themselves rather than to examine him.

Holding to your faith: literally "in the faith" (AB). This is translated as "living the life of faith" in REB. Though Paul does not use the word "Christians," the meaning is that they are to find out whether they are living as Christians should live. The idea of **faith** will have to be translated by a verbal expression in some languages, and this may require that the object of the faith be expressed. Some languages may say "whether you are really true to what you believe."

Do you not realize: here, as frequently in his letters, Paul writes "Do you not know" (see Rom 6.3,16; 1 Cor 3.16; 5.6; 6.2-3). This is a rhetorical question that introduces a well-known or obvious fact. REB, like TEV, changes the form of this question in a way that emphasizes the implied answer: "Surely you recognize that Jesus Christ is among you?"

Jesus Christ is in you: the word **you** is plural in Greek. The Greek word translated as **in** may also be translated as "among" (so REB, FRCL, NBE; and see comment on 13.3). If the RSV interpretation is followed, the focus is more on the indwelling of Christ in the individual. If REB is followed, the focus is on the presence of Christ within the Corinthian community. NJB seems to focus more on the community than the individual, by translating "do you not recognize yourselves as a people in whom Jesus Christ is present?" Either interpretation is possible, and both make sense in the context. Perhaps the fact that each person is to test himself or herself favors the translation **in you**.

It will be noted that RSV has **Jesus Christ**, while TEV, NIV, NAB, and Mft have these names in reverse order. Some Greek manuscripts have the order **Jesus Christ**, and others have the order "Christ Jesus." The editors of the UBS *Greek New Testament* have here followed the reading **Jesus Christ**, considering it to be the original reading. On the order of these two names, see comment on 1.1.

The comparable vocabulary in **test yourselves** and **meet the test** in this verse reflects a similar correspondence in the Greek. It may be possible to show this relationship in the receptor language by using related words. But the translation should not be forced to the point of unnaturalness in order to do this.

13.6 RSV TEV

I hope you will find out that we have not failed. I trust you will know that we are not failures.

If the Corinthians realize that Christ is in them, then they will have proof that Paul is a true apostle, for he was the one who brought them to faith in Christ (1 Cor 4.15)!

I hope: in 1.13 and 5.11 this same word is used to indicate a degree of confidence in the Corinthians, but here it is almost like a command to them to correct their thinking before he comes. However, it would not be appropriate to translate it as a command.

As in verse 4, the pronoun **we** does not include the Corinthians. And as in verse 4, the pronoun **we** may be an epistolary plural. If so, translators may wish to say "that I have not failed" (so NBE, and similarly AT, Mft, and ITCL).

That we have not failed: this continues the image of testing pointed out in the previous verse. Where possible the same kind of terminology should be used to show this relationship.

In the context of this letter, the words **find out that we have not failed** mean that Paul hopes the Corinthians will realize that he has proven himself to be a true apostle (see 12.11-12). The verb may be rendered "discover" (CEV), "come to know" (AB), or "come to recognize" (NJB).

13.7 RSV TEV

But we pray God that you may not do wrong—not that we may appear to have met the test, but that you may do what is right, though we may seem to have failed. We pray to God that you will do no wrong—not in order to show that we are a success, but so that you may do what is right, even though we may seem to be failures.

Paul prays that he will not find the Corinthians guilty as he has accused them of being. He would rather be found to have been wrong in his charges against them and seem to be a failure as an apostle, than for them to be found guilty of sins.

But: although the conjunction used here is often omitted in English versions, it marks something of a contrast between Paul's expectations for the Corinthians (recognition that he is not a failure) and his own action (prayer). AB renders it "yet."

We pray: if this is an epistolary plural (see 13.4), it will be correct to use the first person singular pronoun in this verse and in verses 8 and 9 (so NBE, ITCL, Mft, and AT).

Not that . . . : the words that follow the dashes in RSV and TEV may need to be translated as a separate sentence in many languages. They indicate the purpose of his prayer, and this is framed both negatively and positively. One may say "we don't pray like this in order to justify ourselves, but to get you to do what is right, even if we appear to be failures." Another possible model showing more clearly the continuation of the testing theme can be as follows: "we are not trying to make ourselves look good, but we pray that you will do what is right even if people think that we have failed the test."

13.8   RSV   TEV

For we cannot do anything against the truth, but only for the truth.	For we cannot do a thing against the truth, but only for it.

We again does not include the Corinthian readers.

We cannot do anything against the truth: that is, "we cannot do anything to oppose the truth." The verb with the negative indicates powerlessness. NJB translates "we have no power to resist the truth."

The truth is the gospel or the progress of the gospel.

In the context of chapters 10–13, verse 8 means that when Paul returns to Corinth, he will take the necessary action, depending on whether they have done wrong or have done what is right (verse 8).

In some languages it will be more natural to state the positive side in this verse before the negative: "We can do only those things that advance the truth; we cannot do anything to hold it back."

13.9   RSV   TEV

For we are glad when we are weak and you are strong. What we pray for is your improvement.	We are glad when we are weak but you are strong. And so we also pray that you will become perfect.

We here excludes the readers.

Weak and **strong** here mean that Paul is happy to be wrong or to suffer defeat as long as the Corinthians are living victorious Christian lives. Indeed, Paul prays that they will continue to grow more mature in their Christian living. It should be noted that this verse uses the same vocabulary as in 10.10, where the theme of strength and weakness was introduced. This, then, is the conclusion of the matter.

Your improvement: this wording, as well as the TEV rendering "that you will become perfect," may be misleading. The idea here is not so much that of bringing to perfection something that is already good. It is rather one of restoring something that has been damaged or reinstating something that was lost. Paul used the verb form of this noun in Gal 6.1 to speak of the need to restore a fellow Christian who had sinned. Hence AB, Barrett, and Martin translate "your restoration," while REB speaks of "your amendment."

13.10 RSV TEV

I write this while I am away from you, in order that when I come I may not have to be severe in my use of the authority which the Lord has given me for building up and not for tearing down.	That is why I write this while I am away from you; it is so that when I arrive I will not have to deal harshly with you in using the authority that the Lord has given me—authority to build you up, not to tear you down.

I write this refers to the letter which he is now writing. REB says "In writing this letter." Whether 2 Corinthians was originally one whole letter, or whether it is made up of parts of two or more originally separate letters, is debated by scholars (see "Translating 2 Corinthians," page 3), but in any case Paul is referring to the entire letter which he is writing and not just the immediately preceding words. (See 10.2,8.)

Be severe: although it is not explicitly stated, clearly Paul is talking about being severe with the Corinthian Christians to whom he is writing. This may be directly stated in translation by saying something like "be severe with you," or "treat you with force," or "handle you with a strong hand."

The authority which the Lord has given: this phrase is almost identical with the one in 10.8. **The Lord** here and in 10.8 is probably Christ, since Paul claims to be speaking for Christ (12.19; 13.3).

On **building up** and **tearing down**, see comments on 10.8, where the same words occur in Greek, and where the object is specifically stated as "you" (the Corinthians). Here it may also be necessary to provide the same object for the two verbs. CEV translates "so that I could help you and not destroy you."

E. Conclusion

13.11-14

RSV   TEV

11 Finally, brethren, farewell. Mend   11 And now, my brothers, good-bye!
your ways, heed my appeal, agree with one   Strive for perfection; listen to my appeals;
another, live in peace, and the God of love and   agree with one another; live in peace. And the
peace will be with you. 12 Greet one another   God of love and peace will be with you.
with a holy kiss. 13 All the saints greet you.   12 Greet one another with a brotherly
   14 The grace of the Lord Jesus Christ   kiss.
and the love of God and the fellowship of the   All of God's people send you their greet-
Holy Spirit be with you all.   ings.
                                                    13 The grace of the Lord Jesus Christ,
                                             the love of God, and the fellowship of the Holy
                                             Spirit be with you all.

13.11   RSV   TEV

Finally, brethren, farewell. Mend   **And now, my brothers, good-bye!**
your ways, heed my appeal, agree with   **Strive for perfection; listen to my ap-**
one another, live in peace, and the God   **peals; agree with one another; live in**
of love and peace will be with you.   **peace. And the God of love and peace**
                                             will be with you.

Finally: the word so translated is often used to mark the transition to the
conclusion of one of Paul's letters (compare, for example, 1 Thes 4.1 and 2 Thes
3.1). Several versions translate as TEV "and now" (NAB, REB). NJB has "to end
then . . . ." Others may say "in conclusion" or "now let me finish my letter by
saying . . . ."

On **brethren** see comments on 1.8.

Paul makes four final appeals to the Corinthians: **mend your ways, heed
my appeal, agree with one another**, and **live in peace**. If the first verb
(**farewell** in RSV) is also an imperative, then Paul makes five final appeals.

The Greek word translated as **farewell** in many translations (RSV, TEV,
REB, NIV, FRCL) is the same word that is frequently translated as "rejoice." In
form this verb may be an imperative, as are the following four verbs in verse
11, or an indicative mood verb that simply states a fact. Numerous translations
take this verb as an imperative and translate it as "rejoice" (AB, TOB, NJB, NBE,
Lu). Though this same Greek word is commonly used at the beginning of

letters to mean "greetings," there is no solid evidence that it was ever used at the conclusion of a letter to mean "good-bye." The translation "rejoice" seems preferable.

Mend your ways may be understood in either of two ways: (1) it may refer to something that the Corinthians are to do actively themselves, as in RSV and TEV; or (2) it may be understood in a passive sense. If passive (so KJV, GECL, Lu), the sense is "be restored (or, perfected) [by God? by Paul?]." But it is difficult to see why Paul would appeal to them with regard to something over which they have no control. It seems much more likely that the meaning found in the majority of English versions (RSV, TEV, NAB, REB) is the correct understanding of the text. The sense is then "correct the wrong behavior" or "put things in order" (NRSV). The verb **mend your ways** is from the same root as the noun translated **improvement** in verse 9 (see comments there).

Heed my appeal: the words so translated have two possible meanings: (1) "be exhorted" or (2) "exhort one another." RSV and TEV both choose the first option and translate this verb as passive in meaning, that is, "be exhorted by me" (so also NIV, REB, Lu), even though the form in English is not passive. The other option is, however, equally possible in the context, since Paul is encouraging the readers to live in harmony. In this case the meaning is "encourage one another" (NJB, TOB, Martin, and Barrett). While both interpretations are quite possible, translators will probably want to follow the example of RSV and TEV and translate something like "pay attention to what I have said."

Agree with one another is literally "think the same." RSV translates the same expression as "to live in harmony with one another" in Rom 15.5, and as "be of the same mind" in Phil 2.2.

Live in peace: Paul uses the same verb in Rom 12.18, where he urges the Roman Christians to "live in peace with all people," and in 1 Thes 5.13, where he exhorts the Thessalonian Christians to "live in peace with one another." Here in 2 Corinthians Paul does not specify whether they are to live in peace with non-Christians or among themselves, though the latter seems more likely in the context (so GECL). If the receptor language requires a choice, it is therefore probably better to say "live in peace with each other" or "have peace with one other."

God of love and peace: CEV says "God, who gives love and peace." But perhaps the meaning is not only that God creates love and peace among the believers, but that he also is characterized by love and peace. If translators must decide between these two interpretations, they may choose either as being in agreement with Paul's theology.

Translators in some languages will need to be careful lest the translation suggest that for Paul there is another god (or other gods) who is not the source of love and peace.

13.12-13   RSV   TEV

12 Greet one another with a holy kiss.   12 Greet one another with a
13 All the saints greet you.   brotherly kiss.
                                                    All of God's people send you their
                                                greetings.

Following the UBS *Greek New Testament,* TEV includes these two verses as one verse, numbered 12. Chapter 13, therefore, has fourteen verses in some translations (RSV, REB, SPCL) and 13 in others (TEV, NRSV, FRCL, GECL). But the content of the different versions is the same. If there is already an established tradition in the area of the receptor language, that tradition may be followed. Otherwise it is probably best to follow the verse division of the UBS *Greek New Testament,* which is reflected in TEV.

Greet . . . with a holy kiss: Paul does not specify whether the kiss of greeting should be given only when the believers gather to worship or whether they are to greet each other in this manner in public any time they meet each other. Interpreters are divided on whether Paul's admonition is intended (1) only for the single occasion of hearing this letter read, (2) for any time that Christians gather to worship, or (3) for any time or place where Christians meet each other. If translators must decide between these options, perhaps it is best to follow the first or second.

A holy kiss is difficult to translate in many languages. The same expression is found in a number of other letters of Paul (see Rom 16.16; 1 Cor 16.20; 1 Thes 5.26). The word **holy** is often difficult to render correctly, and some languages do not have a word for **kiss** but use a word that means a sucking on the cheek, such as a mother might do to her baby. In any case this kind of action is not something that would ever take place between adults in many cultures—especially of the same sex. A literal translation will therefore be distracting and misleading. Translators may use a more general expression that basically retains the meaning: "Give one another a Christian greeting," "a warm embrace," or "a warm greeting" (CEV). An article on the subject of "Kissing in the Bible" may be found in *The Bible Translator* (October 1990), pages 409-416.

On **the saints** see 1.1. The Christians who send greetings are Christians in Paul's company or in the place where Paul is staying when he is writing this letter. It may therefore be more in line with Paul's intention to translate "All the people of God who are here . . . ."

The saints greet you: the word **you** is plural. Since the persons giving the greetings are not present in Corinth and therefore cannot greet the Corinthians directly, some translations add the word "send," as in TEV and REB.

13.14   RSV   TEV

The grace of the Lord Jesus Christ and the love of God and the fellowship of[n] the Holy Spirit be with you all.	13 The grace of the Lord Jesus Christ, the love of God, and the fellowship of the Holy Spirit be with you all.

[n] Or *and participation in*

Paul often ends his letters with such a benediction (compare 1 Cor 16.23; Gal 6.18; 1 Thes 5.28; 2 Thes 3.18). Since this whole verse is a wish or prayer of Paul for the Christians at Corinth, it may be necessary in the receptor language to introduce it by saying "It is my desire that . . ." or "I pray that . . ." (CEV).

On **The grace of the Lord Jesus Christ**, see comments on 8.9, and compare 1 Cor 1.3. **Grace** must not be understood as a quality or characteristic of Christ but as something which he does. In some languages it will be more natural to say something like "I pray that the Lord Jesus Christ will show his kindness to you . . . ."

Since the first part of this verse must mean the **grace** that comes from Jesus Christ, the other two parts of the verse probably mean the **love** that God has for them ("May God bless you with his love," CEV) and the **fellowship** that the Holy Spirit creates ("May the Holy Spirit join all your hearts together," CEV). It is possible, however, but not as likely, that Paul refers to love for God and fellowship with the Holy Spirit.

You all: as in Rom 15.33 and 1 Cor 16.24, the second person plural pronoun is accompanied by the inclusive adjective **all**, thus highlighting the extent of Paul's wish for the Corinthians. This comprehensiveness is also emphasized several times earlier in this letter (2.3,5 and 7.13,15).

The following model may be helpful in some languages: "I pray for all of you that the Lord Jesus Christ will continue to be gracious to you, that God will continue to love you, and that the Holy Spirit will unite you in his fellowship."

Some manuscripts add the word "Amen" to the end of this letter (see KJV, RVR), but scholars today agree that this word was later added by a scribe and was not written by Paul. It should therefore not be used in the receptor language.

Bibliography

Texts

The Greek New Testament. Fourth revised edition, 1993. Barbara Aland, Kurt Aland, Johannes Karavidopoulos, Carlo M. Martini, and Bruce M. Metzger, eds. Stuttgart: Deutsche Bibelgesellschaft/United Bible Societies. (Cited as UBS *Greek New Testament*.)

Novum Testamentum Graece. 26th edition, 1979; corrected, 1981. Erwin Nestle and Kurt Aland, eds. Stuttgart: Deutsche Bibelgesellschaft. (Cited as Nestle-Aland.)

Lexicons

Arndt, William F., and F. Wilbur Gingrich. 1979. *A Greek-English Lexicon of the New Testament and Other Early Christian Literature*. Second edition, revised and augmented by F. Wilbur Gingrich and Frederick W. Danker. Chicago and London: The University of Chicago Press.

Nida, Eugene A., and Johannes P. Louw, eds. 1988. *Greek-English Lexicon*, 2 vols. New York: United Bible Societies.

Commentaries

Barrett, Charles K. 1973. *A Commentary on the Second Epistle to the Corinthians* (Harper's New Testament Commentaries) New York: Harper & Row.

Betz, Hans Dieter. 1985. *2 Corinthians 8 and 9* (Hermeneia). Philadelphia: Fortress Press.

Bratcher, Robert G. 1982. *A Translator's Guide to Paul's Second Letter to the Corinthians*. New York: United Bible Societies.

Bruce, Frederick F. 1971. *1 and 2 Corinthians* (New Century Bible Commentary). Grand Rapids, Michigan: Eerdmans.

Danker, Frederick W. 1989. *II Corinthians* (Augsburg Commentary on the New Testament). Minneapolis: Augsburg.

Fisher, Fred. 1975. *Commentary on 1 & 2 Corinthians*. Waco, Texas: Word Books.

Furnish, Victor Paul. 1984. *II Corinthians* (The Anchor Bible 32A). Garden City, N.Y.: Doubleday.

———. 1988. "2 Corinthians," in *Harper's Bible Commentary*, ed. by James L. Mays. San Francisco: Harper & Row, pp. 1190-1203.

Héring, Jean. 1958. *La seconde épître de Saint Paul aux Corinthiens* (Commentaire du Nouveau Testament). Neuchâtel: Delachaux & Niestlé.

Hughes, Philip E. 1962 *The Second Epistle to the Corinthians* (New International Commentary on the New Testament). Grand Rapids: Eerdmans.

Martin, Ralph P. 1986. *2 Corinthians* (Word Biblical Commentary 40). Waco, Texas: Word Books.

Plummer, Alfred. 1915. *The Second Epistle of St Paul to the Corinthians* (International Critical Commentary). Edinburgh: T. & T. Clark.

Strachen, R.H. 1935. *The Second Epistle of Paul to the Corinthians*. London: Hodder & Stoughton.

Talbert, Charles H. 1987. *Reading Corinthians: A Literary and Theological Commentary on 1 and 2 Corinthians*. New York: Crossroad.

Tasker, R.V.G. 1958. *The Second Epistle of Paul to the Corinthians*. Grand Rapids: Eerdmans.

Other Works

Barrett, Charles K. 1982. *Essays on Paul*. Philadelphia: Westminster Press.

Bromily, Geoffrey W., ed. 1979-1988. *The International Standard Bible Encyclopedia*. Four volumes. Grand Rapids: Eerdmans.

Buttrick, George Arthur, ed. 1962. *The Interpreter's Dictionary of the Bible*. 4 vols. Nashville: Abingdon.

Crim, Keith, ed. 1976. *The Interpreter's Dictionary of the Bible*. Supplementary Volume. Nashville: Abingdon.

Freedman, David Noel, ed. 1992. *The Anchor Bible Dictionary.* 6 volumes. New York: Doubleday.

Metzger, Bruce M. 1971. *A Textual Commentary on the Greek New Testament.* London/New York: United Bible Societies.

Moule, C.F.D. 1968. *An Idiom-Book of New Testament Greek.* Cambridge: Cambridge University Press.

Murphy-O'Connor, Jerome. 1991. *The Theology of the Second Letter to the Corinthians.* New York and Cambridge: Cambridge University Press.

Bible Texts and Versions Cited

The Anchor Bible. 1984. Translated by Victor Paul Furnish. Garden City, N.Y.: Doubleday. (Cited as AB.)

Barrett, Charles K. (translation in *The Second Epistle to the Corinthians*). 1973. (Cited as Barrett.)

Die Bibel in heutigem Deutsch: Die Gute Nachricht des Alten und Neuen Testaments. 1982. Stuttgart: Deutsche Bibelgesellschaft. (Cited as GECL.)

La Bible de Jérusalem. 1973. Paris: Éditions du Cerf. (Cited as BJ.)

La Bible en français courant. 1982. Paris: Société biblique française. (Cited as FRCL.)

A Bíblia Sagrada: Tradução na linguagem de hoje. 1988. São Paulo: Sociedade Bíblica do Brasil. (Cited as Brazilian Portuguese common language version, BRCL.)

La Biblia Interconfesional: Nuevo Testamento. 1978. Madrid: BAC-EDICABI-SBU. (Cited as LBI.)

The Catholic Study Bible (The New American Bible). 1990. New York, Oxford: Oxford University Press. (Cited as NAB. When the edition published in 1971 is cited, reference is made to "the first edition of NAB.")

The Complete Bible: An American Translation. 1923. Translated by J.M. Powis Smith and Edgar J. Goodspeed. Chicago: University of Chicago Press. (Cited as AT.)

Contemporary English Version. 1991. New York: American Bible Society. (Cited as CEV.)

Dios Habla Hoy: La Biblia, Versión Popular. 2ª edición. 1983. Nueva York: Sociedad Bíblica Americana. (Cited as SPCL.)

The Everyday Bible: New Century Version. 1988. Dallas, Texas: Word Publishing. (Cited as NCV.)

God's New Covenant: A New Testament Translation. 1989. Translated by Heinz W. Cassirer. Grand Rapids: Eerdmans. (Cited as GNC.)

Good News Bible: The Bible in Today's English Version with Deuterocanonicals/Apocrypha. 1979. New York: American Bible Society. (Cited as TEV.)

Good News for the World (The New Testament in Worldwide English). 1969. Bombay: Soon! Publications. (Cited as GNW.)

Holy Bible (International Children's Bible: New Century Version). 1988. (Cited as NCV.)

The Holy Bible (Authorized or King James Version). 1611. (Cited as KJV.)

The Holy Bible (New Revised Standard Version with Apocrypha). 1989. New York: Division of Christian Education of the National Council of the Churches of Christ in the United States of America. (Cited as NRSV.)

The Holy Bible: Revised Standard Version. 1952, 1971, 1973. New York: Division of Christian Education of the National Council of the Churches of Christ in the United States of America. (Cited as RSV.)

The Holy Bible. 1955. Translated by Ronald A. Knox. London: Burns & Oates. (Cited as Knox.)

El Libro del Pueblo de Dios: La Biblia. 3ª edición. 1987. Madrid, Buenos Aires: Ediciones Paulinas. (Cited as LPD.)

The Living Bible. 1971. Translated by Kenneth Taylor. Wheaton, Illinois: Tyndale House. (Cited as LB.)

Martin, Ralph P. (See the translation in the commentary, *2 Corinthians*). 1986. (Cited as Martin.)

Das Neue Testament und die Psalmen. 1985. Stuttgart: Deutsche Bibelgesellschaft. (Cited as Lu.)

The New English Bible with the Apocrypha. 2nd edition. 1970. London: Oxford University Press, and Cambridge University Press. (Cited as NEB.)

The New Jerusalem Bible. 1985. Garden City, New York: Doubleday. (Cited as NJB.)

The New Testament: A New Translation. 1969. Translated by William Barclay. London: Collins. (Cited as Brc.)

The New Testament: A New Translation. Revised edition. 1935. Translated by James Moffatt. (Cited as Mft.)

The New Testament in Modern English. 1924. Translated by Helen Barrett Montgomery. Valley Forge, Pennsylvania: Judson Press.

The New Testament in Modern English. Revised edition, 1972. Translated by J.B. Phillips. London: Collins. (Cited as Phps.)

The New Testament in the Language of the People. 1937. Translated by Charles Bray Williams. (Cited as Williams.)

The NIV Study Bible (New International Version). 1985. Grand Rapids: Zondervan. (Cited as NIV.)

Nueva Biblia Española. 1975. Madrid: Ediciones Cristiandad. (Cited as NBE.)

The Original New Testament. 1985. Translated by Hugh J. Schonfield. New York: Harper & Row.

Parola del Signore: La Bibbia. Traduzione interconfessionale in lingua corrente. 1985. Torino: Editrice Elle Di Ci/Roma: Alleanza Biblica Universale. (Cited as ITCL.)

The Revised English Bible. 1989. London: Oxford University Press, and Cambridge University Press. (Cited as REB.)

La Sainte Bible. 1910. Translated by Louis Segond. Paris: Alliance biblique universelle (Cited as SE.)

La Sainte Bible (Version établie par les moines de Maredsous). 1973. Paris: Brepols. (Cited as Maredsous.)

La Sainte Bible: Traduite d'après les textes originaux hébreu et grec. 1978. Nouvelle version Segond révisée, deuxième édition. Paris: Société biblique française. (Cited as NVSR.)

La Santa Biblia (Versión de Reina-Valera). Revisión de 1960. México, D.F.: Sociedades Bíblicas en America Latina. (Cited as RVR.)

Traduction œcuménique de la Bible. Seconde Edition. 1982. Paris: Éditions du Cerf / Alliance Biblique Universelle. (Cited as TOB.)

The Translator's New Testament. 1973. London: British and Foreign Bible Society. (Cited as TNT.)

Articles

Carrez, Maurice. 1980. "Le 'nous' en 2 Corinthiens. Paul parle-t-il au nom de toute la communauté, du groupe apostolique, de l'équipe ministérielle ou en son nom personnel? Contribution à l'étude de l'apostolicité dans 2 Corinthiens." *New Testament Studies* 26:474-486.

Ellington, John. 1990. "Kissing in the Bible." *The Bible Translator* 41:409-416.

Ellingworth, Paul. 1992. "Grammar, meaning, and verse divisions in 2 Cor 11.16-29." *The Bible Translator* 43:245-246.

Glossary

This Glossary contains terms that are technical from an exegetical or a linguistic viewpoint. Other terms not defined here may be referred to in a Bible dictionary.

ABSTRACT refers to terms that designate the qualities and quantities (that is, the features) of objects and events but which are not objects or events themselves. For example, "red" is a quality of a number of objects but is not a thing in and of itself. Typical abstracts include "goodness," "length," "breadth," and "time." **ABSTRACT NOUN** is one that refers to a quality or characteristic, such as "beauty" or "darkness."

ACTIVE. See **VOICE**.

ADJECTIVE is a word that limits, describes, or qualifies a noun. In English, "red," "tall," "beautiful," and "important" are adjectives.

ADVERB is a word that limits, describes, or qualifies a verb, an adjective, or another adverb. In English, "quickly," "soon," "primarily," and "very" are adverbs.

ADVERBIAL refers to adverbs. An **ADVERBIAL PHRASE** is a phrase that functions as an adverb. See **PHRASE**.

ADVERSATIVE describes something opposed to or in contrast with something already stated. "But" and "however" are adversative conjunctions.

AGENT is that which accomplishes the action in a sentence or clause, regardless of whether the grammatical construction is active or passive. In "John struck Bill" (active) and "Bill was struck by John" (passive), the agent in either case is "John."

AMBIGUOUS (AMBIGUITY) describes a word or phrase that in a specific context may have two or more different meanings. For example, "Bill did not leave because John came" could mean either (1) "the coming of John prevented Bill from leaving" or (2) "the coming of John was not the cause of Bill's leaving." It is often the case that what is ambiguous in written form is not ambiguous when actually spoken, since features of intonation and slight pauses usually make clear which of two or more meanings is intended. Furthermore, even in written discourse, the entire context normally serves to indicate which meaning is intended by the writer.

ANACHRONISM (ANACHRONISTIC) is an expression that is incorrectly used because it is historically or chronologically misplaced. For example, to refer to Jonah buying a ticket for his sea voyage would be an anachronism, because it introduces a modern custom into an ancient setting.

ANTECEDENT describes a person or thing that precedes or exists prior to something or someone else. In grammar, an antecedent is the word, phrase, or clause to which a pronoun refers.

AORIST refers to a set of forms in Greek verbs which denote an action completed without the implication of continuance or duration. Usually, but not always, the action is considered as completed in past time.

APPOSITION is the placing of two expressions together so that they both refer to the same object, event, or concept; for example, "my friend, Mr. Smith." The one expression is said to be the **APPOSITIVE** of the other.

ARAMAIC is a language that was widely used in Southwest Asia before the time of Christ. It became the common language of the Jewish people in Palestine in place of Hebrew, to which it is related.

ARTICLE is a grammatical class of words, often obligatory, which indicate whether the following word is definite or indefinite. In English the **DEFINITE ARTICLE** is "the," and the **INDEFINITE ARTICLE** is "a" or "an."

ASPECT is a grammatical category that specifies the nature of an action; for example, whether the action is completed, uncompleted, repeated, begun, continuing, increasing in intensity, decreasing in intensity, etc. "Was built" indicates completed aspect, while, "was running" indicates continuing aspect.

BENEFACTIVE refers to goals for whom or which something is done. The pronoun "him" is the benefactive goal in each of the following constructions: "they showed him kindness," "they did the work for him," and "they found him an apartment."

BORROWED TERM refers to a foreign term that is used in another language. (Gos of John) For example, "matador" is a Spanish word that has been borrowed by English speakers for "bullfighter."

CAUSATIVE (CAUSAL) relates to events and indicates that someone or something caused something to happen, rather than that the person or thing did it directly. In "John ran the horse," the verb "ran" is a causative, since it was not John who ran, but rather it was John who caused the horse to run.

CHIASMUS (**CHIASTIC**) is a reversal of words or phrases in the second part of an otherwise parallel construction. For example: "I (1) / was shapen (2) / in iniquity (3) // in sin (3) / did my mother conceive (2) / me (1)."

CLASSIFIER is a term used with another term (often a proper noun) to indicate to what category the latter belongs. "Town" may serve as a classifier in the phrase "town of Bethlehem," and "river" as a classifier in "river Jordan."

CLAUSE is a grammatical construction, normally consisting of a subject and a predicate.

COMMAND. See **IMPERATIVE**.

COMPONENTS are the parts or elements that go together to form the whole of an object. For example, the components of bread are flour, salt, shortening, yeast, and water. The components of the meaning (semantic components) of a term are the elements of meaning that it contains. For example, some of the components of "boy" are "human," "male," and "immature."

COMPOUND refers to forms of words or phrases consisting of two or more parts.

CONCRETE refers to the reality or experience of things or events, particularly in contrast to **ABSTRACT**. The term "child," for example, is concrete, but "childhood" is an abstraction. See **ABSTRACT**.

CONDITION is that which shows the circumstance under which something may be true. In English, a **CONDITIONAL** phrase or clause is usually introduced by "if."

CONJUNCTIONS are words that serve as connectors between words, phrases, clauses, and sentences. "And," "but," "if," and "because" are typical conjunctions in English.

CONSEQUENCE is that which shows the result of a condition or event.

CONSONANTS are symbols representing those speech sounds that are produced by obstructing, blocking, or restricting the free passage of air from the lungs through the mouth. They were originally the only spoken sounds recorded in the Hebrew system of writing; vowels were added later as marks associated with the **CONSONANTS**.

CONSTRUCTION. See **STRUCTURE**.

CONTEXT (**CONTEXTUAL**) is that which precedes and/or follows any part of a discourse. For example, the context of a word or phrase in Scripture would be the other words and phrases associated with it in the sentence, paragraph, section, and even the entire book in which it occurs. The context of a term often affects its meaning, so that a word does not mean exactly the same thing in one context that it does in another context.

CONTRASTIVE expresses something opposed to or in contrast to something already stated. "But" and "however" are **CONTRASTIVE CONJUNCTIONS**.

CULTIC is an adjective formed from the noun "cult"; it is used to describe any custom or action that is required in the performance of religious practices. It is broadly synonymous with the adjectives "ritual" and "ceremonial."

DEFINITE ARTICLE. See **ARTICLE**.

DEMONSTRATIVE PRONOUN refers to one or more specific persons, things, events, or objects by indicating or singling out what is referred to. "That," "this," and "those" are demonstrative pronouns in English. See also **PRONOUN**.

DIRECT ADDRESS, DIRECT DISCOURSE, DIRECT QUOTATION, DIRECT SPEECH. See **DISCOURSE**.

DIRECT OBJECT is the goal of an event or action specified by a verb. In "John hit the ball," the direct object of "hit" is "ball."

DISCOURSE is the connected and continuous communication of thought by means of language, whether spoken or written. The way in which the elements of a discourse are arranged is called **DISCOURSE STRUCTURE**. **DIRECT DISCOURSE** (or, **DIRECT QUOTATION, DIRECT SPEECH**) is the reproduction of the actual words of one person quoted and included in the discourse of another person; for example, "He declared 'I will have nothing to do with this man.' " **INDIRECT DISCOURSE** (or, **INDIRECT QUOTATION, INDIRECT SPEECH**) is the reporting of the words of one person within the discourse of another person, but in an altered grammatical form rather than as an exact quotation; for example, "He said he would have nothing to do with that man."

DYNAMIC EQUIVALENCE (**DYNAMIC RENDERING**) is a type of translation in which the message of the original text is so conveyed in the receptor language that the response of the receptors is (or, can be) essentially like that of the original receptors, or that the receptors can in large measure comprehend the response of the original receptors, if, as in certain languages, the differences between the two cultures are extremely great. In recent years the term **FUNCTIONAL EQUIVALENCE** has been applied to what is essentially the same kind of translation.

EMPHASIS (EMPHATIC) is the special importance given to an element in a discourse, sometimes indicated by the choice of words or by position in the sentence. For example, in "Never will I eat pork again," "Never" is given emphasis by placing it at the beginning of the sentence.

EPISTOLARY PLURAL is the use of the pronoun "we" ("us," "our") instead of "I" ("me," "my") in writing by a single person, for the purpose of achieving a more formal or impersonal effect. It is called the "editorial 'we.' "

EQUIVALENCE: a very close similarity in meaning, as opposed to similarity in form; see **DYNAMIC EQUIVALENCE**. It contrasts with **FORMAL CORRESPONDENCE**.

EVENT is a semantic category of meanings referring to actions, processes, etc., in which objects can participate. In English, most events are grammatically classified as verbs ("run," "grow" "think," etc.), but many nouns may also refer to events, as for example, "baptism," "song," "game," and "prayer."

EXAGGERATION (EXAGGERATE) is a figure of speech that states more than the speaker or writer intends to be understood. For example, "Everyone is doing it" may simply mean "Many people are doing it."

EXCLUSIVE first person plural excludes the person(s) addressed. That is, a speaker may use "we" to refer to himself and his companions, while specifically excluding the person(s) to whom he is speaking. See **INCLUSIVE**.

EXEGESIS (EXEGETICAL) is the process of determining the meaning of a text (or the result of this process), normally in terms of "who said what to whom under what circumstances and with what intent." A correct exegesis is indispensable before a passage can be translated correctly.

EXHORTATION is the verbal act of encouraging, attempting, or urging, to make someone change a course of action or a matter of belief. "Do your best to encourage one another!" is an **EXHORTATION**.

EXPLICIT refers to information that is expressed in the words of a discourse. This is in contrast to implicit information. See **IMPLICIT**.

FEMININE is one of the genders in the Greek language. See **GENDER**.

FIGURE, FIGURE OF SPEECH, or **FIGURATIVE EXPRESSION** involves the use of words in other than their literal or ordinary sense, in order to bring out some aspect of meaning by means of comparison or association. For example, "raindrops dancing on the street," or "his speech was like thunder." **METAPHORS** and **SIMILES** are figures of speech.

FIRST PERSON. See **PERSON**.

FOCUS is the center of attention in a discourse or in any part of a discourse.

FORMAL CORRESPONDENCE or **FORMAL EQUIVALENCE** is a type of translation in which the features of form in the source text have been more or less mechanically reproduced in the receptor language.

FUTURE TENSE. See **TENSE**.

GENDER is any of three grammatical subclasses of Greek nouns and pronouns (called **MASCULINE, FEMININE,** and **NEUTER**), which determine agreement with and selection of other words or grammatical forms. In most languages the classification of nouns is not related to the identity of male or female sex.

GENERAL (GENERIC) has reference to a general class or kind of objects, events, or abstracts; it is the opposite of **SPECIFIC**. For example, the term "animal" is general in relation to "dog," which is a specific kind of animal. However, "dog" is general in relation to the more specific term "poodle."

GRAMMATICAL refers to **GRAMMAR**, which includes the selection and arrangement of words in phrases, clauses, and sentences.

GREEK is the language in which the New Testament was written. It was spoken first by the inhabitants of Greece, which was then the Roman province of Achaia. Greek became the common language of government and commerce in the eastern portion of the Roman empire. It therefore became a common language for many of the early Christians.

HEBREW is the language in which the Old Testament was written. It belongs to the Semitic family of languages. By the time of Christ, many Jewish people no longer used Hebrew as their common language.

HYPOTHETICAL refers to something that is not recognized as a fact but which is assumed to be true to develop an argument or line of reasoning.

IDIOM (IDIOMATIC EXPRESSION) is a combination of terms whose meanings cannot be understood by adding up the meanings of the parts. "To hang one's head," "to have a green thumb," and "behind the eightball" are American English idioms. Idioms almost always lose their meaning or convey a wrong meaning when translated literally from one language to another.

IMMEDIATE CONTEXT is that context which immediately precedes or follows a discourse or segment of discourse, with no intervening context. For example, John 3.17 is a passage in the immediate context of John 3.16.

IMPERATIVE refers to forms of a verb that indicate commands or requests. In "Go and do likewise," the verbs "Go" and "do" are imperatives. In many languages imperatives are confined to the grammatical second person; but some languages have corresponding forms for the first and third persons. These are usually expressed in English by the use of "must" or "let"; for example, "We must not swim here!" or "They must work harder!" or "Let them eat cake!"

IMPLICIT (**IMPLIED**) refers to information that is not formally represented in a discourse, since it is assumed that it is already known to the receptor, or evident from the meaning of the words in question. For example, the phrase "the other son" carries with it the implicit information that there is a son in addition to the one mentioned. This is in contrast to **EXPLICIT** information, which is expressly stated in a discourse. See **EXPLICIT**.

IMPLY. See **IMPLICIT, IMPLIED**.

INCLUSIVE first person plural includes both the speaker and the one(s) to whom that person is speaking. See **EXCLUSIVE**.

INDICATIVE refers to forms of a verb in which an act or condition is stated as an actual fact rather than as a potentiality, a hope, or an unrealized condition. The verb "won" in "The king won the battle" is in the indicative form.

INDIRECT DISCOURSE, INDIRECT QUOTATION, INDIRECT SPEECH. See **DISCOURSE**.

INFINITIVE is a verb form that indicates an action or state without specifying such factors as agent or time; for example, "to mark," "to sing," or "to go."

INTERPRETATION of a text is the exegesis of it. See **EXEGESIS**.

IRONY (**IRONIC, IRONICAL**) is a sarcastic or humorous manner of discourse in which what is said is intended to express its opposite; for example, "That was a smart thing to do!" when intended to convey the meaning "That was a stupid thing to do!"

LITERAL means the ordinary or primary meaning of a term or expression, in contrast with a figurative meaning. A **LITERAL TRANSLATION** is one that represents the exact words and word order of the source language; such a translation is frequently unnatural or awkward in the receptor language.

LITURGICAL refers to liturgy, that is, public worship; more particularly to the prayers, responses, etc. that are often expressed in traditional or archaic language forms.

MANUSCRIPTS are books, documents, or letters written or copied by hand. A **SCRIBE** is one who copies a manuscript. Thousands of manuscript copies of various Old and New Testament books still exist, but none of the original manuscripts. See **TEXT**. **MANUSCRIPT EVIDENCE** (**MANUSCRIPT SUPPORT**) is also called **TEXTUAL EVIDENCE**. See **TEXT, TEXTUAL**.

MARKERS (**MARKING**) are features of words or of a discourse that signal some special meaning or some particular structure. For example, words for speaking may mark the onset of direct discourse, a phrase such as "once upon a time" may mark the beginning of a fairy story, and certain features of parallelism are the dominant markers of poetry. The word "body" may require a marker to clarify whether a person, a group, or a corpse is meant.

MASCULINE is one of the genders in the Greek language. See **GENDER**.

METAPHOR is likening one object, event, or state to another by speaking of it as if it were the other; for example, "flowers dancing in the breeze" compares the movement of flowers with dancing. Metaphors are the most commonly used figures of speech and are often so subtle that a speaker or writer is not conscious of the fact that he or she is using figurative language. See **SIMILE**.

MODIFY is to affect the meaning of another part of the sentence, as when an adjective modifies a noun or an adverb modifies a verb.

MOOD defines the psychological background of the action, and involves such categories as possibility, necessity, and desire. Some languages (for example, Greek) use specific verb forms to express mood.

NEUTER is one of the genders in the Greek language. See **GENDER**.

NOMINAL refers to nouns or noun-like words. See **NOUN**.

NONFIGURATIVE refers to the literal or ordinary sense of an expression. See **FIGURE, FIGURATIVE**.

NOUN is a word that names a person, place, thing, or idea, and often serves to specify a subject or topic of discussion.

NOUN PHRASE. See **PHRASE**.

OBJECT. See **DIRECT OBJECT**.

PARAGRAPH is a distinct segment of discourse dealing with a particular idea, and usually marked with an indentation on a new line.

PARALLEL, PARALLELISM, generally refers to some similarity in the content and/or form of two parts of a construction; for example, "Hear this, all peoples! Give ear, all inhabitants of the world." The structures that correspond to each other in the two statements are said to be parallel. **PARALLELS,** or **PARALLEL PASSAGES,** refers to two or more portions of biblical text that resemble each other, often by using a series of words that are identical. For example, the Lord's Prayer as recorded in Matt 6.9-13 has as its parallel Luke 11.2-4.

PARENTHETICAL STATEMENT is a statement that interrupts a discourse by departing from its main theme. It is frequently set off by marks of parenthesis ( ).

PARTICIPLE is a verbal adjective, that is, a word that retains some of the characteristics of a verb while functioning as an adjective. In "singing children" and "painted house," "singing" and "painted" are participles.

PARTICLE is a small word whose grammatical form does not change. In English the most common particles are prepositions and conjunctions.

PARTICULAR is the opposite of **GENERAL.** See **GENERAL.**

PASSAGE is the text of Scripture in a specific location. It is usually thought of as comprising more than one verse, but it can be a single verse or part of a verse.

PASSIVE. See **VOICE.**

PAST TENSE. See **TENSE.**

PERFECT TENSE is a set of verb forms that indicate an action completed before the time of speaking or writing. For example, in "John has finished his task," "has finished" is in the perfect tense. See also **TENSE.**

PERSON, as a grammatical term, refers to the speaker, the person spoken to, or the person or thing spoken about. **FIRST PERSON** is the person(s) speaking (such as "I," "me," "my," "mine," "we," "us," "our," or "ours"). **SECOND PERSON** is the person(s) or thing(s) spoken to (such as "thou," "thee," "thy," "thine," "ye," "you," "your," or "yours"). **THIRD PERSON** is the person(s) or thing(s) spoken about (such as "he," "she," "it," "his," "her," "them," or "their"). The examples here given are all pronouns, but in many languages the verb forms have affixes that indicate first, second, or third person and also indicate whether they are **SINGULAR** or **PLURAL.**

PERSONAL PRONOUN is one that indicates first, second, or third person. See **PERSON** and **PRONOUN.**

PHRASE is a grammatical construction of two or more words, but less than a complete clause or a sentence. A phrase is usually given a name according to its function in a sentence, such as "noun phrase," "verb phrase," or "prepositional phrase."

PLAY ON WORDS in a discourse is the use of the similarity in the sounds of two words to produce a special effect.

PLURAL refers to the form of a word that indicates more than one. See **SINGULAR**.

POSSESSIVE PRONOUNS are pronouns such as "my," "our," "your," or "his," which indicate possession.

PREFIX is a part of a word that cannot stand alone and which is positioned at the beginning of the word to which it belongs; for example, "*im*possible," or "*re*structure."

PREPOSITION is a word (usually a particle) whose function is to indicate the relation of a noun or pronoun to another noun, pronoun, verb, or adjective. Some English prepositions are "for," "from," "in," "to," and "with."

PRESENT TENSE. See **TENSE**.

PROGRESSIVE is an aspect of an event referring to its continuation or duration. For example, "the bird is singing" is the progressive aspect of "the bird sings."

PRONOUNS are words that are used in place of nouns, such as "he," "him," "his," "she," "we," "them," "who," "which," "this," or "these."

PROPER NAME or **PROPER NOUN** is the name of a unique object, as "Jerusalem," "Joshua," "Jordan." However, the same name may be applied to more than one object; for example, "John" (the Baptist or the Apostle) and "Antioch" (of Syria or Pisidia).

QUALIFY is to limit the meaning of a term by means of another term. For example, in "old man," the term "old" qualifies the term "man."

QUOTATION. See **DISCOURSE**.

READ, READING, frequently refers to the interpretation of the written form of a text, especially under the following conditions: if the available text appears to be defective; or if differing versions of the same text are available; or if several alternative sets of vowels may be understood as correct in languages such as biblical Hebrew, in which only the consonants were written. See also TEXT, TEXTUAL.

RECEPTOR is the person(s) receiving a message. The RECEPTOR LANGUAGE is the language into which a translation is made. For example, in a translation from Hebrew into German, Hebrew is the source language and German is the receptor language.

REDUNDANT refers to anything that is entirely predictable from the context. For example, in "John, he did it," the pronoun "he" is redundant. A feature may be redundant and yet may be important to retain in certain languages, perhaps for stylistic or for grammatical reasons.

REFERENT is the thing(s) or person(s) referred to by a pronoun, phrase, or clause.

REFLEXIVE has to do with verbs where the agent and goal are the same person. Sometimes the goal is explicit (as in "He dresses himself"); at other times it is implicit (as in "He dresses").

RELATIVE CLAUSE is a dependent clause that describes the object to which it refers. In "the man whom you saw," the clause "whom you saw" is relative because it relates to and describes "man."

RELATIVE PRONOUN is a pronoun that refers to a noun in another clause, and which serves to mark the subordination of its own clause to that noun; for example, in "This is the man who came to dinner," "who" is the relative pronoun referring to "the man" in the previous clause. The subordinated clause is also called a relative clause.

RENDER means translate or express in a language different from the original. RENDERING is the manner in which a specific passage is translated from one language to another.

RESTRUCTURE. See STRUCTURE.

RHETORICAL refers to forms of speech that are employed to highlight or make more attractive some aspect of a discourse. A RHETORICAL QUESTION, for example, is not a request for information but is a way of making an emphatic statement.

ROOT is the minimal base of a derived or inflected word. For example, "friend" is the root of "friendliness."

SARCASM (SARCASTIC) is an ironical and frequently contemptuous manner of discourse in which what is said is intended to express its opposite; for example, "What a brilliant idea!" when intended to convey the meaning, "What a ridiculous idea!"

SCRIBE. See **MANUSCRIPT.**

SECOND PERSON. See **PERSON.**

SEMITIC refers to a family of languages that includes Hebrew, Aramaic, and Arabic. Greek belongs to quite another language family, with a distinct cultural background. In view of the Jewish ancestry and training of the writers of the New Testament, it is not surprising that many Semitic idioms and thought patterns (called Semitisms or Hebraisms) appear in the Greek writings of the New Testament.

SENTENCE is a grammatical construction composed of one or more clauses and capable of standing alone.

SEPTUAGINT is a translation of the Hebrew Old Testament into Greek, begun some two hundred years before Christ. It is often abbreviated as LXX.

SIMILE (pronounced SIM-i-lee) is a **FIGURE OF SPEECH** that describes one event or object by comparing it to another, using "like," "as," or some other word to mark or signal the comparison. For example, "She runs like a deer," "He is as straight as an arrow." Similes are less subtle than metaphors in that metaphors do not mark the comparison with words such as "like" or "as." See **METAPHOR.**

SINGULAR refers to the form of a word that indicates one thing or person, in contrast to **PLURAL**, which indicates more than one. See **PLURAL.**

SPECIFIC refers to the opposite of **GENERAL.** See **GENERAL.**

STEM is the base for a specific derivation or inflection. For example, "demonstr-" is the stem of "demonstrable."

STRUCTURE is the systematic arrangement of the elements of language, including the ways in which words combine into phrases, phrases into clauses, clauses into sentences, and sentences into larger units of discourse. Because this process may be compared to the building of a house or bridge, such words as **STRUCTURE** and **CONSTRUCTION** are used in reference to it. To separate and rearrange the various components of a sentence or other unit of discourse in the translation process is to **RESTRUCTURE** it.

STYLE is a particular or a characteristic manner in discourse. Each language has certain distinctive **STYLISTIC** features that cannot be reproduced literally in another language. Within any language, certain groups of speakers may have their characteristic discourse styles, and among individual speakers and writers, each has his or her own style. Various stylistic devices are used for the purpose of achieving a more pleasing style. For example, synonyms are sometimes used to avoid the monotonous repetition of the same words, or the normal order of clauses and phrases may be altered for the sake of emphasis.

SUBJECT is one of the major divisions of a clause, the other being the predicate. In "The small boy walked to school," "The small boy" is the subject. Typically the subject is a noun phrase. It should not be confused with the semantic **AGENT**, or "actor."

SYNONYMS are words that are different in form but similar in meaning, such as "boy" and "lad." Expressions that have essentially the same meaning are said to be **SYNONYMOUS**. No two words are completely synonymous.

SYNTAX is the selection and arrangement of words in phrases, clauses, and sentences.

TEMPORAL refers to time. A **TEMPORAL CLAUSE** is a dependent clause that indicates the time of the action in the main clause; for example, "When the bell rang, the students went home."

TENSE is usually a form of a verb that indicates time relative to a discourse or some event in a discourse. The most common forms of tense are past, present, and future.

TEXT, TEXTUAL, refers to the various Greek and Hebrew manuscripts of the Scriptures. **TEXTUAL EVIDENCE** is the cumulative evidence for a particular form of the text. See also **MANUSCRIPTS**.

TEXTUS RECEPTUS (Latin for "Received Text") is one of the earliest printed forms of the text of the Greek New Testament. Based on very late manuscripts, it contains many changes made by copyists which a modern translation should not follow.

THEME is the subject of a discourse.

THIRD PERSON. See **PERSON**.

TONE is the spirit, character, or emotional effect of a passage or discourse.

TRANSITION in discourse involves passing from one thought-section or group of related thought-sections to another. **TRANSITIONAL** words, phrases, or longer passages mark the connections between two such sets of related sections and help the hearer to understand the connection.

TRANSLATION is the reproduction in a receptor language of the closest natural equivalent of a message in the source language, first, in terms of meaning, and second, in terms of style.

TRANSLITERATE is to represent in the receptor language the approximate sounds or letters of words occurring in the source language, rather than translating their meaning; for example, "Amen" from the Hebrew, or the title "Christ" from the Greek.

TRANSPOSITION (**TRANSPOSE**) is the act, process, or result of exchanging the relative position of two elements, substituting one for the other. For example, the adjectives in "the little laughing girl" may be transposed to "the laughing little girl."

VERBS are a grammatical class of words that express existence, action, or occurrence, such as "be," "become," "run," or "think."

VERBAL has two meanings. (1) It may refer to expressions consisting of words, sometimes in distinction to forms of communication that do not employ words ("sign language," for example). (2) It may refer to word forms that are derived from verbs. For example, "coming" and "engaged" may be called verbals, and participles are called verbal adjectives.

VERSIONS are translations. The ancient, or early, versions are translations of the Bible, or of portions of the Bible, made in early times; for example, the Greek Septuagint, the ancient Syriac, or the Ethiopic versions.

VOICE in grammar is the relation of the action expressed by a verb to the participants in the action. In English and many other languages, the **ACTIVE VOICE** indicates that the subject performs the action ("John hit the man"), while the **PASSIVE VOICE** indicates that the subject is being acted upon ("The man was hit").

Index

This Index includes concepts, key words, and terms for which the Handbook contains a discussion useful for translators. Hebrew and Greek terms have been transliterated and occur in English alphabetical order.

PRINTED IN THE UNITED STATES OF AMERICA